Capital Flows, Financial Markets and Banking Crises

The increasing capital flows in the emerging markets and developed countries have raised various concerns worldwide. One main concern is the impact of the sharp decline of capital flows – so-called sudden stops – on financial markets and the stability of banking systems and the economy. The sudden stops and banking crises have been identified as the two main features of most financial crises, including the recent Asian Financial Crisis and Global Financial Crisis. However, how capital flows and banking crises are connected still remains unanswered.

Most current studies on capital flows are empirical work, which faces various challenges. The challenges include how data has been collected and measured in each country and how sensitive the results are to the data and the adopted methodologies. Moreover, the links between capital flows and banking systems have been neglected. This book helps provide some insight into the challenges faced by empirical studies and the lessons of the recent crises. The book develops theoretical analysis to deepen our understanding on how capital flows, banking systems and financial markets are linked with each other and provides constructive policy implications by overcoming the empirical challenges.

Chia-Ying Chang is a research scholar in the Faculty of Economics at Nagoya City University and an associated member of Macroeconomics Research Unit at the University of Melbourne. She received her PhD in economics from Vanderbilt University, USA. Her research interests include money and banking theory, macroeconomic theory, economic growth and development, industrial organisation and labour economic theory in macroeconomic perspective.

Routledge International Studies in Money and Banking

For a full list of titles in this series, please visit www.routledge.com/series/SE0403

81 **Cultures of Expertise in Global Currency Markets**
Leon Wansleben

82 **The Global Financial Crisis and the New Monetary Consensus**
Marc Pilkington

83 **A New Measure of Competition in the Financial Industry: the Performance-Conduct-structure indicator**
Edited by Jacob A. Bikker and Michiel van Leuvensteijn

84 **Money, Valuation and Growth**
Conceptualizations and contradictions of the money economy
Hasse Ekstedt

85 **European Banking Union**
Prospects and challenges
Edited by Juan E. Castañeda, David G. Mayes and Geoffrey Wood

86 **Wages, Bonuses and Appropriation of Profit in the Financial Industry**
The working rich
Olivier Godechot

87 **Banking and Monetary Policies in a Changing Financial Environment**
A regulatory approach
Wassim Shahin and Elias El-Achkar

88 **Modern Monetary Theory and European Macroeconomics**
Dirk H. Ehnts

89 **Capital Flows, Financial Markets and Banking Crises**
Chia-Ying Chang

Capital Flows, Financial Markets and Banking Crises

Chia-Ying Chang

Routledge
Taylor & Francis Group
LONDON AND NEW YORK

First published 2017
by Routledge

2 Park Square, Milton Park, Abingdon, Oxfordshire OX14 4RN
52 Vanderbilt Avenue, New York, NY 10017

Routledge is an imprint of the Taylor & Francis Group, an informa business

First issued in paperback 2019

British Library Cataloguing-in-Publication Data
A catalogue record for this book is available from the British Library

Library of Congress Cataloging-in-Publication Data
Names: Chang, Chia-Ying, 1972– author.
Title: Capital flows, financial markets and banking crises / by Chia-Ying Chang.
Description: First Edition. | New York, NY : Routledge, 2017. | Series: Routledge international studies in money and banking ; 89 | Includes bibliographical references and index.
Identifiers: LCCN 2016055249 | ISBN 9780415749558 (hardback) | ISBN 9781315469416 (ebook)
Subjects: LCSH: Capital movements. | Banks and banking. | Financial crises. | International finance.
Classification: LCC HG3891 .C496 2017 | DDC 332/.0424—dc23
LC record available at https://lccn.loc.gov/2016055249

ISBN: 978-0-415-74955-8 (hbk)
ISBN: 978-0-367-35058-1 (pbk)

Typeset in Galliard
by Apex CoVantage, LLC

To my parents, my family, and my best friends

Contents

Illustrations

Figures

Tables

Acknowledgements

There have been many challenges during the period of time during which I worked on this research monograph. There are many people to whom I owe my deepest gratitude. Without their support and encouragement, the production of this book would have been impossible. They are my parents, my family and my best friends. I especially owe my big thanks to Louise Altman, who believes in me and has been with me throughout my most difficult time; to John Singleton, who has been very generous with his time in providing me his comments and support; and to Morris Altman, who has supported me since the early stage of the book. Their hard work and passion in economic research and teaching have inspired me enormously. I am very grateful to have them all in my life.

The majority of the book was started and has been completed during my stay at Nagoya City University. The generosity of Taro Akiyama and Kazuyuki Inagaki and the hospitality of Nagoya City University are especially appreciated. Their kindness and friendship have made this book possible. I also want to thank Yong Ling Lam and Samantha Phua for their patience, and the editors and the project manager and her team for their great work throughout the process. The work of Thakishila Gunaratna as a research assistant and the editing of Pam Englert at the early stage of the book are greatly appreciated. The minimal USD$600 approx. (including tax) in 2014 from Victoria University is also acknowledged here. All errors are my own.

Every cloud has a silver lining. The past few years have been very difficult. However, I have been very fortunate to have my family and friends, who have stood by me and supported me through the difficult time. Because of their love and support, I survived that difficult period, and when the working conditions of the place to which I have devoted more than a decade seriously threatened my health and safety, I have had the courage to leave the place so that I could keep and continue to work for my passion in economics. My family and friends and all the people who have inspired and helped me in various ways are my brightest stars in the darkest sky. Because of these great and wonderful people, I gain strength and I see hope. No word can express my deepest gratitude to them.

At the end, I want to dedicate a quote to people who are reading this book.

> *It is often in the darkest skies that we see the brightest stars.*
>
> Richard Evans

If you have not yet found the brightest stars, keep looking and don't give up. While looking for the brightest stars, be one and light a candle for others.

1 Introduction

Globalization has reduced the distances between countries and has sped up the integration of capital markets. In response to capital market integration, countries have started liberalizing/deregulating financial markets. Both the liberalization and deregulation have led to rapid growth in capital flows across countries. The growth of capital flows changes not only the volumes and the frequencies of flows but also their nature and the composition, which could then affect the fundamentals of an economy and have raised many concerns. Thus, the issues related to capital flows have attracted broad attention and discussion, especially in emerging markets.

Capital flows

An increase in capital flows, on one hand, could integrate capital markets across countries and reduce the frictions of financial markets. On the other hand, the associated contagion effects, also called spill-over effects, could shake the stability of the banking system and the financial markets and hence expose the economy to international credit risks and ultimately lead the economy to overseas-originated financial crises. While enjoying the benefits brought by increasing capital flows, the countries, especially emerging economies, are motivated to manage increasing capital flows to prevent contagion effects as well as overseas-originated crises. Amongst all management on capital flows, capital controls are the most popular and controversial policies. Their effectiveness as well as their pros and cons have been under debate for several decades since the 1970s. The results of the debates are inconclusive. The inconclusive results from this debate and the mixed results from decades of research also reflect in reality that while some countries move from free flows to capital controls, other countries move from capital controls to free flows through the liberalization of capital controls and/or accounts.

In general, capital controls were adopted widely before the 1970s but were removed gradually to promote free flows after the 1970s. Controls became popular and were implemented once again in the 1990s. During 1990–1997, prior to the Asian Financial Crisis, the implemented capital controls were mainly on inflows [Edwards (2009a, 2009b), Johnson et al (2007)], such as in Thailand, Malaysia, Philippines, Indonesia, Czech Republic, Colombia and Brazil.

Different from these countries, Spain was one of few which implemented controls on outflows. After the crisis in 1997, countries such as Thailand, Malaysia and Brazil added controls on outflows, in addition to their existing inflow controls. Although not affected by the Asian Financial Crisis, Argentina has joined the club to implement inflow controls.

It has been more than four decades since the 1970s, when controls were adopted broadly. Today, countries hold different views on promoting and opposing controls. While opposing each other's view on capital controls, some countries are in fact switching between implementing and liberalizing controls. The switch back and forth between implementation and liberalization of capital controls increases the challenges researchers face in analysing capital flows, especially when conducting empirical studies. As one may know, it takes time for specific policies and the removal of policies to have impacts on the economy. When and how these impacts take place and how long the effects last depend on economic conditions, which vary across countries and across time. Thus, the frequency of switching between implementation and liberalization of capital controls makes it more difficult to analyse the impacts of capital controls and the removal of capital controls, especially for empirical studies. This may explain why despite the continuous development in the methodology of research on capital flows, several key issues surrounding capital flows remain unanswered, while new and more complex issues concerning capital flows keep arising. By summarizing the issues, old and new, one can easily find that most issues are related to the linkages between capital flows, the stability of banking/financial systems and the associated crises, the effectiveness of capital controls and macroeconomic variables such as output and growth.

There is no doubt that the methodologies and datasets adopted are as important as their findings. As shown in the literature, the datasets adopted vary across studies. Depending on the definitions and measurements of the datasets, the results can be sensitive to both methodologies and datasets. Without the knowledge of the definitions and measurements adopted in all datasets used in all countries in empirical studies, it is difficult to provide insights on suitable datasets to be adopted when studying capital flows. Meanwhile, each methodology adopted to study capital flows has its own features and tends to drive specific results [Forbes (2012)]. In order to fit into specific methodologies, some studies may have treated and/or adjusted data. The treatments and the adjustments may have affected the results. The comments regarding suitable datasets and methodologies to be adopted will be left to the experts who have knowledge on various datasets and methodologies. The focus of the book will be to use the information adopted and the results obtained in the empirical studies to compare consistencies and inconsistencies in various topics and then use the theoretical analysis to identify possible factors which might be useful to explain why these inconsistencies in the empirical studies emerge. The introduction of each chapter is presented to draw information from empirical studies in order to develop the theoretical framework and address the related issues relevant to the chapter topic. The details underlying mapping of the theoretical and empirical analysis will be discussed in Chapter 7.

To understand the issues related to capital flows, we must return to the sources of flows, which are the capital accounts showing the components of flows. Capital accounts can be divided into four categories: (1) foreign direct investment (FDI); (2) foreign portfolio investment (FPI); (3) other investment; and (4) the reserve accounts held by the central banks. Among these, this book focuses on the first three categories. This is because the reserve accounts (the fourth category) has a different nature from the other three due to the role and the strategies of the central banks. Among the first three, FDI flows are often considered long-run (LR) flows and more stable, while both FPI flows and other investments are often considered short-run (SR) flows and more volatile. The nature of FDI LR flows and FPI SR flows are different from each other. Moreover, FDI and FPI flows serve different purposes and play different roles and hence have different impacts on the economy. Therefore, it is important to differentiate FDI flows from FPI flows and to incorporate their features while conducting analysis on capital flows, whether it is theoretical or empirical.

The limitation of specific datasets

Despite the importance of differentiating the types of flows in any analysis, the available datasets may not provide the differentiations between LR and SR flows. Moreover, some of the datasets provide only annual data, and some datasets provide only net flows. These datasets not only fail to differentiate the types of flows but also neglect the possibility of seasonal effects and have mixed the changes of flows to/from various industries. The empirical studies which employ these datasets may provide non-intuitive results without sensible explanations, increase unnecessary confusion in the current literature and/or make it more difficult to solve the puzzle and to move the current capital flows/controls debates forward.

Take the famous Feldstein-Horioka-puzzle as an example. Many research works have attempted to explain the puzzle. The puzzle states strong correlation between domestic saving and investment and implies low capital mobility and less perfect capital market, as assumed in the literature. Among the studies seeking to explain the puzzle, one main stream of research shows that the puzzle is for average LR capital but not for SR capital [Abbott and Vita (2003), Bai and Zhang (2010), Chang and Smith (2014), Coakley et al (1996), Sinn (1992)]. Another stream of research attributes specific country factors to the puzzle [Abbott and Vita (2003), Chen and Shen (2015), Corbin (2001)]. The specific country factors include home bias portfolio preferences [Feldstein (1983)], interest rate differential, currency premium [Corbin (2001)] and regime switching on capital controls [Abbott and Vita (2003), Chen and Shen (2015), Corbin (2001)]. By gathering the literature on the Feldstein-Horioka-puzzle, one can conclude that the key to solving the puzzle is not only to find ways to differentiate SR and LR capital flows but also to find the specific country factors, such as capital controls, which may drive specific results. The puzzle will not be solved and would become even more confusing when the empirical studies adopt specific datasets that do not have the qualities needed to assist in solving the puzzle.

Mixed results of liberalizations and controls

More mixed and confusing results in empirical studies are also found in the liberalization of capital accounts and the associated changes on output and growth. Some research finds that liberalization will promote growth, while others find that liberalization will harm growth. To be more specific, Eichengreen (2004, chapter 3) provides evidence showing that the positive effects of liberalization do not apply to most countries and that the robustness of the positive effect holds only for the post–1982 period and for high-income countries. For the countries with weak contract and law enforcement, the positive effect of liberalization cannot be found. Meanwhile, most views opposing liberalization are based on the contagion effects which may lead the countries to currency crises. There is no doubt that a sharp increase in capital flows would cause exchange rate fluctuations. However, moving from exchange rate fluctuations to currency crises is a very strong statement. One argument against this statement is that depending on changes in the direction of capital flows, an increase in capital flows may magnify (or offset) the size of movements on the exchange rate and hence worsen (improve) economic conditions caused by currency crises. Moreover, the volatility of the exchange rate does not depend on capital flows alone. The volatility of the exchange rate depends strongly on the country's domestic fundamentals and its exposure to global risks, which would also determine how contagion effects would spread out to one country. In other words, the studies focusing on the effects of flows on currency crises can easily overstate/understate the impacts of flows on the exchange rate by failing to account for the influences of other macro factors which may not be related to capital flows. Hence, such studies miss the big picture of the real impacts of capital flows on the economy. Not to mention that for a fixed-exchange-rate regime, there is no room for exchange rate volatility, while for a flexible-exchange-rate regime, the existing theory that proves exchange rate indeterminacy has shown that the volatility of exchange rate is inevitable. To avoid the complications and confusion brought by the exchange rate, this book will focus on the impacts of capital flows on the banking system, the financial markets and macroeconomic variables in a real economy.

There are several reasons this book focuses on the linkages of capital flows/controls to the financial markets and the stability of banking systems as well as the possibility of banking crises. First, most capital flows, whether SR or LR, are through the banking systems of countries. Grittersova (2014) studies 18 advanced countries during 1960–2005 and shows that the financial liberalizations started in the 1990s have increased the role of banks and related financial institutions. Therefore, the changes of capital flows would affect banks' assets and liabilities and the banks' exposure to international credit defaults as well as other risks. Depending on bank governance, the changes of capital flows may affect the stability of banking systems. Second, the stability of banking systems is related to the possibility of bank runs and hence banking crises. To understand crises well, it is important to clarify the definition of crises. Banking crises, based on the definition of Allen and Gale (2007b, p 10), are defined as "*financial distress that is severe enough to result in the erosion of most or all of the capital in the banking system*". Also in Allen and Gale (2007b, p 10), currency crises are defined as "*a forced change in parity, abandonment of a pegged exchange rate or an international rescue*". Both banking crises and currency crises are classified as the two key features of financial crises [Tirole (2002), chapter 1]. Financial crises are defined as "*a disturbance to financial markets, associated typically with falling asset prices and insolvency among debtors and intermediaries, which spread through the financial system, disrupting the market's capacity to allocate capital*", according to Eichengreen and Portes (1987, page i). Regarding the frequency of the occurrence of banking crises, Tirole (2002, chapter 1) finds that banking crises have occurred more often in recent decades after the 1970s. Expanding to historical data, Eichengreen et al (2008) find that 50 per cent of financial crises have coincided with banking crises and only 2 per cent have coincided with currency crises. Focusing on the recent period after 1973, both Bordo et al (2001) and Allen and Gale (2007b, chapter 1) find that banking crises have occurred more frequently after 1973. Moreover, Tirole (2002, chapter 1) points out that starting in the 1970s, the crises have been related to bank failures which were not the case in the period prior to the 1970s when banking systems were highly regulated and banking activities were limited. In the 1970s, banking systems were deregulated jointly with financial liberalization as well as the liberalization of capital accounts/controls. Because the liberalization of capital accounts is defined as "easing the restrictions of capital flows across a country's borders", based on Kose and Prasad (IMF, 2012), it is also called the liberalization of capital controls in many studies.

The role change of the banking systems

While the deregulation of banking systems and financial liberalization have expanded banks' activities, the liberalization of capital accounts/controls has led to the rapid growth of capital flows, which has, in turn, increased the role of banking systems and provided the banking system more opportunities to involve and to engage in new activities at an international level. The increasing activities involved by the banks have expanded the roles of banks to be not only a middleman and a portfolio manager but also to be a major player in the financial markets. As a major player, the banks would seek maximum profits. This implies that the traditional way to model banks as zero profit is no longer suitable for the modern economy. The policies which draw from the models with zero-profit banks must be revisited.

When banks seek to maximize profits, on one hand, the profits of the banks may serve to finance liquidity shortfalls and reduce the probability of bank runs and banking crises. On the other hand, the goal to maximize profits may have the banks overlook/mismanage risks and expose themselves to various credit defaults and global risks. The exposure to global risks would make the banks more vulnerable and sensitive to the shocks and contagion effects and hence increase the probability of bank runs and banking crises. When capital flows are added to the analysis, it is not only the banking system but also the sectors to/from which the flows are injected/withdrawn that would be affected by the fluctuations of capital flows. How the fluctuations would benefit or damage the economy would depend on the directions of the flows, which may magnify or offset the contagion effects originated domestically and/or overseas. Therefore, it has become more important and urgent to understand better how the economy is affected by the deregulation of the banking system and the liberalization of capital flows if one wishes related policies implemented/liberalized to do a better job to stop the economy from bleeding or to divert the economy from crises instead of worsening the economy. This is why the analysis in this book will discuss the cases with and without capital flows as well as having a separate chapter (Chapter 5) to discuss bank governance.

The banking system without capital flows has its own inherent problems. As well, as documented by current banking literature, liquidity shortfalls are one of the key problems of the banking system. When the liquidity problems are not resolved in time, bank insolvency and bank runs are inevitable. The causes of liquidity shortfalls vary in different cases, situations and countries. The causes include the mismatch of maturity [Tirole (2002, chapter 2)] and the panic of creditors [Diamond and Dybvig (1983)], as well as risk-taking behaviours of the banks [Calomiris (2009)]. Note that the implicitly assumed zero-profit banks in the traditional literature have left the banks little space to absorb shocks and increased the possibility of bank runs. This assumption has been severely criticized. The bank runs would then interrupt the financial and other economic activities and drive the economy into crises and recessions. To prevent bank runs and their associated crises and recessions, central banks and international organizations, such as the International Monetary Fund (IMF), have provided short-term lending facilities to resolve the liquidity problems of banks. Despite various sources of liquidity provision, bank runs and banking crises continue to occur, as shown in the most recent crises. When more countries experience bank runs and banking crises which require liquidity provision to be in place, the promise of the IMF to provide lending has in turn threatened the financial positions of many central banks and the IMF. Does it mean that liquidity provision is insufficient in preventing banking crises? If so, what more can be done to prevent bank runs and crises? It is also one of the goals of the book to address these questions by modelling profit-maximizing banks to identify the circumstances in which liquidity provision would be effective or ineffective.

The format and the impacts of capital controls

To limit the exposure to global risks without restoring bank regulations, capital controls have been popularly adopted as macro-prudential policies. Capital controls aim to restrict flows and can be implemented in various ways and formats. However, the impacts of controls are not limited to flows but also to the sectors connecting to the flows. Unfortunately, the associated impacts on the connecting sectors by capital controls are not always desirable. Depending on the ways and formats of capital controls as well as economic conditions, capital controls would affect the economy through various channels. Therefore, it is important to be cautious when assessing the real impacts of capital controls by conducting analysis in various ways and tackling the issues from various angles to get a better picture of the real impacts of capital controls before implementing/liberalizing capital controls.

The effectiveness of capital controls

Depending on the goals one wishes to achieve, there are many definitions of the effectiveness of capital controls. In general, according to Edwards (2001, 2007a, 2007b), the goals of capital controls can be summarized as (1) restricting the volumes and compositions of flows, (2) gaining monetary autonomy and (3) reducing fluctuations and preventing crises. Empirically, the findings regarding the effectiveness of capital controls are mixed in several ways.

One example regards the effects of controls on capital flows. Forbes and Warnock (2012) find that capital controls have little association with foreign-driven capital flows. However, El-Shagi (2010) discovers that capital controls can restructure capital flows without distortion but does not specify whether the capital flows to be restructured by controls are limited to foreign- or domestic-driven flows. Without the specification of foreign-/domestic driven flows, it is difficult to conclude whether the two results are inconsistent. Another example regards general versus specific patterns of flow. Forbes and Warnock (2012) focus on general patterns of flow waves during specific periods. Meanwhile, El-Shagi (2010) focuses on the panel data of specific countries. If the patterns found in specific countries differ from Forbes and Warnock (2012), should the results be considered as inconsistent? Note that patterns may depend on the datasets and the methodology adopted for the empirical studies. Various datasets may have different definitions and measurements both within and across countries and across time. While using the term "capital flows", some studies analyse gross flows; some use net flows; some did not mention whether it is gross or net flows. Therefore, it has been challenging to compare various empirical studies related to capital flows and controls.

In order to overcome the challenges of empirical studies, Eichengreen (2004, p 51) takes the first step by exploring the problems and limitations of the measures based on statute, on actual flows and on asset prices. He concludes that with various measures, the results of studying the effectiveness of capital account liberalization are various and inconsistent, and that the consistency depends crucially on the measures and the data. Therefore, although it is challenging to unify the definitions and measures of datasets, especially for historical datasets, it is important and crucial to take steps to clarify specific issues of debates and to understand better various empirical studies on capital flows.

Note that the challenges mentioned earlier have not accounted for the policy shifts between various capital controls as well as on and off controls from time to time. Even though some challenges may be overcome by further developments in empirical methodology and measurements, some challenges require a structured theoretical analysis to clear the road for the next step or directions. These challenges explain why Magud and Reinhart (2007) call for the development of a unified theoretical framework to resolve the existing apple-to-orange problems in empirical studies on the effectiveness of capital controls. Through a theoretical framework, specific complications can be simplified, and some challenges faced by empirical studies can be overcome. By connecting flows with financial markets and banking systems in a theoretical framework, we can analyse the circumstances in which contagion effects are more likely to occur and in which the banking system would be more fragile. With the assistance of theoretical analysis, we can then identify the real impacts of capital flows and controls on the financial markets, the banking system and the economy and find mechanisms with which to prevent contagion effects associated with flows. Based on the analysis, we may find those factors that are the causes of inconsistent results in empirical findings.

Theoretical frameworks

In macroeconomics, there are theoretical frameworks that can be the candidates for analysing the increasing role of banks and the linkages to capital flows. Acemoglu (2009, chapter 19) extends an infinite-horizon model of trade to analyse the direction of flows and to show how flows depend on the returns of the capital–labour ratio. Bencivenga and Smith (1991) adopt an overlapping-generations model to analyse the roles of financial intermediation on growth. Diamond and Dybvig (1983, 1986) extend an overlapping-generations model to address bank runs and demonstrate the fragility of the banking system. Following Diamond and Dybvig (1983), the overlapping-generations model has been widely extended to discuss various circumstances of bank runs and the fragility of the banking system. The recent work of Gertler and Kiyotaki (2015) opens the door for an infinite-horizon model to incorporate banking systems to discuss the possibility of bank runs.

Infinite-horizon and overlapping-generations models have their own advantages and disadvantages. Depending on the features to incorporate and the purposes of the analysis, one type of model can be more appropriate than the other. In this book, I extend the overlapping-generations framework for its key feature to incorporate the dynamics of the decisions made by different generations. The feature will provide the space to analyse the amount of periods it will take to affect the banking system and the economy, as some effects may take time to surface, including the effects of flows. Depending on the topics, the models of each chapter would incorporate the specific features of capital flows, the banking system and the financial markets. Moreover, while an overlapping-generations framework has been adopted to analyse bank runs and financial assets, it also suits the purposes of the chapters to analyse the stability of banking systems and the financial markets. Therefore, the overlapping-generations framework is adopted here to analyse various issues related to capital flows and controls and banking crises.

In this book, an open-economy, three-period-lived overlapping-generations model is constructed to incorporate the features of capital flows, the financial markets and the banking system. There are agents of different types as well as financial markets and the banking system. The banks, also called financial intermediaries, are assumed to serve primarily as middlemen and as portfolio managers in the analysis which focuses on capital flows and growth. The assumption is then relaxed, and the banks are assumed to maximize their own profits in the analysis which then focuses on the fluctuations of capital flows, capital controls and bank governance. The decisions made (and expected to be made) by the agents of different generations would affect the decision of the banks, which would have impacts on the situations of the financial markets and capital flows and hence the economy and the decision making of the agents of different generations. The realized as well as the expected outcome would then affect the decisions of the agents in the following period and affect the economic outcome. The dynamics across various agents and sectors need not be unidirectional. The features of overlapping-generations frameworks provide the space to peel away the interactions of various sectors carefully before and after incidences period by period. This allows us to identify when specific crucial factors take place underneath and when the effects would surface and show the impacts.

The rest of the book is organized in the following order. Chapters 2 and 3 are both on growth aspects. While Chapter 2 focuses on long-term foreign direct investment flows, Chapter 3 focuses on short-term flows, portfolios and other investment. Chapter 4 discusses the change of capital flows and their relations to the stability of the financial markets and the banking system. Chapter 5 concentrates on the banking system to analyse the effectiveness of the facilities used to prevent the runs. Combining what has been learned in Chapters 4 and 5 on capital flows and the stability of the banking system, I introduce capital controls in Chapter 6 to analyse whether such implementation can make a difference in preventing banking crises. This is followed by Chapter 7, in which I combine current studies in various literatures to look at the missing pieces and the possible steps in both theories and empirics to further understand the flows and related policies as well as their impacts. The conclusion is provided in Chapter 8.

To be more specific, as long-term capital flows, foreign direct investment has been considered as the steady component of capital flows. Based on the existing theory analysing various types of foreign direct investment projects, FDI flows should have positive effects on both home and host countries' growth. However, the empirical studies have found mixed and inconsistent results even for the same countries as well as for the countries at similar development stages. Chapter 2 develops a model incorporating the key features of FDI projects and analyses both the short-term and the long-term impacts on the banks' role as a portfolio manager and hence economic growth.

The short-term capital flows often refer to portfolio and other investments. The short-term flows are sensitive to economic conditions and shocks. The economic conditions are the conditions of all countries involved in the investors' investment portfolios, not limited to those of the host countries. Thus, the short-term capital flows tend to fluctuate more frequently than long-term flows and are considered as one main cause of "sudden stops". Extending the theoretical model of Chapter 2, Chapter 3 analyses how the short-term flows might affect the portfolios of the financial intermediaries and hence economic growth of both the home and the host countries. This is followed by discussion on how economic growth might affect portfolio capital flows in return.

One argument on capital flows benefitting both home and host countries is based on deepening financial development. Chapter 4 looks into the channels of how capital flows affect the financial markets and the ability of capital flows to shake the stability of the banking system. To do so, this chapter analyses the financial markets and the stability of banking systems in both home and host countries with and without capital flows as well as the consequences of sudden stops.

Banking crises have occurred more frequently after deregulations in financial markets, which may and may not be related to capital flows. In response to banking crises, short-term lending facilities have been considered as the elixir to rescue banks from crises. Thus, such lending facilities have been provided by central banks and international organizations. Unfortunately, banking crises do not stop occurring. The banking crises in the Global Financial Crisis in 2008 were the most recent examples. Do lending facilities fail to prevent banking crises? Or are there problems in the banking system which prevent lending facilities from being effective? Chapter 5 examines the limitations of lending facilities in preventing banking crises and asks whether there exists an alternative way to improve the effectiveness of lending facilities in preventing banking crises without capital flows. Focusing on the banking system without capital flows allows us to deepen our understanding of the issues existing in the banking system when capital flows have not yet taken place.

Since the 1990s, capital controls have been implemented to prevent contagion effects via financial liberalizations and hence to prevent the countries from experiencing banking crises. Have capital controls been effective in achieving the goal of preventing banking crises? There are various types of capital controls. Some countries control either inflows or outflows, and some control both flows. Are controls in one specific direction more effective in preventing the crises? Is one specific control more suitable for certain countries than other controls? Chapter 6 examines the effectiveness of various types of capital controls in preventing banking crises. The chapter also evaluates the cost and the benefits of implementing capital controls.

The issues of capital flows and their connections to the stability of banking systems and crises have been challenges to empirical studies. The challenges include data limitation, issues of measurement and methodology adopted. Thus, empirical findings related to capital flows are sensitive to the datasets, the methodology and the countries. The sensitive findings in empirical work have led to inconsistency and generate various debates on capital flows, financial liberalizations and the stability of banking systems. Chapter 7 summarizes the findings of current empirical studies related to capital flows and financial markets. Then, connecting what has been learned in theoretical analyses in the previous chapters, this chapter discusses what can be done in empirical studies to narrow the gap and to contribute to the current debate. Moreover, this chapter takes a step further to discuss policy implications, especially on the policies related to capital flows, the financial de(regulations) and the stability of banking systems. This is followed by the conclusion in Chapter 8.

Chapter 8 summarizes the key features and conclusions of each chapter and highlights the main policy implications as well as possible extensions for further theoretical and empirical studies.

2 Long-term foreign direct investment and economic growth

Introduction: the background and the facts

From 1980 to 2004, the capital flows caused by foreign direct investment (FDI thereafter) have counted for 2 per cent to 10 per cent of global fixed capital formation. Although the share 2 per cent to 10 per cent seems small, the actual size of fixed capital formation caused by FDI is large. To illustrate, the amount of fixed capital formation is equivalent to the payments of approximately 14 per cent of manufacturing jobs in the United States and 20 per cent in Europe.[1] Both the United States and Europe have been the two main sources of the world outward FDI since World War II in the 1960s. The outward FDI from these two regions has remained significant even after the emerging markets joined them to become the sources of outward FDI in the 1980s. Due to the significant impacts of FDI on the economies, both the home (source) and the host (destination) economies and the connections of FDI to the production sectors, the increasing FDI has attracted broad attention and raised various concerns.

In response to the concerns of FDI, there have been many empirical studies analysing its impacts on productivity, employment and growth in the host countries but not the home countries. It is not until the recent decade, when increased unemployment in the advanced countries has attracted broad attention and held FDI countable for the loss of jobs, that some studies have started to work on the impacts of FDI on home employment [Marin (2004)]. Meanwhile, the lack of theoretical analysis increases the difficulties in understanding the causes of the mixed and inconsistent results in the empirical studies. Therefore, it is the goal of this chapter to develop a theoretical framework to analyse various impacts of FDI on macro variables, such as productivity, employment, portfolio decision and economic growth, both in the short run (SR) and in the long run (LR), for both the home and the host countries.

Before moving to the theoretical analysis, it is important to look at the current empirical findings which are summarized based on their findings in terms of employment, productivity and/or growth in the home and the host countries.

SR home employment

It has been well documented that FDI would increase employment in the host countries due to an increase in labour demand. The impact on the home employment, however, is still under debate. Concerning the loss of jobs in the home country caused by FDI, Marin (2004) investigates 2,200 investment projects of 660 firms in Germany and Austria to Eastern Europe during 1990–2001 and shows that outward FDI has directly caused 90,000 lost jobs in Germany and 24,000 in Austria. The numbers of jobs lost to outward FDI are equivalent to 0.25 per cent and 0.75 per cent loss of total employment in Germany and Austria, respectively. Similarly, Debaere, Lee, and Lee (2010), Elia, Mariotti, and Piscitello (2009) and Lee, Lin, and Tsui (2009) find that outward FDI is one main cause of the reduction of home employment. While the findings of Debaere et al (2010) come from taking the approach of multinational corporations, the findings of Elia et al (2009) come from investigating Italian firms during 1996–2002, and the findings of Lee et al (2009) come from studying four Asian Tigers losing home employment due to outward FDI to China.[2]

Meanwhile, there are also studies finding positive and/or neutral effects of FDI on home employment [Masso, Varblane, and Vahter (2008) and Federico and Minerva (2008)]. To be more specific, Masso et al (2008) use firm-level data of Estonia during 1995–2002 and find positive effects of outward FDI on home employment. The positive effects are stronger in service firms than in manufacturing firms and stronger after 1999 when macro performances were better. In other words, the effects of outward FDI on home employment may depend on the sectors and macro performances, at least for Estonia. One may come to a similar conclusion when comparing the work of both Federico and Minerva (2008) and Imbriani, Pittiglio, and Reganati (2011) on Italy. Federico and Minerva (2008) investigate Italy's 12 manufacturing industries and 103 administrative provinces during 1996–2001 and find non-negative effects on home employment when controlling for local industrial structure and area fixed effects. Imbriani et al (2011) use Italy's firm-level data from 2003–2006 and find a loss of home employment in the service sector but not the manufacturing sector. In addition to sectors and macro performances, the effects of outward FDI on home employment may also be country dependent. By investigating multinational enterprises (MNEs) of OECD countries, Molnar, Pain, and Taglioni (2008) find that outward FDI has negative effects on Japan's home employment but has positive effects on the United States' home employment. Lipsey (2004) attributes these differences to the reallocation of parent firms in the home country. That is, the parent firms of the United States have been reallocated to capital-intensive production, but such reallocation does not appear in Japan.

Home productivity and growth

In terms of the effects of FDI on home productivity and growth, the results of empirical studies are also mixed. Focusing on home productivity, Braconier, Ekholm, and Knarvik (2001), Bitzer and Gorg (2009) and Hijzen, Jean, and Mayer (2011) find that outward FDI has negative impacts on home productivity, while Herzer (2010) finds that outward FDI has positive impacts on home total factor productivity. It is unclear whether these studies share the same definition of (total factor) productivity. In addition to the countries included in the studies and the definition of home productivity in each study, one explanation which may contribute to the different effects is the roles of the countries as both the home and the host countries. Moreover, most empirical studies do not specify whether the results are for SR or for LR. This is mainly because the openness to FDI can be limited to specific industries and extended gradually to other industries. Because we do not know the time at which the specific industries were opened to FDI flows, it is difficult to determine whether the results are for SR or for LR.

Since the definitions of home productivity can be different across countries, the different definitions might cause differences in the effects of outward FDI on the home country. The problem of different definitions, however, does not apply to home growth. The definition of home growth is the same across countries. That is the change of gross domestic product (GDP) of a country. Yet when gathering empirical studies to compare, there are also inconsistencies in home growth. According to Lee (2010), the positive causality between outward FDI and home growth is only for LR. The causality for SR, however, is non-positive. Meanwhile, the results of positive effects of FDI on home growth are found in Zhang (2013), Herzer (2012) and Herzer (2008).[3]

If we focus on the majority of results, the results of positive impacts of FDI on home growth while having negative impacts on home productivity and mixed/negative impacts on home employment have raised more questions than answers. For example, how could outward FDI increase home growth while reducing home productivity, capital and employment? Since growth is defined as an increase in output which relies on an increase in productivity, capital and/or employment, how could outward FDI increase home output while lowering productivity, lowering capital and lowering employment? If the loss of employment caused by outward FDI is due to a decrease in labour demand and capital, what is left in the home country to improve the home countries' growth in the LR? Are there other factors for the home countries which have been neglected but crucial to the results? These are important questions to think prior to applying the results of the empirical studies to conduct policies. Possible answers will be discussed in Chapter 7 when we map the theoretical results to empirical findings.

Host productivity and growth

The mixed results of FDI on productivity and growth are not only for the home countries but also for the host countries. Bodman and Le (2013), Lee (2007) and Narula and Driffield (2012) find positive impacts of inward FDI on host productivity. Narula and Driffield (2012) reach the conclusion after reviewing various articles. While Lee (2007) studies nine OECD countries during 1971–1999 and claims that his finding is for LR, Bodman, and Le (2013) study OECD countries during 1982–2003 and attribute the positive effects to the improvement of the host absorptive capacity.

The impacts of FDI have been found negative/non-positive on host growth by Azman-Saini, Baharumshah, and Law (2010), Mencinger (2003) and

Nunnenkamp (2004). Mencinger (2003) uses the panel data of eight EU transition countries in 1994–2001; Nunnenkamp's (2004) finding is based on the panel data of the developing countries; Azman-Saini et al (2010) use the panel data of 85 countries during 1976–2004 and attribute the negative effects to economic freedom.

The positive effects of FDI on host growth have also been found in many other studies. This includes the studies focusing on one country and a group of host countries, regardless of the development stages [Borenszrein, De Gregorio, and Law (1998), Cipollina et al (2012) and Stehrer and Woerz (2009)], the located regions [Bengoa and Sancgez-Eobles (2003), Campos and Kinoshita (2002),[4] Kornecki (2008), Moudatsou (2003), Sghaier et al (2013) and Wang (2009)] and the relations of the origins of FDI [Kim, Lyn, and Zychowicz (2003), Poon and Thompson (1998)].[5] Other studies on the effects of FDI on macro variables without specifying the lengths of periods covered include Asiedu (2004) and Razin (2003). Asiedu (2004) uses the panel data of Africa and finds positive effects on host wage income and employment. Razin (2003) surveys theories and empirical studies and concludes positive effects on growth rates. Note that growth rate is based on the output level of the previous year. The positive effects on the host growth rate would require output growing at an increasing rate. The result is stronger than positive effects on growth.

The gap and the contributions of theoretical analysis

When looking at the datasets adopted to study FDI effects in empirical studies, many studies have used the datasets of multinational enterprises (MNEs). It is important to note that the performances of MNEs do not represent the performance of a country. Using the performances of MNEs to represent a country's performance is misleading and will lead to biased policies, which will bring unexpected consequences. The gap of performances between a country and MNEs is well documented in Nachum, Jones, and Dunning (2001). Nachum et al (2001) use the datasets of the UK in the last century and the share of the UK to OECD as the measurements and show that while the share of UK output in OECD output has been declining, the performances of MNEs in the UK have been consistently better, especially after the 1960s. Therefore, it is important to pay attention to the empirical studies using the datasets of MNEs to represent the performances of a country, especially on macro variables, such as productivities, capital investment, employment, output and growth.

As mentioned, the inconclusive and mixed results of FDI in both home and host countries in the existing literature may have raised more questions than answers. The causes of the mixed results can be various definitions and measurements as well as the methodologies and their associated adjustments and features. The causes can also be specific situations faced by the countries and sectors during a particular period of time that lead to a large range of results. As researchers, we can either be satisfied with the interpretation or we can own the responsibilities to engage in deeper analysis, both theory and empirics, based on the development of the literature to better understand the consistencies and inconsistencies to move the current debates forward. One important step for empirical studies would be to develop methodologies to adjust the gaps of definitions and measurements across datasets and to conduct sensitivity and robustness tests of the existing literature. What the theoretical analysis could do is to look into the inconclusive and mixed results of empirical studies to identify the key factors which have been missed in current empirical research and might be crucial in leading to the inconsistent conclusions. Such theoretical analysis is important in building up the bridge in current empirical studies.

In this chapter, I construct a theoretical model to incorporate the general features of FDI. The theoretical model extends the three-period-lived overlapping-generations framework of Bencivenga and Smith (1991) and Chang (2010, 2012) to an open economy with two countries. The framework incorporates an explicit banking sector and FDI conducted by the firms. The banking sector, so-called banks (or finanicial intermediaries, the FIs), would serve as a portfolio manager for the depositors and as a central planner for the economy. The role of central planner implies zero profit of the banks and rules out the possibility of bank runs, so that the theoretical analysis can focus on the effects of FDI on economic growth.[6] FDI is assumed to be conducted by the firms, which would relocate the production in the host country. The relocation of production and/or corporations and firms is a common feature of firms conducting FDI. The feature applies not only to MNEs but also to domestic firms. There are many reasons firms would conduct FDI.[7] The theoretical framework focuses on FDI which takes advantage of cheap labour cost. The cheap labour cost is assumed to be due to the large population of the host country. It is similar to FDI flowing from developed to emerging/developing economies.

Consequently, in the SR when wage income has not yet adjusted fully to the openness of FDI, the home country would experience an increase in unemployment and a decrease in the rate of return of capital but an increase in the growth rate due to the portfolio adjustment by the banks. Meanwhile, the host country would experience an increase in the rate of return of capital but a decrease in the growth rate. In the LR, when the wage income would fully adjust to the openness of FDI, the home country would experience a decrease in wage income due to the lack of labour demand, while the host country would experience an increase in wage income. The changes of both the rates of return of capital and the growth rates, however, would depend on the presence of the scale effects for both the home and the host countries.

The organization of the chapter is as follows. The second section describes the environment of the model. The model of this chapter is used as a framework which would be modified to incorporate specific features of the topics in each of the following chapters. The third section provides the results of the analysis, which starts with a closed economy, followed by an open economy which allows for FDI flows in the SR and in the LR. The fourth section discusses the role of return flows in both countries, and the fifth section concludes the main results.

The theoretical framework

The agents

The home country and the host country are assumed to be symmetric except for the technology level and the population growth rates. Let superscript asterisk denote the variables of the host country. It is assumed that the technology level in the home country is more advanced than the host country, $A_t > A_t^*$. The populations of the two countries in period t are defined as: $N_t = (1 + n)^2\ N_{t-2}$, and $N_t^* = \left(1+n^*\right)^2 N_{t-2}^*$, where n and n^* represent the population growth rates of the home and the host country, respectively. The population growth rates of the two countries are assumed to be constant, and the growth rate of the home country is assumed lower than that of the host country, $n < n^*$. By normalizing both N_{t-2} and N_{t-2}^* to one, the relations of the populations between the two countries can be simplified to: $N_t \ / \ N_t^* = \left[\left(1+n\right) / \left(1+n^*\right)\right]^2$.

There are two financial assets. One is a liquid asset, and the other is an illiquid asset. It is assumed that the returns of the two assets are exogenous and without default risk and that the access to invest into the two assets is for banks only. The roles of the banks are to serve as portfolio managers for the agents and as central planners to determine the portfolio which would provide the returns to maximize the utility of the agents. The banks are assumed identical, and the agents of different types are assumed equally distributed in the economy. So the problems faced by each bank would be identical. One can read the banks' roles as the roles of the banking system as a whole. As central planners, the banks are assumed to have zero profit, and there is no possibility of bank runs, and neither are the incentive problems, such as the moral hazard and adverse selection problems of the banks.

Each agent is assumed to be born identical and would live for three periods: young, middle-aged and old. When young, every agent would be endowed with one unit of labour, which must be provided in-elastically to earn wage income w_t. At the beginning of the middle age, each agent would learn his/her own type, which would be determined exogenously. There are three types: non-entrepreneurs, non-relocated entrepreneurs and relocated entrepreneurs. One agent would be assigned to one type. The type would remain with the agent throughout the lifetime. The probability for an agent to be an entrepreneur is π and to be a non-entrepreneur is $(1 - \pi)$. The probability for an entrepreneur to be a non-relocated one is $(1 - \beta)$ and to be a relocated one is β. The two probabilities are assumed to be independent of each other. So the probability for an agent to be a relocated entrepreneur would be $\pi\beta$ and to be a non-relocated entrepreneur would be $\pi(1 - \beta)$. An agent's type is assumed to be private information to the agent only. The distribution of the types, however, is public information.

There are two types of goods: output goods and capital goods. It is assumed that capital goods can only be used to produce and are not consumable or tradable. Utility can be obtained by consuming output goods. Both capital and output goods are assumed to perish fully if not used or consumed. Free disposal is also assumed for both capital and output goods to prevent the costs of disposal from distorting the allocation of consumption and production.

After providing the unit of labour, the young would receive wage income w_t, which is paid in the form of output goods. It is assumed that the agents value both the middle-aged consumption ($c_{2,t+1}$) and the old consumption ($c_{3,t+2}$). Therefore, in order to store the value of w_t for both $c_{2,t+1}$ and $c_{3,t+2}$, the young would deposit w_t into the banks. The utility function of an agent is assumed in the form of:

$$u\left(c_{1,t}, c_{2,t+1}, c_{3,t+2}\right) = -\frac{\left[c_{2,t+1} + \phi\left(c_{3,t+2} + \sigma c^{*}_{3,t+2}\right)\right]^{-\gamma}}{\gamma} \tag{2.1}$$

where γ represents the elasticity of intertemporal substitution, $\gamma > -1$. The value of ϕ represents the relative weight of $c_{3,t+2}$ to $c_{2,t+1}$. Depending on the type of agents, the value of ϕ would be:

$$\phi = \begin{cases} 0, \text{ for all non} - \text{entrepreneurs,} \\ 1, \text{ for all entrepreneurs, whether relocating or not.} \end{cases}$$

The value of σ represents the marginal rate of substitution between home goods and host goods, $0 < \sigma < 1$.[8] To complete the model, the initial old in period 1 is endowed with $c_{3,1}$ goods to consume. Each initial middle-aged entrepreneur is endowed with k_1 capital goods, and each initial middle-aged non-entrepreneur is endowed with $c_{2,1}$ output goods.

The firms

To produce output goods would require both labour (L_t) and capital goods (k_t) as inputs. The production function is assumed in the form of $Y_t = A_t \bar{k}_t^{\delta} k_t^{\theta} L_t^{1-\theta}$, where $\theta \in [0,1]$. The variable k_t represents capital goods invested in production by an entrepreneur; the variable $\bar{k}_t$ represents the average capital goods per entrepreneur in the economy; the variable δ represents the scale effect of the economy. The value of δ is assumed equal to $(1 - \theta)$ when the economy has positive externality to production and equal to zero when the scale effects disappear. As shown in the literature, the scale effects exist in the SR but may or may not disappear in the LR, depending on the economic conditions. At $\delta = 0$ in the absence of scale effects, the production function returns to constant return to scale: $Y_t = A_t k_t^{\theta} L_t^{1-\theta}$. The problem faced by the entrepreneur is to choose L_t to maximize the capital gains:

$$Max_{L_t} \left\{Y_t - w_t L_t\right\}, \tag{2.2}$$

which would give the rate of return of capital goods: $ROR(k_t) = (Y_t - w_t L_t)/k_t$.

The banks

The banks play two roles: portfolio managers and central planners. As portfolio managers, the banks would allocate w_t which is deposited by the young between liquid and illiquid assets. The liquid assets would take one period to mature and would provide the rate of return v in output goods at maturity. The illiquid assets would take two periods to mature and would provide the rate of return R

in capital goods at maturity. If liquidating prematurely, the illiquid assets would provide the rate of return χ in output goods, which is less than the return rate of the liquid assets, $0 \leq \chi < \upsilon < R$. The returns of both the liquid and illiquid assets are assumed to be exogenous and are shown in Table 2.1. The banks would then determine the rates of return to the depositors at the time of withdrawals.

As central planners, the banks would choose the investment portfolio and the returns to withdrawals which would maximize the utility of the agents based on the distribution of the types. There are two returns to the withdrawals to be determined by the banks: the withdrawals one period and two periods after the deposits. It is assumed that the banks would not leverage. That is, the banks would operate as *fully funded*, meaning that the returns of the assets whose resources were the depositors of generation t would be returned to the withdrawals of the same generation.

Since the returns of the assets must meet the returns to the withdrawals, the banks must satisfy the following three budget constraints. The three budget constraints are for one period after deposit and for two periods after deposits in capital goods and in output goods. Let $z_t \in [0,1]$ denote the fraction of w_t invested in liquid assets, and let $q_t \in [0,1]$ denote the fraction of w_t invested in illiquid assets. Without reserve requirements, all deposits would be invested in the two assets: $z_t + q_t = 1$. Let $\{r_{1t+1}, r_{2t+2}, \tilde{r}_{2t+2}\}$ denote the rates of returns to the withdrawals, where r_{1t+1} represents the rate of return in output goods to the withdrawals one period after deposit; r_{2t+2} and $\tilde{r}_{2t+2}$ represent the rates of returns in capital goods and output goods, respectively, for the withdrawals two periods after deposit. Therefore, the banks' budget constraints can be written as:

$$(1-\pi)(1+n)^2 r_{1t+1} = \alpha_{1t+1} z_t \upsilon + \alpha_{2t+1} q_t \chi, \tag{2.3}$$

$$\pi(1+n)^2 r_{2t+2} = (1-\alpha_{2t+1}) R q_t, \tag{2.4}$$

$$\pi(1+n)^2 \tilde{r}_{2t+2} = (1-\alpha_{1t+1}) z_t, \tag{2.5}$$

where $\alpha_{1t+1}(\alpha_{1t+1})$ represents the fraction of the liquid (illiquid) assets which are liquidated one period after deposit. Equation (2.3) is for the withdrawals one period after deposit. Both equations (2.4) and (2.5) are for the withdrawals two periods after deposits, but equation (2.4) is paid in capital goods, while equation (2.5) is paid in output goods. The timeline of the withdrawals, consumption, relocation and production of the agents of different types and of the banks is shown in Figure 2.1.

Table 2.1 The rates of returns of assets

	t (investment)	*t + 1 (returns)*	*t + 2 (returns)*
Liquid assets	1	υ (output goods)	
Illiquid assets	1		R (capital goods)
Premature Illiquid assets	1	χ (output goods)	

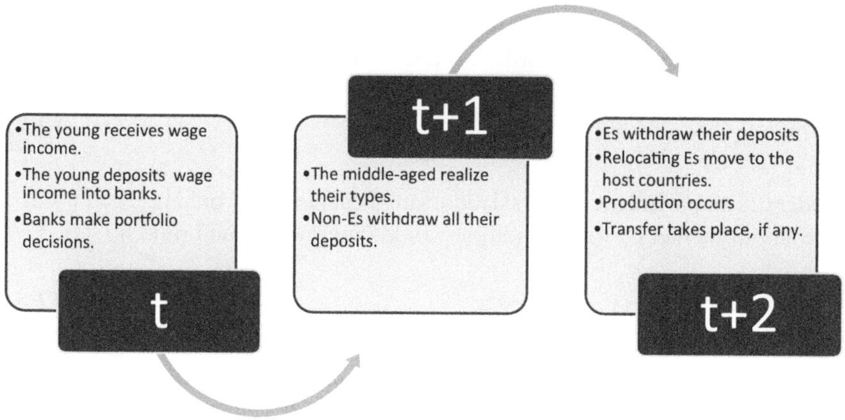

Figure 2.1 The timeline of events
("Es" is the abbreviation of "entrepreneurs")

Since the young who deposit into the banks can be in either type, the objective function of the banks as central planners would be the expected utility function of agents based on the distribution of the types. Moreover, the identical banks and equally distributed agent types imply that one can write the problem faced by the banking system as a whole for the economy. In a closed economy when all entrepreneurs would produce in the domestic country, the the banking system's objective function would be:

$$\max\left\{\begin{array}{c} -\left(\dfrac{1-\pi}{\gamma}\right)\left(r_{1t+1}w_t\right)^{-\gamma} \\ -\dfrac{\pi}{\gamma}\left[ROR\left(k_t\right)r_{2t+2}w_t+\tilde{r}_{2t+2}w_t\right]^{-\gamma} \end{array}\right\} \tag{2.6}$$

where $ROR(k_t)r_{2t+2}w_t$ represents net capital gains of an entrepreneur, since capital goods are spent on production, which provides the rate of return of capital. The task of the banks would be choosing the values of $\{z_t, q_t, \alpha_{1t+1}, \alpha_{2t+1}, r_{1t+1}, r_{2t+2}, \tilde{r}_{2t+2}\}$ to maximize equation (2.6) subject to equations (2.3) to (2.5).

The results

In this section, the results of three cases are analysed: a closed economy and an open economy with FDI flows in the SR and in the LR. The difference between SR and LR in an open economy is the adjustment of w_t. In an open economy in the SR, w_t is assumed to be not yet adjusted to the openness of FDI and would remain the same as a closed economy. In the LR, w_t is assumed to be adjusted fully to the openness of FDI. The variable A_t is assumed to be summarizing both the technology level and total factor productivity.

A closed economy

In a closed economy without FDI flows, the labour demand of each entrepreneur is obtained by taking the first-order condition of equation (2.2) with respect to L_t:

$$L_t = k_t \left[\frac{(1-\theta) A_t \bar{k}_t^{\delta}}{w_t} \right]^{1/\theta}. \tag{2.7}$$

Under full employment, the total labour supply in period t would be $N_t = (1+n)^2$. The labour market clearing condition would determine equilibrium w_t:

$$w_t = \left(\frac{\pi}{(1+n)^2} \right)^{\theta} (1-\theta) A_t \bar{k}_t^{\delta} k_t^{\theta}, \tag{2.8}$$

which is decreasing in n, implying that the higher the population growth rate is, the lower the wage income would be. The value of w_t can then be plugged into equation (2.2) to derive capital gains and $ROR(k_t)$:

$$ROR(k_t) = A_t \theta \left(\frac{(1+n)^2}{\pi} \right)^{1-\theta} \bar{k}_t^{\delta} k_t^{\theta-1}, \tag{2.9}$$

where $ROR(k_t)$ is the same as the marginal productivity of capital MPK_t in this model.

In order for the entrepreneurs to conduct production, the incentive constraint must hold: $ROR(k_t) r_{2t+2} > r_{1t+1} > 0$. So the entrepreneurs would withdraw two periods after deposit, at the maturity of the illiquid assets, to obtain capital goods to produce. As central planners, the banks (banking system) would maximize the returns to the withdrawals. That is to minimize the fraction of illiquid assets to be liquidated prematurely. One equilibrium liquidation would be $\{\alpha_{1t}, \alpha_{2t}\} = \{1, 0\}$, which can be plugged into equations (2.3) to (2.5) to derive the equilibrium returns to the withdrawals:

$$\{r_{1t+1}, r_{2t+2}, \tilde{r}_{2t+2}\} = \left\{ \left(\frac{v}{(1-\pi)(1+n)^2} \right)(1-q_t), \left(\frac{R}{\pi(1+n)^2} \right) q_t, 0 \right\}. \tag{2.10}$$

By substituting equation (2.10) into (2.2) and taking the first-order condition with respect to q_t, one can obtain the equilibrium portfolio allocation:

$$\{z_t, q_t\} = \left\{ \frac{1}{1+\Phi}, \frac{\Phi}{1+\Phi} \right\}, where\, \Phi \equiv \left(\frac{\pi}{1-\pi} \right) \left[\frac{ROR(k_t) R}{v} \right]^{\frac{-\gamma}{1+\gamma}}. \tag{2.11}$$

As shown in equation (2.11), q_t is decreasing in $ROR(k_t)R$ and increasing in v and π. At a higher $ROR(k_t)R$, the central planner needs not place as high q_t to keep/improve the entrepreneurs' utility level. Hence, more deposits would be invested in the liquid assets (an increase in z_t) to improve the non-entrepreneurs' utility level. When this is done, the economy's welfare is improved. Similar argument can be applied to an increase in v but in the opposite direction. Meanwhile, an increase in π means a higher demand for capital goods, so the banks must increase q_t.

Since capital goods are crucial for output production, one definition of growth rate is capital accumulation rate: $\mu_{t+2} \equiv k_{t+2} / k_t = r_{2t+2} w_t / k_t$:

$$\mu_{t+2} = \frac{r_{2t+2} w_t}{k_t} = \left(\frac{R}{\pi(1+n)^2} \right)(1-\theta) \left(\frac{\pi}{(1+n)^2} \right)^{\theta} q_t A_t \bar{k}_t^{\delta} k_t^{\theta-1}, \tag{2.12}$$

where μ_{t+2} is increasing in R, q_t, A_t and $(1 - \theta)$, but decreasing in π and $(1 + n)$. In fact, R has both a positive direct effect and a negative indirect effect on μ_{t+2} via q_t, as explained earlier. When the direct effect dominates, an increase in R would promote μ_{t+2}. An increase in π would have an overall negative effect on μ_{t+2}, since the negative effect via r_{2t+2} is stronger than the positive effect via w_t. An increase in A_t would have direct positive impacts on μ_{t+2} but would have negative indirect impacts on μ_{t+2} via q_t due to its positive effects on $ROR(k_t)$. When the direct effect dominates, an increase in A_t would increase μ_{t+2}, which is consistent with the findings in current literature in both theory and empirics. Moreover, in the presence of scale effects, $\delta = 1 - \theta$, at $\bar{k}_t = k_t$, μ_{t+2} is independent of capital goods k_t. In the absence of scale effects, $\delta = 0$, μ_{t+2} is decreasing in k_t. Applying the analysis to the host country, one can find that the countries with a higher technology level and a lower population growth rate ($A_t^* < A_t$, and $n^* > n$) tend to have higher wage income and a higher growth rate ($w_t^* < w_t$ and $\mu_{t+2}^* < \mu_{t+2}$). As mentioned in the first section, these countries tend to be the sources of FDI, such as the United States and Europe since the 1960s and emerging markets after the 1980s.

An open economy in the SR

It is assumed that FDI flows are opened in both countries in period t. Having a higher technology level and a lower population growth rate ($A_t^* < A_t$ and $n^* > n$), the home country would have higher wage income than the host country $w_t^* < w_t$. To take advantage of cheap labour costs in the host country, the home (host) country in the model would be the source (destination) of FDI in an open economy: $\beta^{SR} > 0$ and $\beta^{SR*} = 0$. In the SR, $w_t^{SR} = w_t$ [equation (2.8)].

The home country (SR)

In period t, FDI outflows from the home country is due to the relocated entrepreneurs of generation t–2, who take capital goods to the host country to produce. The outflow FDI would reduce the average capital goods per non-relocated home entrepreneur to $(1-\beta^{SR})\bar{k}_t$[9], which would change the production to $Y_t^{SR} = A_t\left[(1-\beta^{SR})\overline{k_t^{SR}}\right]^{\delta} (k_t^{SR})^{\theta} (L_t^{SR})^{1-\theta}$. Accordingly, the labour demand per entrepreneur would change to:

$$L_t^{SR} = \left[\frac{(1-\theta) A_t \left[(1-\beta^{SR})\bar{k}_t\right]^{\delta}}{w_t} \right]^{1/\theta} k_t.$$

By plugging w_t [equation (2.8)] into L_t^{SR}, the equilibrium L_t^{SR} would be:

$$L_t^{SR} = \frac{(1+n)^2 (1-\beta^{SR})^{\frac{\delta}{\theta}}}{\pi}, \tag{2.13}$$

where $L_t^{SR} < L_t$, lower than that in the closed economy [equation (2.7)]. The decrease in labour demand would generate unemployment:

$$UE_t = (1+n)^2 \left[1-(1-\beta^{SR})^{1+\frac{\delta}{\theta}}\right], \tag{2.14}$$

where UE_t is increasing in β^{SR}, indicating that more FDI outflows would cause higher home unemployment in the SR. The result of the loss of home employment to outward FDI supports the findings of Debaere et al (2010), Elia et al (2009), Lee et al (2009) and Marin's (2004) but not the findings of Masso et al (2008) and Federico and Minerva (2008). One possible explanation is that the period covered in Masso et al (2008) is when Estonia experienced particularly better macro performances, and it is unclear that the sample of firms in the manufacturing and administrative sectors selected by Federico and Minerva (2008) could represent general macro-economy of Italy. More comparison between theoretical and empirical findings will be discussed in Chapter 7.

By plugging equation (2.13) into (2.2), one can derive $ROR(k_t^{SR})$:

$$ROR(k_t^{SR}) = \theta\left(\frac{(1+n)^2}{\pi}\right)^{1-\theta} (1-\beta^{SR})^{\frac{\delta}{\theta}} A_t \left(\overline{k_t^{SR}}\right)^{\delta} (k_t^{SR})^{\theta-1}, \tag{2.15}$$

where $ROR(k_t^{SR}) < ROR(k_t)$, lower than that in the closed economy, and is decreasing in β^{SR} and π but increasing in $(1 + n)$. As mentioned in the first section, most studies finding negative effects of outward FDI on home productivity [Braconier et al (2001), Britzer and Gorg (2009), Hijzen et al (2011)] have covered a long period of time. However, without knowing specific industries and countries which were opened to FDI flows, especially for studies which include a group of countries, it is difficult to conclude whether their effects are for SR or for LR.

The loss of employment means only a fraction of the employed young would have w_t to deposit. Accordingly, the problem of the banks would be modified to:

$$Max \left\{ \begin{array}{c} -\left(\dfrac{(1-\beta^{SR})^{\frac{\delta}{\theta}+1}(1+n)^2(1-\pi)}{\gamma}\right)\left(r_{1t+1}^{SR} w_t\right)^{-\gamma} \\ -\dfrac{(1-\beta^{SR})^{\frac{\delta}{\theta}+1}(1+n)^2\pi}{\gamma}\left\{\begin{array}{l} \beta^{SR}\left[(1-\tau)ROR(k_t^{SR*})r_{2t+2}^{SR} w_t + \tilde{r}_{2t+2}^{SR} w_t\right] \\ +(1-\beta^{SR})\left[ROR(k_t^{SR})r_{2t+2}^{SR} w_t + \tilde{r}_{2t+2}^{SR} w_t\right] \end{array}\right\}^{-\gamma} \end{array} \right\}, \tag{2.16}$$

subject to:

$$\left(1-\beta^{SR}\right)^{\frac{\delta}{\theta}+1}(1+n)^2(1-\pi)r_{1t+1}^{SR} = \alpha_{1t+1}^{SR} z_t^{SR} \upsilon + \alpha_{2t+1}^{SR} q_t^{SR} \chi,$$
$$\left(1-\beta^{SR}\right)^{\frac{\delta}{\theta}+1}(1+n)^2 \pi r_{2t+2}^{SR} = \left(1-\alpha_{2t+1}^{SR}\right) R q_t^{SR}, \tag{2.17}$$
$$\left(1-\beta^{SR}\right)^{\frac{\delta}{\theta}+1}(1+n)^2 \pi \tilde{r}_{2t+2}^{SR} = \left(1-\alpha_{1t+1}^{SR}\right) z_t^{SR} \upsilon.$$

The modifications show that in the face of unemployment, the banks' objective function is limited to the depositors who are the employed young. In other words, the banks' role is restricted to the employed agents only, rather than the whole economy, which includes the unemployed workers. Moreover, in the fully funded system, the investment portfolios decided by the banks would be modified in period t in response to the openness of FDI. The investment portfolios made in period t would not receive the returns of the illiquid assets until period $t+2$. This implies that some effects of FDI would take two periods to surface. These effects which appear in period $t+2$ are important, as the returns of illiquid assets at maturity would be capital goods, which have direct effects on economic growth.

In order for the entrepreneurs to take capital goods to produce, the incentive constraint for production must hold: $(1-\tau)ROR\left(k_t^{SR*}\right)r_{2t+2}^{SR} = ROR\left(k_t^{SR}\right) r_{2t+2}^{SR} > r_{1t+1}^{SR} > 0$, where τ represents the outflow tax rate charged by the host country. By substituting equation (2.15) into $ROR\left(k_t^{SR}\right)$, one can simplify the incentive constraint to:

$$k_t^{SR} < \widehat{k_t^{SR}},\ where\ \widehat{k_t^{SR}} \equiv \left[\frac{\theta A_t R}{\upsilon}\left(\frac{q_t^{SR}}{1-q_t^{SR}}\right)\left(\frac{1-\pi}{\pi}\right)\right]^{\frac{1}{1-\theta}}\left(\frac{(1+n)^2}{\pi}\right)\left(1-\beta^{SR}\right)^{\frac{\delta}{\theta(1-\theta)}} \left(\overline{k_t^{SR}}\right)^{\frac{\delta}{1-\theta}}, \tag{2.18}$$

which shows that at $k_t^{SR} < \widehat{k_t^{SR}}$, the entrepreneurs would withdraw at the maturity of illiquid assets and obtain capital goods to start production. The reason why it requires k_t^{SR} sufficiently small is because $ROR\left(k_t^{SR}\right)$ is decreasing in k_t^{SR}. The higher the amount of k_t^{SR} is, the lower $ROR\left(k_t^{SR}\right)$ would be and the less likely for the incentive constraint to hold.

When the incentive constraint holds, one equilibrium for liquidation and the returns to the withdrawals would be: $\left\{\alpha_{1t+1}^{SR}, \alpha_{2t+1}^{SR}\right\} = \{1,0\}$, $\tilde{r}_{2t+2}^{SR} = 0$, and

$$\left\{r_{1t+1}^{SR}, r_{2t+2}^{SR}\right\} = \left\{\left(\frac{\upsilon}{(1-\pi)\left(1-\beta^{SR}\right)^{\frac{1}{\theta}}(1+n)^2}\right)\left(1-q_t^{SR}\right), \left(\frac{R}{\pi\left(1-\beta^{SR}\right)^{\frac{1}{\theta}}(1+n)^2}\right) q_t^{SR}\right\},$$

where both r_{1t+1}^{SR} and r_{2t+2}^{SR} are increasing in employment factor, $\left(1-\beta^{SR}\right)^{\frac{1}{\theta}}$. The higher the employment is, the lower the returns to each withdrawal would be. The investment portfolio would change to:

$$\left\{z_t^{SR}, q_t^{SR}\right\} = \left\{\frac{1}{1+\Phi^{SR}}, \frac{\Phi^{SR}}{1+\Phi^{SR}}\right\}, \tag{2.19}$$

where $\Phi^{SR} \equiv \left(\frac{\pi}{1-\pi}\right)\left(\frac{R}{v}\right)^{\frac{-\gamma}{1+\gamma}}\left[\beta^{SR}(1-\tau)ROR\left(k_t^{SR*}\right)+\left(1-\beta^{SR}\right)ROR\left(k_t^{SR}\right)\right]^{\frac{-\gamma}{1+\gamma}}$.

Equation (2.19) shows that q_t^{SR} is increasing in outward FDI factors, τ and β^{SR}. The result is due to the role of the banks as central planners. To compensate for the loss of capital gains of home production caused by outward FDI, the banks would invest more in the illiquid assets in order to provide more capital goods as the returns to the entrepreneurs to stimulate capital gains. As a result, the increase in r_{2t+2}^{SR} would increase the SR home growth rate at $t+2$:

$$\mu_{t+2}^{SR} = \left(\frac{R}{\pi\left(1-\beta^{SR}\right)^{\frac{1}{\theta}}(1+n)^2}\right) q_t^{SR}\left(\frac{\pi}{(1+n)^2}\right)^{\theta}(1-\theta)A_t\left(\overline{k_t^{SR}}\right)^{\delta}\left(k_t^{SR}\right)^{\theta-1}, \quad (2.20)$$

where $\mu_{t+2}^{SR} > \mu_t$ and is increasing in β^{SR} when the direct effects dominate. The result shows that outward FDI would promote the SR home growth rate, mainly because of the central planner role of the banks in adjusting investment portfolios. For similar reasons, although there are studies which find positive effects of FDI on home growth [Zhang (2013), Herzer (2012) and Herzer (2008)], it is difficult to know whether their results are for SR or for LR. Without the details of the openness to FDI of each country, especially when some do not specify the covered period [Herzer (2012)], it is difficult to compare the theoretical results to theirs.

The host country (SR)

The openness to FDI would bring the host country inward FDI, which would increase the average capital stock of the host country to $\left[\overline{k}_t^{SR*}+\left(\pi\beta^{SR}/\pi^*\right)\overline{k}_t^{SR}\right]$. By defining $\overline{k}_t^{SR*} = \xi\overline{k}_t^{SR}$, the average capital stock of the host country can be simplified to $\left[1+\left(\pi\beta^{SR}/\xi\pi^*\right)\right]\left(\overline{k}_t^{SR*}\right)$. The host production function can then be modified to:

$$Y_t^{SR*} = A_t^*\left[1+\left(\frac{\pi\beta^{SR}}{\pi^*\xi}\right)\right]^{\delta^*}\left(\overline{k}_t^{SR*}\right)^{\delta^*}\left(k_t^{SR*}\right)^{\theta^*}\left(L_t^{SR*}\right)^{1-\theta^*}.$$

Provided $w_t^{SR*} = w_t^* = \left(\pi^*/\left(1+n^*\right)^2\right)^{\theta^*}\left(1-\theta^*\right)A_t^*\left(\overline{k}_t^*\right)^{\delta^*}\left(k_t^*\right)^{\theta^*}$ [equation (2.8)], the labour per entrepreneur would become:

$$L_t^{SR*} = \frac{\left(1+n^*\right)^2}{\pi^*\left(1+\frac{\pi\beta^{SR}}{\pi^*}\right)},$$

and the rate of return of host capital would be:

$$ROR\left(k_t^{SR*}\right) = A_t^*\left[\frac{\left(1+n^*\right)^2}{\pi^*}\right]^{1-\theta^*}\frac{1}{\left(1+\frac{\pi\beta^{SR}}{\pi^*}\right)}\left[\left(1+\frac{\pi\beta^{SR}}{\pi^*\xi}\right)^{\delta^*}\left(1+\frac{\pi\beta^{SR}}{\pi^*}\right)^{\theta^*} - \left(1-\theta^*\right)\right]\left(\overline{k}_t^{SR*}\right)^{\delta^*}\left(k_t^{SR*}\right)^{\theta^*-1}, \quad (2.21)$$

where $ROR\left(k_t^{SR*}\right) > ROR\left(k_t^*\right)$. Equation (2.21) shows that $ROR\left(k_t^{SR*}\right)$ is decreasing in k_t^{SR*} and is increasing in $(1 + n^*)$ and β^{SR} at $\xi = 1$ and in the presence of the scale effect $\delta^* = 1 - \theta^*$. This implies that the inward FDI would improve host productivity in the SR. Similarly, without the details of the openness to FDI of each country, although some studies have covered a long period of time [Bodman and Le (2013)], it is difficult to tell whether the empirical results are for SR or for LR and to compare theoretical and empirical results on productivity.

The relocated home entrepreneurs would increase labour demand in the host country, which would remain at full employment after the openness to FDI. To satisfy the incentive constraint for the entrepreneurs to produce would require k_t^{SR*} to be sufficiently small:

$$k_t^{SR*} < \widehat{k_t^{SR*}}$$

where

$$\widehat{k_t^{SR*}} \equiv \left[\frac{\left(1+n^*\right)^2}{\pi^*}\right]^{1-\theta^*} \left\{ A_t^* \frac{1}{\left(1+\frac{\pi\beta^{SR}}{\pi^*}\right)} \left[\left(1+\frac{\pi\beta^{SR}}{\pi^*\xi}\right)^{\delta^*}\left(1+\frac{\pi\beta^{SR}}{\pi^*}\right)^{\theta^*} - \left(1-\theta^*\right)\right] \left(\frac{R}{\upsilon}\right)\left(\frac{q_t^{SR*}}{1-q_t^{SR*}}\right)\left(\frac{1-\pi^*}{\pi^*}\right) \right\}^{\frac{1}{1-\theta^*}} \left(\bar{k}_t^{SR*}\right)^{\frac{\delta^*}{1-\theta^*}}$$

Equilibrium liquidation decision $\left\{\alpha_{1t+1}^{SR*}, \alpha_{2t+1}^{SR*}\right\} = \{1, 0\}$ would give the returns to withdrawals: $\tilde{r}_{2t+2}^{SR*} = 0$ and

$$\left\{r_{1t+1}^{SR*}, r_{2t+2}^{SR*}, \tilde{r}_{2t+2}^{SR*}\right\} = \left\{\left(\frac{\upsilon}{\left(1-\pi^*\right)\left(1+n^*\right)^2}\right)\left(1-q_t^{SR*}\right), \left(\frac{R}{\pi^*\left(1+n^*\right)^2}\right)q_t^{SR*}, 0\right\}.$$

The portfolio allocation would be:

$$\left\{z_t^{SR*}, q_t^{SR*}\right\} = \left\{\frac{1}{1+\Phi^{SR*}}, \frac{\Phi^{SR*}}{1+\Phi^{SR*}}\right\}, \; \Phi^{SR*} \equiv \left(\frac{\pi^*}{1-\pi^*}\right)\left(\frac{R}{\upsilon}\right)^{\frac{-\gamma}{1+\gamma}}\left[ROR\left(k_t^{SR*}\right)\right]^{\frac{-\gamma}{1+\gamma}}.$$

where q_t^* is decreasing in $(1 + n^*)$ via $ROR\left(k_t^{SR*}\right)$ and decreasing in FDI factors π and β^{SR}. The host growth rate would be:

$$\mu_{t+2}^{SR*} = \frac{R}{\pi^*} q_t^{SR*} \left(\frac{\pi^*}{\left(1+n^*\right)^2}\right)^{\theta^*} \left(1-\theta^*\right) A_t^* \left(\bar{k}_t^{SR*}\right)^{\delta^*} \left(k_t^{SR*}\right)^{\theta^*-1}, \tag{2.22}$$

where $\mu_{t+2}^{SR*} < \mu_t^*$, and μ_{t+2}^{SR*} is decreasing in FDI factors, π and β^{SR}, via q_t^{SR*}. This is mainly due to the central planner role played by the banks. The higher $ROR\left(k_t^{SR*}\right)$ would lead the banks to reduce q_t^{SR*} and hence decrease μ_{t+2}^{SR*}. The result of negative effects on host growth supports the findings of Mencinger (2003) and

Nunnenkamp (2004) but not the findings of Campos and Kinoshita (2002). Although both Mencinger (2003) and Campos and Kinoshita (2002) cover short periods of time, it is unclear whether the results come from the openness to FDI. This is because depending on economic conditions, the effects of FDI may take specific periods of time to surface. For the studies which cover a short period of time, it is also important to ensure there were not significant policies prior to the openness to FDI, and cause such effects which may be misunderstood as the effects of FDI.

SR return flows and the relocation rate

After production, the relocated entrepreneurs have options on whether to consume the home or the host products. To simplify the model, it is assumed that the relocated entrepreneurs must flow capital gains to the home country if choosing to consume home products and that the entrepreneurs would choose either home or host products to consume but not both. As mentioned, the return flows would be costly to the relocated entrepreneurs. The cost would be the tax rate on the return flows.[9] However, consuming host product would cost $MRS = \sigma$, as indicated in the utility function [equation (2.1)]. For a relocated entrepreneur to conduct return flows would require:

$$(1-\tau) \geq \sigma \tag{2.23}$$

Having return flows available, the no-arbitrage condition states that the old consumption of home entrepreneurs, whether relocated or not, must be the same. Let $c_{3,t+2}^{NR}\left(c_{3,t+2}^{R}\right)$ denote old consumption of a non-relocated (relocated) entrepreneur. The non-arbitrage condition indicates: $c_{3,t+2}^{NR} = c_{3,t+2}^{R}$. Since $c_{3,t+2}^{NR} = ROR\left(k_t^{SR}\right)k_t$, and $c_{3,t+2}^{R} = (1-\tau)ROR\left(k_t^{SR*}\right)k_t$, the arbitrage condition can be used to derive the equilibrium relocation rate, β^{SR}. By combining with equations (2.15) and (2.21), the arbitrage condition can be written as:

$$(1-\tau)A_t^*\left[\frac{\left(1+n^*\right)^2}{\pi^*}\right]^{1-\theta^*}\frac{1}{\left(1+\frac{\pi\beta^{SR}}{\pi^*}\right)}\left[\left(1+\frac{\pi\beta^{SR}}{\pi^*\xi}\right)^{\delta^*}\left(1+\frac{\pi\beta^{SR}}{\pi^*}\right)^{\theta^*}-\left(1-\theta^*\right)\right]$$

$$\left(\bar{k}_t^{SR*}\right)^{\delta^*}\left(k_t^{SR*}\right)^{\theta^*-1} = \theta\left(\frac{(1+n)^2}{\pi}\right)^{1-\theta}\left(1-\beta^{SR}\right)^{\frac{\delta}{\theta}}A_t\left(\overline{k_t^{SR}}\right)^{\delta}\left(k_t^{SR}\right)^{\theta-1}, \tag{2.24}$$

where β^{SR} is increasing in $\left(A_t / A_t^*\right)$, $[(1+n)/(1+n^*)]$ and τ but decreasing in (π / π^*). The result implies that the relative economic conditions of the home and the host countries matter to FDI flows, at least for FDI aiming to take advantage of cheap labour costs. When technology (A_t) would increase w_t, the improvement of home technology would encourage FDI to the host countries with less advanced technology. The trend of FDI flows may decrease when A_t^* starts catching up A_t and reduces the ratio $\left(A_t / A_t^*\right)$. The result is consistent with the findings of Das (2013), who uses panel data of developing countries during the period of 1996–2010 and finds that technology investment in the home countries could encourage outward FDI from developing countries. Meanwhile, a higher tax rate on return flows (τ) would require more FDI (a higher β^{SR}) in the first place in order to consume at a similar level to that of the non-relocated entrepreneur. The relative ratios of populations $[(1+n)/(1+n^*)]$ and the proportion of entrepreneurs (π / π^*) are two interesting factors which imply that the intensity of entrepreneurs of a country may serve as an important indicator for FDI flows and may assist in determining FDI flows of specific industries.

An open economy in the LR

Recall that LR is when w_t would adjust fully to the openness of FDI. As shown in the SR, it takes at least two periods for some effects of SR to surface. To avoid confusion between SR and LR, it is assumed that it would take three periods for LR to take place, that is, it is until period $t+3$, when w_t would adjust fully to the openness of FDI and when full employment would be restored in the home country. Meanwhile, since the scale effects may or may not exist in the LR due to various economic conditions, the analysis would discuss both cases: the case for the presence of the scale effects ($\delta = 1-\theta$) and the case for the absence of the scale effects ($\delta = 0$).

The home country (LR)

In the LR in period $t+3$, w_t would adjust fully to the reduction of the average capital stock to $\left(1-\beta^{LR}\right)\overline{k_{t+1}^{LR}}$, and full employment would be restored. Therefore, labour supply per non-relocated home entrepreneur would be:

$$L_{t+3}^{LR} = \frac{(1+n)^2}{\pi\left(1-\beta^{LR}\right)}, \tag{2.25}$$

and the wage income would be:

$$w_{t+3}^{LR} = A_{t+3}(1-\theta)\left[\frac{\pi\left(1-\beta^{LR}\right)}{(1+n)^2}\right]^{\theta}\left[\left(1-\beta^{LR}\right)\overline{k_{t+3}^{LR}}\right]^{\delta}\left(k_{t+3}^{LR}\right)^{\theta}, \tag{2.26}$$

where $w_{t+3}^{LR} < w_t$ and w_{t+3}^{LR} is decreasing in the FDI factor, β^{LR}, regardless of the presence of the scale effects. The result is consistent with Gopinath and Chen (2003).[10] Moreover, the wage income in the presence of the scale effects $\left(w_{t+3}^{LR,S}\right)$ is higher than the wage income in the absence of the scale effects $\left(w_{t+3}^{LR,NS}\right)$, $w_{t+3}^{LR,S} > w_{t+3}^{LR,NS}$. The FDI factor, β^{LR}, would affect $w_{t+3}^{LR,NS}$ more severely.

The value of w_{t+3}^{LR} [equation (2.26)] can then be plugged into capital gains and derive $ROR\left(k_{t+3}^{LR}\right)$:

$$ROR\left(k_{t+3}^{LR}\right) = \theta A_{t+1}\left[\frac{(1+n)^2}{\pi\left(1-\beta^{LR}\right)}\right]^{1-\theta}\left[\left(1-\beta^{LR}\right)\overline{k_{t+3}^{LR}}\right]^{\delta}\left(k_{t+3}^{LR}\right)^{\theta-1}, \tag{2.27}$$

where the absence of the scale effect would increase $ROR\left(k_{t+3}^{LR}\right)$: $ROR\left(k_{t+3}^{LR,NS}\right) > ROR\left(k_{t+3}^{LR,S}\right) = ROR\left(k_{t-1}\right) > ROR\left(k_{t}^{SR}\right)$. Because of the fully adjusted w_{t+3}^{LR} in the LR, the scale effects would offset the effects of outward FDI on $ROR\left(k_{t+3}^{LR}\right)$ and reduce $ROR\left(k_{t+3}^{LR,S}\right)$ back to the same level as the closed economy, $ROR\left(k_{t-1}\right)$, which is still higher than $ROR\left(k_{t}^{SR}\right)$. In general, the effect of outward FDI, β^{LR}, on $ROR\left(k_{t+1}^{LR}\right)$ is negative in the SR but non-negative in the LR. The theoretical result for LR productivity is consistent with the findings of Herzer (2011), which claims that his findings are for LR. If so, the theoretical result suggests that the scale effects of 33 countries included in Herzer (2011) may be absent.

The change of w_{t+3}^{LR} and $ROR\left(k_{t+3}^{LR}\right)$ would change the problem faced by the banks to:

$$Max\left\{\begin{array}{c} -\left(\dfrac{(1-\pi)}{\gamma}\right)\left(r_{1t+4}^{LR}w_{t+3}^{LR}\right)^{-\gamma} \\ -\dfrac{\pi}{\gamma}\left\{\begin{array}{l}\beta^{SR}\left[(1-\tau)ROR\left(k_{t+3}^{LR*}\right)r_{2t+5}^{LR}w_{t+3}^{LR}+\tilde{r}_{2t+5}^{LR}w_{t+3}^{LR}\right] \\ +\left(1-\beta^{LR}\right)\left[ROR\left(k_{t+3}^{LR}\right)r_{2t+5}^{LR}w_{t+3}^{LR}+\tilde{r}_{2t+5}^{LR}w_{t+3}^{LR}\right]\end{array}\right\}^{-\gamma}\end{array}\right\}$$

$$(1-\pi)r_{1t+4}^{LR} = \alpha_{1t+4}^{LR}z_{t+3}^{LR}v + \alpha_{2t+4}^{LR}q_{t+3}^{LR}\chi,$$

$$\pi r_{2t+5}^{LR} = \left(1-\alpha_{2t+4}^{LR}\right)Rq_{t+3}^{LR},$$

$$\pi\tilde{r}_{2t+5}^{LR} = \left(1-\alpha_{1t+4}^{LR}\right)vz_{t+3}^{LR},$$

where r_{1t+4}^{LR} represents the returns to the withdrawals in period $t+4$, one period after deposits in period $t+3$, and r_{2t+5}^{LR} represents the returns to the withdrawals in period $t+5$, two periods after the deposits. As shown in equation (2.27), $ROR\left(k_{t+3}^{LR}\right)$ is decreasing in k_{t+3}^{LR}. In order for the entrepreneurs to produce, the incentive constraint, $ROR\left(k_{t+3}^{LR}\right)r_{2t+5}^{LR} > r_{1t+4}^{LR}$, must hold. It implies:

$$k_{t+3}^{LR} < \widehat{k_{t+3}^{LR}},$$

where

$$\widehat{k_{t+3}^{LR}} \equiv \left[\frac{\theta A_{t+3}R}{v}\left(\frac{q_{t+3}^{LR}}{1-q_{t+3}^{LR}}\right)\left(\frac{1-\pi}{\pi}\right)\right]^{\frac{1}{1-\theta}}\left[\frac{(1+n)^2}{\pi\left(1-\beta^{LR}\right)}\right]\left[\left(1-\beta^{LR}\right)\overline{k_{t+3}^{LR}}\right]^{\frac{\delta}{1-\theta}}. \tag{2.28}$$

Accordingly, one equilibrium liquidation $\left\{\alpha_{1t+1}^{LR}, \alpha_{2t+1}^{LR}\right\} = \{1,0\}$ would give the equilibrium returns to the withdrawals:

$$\left\{r_{1t+4}^{LR}, r_{2t+5}^{LR}, \tilde{r}_{2t+5}^{LR}\right\} = \left\{\left(\frac{v}{(1-\pi)(1+n)^2}\right)\left(1-q_{t+3}^{LR}\right), \left(\frac{R}{\pi(1+n)^2}\right)q_{t+3}^{LR}, 0\right\},$$

and the portfolio allocation:

$$\left\{z_{t+3}^{LR}, q_{t+3}^{LR}\right\} = \left\{\frac{1}{1+\Phi^{LR}}, \frac{\Phi^{LR}}{1+\Phi^{LR}}\right\},$$

where $\Phi^{LR} \equiv \frac{\pi}{1-\pi}\left(\frac{R}{v}\right)^{\frac{-\gamma}{1+\gamma}}\left[\beta^{LR}(1-\tau)ROR\left(k_{t+3}^{LR*}\right)+\left(1-\beta^{LR}\right)ROR\left(k_{t+3}^{LR}\right)\right]^{-\frac{\gamma}{1+\gamma}}$.

Therefore, the LR home growth rate in period $t+5$ would be:

$$\mu_{t+5}^{LR} = \left(\frac{R}{\pi(1+n)^2}\right) q_{t+3}^{LR} A_{t+5}(1-\theta)\left[\frac{\pi\left(1-\beta^{LR}\right)}{(1+n)^2}\right]^{\theta}\left[\left(1-\beta^{LR}\right)\overline{k_{t+5}^{LR}}\right]^{\delta}\left(k_{t+5}^{LR}\right)^{\theta-1}, \tag{2.29}$$

where μ_{t+5}^{LR} is decreasing in FDI factor β^{LR}. In terms of the scale effects, $\mu_{t+3}^{LR,NS} < \mu_{t+3}^{LR,S}$ due to $w_{t+3}^{LR,NS} < w_{t+3}^{LR,S}$ and $q_{t+3}^{LR,NS} < q_{t+3}^{LR,S}$ $\left(\because ROR\left(k_{t+5}^{LR,NS}\right) > ROR\left(k_{t+5}^{LR,S}\right)\right)$, meaning the presence of the scale effects would give a higher home growth rate. The comparison to SR is more complicated. The two main components of μ_{t+5}^{LR} are w_{t+3}^{LR} and r_{2t+5}^{LR}. A lower LR wage income $w_{t+3}^{LR} < w_t^{SR} = w_t$ would reduce μ_{t+5}^{LR}. A higher $ROR\left(k_{t+3}^{LR}\right)$ would reduce q_{t+3}^{LR} and r_{2t+5}^{LR} and hence lower μ_{t+5}^{LR}. So the home growth rate would be lower in the LR than SR: $\mu_{t+5}^{LR} < \mu_{t+2}^{SR}$. One review work which focuses on growth rate is Razin (2003), which concludes positive effects on growth rates but does not specify whether it is for SR or LR. Most empirical studies focus on growth rather than growth rate and have mixed results, as mentioned in the first section. These differences make the comparison between theoretical and empirical studies more complicated. The details of the comparison will be discussed in Chapter 7.

The host country (LR)

The inward FDI has increased the host country's average capital stock per entrepreneur to $\left[\bar{k}_{t+3}^{*} + \left(\pi\beta^{LR} / \pi^{*}\right)\bar{k}_{t+3}\right]$. At $\bar{k}_{t+3}^{*} = \xi\bar{k}_{t+3}$, where ξ is constant, the average capital stock per entrepreneur can be simplified to $\left[1+\left(\pi\beta^{LR} / \xi\pi^{*}\right)\right]\left(\bar{k}_{t+3}^{*}\right)$. Therefore, the host production function would change to:

$$Y_{t+3}^{LR*} = A_{t+3}^{*}\left[\left(1+\frac{\pi\beta^{LR}}{\pi^{*}\xi}\right)\left(\bar{k}_{t+3}^{LR*}\right)\right]^{\delta^{*}}\left(k_{t+3}^{LR*}\right)^{\theta^{*}}\left(L_{t+3}^{LR*}\right)^{1-\theta^{*}}.$$

The labour demand per entrepreneur would be:

$$L_{t+3}^{LR*} = \left[\frac{A_t^{*}\left(1-\theta^{*}\right)}{w_{t+3}^{LR*}}\right]^{\frac{1}{\theta^{*}}}\left[\left(1+\frac{\pi\beta^{LR}}{\pi^{*}\xi}\right)\left(\bar{k}_{t+3}^{LR*}\right)\right]^{\frac{\delta^{*}}{\theta^{*}}} k_{t+3}^{LR*}.$$

The market clearing condition gives

$$L_{t+3}^{LR*} = \frac{\left(1+n^{*}\right)^2}{\pi^{*}\left(1+\frac{\pi\beta^{LR}}{\pi^{*}}\right)},$$

where $L_{t+3}^{LR*} < L_{t+3}^{*}$. This is because the relocated home entrepreneurs would share the existing labour supply of the host country. So the amount of labour distributed to each entrepreneur would be lower. The result is supported by the evidence of Slovenia [Zajc, Kejzar, and Kumar (2006)].[11] In the LR, w_{t+3}^{LR*} would adjust fully to the openness of FDI and would change to:

$$w_{t+3}^{LR*} = A_{t+3}^{*}\left(1-\theta^{*}\right)\left[\frac{\pi^{*}}{\left(1+n^{*}\right)^{2}}\left(1+\frac{\pi\beta^{LR}}{\pi^{*}}\right)\right]^{\theta^{*}}\left[\left(1+\frac{\pi\beta^{LR}}{\pi^{*}\xi}\right)\left(\bar{k}_{t+3}^{LR*}\right)\right]^{\delta^{*}}\left(k_{t+3}^{LR*}\right)^{\theta^{*}}, \tag{2.30}$$

where $w_{t+3}^{LR*} > w_{t}^{*}$, and w_{t+3}^{LR*} is increasing in FDI factors, π and β^{LR}. The increase in w_{t+3}^{LR*} is due to the increase in labour demand. At $\left(\bar{k}_{t+3}^{LR*}\right) > \left(1+\pi\beta^{LR}/\pi^{*}\right), w_{t+3}^{LR*}$ in the presence of the scale effects is larger than that in the absence of the scale effects: $w_{t+3}^{LR*,S} > w_{t+3}^{LR*,NS}$. The increase in w_{t+3}^{LR*} is supported by the evidence found in Africa [Asiedu (2004)].

The values of L_{t+3}^{LR*} and w_{t+3}^{LR*} [equation (2.30)] can then be substituted into Y_{t+3}^{LR*} to obtain $ROR\left(k_{t+3}^{LR*}\right)$:

$$ROR\left(k_{t+3}^{LR*}\right) = \theta^{*}\left[\frac{\left(1+n^{*}\right)^{2}}{\pi^{*}\left(1+\frac{\pi\beta^{LR}}{\pi^{*}}\right)}\right]^{1-\theta^{*}} A_{t+3}^{*}\left[\left(1+\frac{\pi\beta^{LR}}{\pi^{*}\xi}\right)\left(\bar{k}_{t+3}^{LR*}\right)\right]^{\delta^{*}}\left(k_{t+3}^{LR*}\right)^{\theta^{*}-1}, \tag{2.31}$$

where $ROR\left(k_{t}^{LR*}\right)$ is decreasing in k_{t}^{LR*} and $ROR\left(k_{t+3}^{LR*,NS}\right) < ROR\left(k_{t+3}^{LR*,S}\right) < ROR\left(k_{t}^{SR*}\right)$, implying that the scale effects are crucial in determining $ROR\left(k_{t+3}^{LR*}\right)$. In the presence of the scale effects ($\delta^{*} = (1-\theta)^{*}$), $ROR\left(k_{t+3}^{LR*,S}\right)$ is independent of β^{LR}. In the absence of the scale effects ($\delta^{*} = 0$), however, $ROR\left(k_{t+3}^{LR*,NS}\right)$ is decreasing in β^{LR}. Note that the result has not yet counted for technology diffusion. When technology spill-over is sufficiently strong (an increase in A_{t}^{*}), the LR effects of FDI on productivity may turn positive. The positive effect is also supported by Lee (2007), who studies nine OECD countries during 1971–1999.

Provided $ROR\left(k_{t+3}^{LR*}\right)$, the incentive constraint for the entrepreneurs to produce requires

$$k_{t+3}^{LR*} < \widehat{k_{t+3}^{LR*}}$$

where

$$\widehat{k_{t+3}^{LR*}} \equiv \left[\frac{A_{t+3}^{*}R}{\upsilon}\left(\frac{q_{t+3}^{LR*}}{1-q_{t+3}^{LR*}}\right)\left(\frac{1-\pi^{*}}{\pi^{*}}\right)\right]^{\frac{1}{1-\theta^{*}}}\left(\pi^{*}\right)^{-1}\left[1+\frac{\pi\beta^{LR}}{\pi^{*}}\left(\frac{1+n}{1+n^{*}}\right)\right]^{\frac{\delta^{*}}{1-\theta^{*}}-1}\left(\bar{k}_{t+3}^{LR*}\right)^{\frac{\delta^{*}}{1-\theta^{*}}}. \tag{2.32}$$

When the incentive constraint holds, one equilibrium liquidation would be $\left\{\alpha_{1t+4}^{LR*}, \alpha_{2t+5}^{LR*}\right\} = \{1,0\}$, which gives the equilibrium returns to withdrawals:

$$\left\{r_{1t+4}^{*}, r_{2t+5}^{*}, \bar{r}_{2t+5}^{*}\right\} = \left\{\left(\frac{\upsilon}{1-\pi^{*}}\right)\left(1-q_{t+3}^{LR*}\right), \left(\frac{R}{\pi^{*}}\right)q_{t+3}^{LR*}, 0\right\},$$

and the equilibrium portfolios:

$$\left\{z_{t+3}^{LR*}, q_{t+3}^{LR*}\right\} = \left\{\frac{1}{1+\Phi^{LR*}}, \frac{\Phi^{LR*}}{1+\Phi^{LR*}}\right\},$$

$$\text{where } \Phi^{LR*} \equiv \left(\frac{\pi^*}{1-\pi^*}\right)\left(\frac{R}{\upsilon}\right)^{\frac{-\gamma}{1+\gamma}}\left[ROR\left(k_{t+3}^{LR*}\right)\right]^{\frac{-\gamma}{1+\gamma}},$$

where q_{t+3}^{LR*} depends on $ROR\left(k_{t+3}^{LR*}\right)$, which depends on the scale effects. In the presence of the scale effects, $q_t^{LR*,S}$ is independent of β^{LR}. In the absence of the scale effects, $q_t^{LR*,NS}$ is increasing in β^{LR}. Compared to SR, the portfolios would be ranked as: $q_t^{LR*,NS} > q_t^{LR*,S} > q_t^{SR*}$, implying that the banks would invest more in illiquid assets in the absence of the scale effects in the LR after w_{t+3}^{LR*} responds fully to the openness of FDI. Accordingly, the LR host growth rate would be:

$$\mu_{t+5}^{LR*} \equiv \frac{R}{\pi^*} q_{t+3}^{LR*} A_t^*\left(1-\theta^*\right)\left[\frac{\pi^*}{\left(1+n^*\right)^2}\left(1+\frac{\pi\beta^{LR}}{\pi^*}\right)\right]^{\theta^*}\left[\left(1+\frac{\pi\beta^{LR}}{\pi^*\xi}\right)\left(\bar{k}_{t+3}^{LR*}\right)\right]^{\delta*}\left(k_{t+3}^{LR*}\right)^{\theta^*-1},$$

where $\mu_{t+2}^{LR*,NS} > \mu_{t+2}^{LR*,S} > \mu_{t+2}^{SR*}$ due to $q_t^{LR*,NS} > q_t^{LR*,S} > q_t^{SR*}$ and $w_t^{LR*} > w_t^*$. The result of positive effects on μ_{t+5}^{LR*} is consistent with many empirical studies. The studies include the ones focusing on a single country [Arisoy (2012), Baliamoune-Lutz (2004), Barry and Bradley (1997), Barry and Kearney (2006), Hassen and Anis (2012), Manova, Wei, and Zhang (2015), Tuan, Ng, and Zhao (2009)], on a group of countries based on development stages [Borenszrein et al (1998), Cipollina et al (2012), Stehrer and Woerz (2009)] and on the regions [Bengoa and Sancgez-Eobles (2003), Kornecki (2008), Moudatsou (2003), Sghaier et al (2013), and Wang (2009)], except for the findings of Belloumi (2014) in Tunisia during 1980–2008 and Shawa and Shen (2013), who show that the causality between FDI and growth is not found in Tanzania during 1980 to 2012.

LR return flows and the relocation rate

The LR FDI flows β^{LR} would be determined by the no-arbitrage condition $c_{3,t+2}^{NR} = c_{3,t+2}^{R}$. By substituting equations (2.27) and (2.31) into $ROR\left(k_t^{LR}\right)k_t = (1-\tau)ROR\left(k_t^{LR*}\right)k_t$, one gets

$$(1-\tau)\theta^*\left[\frac{\left(1+n^*\right)^2}{\pi^*\left(1+\frac{\pi\beta^{LR}}{\pi^*}\right)}\right]^{1-\theta*} A_t^*\left[\left(1+\frac{\pi\beta^{LR}}{\pi^*\xi}\right)\left(\bar{k}_t^{LR*}\right)\right]^{\delta*}\left(k_t^{LR*}\right)^{\theta*-1}$$
$$= \theta A_t\left[\frac{(1+n)^2}{\pi\left(1-\beta^{LR}\right)}\right]^{1-\theta}\left[\left(1-\beta^{LR}\right)\overline{k_t^{LR}}\right]^{\delta}\left(k_t^{LR}\right)^{\theta-1}, \tag{2.33}$$

where the scale effects are crucial to the value of β^{LR}. In the presence of the scale effects, $\beta^{LR,S}$ is indeterminate, meaning that any value of $\beta^{LR,S} \in [0,1]$ is an equilibrium. In the absence of the scale effects, $\beta^{LR,NS}$ is decreasing in τ, $((1+n)/(1+n^*))$ and $\left(A_t / A_t^*\right)$ but increasing in (π / π^*). The result implies that an increase in the host tax rate on the return flows τ, the relative technology $\left(A_t / A_t^*\right)$ or the relative population growth rate $((1+n)/(1+n^*))$ would discourage FDI outflows from the home country in the LR (a decrease in β^{LR}). Compared to SR, one can find that the factors, τ, $((1+n)/(1+n^*))$ and $\left(A_t / A_t^*\right)$, which would increase β^{SR}, would turn to decrease $\beta^{LR,NS}$, while the factor (π / π^*), which reduces β^{SR}, would turn to increase $\beta^{LR,NS}$. In other words, in the LR, the presence of the scale effects matters to the results. Moreover, when w_{t+3}^{LR*} responds fully to the openness of FDI, the effects of specific factors could be reversed. The results demonstrate the importance of the scale effects and the differentiation between SR and LR.

Discussion: no return flows

The analysis so far has assumed the satisfaction of condition [equation (2.23)], meaning that the relocated entrepreneur could conduct return flows to consume home product. In fact, the return flows may not occur should the condition [equation (2.23)] fail to hold: $(1-\tau) < \sigma$. At $(1-\tau) < \sigma$, either σ is sufficiently high (host products and home product are closed to perfect substitute) or τ is sufficiently low, so the relocated entrepreneurs would consume host products and would not conduct return flows.

In the SR, without return flows (NR), $c_{3,t+2}^{R,\,SR} = \sigma ROR\left(k_t^{SR*}\right)k_t$. The no-arbitrage condition which would determine $\beta^{NR,SR}$ would become:

$$\sigma A_t^*\left[\frac{\left(1+n^*\right)^2}{\pi^*}\right]^{1-\theta^*}\frac{1}{\left(1+\dfrac{\pi\beta^{NR,SR}}{\pi^*}\right)}\left[\left(1+\frac{\pi\beta^{NR,SR}}{\pi^*\xi}\right)^{\delta^*}\left(1+\frac{\pi\beta^{NR,SR}}{\pi^*}\right)^{\theta^*}-\left(1-\theta^*\right)\right]$$

$$\left(\overline{k}_t^{SR*}\right)^{\delta^*}\left(k_t^{SR*}\right)^{\theta^*-1}=\theta\left(\frac{\left(1+n\right)^2}{\pi}\right)^{1-\theta}\left(1-\beta^{NR,SR}\right)^{\frac{\delta}{\theta}}A_t\left(\overline{k_t^{SR}}\right)^{\delta}\left(k_t^{SR}\right)^{\theta-1}, \tag{2.34}$$

where $\beta^{NR,SR}$ is decreasing in σ, implying that the closer perfect substitutes the host products are to the home products ($\sigma \approx 1$), the lower FDI flows would be (a smaller $\beta^{NR,SR}$). A decrease in $\beta^{NR,SR}$ would lower $ROR\left(k_t^{NR,SR*}\right)$ and increase $ROR\left(k_t^{NR,SR}\right)$. In turn, a higher $q_t^{NR,SR*}$ would increase the host growth rate $\mu_t^{NR,SR*}$, and a smaller $q_t^{NR,SR}$ would decrease the home growth rate $\mu_t^{NR,SR}$ in the SR. In other words, without return flows, the host country would experience a higher growth rate, while the home country would experience a lower growth rate.

In the LR without return flows, the no-arbitrage condition to determine $\beta^{NR,LR}$ would change to:

$$\sigma\theta^*\left[\frac{\left(1+n^*\right)^2}{\pi^*\left(1+\dfrac{\pi\beta^{NR,LR}}{\pi^*}\right)}\right]^{1-\theta^*}A_t^*\left[\left(1+\frac{\pi\beta^{NR,LR}}{\pi^*\xi}\right)\left(\overline{k}_t^{LR*}\right)\right]^{\delta^*}\left(k_t^{LR*}\right)^{\theta^*-1}$$

$$=\theta A_t\left[\frac{\left(1+n\right)^2}{\pi\left(1-\beta^{NR,LR}\right)}\right]^{1-\theta}\left[\left(1-\beta^{NR,LR}\right)\overline{k_t^{LR}}\right]^{\delta}\left(k_t^{LR}\right)^{\theta-1} \tag{2.35}$$

,

where the scale effects are crucial in determining $\beta^{NR,LR}$. In the presence of the scale effects ($\delta^* = 1 - \theta^*$), $\beta^{NR,LR}$ is indeterminate, meaning that any value of $\beta^{NR,LR} \in [0,1]$ is an equilibrium. In the absence of the scale effects ($\delta^* = 0$), $\beta^{NR,LR}$ is increasing in σ, meaning that the closer to perfect substitutes the host products are to the home products, the higher the LR FDI flows would be (a higher $\beta^{NR,LR}$).

Based on equations (2.28) and (2.32), without return flows, the higher LR FDI flows would increase both $\widehat{k_t^{LR}}$ and $\widehat{k_t^{LR*}}$, implying that the incentive constraints for the entrepreneurs to produce in both home and host countries are more likely to hold. Meanwhile, a higher $\beta^{NR,LR}$ would increase $ROR\left(k_t^{NR,LR*}\right)$, which would lower $q_t^{NR,LR*}$ but would decrease $ROR\left(k_t^{NR,LR}\right)$, which would increase $q_t^{NR,LR}$. Also, an increase in $\beta^{NR,LR}$ would increase w^{LR*} but would reduce w^{LR}. The movements of $q_t^{NR,LR*}$ and w^{LR*} would drive the growth rate to the opposite directions and leave the overall effects on the growth rates ambiguous for both the home and the host countries in the LR.

Conclusion

In this chapter, a three-period-lived overlapping-generations framework is developed to analyse both SR and LR impacts of FDI on home and host countries. To concentrate on economic growth, it is assumed that the banks serve as portfolio managers and as central planners. As demonstrated, it is found that the portfolio allocations are crucial in adjusting the effects of FDI on the economic growth rate. The portfolio allocations, on one hand, would be affected by the openness of FDI; on the other hand, it would then affect the economic growth rates of the home and the host countries both in the SR and in the LR.

To be more specific, in the SR, when wage income has not yet adjusted fully to the openness of FDI, the home country would experience an increase in unemployment and a decrease in the rate of return of capital but an increase in the growth rate due to portfolio adjustments by the banks. Meanwhile, the host country would experience an increase in the rate of return of capital but a decrease in the growth rate. Note that it would take two periods for the effects on the growth rates to surface in the SR. Different from SR, the wage income would adjust fully to the openness of FDI in the LR. Therefore, in the LR, the wage income would decrease in the home country but would increase in the host country due to the shift of labour demand caused by FDI. Another important factor in the LR is the scale effects, which are crucial in determining the rates of return of capital and the growth rates of both the home and the host countries in the LR. One factor which is often neglected in the analysis is return flows, which is crucial in economic growth rates for both the home and the host countries, especially for the SR. The lack of return flows would be harmful for the home growth rate but beneficial for the host growth rate.

As described in the first section, the findings of empirical studies on FDI are mixed. Therefore, the theoretical results are consistent with the findings of some studies but not all. There are several interpretations regarding the consistencies and inconsistencies, which will be discussed in Chapter 7.

Notes

1 Note that this does not imply that FDI is the cause of the loss of jobs.
2 To be more specific, by taking the approach of multinational corporations, Debaere et al (2010) find the loss of employment in the home countries when the FDI outflows to less advanced countries. Elia et al (2009) investigate Italian firms from 1996–2002 and find that outward FDI has negative impacts on labour demand in the home country. Lee et al (2009) also find the loss of employment in the home countries in four tigers in Asia to outward FDI to China.
3 Herzer (2012) studies Germany's growth without mentioning the covered period.
4 Campos and Kinoshita (2002) is based on the data of 25 Central and Eastern European and the former Soviet Union transition countries during 1990–1998.
5 More comparisons among these studies are discussed in Chapter 7.
6 The issues related to the banks will be discussed in Chapter 5.
7 Depending on the relative economic conditions of the home and the host countries, the types of firms conducting FDI are different. For example, the types of firms that relocate from developing to developed countries would be different from the types of firms that relocate from developed to developing countries.
8 The higher the value of σ is, the closer to perfect substitute the host product would be to the home product.
9 There are various forms of costs associated with capital flows. Some are in the form of a tax rate to the volume of capital flows. Some are in the form of sunk costs. The sunk costs associated with each transfer are closed to zero when the volume of flow is sufficiently large. Therefore, most countries use tax rate to control flows. It is also in the interest of the chapter to assume the tax rate as the costs for return flows to reflect the facts.
10 Gopinath and Chen (2003) examine time series data for 26 countries (15 developed and 11 developing) and confirm the proposition which states that capital inflows (outflows) increase (lower) wages in the host (home) countries due to the changes in the relative factor endowments.
11 Zajc and Kumar (2006) study the Slovenian manufacturing sector during 1994–2003 and find that specific firms in the host country experience a decrease in their employment after FDI.

3 Short-term portfolio flows and economic growth

Introduction: the facts and the issues

The focus of this chapter turns to foreign portfolio investment (FPI) flows, which include both portfolio flows and other investment and are often considered as SR flows. As is well documented, FPI flows tend to be more sensitive to the shocks and changes of economic conditions; therefore, they would appear to be more volatile than LR FDI flows [Levchenko and Mauro (2007)]. To be more specific, Goldstein and Razin (2006) show that liquidity shocks make investors sell early and lead to volatile FPI flows. Bohn and Tesar (1996) test US investors' foreign portfolios and find that the investors would chase the markets with high expected returns even though such investment may not be at the right time and at the right place. Brook (2004) finds that the net portfolio flows from the euro area to US stock market reflect the differences in expected productivity growth. To reduce volatility, Hegerty (2011) suggests that more financial integration might be important. The suggestion of Hegerty (2011) highlights the connections between FPI flows and financial markets which have attracted broad attention.

FPI and financial markets

FPI flows are connected to the financial markets closely. That is mainly because FPI tend to flow in and out of one country via its financial markets, regardless of the home or the host countries. Since FPI flows do not connect as closely to the production sector as FDI flows, the earnings from FPI tend to flow back to the home countries. Moreover, most flows between countries are through the banks, which play a crucial role in the financial markets. Therefore, the development and the openness of financial markets would affect the composition, the volumes and the volatility of FPI flows [Bartokova (2011)]. Errunza (2001) finds that the benefits of FPI for the host country would depend on the openness of its capital markets. The connections between FPI flows and financial markets would then affect the macro economy. To be more specific, Gur (2015) finds that with financial integration, FPI could improve employment growth, while Choong, Lam, and Yusop (2010a, 2010b) find that the effects of FPI on growth would depend on the development of the financial sector. Meanwhile, both Agbloyor et al (2014) and Popov (2014) find that FPI has negative impacts on host growth.

To reduce/alter the negative impacts, Agbloyor et al (2014) suggest financial development, while Popov (2014) highlights the importance of financial openness. Abid and Bahloul (2011) test the data of MENA countries as the destinations of FPI and find that reducing restrictions is important to attract FPI flows.

In terms of the restrictions of financial openness and integrations, both Kinda (2012) and Lajuni, Yee, and Ghazali (2008) refer the restrictions to capital controls, which have been found to be important for FPI flows; however, the effects of capital controls on FPI seem country dependent. According to Jongwanich, Bautista, and Lee (2011), capital controls have no effect for FPI in Thailand, only in Malaysia. The causality between FPI and the financial markets may not be uni-directional. Poshakwale and Thapa (2010) show that FPI leads to a greater integration of equity markets. The result is supported by the evidence found in Asian markets [Poshakwale and Thapa (2009)].

FPI flows and macro variables

The high volatility of FPI flows has raised a great concern since the volatility would increase uncertainty and could lead to sudden stops, which are defined as a sudden slowdown on capital flows and are often followed by a sharp decline of macro performances, including a decrease in output, the growth rate and other macro variables.

The concerns of the negative impacts of FPI on macro performances have been confirmed by Agbloyor et al (2014), Popov (2014) and Shen, Lee, and Lee (2010), who have found negative impacts of FPI on growth. Debbiche and Rahmouni (2015), however, argue that the impacts would be positive when counting for total capital flows. It is clear that the argument of Debbiche and Rahmouni (2015) is weak, since total capital flows include LR FDI flows, which may dominate the effects of total capital flows on growth. So the conclusion reached by Debbiche and Rahmouni (2015) does not necessarily contradict the result of the negative effects on growth found by Agbloyor et al (2014), Popov (2014) and Shen et al (2010). To interpret the differences, Ben Naceur, Bakardzhieva, and Kamar (2012) discover that it is the exchange rate appreciation associated with FPI that jeopardizes exports and growth. Meanwhile, Boero, Mavromatis, and Taylor (2015) use FPI-to-FDI ratio and find that host productivity becomes unaffected by the changes of the ratio.

In terms of causality between FPI and growth, Bhattacharya and Bhattacharya (2012) find unidirectional causality of FPI on growth. However, Baek (2006), Duasa and Kassim (2009) and Garg and Dua (2014) find that the causality is the opposite. To be more specific, Duasa and Kassim (2009) show that growth can affect FPI flows. Garg and Dua (2014) discover that growth would determine portfolio flows. Baek (2006) uses the data of Latin America and confirms the causality of growth on FPI flows.

Some studies discover that it is other factors which drive the sign of the effects of FPI on growth. For example, while de Vita and Kyaw (2009) find that to obtain positive effects of FPI on growth, one country must have sufficient economic development and the absorption of capacity, Berument et al (2015) show that it is the composition of flows which affects the sign of the effects of FPI on macroeconomic variables, including output.

FPI (and its volatility) and financial crises/risks

Instead of using FPI flows, one research stream advocates that it is the FPI volatility that affects the performances of macro variables and hence leaves one country more exposed to financial risks. Lee et al (2013) find that the volatility of net flows would make the country more exposed to contagion effects. Uctum and Uctum (2011) confirm that FPI is sensitive to global financial conditions. Brink and Viviers (2003) find that volatile FPI could cause financial risks and should be managed. Thus, to reduce the volatility of macro variables, one must reduce the volatility of FPI.

To reduce the volatility of FPI, Kanayo and Emeka (2012) suggest not encouraging FPI flows to prevent the adverse effects of FPI flows, while Chakraborty and Boasson (2013) suggest doing so through the improvement of financial openness. However, according to Agbloyor et al (2014) and Popov (2014), the improvement of financial openness may reduce the negative impacts of FPI flows on growth, but there is no evidence to support the ideas that the improvement of financial openness may reduce the volatility of flows. Instead, the improvement of openness would, in fact, attract FPI flows [Abid and Bahloul (2011)].

Different from most studies, Joyce (2011) argues that FPI equity liabilities would reduce the incidence of banking crises, while Kandil (2011) argues that FPI would finance current account deficits in both the developed and developing countries. Unfortunately, to hold the arguments of both Joyce (2011) and Kandil (2011) would require steady FPI flows. Both arguments have neglected the volatility of FPI flows, which is the core concern of FPI flows.

FPI and stock markets

Since FPI flows often enter a country through the financial markets, some research narrows down the financial markets to the equity/stock markets and studies the connections between FPI flows and the equity/stock markets [Karolyi (2002), Osazee and Idolor (2014), Thapa and Poshakwale (2012), and Todea and Plesoianu (2013)]. Osazee and Idolor (2014) find that FPI is attracted to the expansion of the stock markets. Thapa and Poshakwale (2012) show that FPI allocation is country specific and would depend on the characteristics of the equity markets. Looking at the causality in the other direction, Todea and Plesoianu (2013) find that FPI would affect information efficiency of the stock market, and Karolyi (2002) finds the positive effects of FPI on the stock markets.

There are also studies which discover that the impacts of FPI on individual firms' performances in the stock/equity markets would depend on both economic boom/recession and on the size of the firms. In the aspect of boom/recession, Hsu (2013) finds that the FPI favoured equities perform better in the boom but not in recession, while Hsu, Huang, and Ntoko (2013) show that although FPI favoured equities have lower volatility, these equities would have higher premium at the time of financial crises. In the aspect of the size of the firms, it is found that FPI reaches out to the small firms via banking channels [Knill (2013)] and that small firms have restricted access to finance when the volatility of FPI is high [Knill and Lee (2014)]. Thus, the volatility of FPI might hinder the growth of small firms [Knill (2005)]. In other words, FPI would affect the performances of the firms through the equity/stock markets. The performances of firms would, in turn, affect output and economic growth.

FPI and other factors

Apparently, the connections of FPI flows are not limited to the variables mentioned earlier but also to other factors. The factors include the network [Leblang (2010)], international reserves [Qian and Steiner (2014)], investors' protection [Poshakwale and Thapa (2011)], market entry costs/geographical distance [Araujo, Lastauskas, and Papageorgiou (2015), Sarisoy Guerin (2006)], investment barriers and riskiness [Liljeblom and Loflund (2005), Tabova (2013)], the risks of detecting invasion [Hanlon, Maydew, and Thornock (2015)], economic development [de Vita and Kyaw (2009)], culture distance [Aggarwal, Kearney, and Lucey (2012)] and corporate social responsibility [Suzuki, Tanimoto, and Kokko (2010)]. Also, FPI flows are connected with policies, especially the policies which reduce the institutional constraints and barriers [Abid and Bahloul (2011), Bartram and Dufey (2001)]. As for the home countries, Giofre (2014) suggests that high home protection would reduce the sensitivity of FPI outflows, while Lee and Park (2013) show that FPI outflows from Eastern Asia to the US are due to excessive savings and foreign reserves.

Theoretical framework

Based on empirical findings, it is clear that FPI flows and financial markets are strongly connected. However, FPI flows tend to have negative impacts on economic growth. Among the suggestions to reduce the negative impacts of FPI flows, financial development has been strongly recommended by many studies. Financial development, on one hand, would, in fact, attract FPI; on the other hand, the volatility of FPI flows would increase financial risks and must be managed. Unfortunately, the differentiation between SR and LR effects of FPI on the economy has been neglected. The bank channel, which plays an important role in transmitting FPI flows to financial risks and macro outcome of a country, has been hardly discussed. Moreover, only a few countries are purely a home or a host country of FPI flows. Depending on the destinations/origins of FPI flows, most countries have the roles of both a home and a host country. To differentiate one country's role as a home and a host country would require the empirical studies to separate FPI inflows and outflows and their destinations and origins. However, it seems that most empirical studies have neglected this step. Without the step, it is challenging to identify whether the empirical results are for the countries as home or host countries and to understand how financial risks are transmitted in a country through FPI flows. These challenges faced by the empirical studies can be overcome by theoretical analysis. It is the goal of this chapter to construct a theoretical framework to analyse the effects of FPI flows on economic growth via banking channel in the SR and in the LR for both the home and the host countries.

The theoretical framework extends the three-period-lived overlapping-generations model in Chapter 2 with some modifications to adapt the features of FPI flows. It is assumed that the relocated home entrepreneurs would conduct FPI flows to invest in the host loan market via banks, which also serve as central planners. To do so, the relocated entrepreneurs would withdraw at middle age for the investment. The same as in Chapter 2, the banks would operate in a fully funded way. Therefore, there would be no incentive problems of the banks, and there would be no bank runs or banking crises. So the chapter can focus on how portfolio investment may influence the effects of FPI on the macro variable and economic growth.

Consequently, it is found that FPI has negative impacts on the growth rate of both the home and the host countries. The openness of FPI could cause liquidity shortage of the banks in the home country. If the liquidity shortage is not assisted promptly and appropriately, bank runs would be inevitable. The bank runs and banking crises would lead to disruption in economic activities. To reduce the possibility of bank runs due to the openness of FPI, providing lending facilities to the banks together with assisting the banks to manage risks would be helpful.

The rest of the chapter is organized as follows. The second section highlights the key features, which have been modified to address FPI. The third section provides the results of a closed economy, of both the home and the host countries in the SR and in the LR, followed by conclusion in the fourth section. The policies related to FPI flows will be discussed in chapter 7.

The theoretical framework

The basic framework is similar to the one in Chapter 2 with some modifications, which are made to catch the features of SR FPI flows. Following the three-period-lived overlapping-generations framework of Chapter 2, every agent is born identical with one unit of labour when young and nothing when middle-aged and when old. The unit of labour must be supplied for production in-elastically to earn wage income. It is assumed that all agents value both middle-aged ($c_{2,\, t+1}$) and old consumption ($c_{3,\, t+2}$) but not young consumption. All goods are assumed to perish fully within one period. To store the value of the wealth, the young would deposit the wage income into the banks, which are assumed to have exclusive access for asset investment.

The agents would learn their types at the beginning of turning middle aged. The type of an agent is exogenously determined and would stay with the agent throughout the lifetime. There are three types: non-entrepreneurs, non-relocated entrepreneurs and relocated entrepreneurs. The probability for an agent to become a non-entrepreneur would be $(1 - \pi)$, a non-relocated entrepreneurs would be $\pi(1 - \beta)$ and a relocated entrepreneur would be $\pi\beta$. The type of an individual is assumed to be private information, while the distribution of the types would be public information.

The banks are assumed to be playing two roles: portfolio manager and central planner. As portfolio managers, the banks would invest assets and provide returns to the withdrawals for the agents. As central planners, the banks would have zero profit and would aim to invest and provide returns to maximize the utility of the depositors. In other words, the banks would operate in a fully funded way and would have no incentive problem.

There are two types of assets available for the banks to invest: SR and LR assets. The SR assets would take one period to mature, while the LR assets would take two periods to mature. Similar to Chapter 2, the LR assets are assumed to be exogenous with returns R in capital goods at maturity and χ in output goods if liquidated prematurely. Different from Chapter 2, the SR assets are assumed to be the loans demanded by the non-relocated entrepreneurs, who would produce and repay the loans at the rate $(1 + i_t)$ at the end of the period, where $\chi < (1 + i_t) < R$.

The SR FPI means investment in host loans by the home relocated entrepreneurs. To focus on the analysis of FPI, it is assumed that the relocated home entrepreneurs would conduct only FPI instead of FDI. Since it takes one period to receive the returns of loans, the relocated home entrepreneurs would withdraw their deposits to invest in the host loans after learning their types at middle age in order to obtain the returns for old consumption. Investing in and obtaining the returns of host loans would be done via banks. So the relocated home entrepreneurs would not move to the host country and would consume home products only. The utility function of an agent would be in the form of:

$$u\left(c_{2,\,t+1}, c_{3,\,t+2}; \phi\right) = -\frac{\left(c_{2,t+1} + \phi c_{3,t+2}\right)^{-\gamma}}{\gamma}, \tag{3.1}$$

where ϕ represents the substitution rate between $c_{2,t+1}$ and $c_{3,t+2}$. The timeline of various activities is depicted in Figure 3.1.

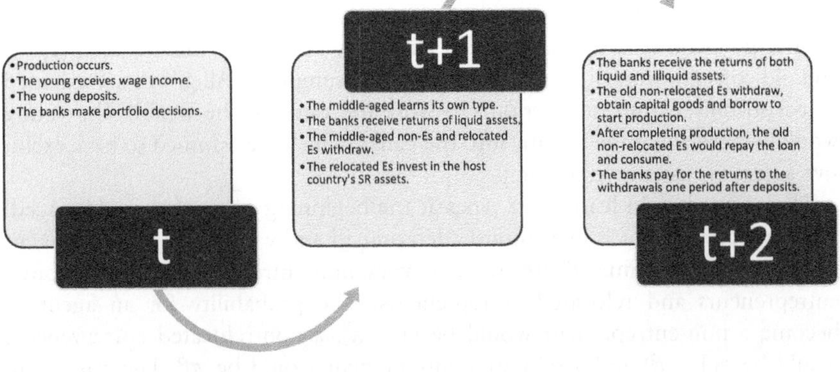

Figure 3.1 The timeline of the activities

The production and the debt market

The output of the home country would be produced by the non-relocated home entrepreneurs. The production would require both capital goods and labour as inputs. The production would be in the form of:

$$Y_t = A_t \bar{k}_t^{\delta} k_t^{\theta} L_t^{1-\theta}, \tag{3.2}$$

where $\bar{k}_t$ represents the average capital goods per non-relocated entrepreneur.[1] To start production, the non-relocated entrepreneurs must have output goods available to pay for wage income. However, by withdrawing at the maturity of LR assets, the non-relocated entrepreneurs have capital goods only. Therefore, in order to start production, the non-relocated entrepreneurs must borrow from the banks. The amount which one non-relocated entrepreneur would borrow would be:

$$b_t = w_t L_t,$$

at the cost of $(1 + i_t)$. It is assumed that there is no credit rationing and that there is no uncertainty for production. Thus, the capital gains earned by a non-relocated entrepreneur would be:

$$\max_{L_t} \left\{ A_t \bar{k}_t^{\delta} k_t^{\theta} L_t^{1-\theta} - (1+i_t) w_t L_t \right\}, \tag{3.3}$$

which provides the rate of return of capital $ROR(k_t)$:

$$ROR(k_t) = \frac{\left[A_t \bar{k}_t^{\delta} k_t^{\theta} L_t^{1-\theta} - (1+i_t) w_t L_t \right]}{k_t}, \tag{3.4}$$

After the loans are repaid before the end of the period, the banks would then pay for the returns to the withdrawals one period after deposits.

The banks

As central planners, the problem faced by the home banks would be

$$\max \left\{ -\left(\frac{1-\pi}{\gamma}\right) (r_{1t+1} w_t)^{-\gamma} - \frac{\pi}{\gamma} \left[\beta (1+i_{t+1}^{*}) r_{1t+1} w_t + (1-\beta) ROR(k_t) r_{2t+2} w_t \right]^{-\gamma} \right\}, \tag{3.5}$$

subject to:

$$(1-\pi(1-\beta))(1+n)^2 r_{1t+1} = \alpha_{1t+1} z_t (1+i_t) + \alpha_{2t+1} q_t \chi, \tag{3.6}$$

$$\pi(1-\beta)(1+n)^2 r_{2t+2} = (1-\alpha_{2t+1}) R q_t, \tag{3.7}$$

$$\pi(1-\beta)(1+n)^2 \tilde{r}_{2t+2} = (1-\alpha_{1t+1})(1+i_t) z_t. \tag{3.8}$$

Equation (3.5) shows the expected utility of an agent. As shown in equation (3.5), the first term represents the utility of a non-entrepreneur, the second term the utility of a relocated entrepreneur and the third term the utility of a non-relocated entrepreneur. The banks would operate in a fully funded way as described in Chapter 2. The budget constraints must be modified accordingly: equations (3.6) through (3.8) are the budget constraints of the banks for the returns to the withdrawals one period after deposits [equation (3.6)] and two periods after deposits in capital goods [equation (3.7)] and in output goods [equation (3.8)].

The results

In this section, the results of a closed economy and of an open economy in the SR and in the LR are analysed. Similar to Chapter 2, the difference between SR and LR is the adjustment of wage income w_t. In the SR, w_t has not yet adjusted to the openness of FPI and is assumed to be the same as the closed economy, $w_t^{SR} = w_t$ while in the LR, w_t has fully adjusted to the openness of FPI. It is assumed that the openness of FPI would take place in period t.

A closed economy

In a closed economy, there would be no FPI, so the relocated entrepreneurs would withdraw at the maturity of the LR assets to obtain capital goods to start production, just like the non-relocated entrepreneurs. Therefore, the labour demand per entrepreneur would be:

$$L_t = k_t \left[\frac{(1-\theta) A_t \bar{k}_t^{\delta}}{(1+i_t) w_t} \right]^{1/\theta}, \tag{3.9}$$

and total labour supply in period t would be: $N_t = (1 + n)^2$. The labour market clearing condition would determine w_t:

$$w_t = \left(\frac{\pi}{(1+n)^2} \right)^{\theta} \frac{(1-\theta) A_t \bar{k}_t^{\delta} k_t^{\theta}}{(1+i_t)}, \tag{3.10}$$

where w_t is decreasing in $(1 + i_t)$. Combining equations (3.10) and (3.4) gives $ROR(k_t)$:

$$ROR(k_t) = A_t \theta \left(\frac{(1+n)^2}{\pi} \right)^{1-\theta} \bar{k}_t^{\delta} k_t^{\theta-1}. \tag{3.11}$$

Similar to Chapter 2, given $ROR(k_t)$ [equation (3.11)], in order for the entrepreneurs to produce, the incentive constraint, $ROR(k_t) r_{2t+2} > r_{1t+1} > 0$, must hold.[2] The problem faced by the banks would be:

$$\begin{aligned} &\max \left\{ -\left(\frac{1-\pi}{\gamma} \right) (r_{1t+1} w_t)^{-\gamma} - \frac{\pi}{\gamma} \left[ROR(k_t) r_{2t+2} w_t + \tilde{r}_{2t+2} w_t \right]^{-\gamma} \right\}, \\ &\pi (1+n)^2 \tilde{r}_{2t+2} = (1-\alpha_{1t+1})(1+i_t) z_t \cdot \\ &\pi (1+n)^2 r_{2t+2} = (1-\alpha_{2t+1}) R q_t, \end{aligned} \tag{3.12}$$

At the liquidation decision $\{\alpha_{1t+1}, \alpha_{2t+1}\} = \{1,0\}$, the returns to the withdrawals would be:

$$\left\{r_{1t+1}, r_{2t+2}, \tilde{r}_{2t+2}\right\} = \left\{\left(\frac{(1+i_t)}{(1-\pi)(1+n)^2}\right)(1-q_t), \left(\frac{R}{\pi(1+n)^2}\right)q_t, 0\right\}. \tag{3.13}$$

Therefore, the equilibrium portfolio allocation would become:

$$\{z_t, q_t\} = \left\{\frac{1}{1+\Phi}, \frac{\Phi}{1+\Phi}\right\}, where\, \Phi \equiv \left(\frac{\pi}{1-\pi}\right)\left[\frac{ROR(k_t)R}{(1+i_t)}\right]^{\frac{-\gamma}{1+\gamma}}, \tag{3.14}$$

where q_t is increasing in $(1 + i_t)$ and is decreasing in $ROR(k_t)$, meaning that a higher $(1 + i_t)$ would lead the banks to invest more towards the LR assets. Similar to what has been explained in Chapter 2, this is because of the role of the banks as central planners to balance the returns to various types of depositors in order to maximize the expected utility. Therefore, the growth rate μ_{t+2} would be:

$$\mu_{t+2} = \frac{r_{2t+2}w_t}{k_t} = \left(\frac{R}{\pi(1+n)^2}\right)(1-\theta)\left(\frac{\pi}{(1+n)^2}\right)^{\theta} q_t \frac{A_t \bar{k}_t^{\delta} k_t^{\theta-1}}{(1+i_t)}. \tag{3.15}$$

As shown in equation (3.15), $(1 + i_t)$ would affect μ_{t+2} via both w_t and q_t, but in opposite directions. The effect via w_t is negative, while the effect via q_t is positive. When the effect via w_t dominate, μ_{t+2} would be decreasing in $(1 + i_t)$.

An open economy in the short run (SR)

Since the investors' foreign portfolio would chase the markets with high returns [Bohn and Tesar (1996)], it is assumed that the returns of host loans would be higher than the returns of home loans, $(1+i_t^*) > (1+i_t)$. Therefore, the home relocated entrepreneurs would invest in the host loans when the openness of FPI takes place in period t, $\beta^{SR} > 0$, but the host entrepreneurs would not invest in the home loans $\beta^{SR*} = 0$. In the SR, w_t has not yet adjusted to the openness of FPI flows and is assumed to be the same as the wage income in the closed economy, $w_t^{SR} = w_t$.

The home country (SR)

In period t when the countries are open for FPI, the middle-aged relocated entrepreneurs would withdraw their deposits to invest in the host loans. Since the banks operate in a fully funded way, the returns to the withdrawals would be from the returns of the asset investment which are from the deposits of the agents of the same generation. In period t, the returns to the withdrawals one period after the deposits would be from the returns of the assets which were invested in period t–1. So the budget constraints faced by the banks would be:

$$(1-\pi)(1+n)r_{1t-1,t} = \alpha_{1t-1,t}z_{t-1}(1+i_{t-1}) + \alpha_{2t-1,t}q_{t-1}\chi,$$

$$\pi(1+n)r_{2t-1,t+1} = (1-\alpha_{2t-1,t})Rq_{t-1}, \tag{3.16}$$
$$\pi(1+n)\tilde{r}_{2t-1,t+1} = (1-\alpha_{1t-1,t})z_{t-1}.$$

At $\{\alpha_{1t-1,t}, \alpha_{2t-1,t}\} = \{1,0\}$, the returns to the withdrawals that were stated on the deposit contracts would be:

$$\{r_{1t-1,t}, r_{2t-1,t+1}, \tilde{r}_{2t-1,t+1}\} = \left\{\left(\frac{(1+i_{t-1})}{(1-\pi)(1+n)}\right)(1-q_{t-1}), \left(\frac{R}{\pi(1+n)}\right)q_{t-1}, 0\right\}. \tag{3.17}$$

Provided the objective function, the equilibrium portfolio would be similar to what is shown in equation (3.14):

$$\{z_{t-1}, q_{t-1}\} = \left\{\frac{1}{1+\Phi}, \frac{\Phi}{1+\Phi}\right\}, \ where\ \Phi \equiv \left(\frac{\pi}{1-\pi}\right)\left[\frac{ROR(k_{t-1})R}{(1+i_{t-1})}\right]^{\frac{-\gamma}{1+\gamma}}.$$

To pay for the unexpected withdrawals by the relocated home entrepreneurs, the home banks must liquidate LR assets. By taking the differences between equations (3.6) and (3.16), one can obtain the fraction of LR assets $\alpha_{2t-1,t}$ which must be liquidated for unexpected withdrawals, $\alpha_{2t-1,t}\, q_{t-1}\chi \geq \pi\beta\,(1+n)\, r_{1t-1,t}$, which gives:

$$\widetilde{\alpha_{2t-1,t}} \leq \alpha_{2t-1,t} \leq 1,$$
$$where\ \widetilde{\alpha_{2t-1,t}} \equiv \frac{\pi\beta}{(1-\pi)} \frac{(1+i_{t-1})}{\chi} \frac{(1-q_{t-1})}{q_{t-1}}, \tag{3.18}$$

where $\widetilde{\alpha_{2t-1,t}}$ is increasing in β but decreasing in q_{t-1}, implying that a higher β and a lower q_{t-1} would make it difficult for the home banks to liquidate sufficient amount to meet the unexpected withdrawals. Meanwhile, $\widetilde{\alpha_{2t-1,t}} \leq 1$ can be combined with equation (3.14) to show the upper bound of $(1 + i_{t-1})$:

$$(1+i_{t-1}) < \left(\frac{\chi}{\beta}\right)^{1+\gamma}\left[ROR(k_{t-1})R\right]^{-\gamma} \equiv \overline{(1+i_{t-1})}, \tag{3.19}$$

where $\overline{(1+i_{t-1})}$ is increasing in χ, but is decreasing in $ROR(k_{t-1})$, R, and β. The upper bound shows that more FPI (a higher β) would reduce $\overline{(1+i_{t-1})}$ which will make equation (3.19) more difficult to hold. When equation (3.19) fails to hold, $\widetilde{\alpha_{2t-1,t}} > 1$, the home banks cannot repay the unexpected withdrawals even after liquidating the entire LR assets, and home bank runs in period *t* would be inevitable. Therefore, in order not to have bank runs in period *t*, equation (3.19) must hold.

When equations (3.18) and (3.19) hold, the home banks manage to liquidate sufficient amounts of LR assets for the unexpected withdrawals and prevent bank runs. Since the banking system operates in a fully funded way, in period *t*, the unexpected withdrawals of middle-aged relocated entrepreneurs of generation

t–1 would not affect the returns in capital goods to the old entrepreneurs of generation t–2 to start production. Since the openness of FDI does not start until period t, none of the entrepreneurs of generation t–2 conducts FPI, and all entrepreneurs of generation t–2 would start production in the home country. Thus, the growth rate of the home country would be the same as in the closed economy: $\mu_{t+1}^{SR} = \mu_t$. The result shows that the effects of FPI may not appear in the the same period as the openness of FPI, especially when the banking system is fully funded.

After the liquidation of LR assets in period t for unexpected withdrawals, the fraction of LR assets left would be $(1 - \alpha_{2t-1,t})$, which would generate capital goods $(1 - \alpha_{2t-1,t})Rq_{t-1}$ in period $t+1$ for the old non-relocated entrepreneurs of generation t–1. Therefore, the amount of capital goods received by each non-relocated old home entrepreneur would be:

$$\widehat{r_{2t-1,t+1}^{SR}} = \frac{R\left(1-\alpha_{2t-1,t}\right)}{\pi(1-\beta)(1+n)} q_{t-1}, \tag{3.20}$$

where $\widehat{r_{2t-1,t+1}^{SR}} < r_{2t-1,t+1}$ [equation (3.17)] since $\alpha_{2t-1,t} > \beta$ [equation (3.18)]. On one hand, the result indicates that the home banks fail the demand deposits, which stated the payments to the home non-relocated entrepreneurs as shown in equation (3.17). Failing demand deposits would lead to bank runs. On the other hand, although less than expected, the amount of capital goods could change home production in period $t+1$ to:

$$Y_{t+1} = A_{t+1}\overline{k}_{t+1}^{\delta} k_{t+1}^{\theta} L_{t+1}^{1-\theta},$$

$$\textit{Where } k_{t+1} = \frac{\left(1-\alpha_{2t-1,t}\right)}{\left(1-\beta\right)} k_{t-1}, \text{ and } \overline{k_{t+1}} = \overline{k_{t-1}}. \tag{3.21}$$

At $w_{t+1}^{SR} = w_t$ [equation (3.10)], the labour demand would become:

$$L_{t+1} = \frac{\left(1-\alpha_{2t-1,t}\right)}{\left(1-\beta\right)}\left(\frac{\left(1+n\right)^2}{\pi}\right)\left(1+i_t\right)^{1/\theta}, \tag{3.22}$$

which gives employment:

$$E_{t+1} = \pi(1 - \beta)(1 + n)L_{t+1},$$

and would lead to unemployment:

$$UE_{t+1} = (1 + n)^3 \left[1 - (1-\alpha_{2t-1,t})(1 + i_t)^{1/\theta}\right], \tag{3.23}$$

where UE_{t+1} is increasing in $\alpha_{2t-1,t}$, implying that the more LR assets liquidated for the withdrawals of the relocated home entrepreneurs to conduct FPI are, the higher home unemployment will be. The $ROR\left(k_{t+1}^{SR}\right)$ would change to:

$$ROR\left(k_{t+1}^{SR}\right) = \left(\frac{1+i_t}{1+i_{t+1}}\right)^{\frac{1-\theta}{\theta}} ROR\left(k_t\right), \tag{3.24}$$

where $ROR\left(k_{t+1}^{SR}\right)$ is decreasing in $(1 + i_{t+1})$ but increasing in $(1 + i_t)$. At $(1 + i_t) < (1 + i_{t+1})$, $ROR\left(k_{t+1}^{SR}\right) < ROR\left(k_t\right)$, which would lead to a tighter incentive constraint for the home non-relocated entrepreneurs to produce: $ROR\left(k_t^{SR}\right)\widehat{r_{2t-1,t+1}^{SR}} > r_{1t,t+1}^{SR} > 0$, which requires $\alpha_{2t-1,t}$ to be sufficiently small:

$$\alpha_{2t-1,t} < 1 - \frac{r_{1t,t+1}^{SR}\pi(1-\beta)(1+n)}{ROR\left(k_{t+1}\right)Rq_{t-1}} \equiv \widehat{\alpha_{2t-1,t}}, \tag{3.25}$$

Equation (3.25) can be combined with equation (3.18) to determine the range of $\alpha_{2t-1,t}$:

$$\widetilde{\alpha_{2t-1,t}} \leq \alpha_{2t-1,t} < \widehat{\alpha_{2t-1,t}} \leq 1. \tag{3.26}$$

When equation (3.26) holds, the home banks would not run in period t, and the home non-relocated entrepreneurs would have the incentive to start production. However, due to failing demand deposits, bank runs in the end of period $t+1$ would be inevitable. Meanwhile, the home growth rate in period $t+1$ would be:

$$\mu_{t+1}^{SR} = \frac{\widehat{r_{2t-1,t+1}^{SR}}w_{t+1}}{k_{t-1}} = \frac{R\left(1-\alpha_{2t-1,t}\right)}{\pi(1-\beta)(1+n)}q_{t-1}\left(\frac{\pi}{(1+n)^2}\right)^{\theta}\frac{(1-\theta)A_{t+1}\bar{k}_{t+1}^{\delta}k_t^{\theta-1}}{\left(1+i_t\right)}, \tag{3.27}$$

where μ_{t+1}^{SR} is decreasing in $\alpha_{2t-1,t}$ and $(1 + i_t)$, implying that FPI, which would lead the relocated entrepreneurs to withdraw their deposits unexpectedly, would reduce the home growth rate. Meanwhile, when w_{t+1} has not yet adjusted fully to the openness of FPI, the past interest rate $(1 + i_t)$ would have negative lasting impacts via w_{t+1} and q_{t-1} on the home growth rate in period $t+1$. The result shows that the openness of FPI would have long-lasting effects on the home countries, especially when the adjustments to the openness is slow.

Regarding bank runs, there are two aspects to discuss when equation (3.26) does not hold. First, at $\alpha_{2t-1,t} < \widetilde{\alpha_{2t-1,t}}$, the home banks fail to meet demand deposits of the unexpected withdrawals of the relocated home entrepreneurs and hence would run in period t. Knowing that banks might run in period t due to failing demand deposit, the non-relocated entrepreneurs would join the line to withdraw in period t and speed up bank runs. Second, at $\alpha_{2t-1,t} > \widehat{\alpha_{2t-1,t}}$, the non-relocated entrepreneurs would have no incentive to produce and would liquidate early in period t to obtain output goods to consume or to reinvest for old consumption and speed up bank runs in period t. Should either situation occur and bank runs in period t, there would not be capital goods left in period $t+1$, and the home growth rate in period $t+1$ would be zero, $\mu_{t+1}^{SR} = 0$.

The host country (SR)

As a recipient of FPI with $\left(1+i_t^*\right) > \left(1+i_t\right)$, the host entrepreneurs would withdraw at the maturity of LR assets to obtain capital goods to produce. Therefore, there would be no unexpected withdrawal for the host banks. However, the FPI inflows would cause the host banks to revise the budget constraint for SR withdrawals in period t to:

$$\left[\left(1-\pi^*\right)\left(1+n^*\right)^2+\pi\beta(1+n)\right]r_{1t,t+1}^{SR*}=\alpha_{1t,t+1}^* z_t^{SR*}\left(1+i_t^*\right)+\alpha_{2t,t+1}^* q_t^{SR*}\chi, \quad (3.28)$$

where $\pi\beta(1+n)$ represents FPI conducted by the home relocated entrepreneurs. At the liquidation decision $\{\alpha_{1t,t+1}^*, \alpha_{2t,t+1}^*\}=\{1,0\}$, the returns to the withdrawals would change to:

$$r_{1t,t+1}^{SR*}=\frac{\left(1+i_t^*\right)\left(1-q_t^{SR*}\right)}{\left[\left(1-\pi^*\right)\left(1+n^*\right)^2+\pi\beta(1+n)\right]}, \quad (3.29)$$

$$\{r_{2t,t+2}^{SR*}, \tilde{r}_{2t,t+2}^{SR*}\}=\left\{\left(\frac{R}{\pi^*\left(1+n^*\right)^2}\right)q_t^{SR*}, 0\right\}.$$

As central planners, the host banks would maximize the utility of the host agents. So the objective function would be:

$$\max\left\{-\left(\frac{1-\pi^*}{\gamma^*}\right)\left(r_{1t,t+1}^* w_t^*\right)^{-\gamma^*}-\frac{\pi^*}{\gamma^*}\left[ROR\left(k_{t+2}^*\right)r_{2t,t+2}^* w_t^*+\tilde{r}_{2t,t+2}^* w_t^*\right]^{-\gamma^*}\right\}.$$

Solving the problem, the equilibrium portfolio would be:

$$\{z_t^{SR*}, q_t^{SR*}\}=\left\{\frac{1}{1+\Phi^{SR*}}, \frac{\Phi^{SR*}}{1+\Phi^{SR*}}\right\},$$

$$\textit{where } \Phi^{SR*}\equiv\left(\frac{\pi^*}{1-\pi^*}\right)^{\frac{1}{\gamma^*+1}}\left[\frac{ROR\left(k_{t+2}^*\right)R}{\pi^*\left(1+n^*\right)^2}\frac{\left[\left(1-\pi^*\right)\left(1+n^*\right)^2+\pi\beta(1+n)\right]}{\left(1+i_t^*\right)}\right]^{\frac{-\gamma^*}{1+\gamma^*}}, \quad (3.30)$$

where q_t^{SR*} is decreasing in FPI factor, $\pi\beta(1+n)$, implying that FPI flows would reduce $r_{1t,t+1}^{SR*}$. A lower $r_{1t,t+1}^{SR*}$ would lead the host banks to invest more in SR loans and crowd out the investment in LR assets (a lower q_t^{SR*}). Consequently, the host growth rate would become:

$$\mu_{t+2}^{SR*}=\left(\frac{R}{\pi^*\left(1+n^*\right)^2}\right)q_t^{SR*}\left(\frac{\pi^*}{\left(1+n^*\right)^2}\right)^{\theta^*}\frac{\left(1-\theta^*\right)A_t^*\left(\bar{k}_t^*\right)^{\delta}\left(k_t^*\right)^{\theta^*-1}}{\left(1+i_t^*\right)}, \quad (3.31)$$

where μ_{t+2}^{SR*} is decreasing in FPI factor, $\pi\beta(1+n)$, via q_t^{SR*}. Note that the effects of FPI on the host growth rate do not take place until two periods after the openness to FPI.

An open economy in the LR

In the LR, the wage income has fully adjusted to the openness of FPI. As mentioned in the SR analysis, FPI outflows may lead the home country to have bank runs in both periods t and $t+1$. To discuss the LR effects would require the home country to survive the turmoil in the SR. Since the effects of FPI would take up to two periods to surface, such as in the host country, it is assumed that it is until period $t+3$ when the wage income finally adjusts fully to the openness of FPI to avoid the confusion between SR and LR effects.

The home country in the LR

In the LR, the wage income w_{t+3}^{LR} would have fully adjusted to the openness of FPI, and full employment would be restored in the home country. Provided the labour demand per non-relocated entrepreneur [equation (3.9)]

$$L_{t+3} = k_{t+3}\left[\frac{(1-\theta)A_{t+3}\bar{k}_{t+3}^{\delta}}{(1+i_{t+3})w_{t+3}}\right]^{1/\theta},$$

and the labour market clearing condition:

$$(1+n)^5 = \pi(1-\beta)(1+n)^3 L_{t+3}^{LR}, \tag{3.32}$$

the wage income in LR would become

$$w_{t+3}^{LR} = \left(\frac{\pi(1-\beta)}{(1+n)^2}\right)^{\theta}\frac{(1-\theta)A_{t+3}\bar{k}_{t+3}^{\delta}k_{t+3}^{\theta}}{(1+i_{t+3})}, \tag{3.33}$$

where w_t is decreasing in FPI factors, β. This is because FPI outflows has reduced the number of home entrepreneurs who would conduct output production at home and hence reduce total labour demand. The lower w_{t+3}^{LR} would then change $ROR(k_{t+3}^{LR})$ to:

$$ROR(k_{t+3}^{LR}) = A_{t+3}\theta\left(\frac{(1+n)^2}{\pi(1-\beta)}\right)^{1-\theta}\bar{k}_{t+3}^{\delta}k_{t+3}^{\theta-1}, \tag{3.34}$$

where $ROR(k_{t+3}^{LR})$ is increasing in FPI factor, β due to a lower w_{t+3}^{LR}.

Accordingly, the home banks would have adjusted the objective function and budget constraints to:

$$\max\left\{-\left(\frac{1-\pi(1-\beta)}{\gamma}\right)\left(r_{1t+3,t+4}w_{t+3}^{LR}\right)^{-\gamma} - \frac{\pi(1-\beta)}{\gamma}\left[ROR(k_{t+3})r_{2t+3,t+5}w_{t+3}^{LR} + \tilde{r}_{2t+3,t+5}w_{t+3}^{LR}\right]^{-\gamma}\right\},$$

$$\begin{aligned}(1-\pi(1-\beta))(1+n)^3 r_{1t+3,t+4} &= \alpha_{1t+3,t+4}z_{t+3}(1+i_{t+3}) + \alpha_{2t+3,t+4}q_{t+3}\chi,\\ \pi(1-\beta)(1+n)^3\tilde{r}_{2t+3,t+5} &= (1-\alpha_{1t+3,t+4})(1+i_{t+3})z_{t+3}.\\ \pi(1-\beta)(1+n)^3 r_{2t+3,t+5} &= (1-\alpha_{2t+3,t+4})Rq_{t+3},\end{aligned} \tag{3.35}$$

At the liquidation decision $\{\alpha_{1t+3,t+4}, \alpha_{2t+3,t+4}\} = \{1,0\}$, the returns to the withdrawals would be:

$$\begin{Bmatrix} r_{1t+3,t+4} \\ r_{2t+3,t+5} \\ \tilde{r}_{2t+2,t+4} \end{Bmatrix} = \begin{Bmatrix} \left(\dfrac{(1+i_{t+3})}{(1-\pi(1-\beta))(1+n)^3}\right)(1-q_{t+3}) \\ \left(\dfrac{R}{\pi(1-\beta)(1+n)^3}\right)q_{t+3} \\ 0 \end{Bmatrix}, \tag{3.36}$$

and the equilibrium portfolio allocation would be:

$$\{z_{t+3}, q_{t+3}\} = \left\{\frac{1}{1+\Phi}, \frac{\Phi}{1+\Phi}\right\}, \textit{ where } \Phi \equiv \left(\frac{\pi(1-\beta)}{1-\pi(1-\beta)}\right)\left[\frac{ROR(k_{t+3})R}{(1+i_{t+3})}\right]^{\frac{-\gamma}{1+\gamma}}, \tag{3.37}$$

where q_{t+3} is decreasing in FPI factor, β. This is because more FPI outflows (an increase in β) would reduce $r_{1t+3,t+4}$ and increase $r_{2t+3,t+5}$. In order to compensate the lower $r_{1t+3,t+4}$, the home banks would invest more in SR loans, which would crowd out the investment in LR assets (a decrease in q_{t+3}). A higher $r_{2t+3,\,t+5}$ and a lower q_{t+3} would then change the home LR growth rate to:

$$\mu_{t+5}^{LR} = \left(\frac{R}{\pi(1-\beta)(1+n)^3}\right)q_{t+3}\left(\frac{\pi(1-\beta)}{(1+n)^2}\right)^{\theta}\frac{(1-\theta)A_{t+3}\bar{k}_{t+3}^{\delta}k_{t+3}^{\theta}}{(1+i_{t+3})}, \tag{3.38}$$

where μ_{t+5}^{LR} is decreasing in $(1 + i_{t+3})$, but the effect of FPI factor β on the home LR growth rate is more complicated. In the LR, FPI outflows would affect μ_{t+5}^{LR} via both w_{t+3}^{LR} and $r_{2t+3,t+5}$ but in the opposite directions. On one hand, FPI outflows would lower labour demand and w_{t+3}^{LR}, which would be harmful for μ_{t+5}^{LR}. On the other hand, FPI outflows would affect $r_{2t+3,t+5}$ both directly and indirectly. The direct impact of FPI on $r_{2t+3,t+5}$ is positive, but the indirect impact is negative via q_{t+3} due to a higher $ROR(k_{t+3})$. If the effects via w_{t+3}^{LR} dominate, FPI flows would have negative impacts on μ_{t+5}^{LR}.

The host country in the LR

Since FPI inflows do not bring in labour demand, the host wage income in the LR would remain the same:

$$w_{t+3}^{LR*} = \left(\frac{\pi^*}{(1+n^*)^2}\right)^{\theta^*}\frac{(1-\theta^*)A_{t+3}^*\left(\bar{k}_{t+3}^*\right)^{\delta^*}\left(k_{t+3}^*\right)^{\theta^*}}{(1+i_{t+3}^*)}, \tag{3.39}$$

which can be combined with equilibrium labour to derive $ROR\left(k^{*}_{t+3}\right)$:

$$ROR(k^{*}_{t+3}) = A^{*}_{t+3}\theta^{*}\left(\frac{(1+n^{*})^{2}}{\pi^{*}}\right)^{1-\theta^{*}}(\bar{k}^{*}_{t+3})^{\delta^{*}}(k^{*}_{t+3})^{\theta^{*}-1} \tag{3.40}$$

Because of FPI inflows, the host bank's budget constraint for the SR withdrawals would change to:

$$\left[\left(1-\pi^{*}\right)\left(1+n^{*}\right)^{3}+\pi\beta(1+n)^{2}\right]r^{LR*}_{1t+3,t+4}=\alpha^{*}_{1t+3,t+5}z^{LR*}_{t+3}\left(1+i^{*}_{t+3}\right)+\alpha^{*}_{2t+3,t+4}q^{LR*}_{t+3}\chi.$$

At the liquidation decision $\left\{\alpha^{*}_{1t+3,t+4},\alpha^{*}_{2t+3,t+4}\right\}=\{1,0\}$, the returns to the withdrawals would be:

$$\left\{r^{LR*}_{1t+3,t+4},r^{LR*}_{2t+3,t+5},\tilde{r}^{LR*}_{2t+3,t+5}\right\}=\left\{\frac{z^{LR*}_{t+3}\left(1+i^{*}_{t+3}\right)}{\left[\left(1-\pi^{*}\right)\left(1+n^{*}\right)^{3}+\pi\beta(1+n)^{2}\right]},\left(\frac{R}{\pi^{*}\left(1+n^{*}\right)^{3}}\right)q^{LR*}_{t+3},0\right\}, \tag{3.41}$$

and the equilibrium portfolio allocation would be:

$$\left\{z^{LR*}_{t+3},q^{LR*}_{t+3}\right\}=\left\{\frac{1}{1+\Phi^{LR*}},\frac{\Phi^{LR*}}{1+\Phi^{LR*}}\right\},$$

where $$\Phi^{LR*}\equiv\left(\frac{\pi^{*}}{1-\pi^{*}}\right)^{\frac{1}{\gamma^{*}+1}}\left[\frac{ROR\left(k^{*}_{t+3}\right)R}{\pi^{*}\left(1+n^{*}\right)^{3}}\frac{\left[\left(1-\pi^{*}\right)\left(1+n^{*}\right)^{3}+\pi\beta(1+n)^{2}\right]}{\left(1+i^{*}_{t+3}\right)}\right]^{\frac{-\gamma^{*}}{1+\gamma^{*}}} \tag{3.42}$$

where q^{LR*}_{t+3} is decreasing in β due to the role of the banks as central planners to maximize the expected utility of the agents.

Given $ROR\left(k^{*}_{t+3}\right)$, $r^{LR*}_{1t+3,t+4}$, and $r^{LR*}_{2t+3,t+5}$, the incentive constraint for the entrepreneurs to produce must hold: $ROR\left(k^{*}_{t+3}\right)r^{LR*}_{2t+3,t+5}>r^{LR*}_{1t+3,t+4}>0$. Since more FPI flows (a higher β) would reduce q^{LR*}_{t+3} and $r^{LR*}_{2t+3,t+5}$, the incentive constraint would be tighter after the openness of FPI. When the incentive constraint holds, the host growth rate would be:

$$\mu^{LR*}_{t+5}=\left(\frac{R}{\pi^{*}\left(1+n^{*}\right)^{3}}\right)q^{LR*}_{t+3}\left(\frac{\pi^{*}}{\left(1+n^{*}\right)^{2}}\right)^{\theta^{*}}\frac{\left(1-\theta^{*}\right)A^{*}_{t+3}\left(\bar{k}^{*}_{t+3}\right)^{\delta^{*}}\left(k^{*}_{t+3}\right)^{\theta^{*}}}{\left(1+i^{*}_{t+3}\right)}, \tag{3.43}$$

where μ^{LR*}_{t+5} is decreasing in β via q^{LR*}_{t+3}, implying that FPI inflows would crowd out the investment in the LR assets in the host country and reduce the host growth rate in the LR.

Note that the results are based on the assumption of exogenously determined interest rates of both the home and the host countries, $\left(1+i_{t+3}\right)$ and $\left(1+i^{*}_{t+3}\right)$. When the assumption is relaxed to allow for both $\left(1+i_{t+3}\right)$ and $\left(1+i^{*}_{t+3}\right)$ to be determined endogenously, some of the results may be affected. For example, FPI flows from the home to the host country would reduce the loan supply of the home country but would increase the loan supply of the host country. Consequently, a higher $\left(1+i_{t+3}\right)$ and a lower $\left(1+i^{*}_{t+3}\right)$ would shrink the gap between $\left(1+i_{t+3}\right)$ and $\left(1+i^{*}_{t+3}\right)$. When the gap shrinks to a specific level, FPI flows may cease because of home bias. The changes of $\left(1+i_{t+3}\right)$ and $\left(1+i^{*}_{t+3}\right)$ would in turn affect the wage income and the growth rates of both home and the host countries. The details when interest rates would be endogenously determined would be analysed in Chapter 4.

The conclusion

This chapter examines SR FPI flows and the impacts to the home and the host countries in the SR and in the LR. For the home country in the SR, the openness of FPI flows which would lead to unexpected withdrawals would cause inevitable bank runs either in period t or in period $t+1$, depending on two conditions. The two conditions are (1) a sufficient amount of liquidation to pay for unexpected withdrawals and (2) the satisfaction of incentive constraints for the entrepreneurs to produce. When both conditions hold, the bank runs would be deferred to period $t+1$ due to failing demand deposits; otherwise, the bank runs would occur in period t.

At the time of bank runs, the amount of output goods produced during that period may remain positive but would reduce to zero in the following period. This is because the banks are assumed to be operating in a fully funded way and serving as central planners, and there is no incentive or moral problems of the banks. The result shows that even for a relative secure banking system with zero profit and without leverage or incentive problems, bank runs can be inevitable in response to the openness of FPI for the home country. To prevent bank runs would require lending facilities from the central banks and/or international organizations, such as the International Monetary Fund (IMF).

After surviving SR turmoil, in the LR after wage income fully adjusts to the openness of FPI, the home country would experience a lower wage income due to a decrease in labour demand. The lower wage income would boost the productivity and reduce the portfolio allocation towards LR assets. When the effects via wage income dominate, FPI may reduce the home growth rate in the LR.

As the recipients of the FPI, the host countries are less likely to experience bank runs. However, even without affecting host employment, FPI would crowd out the investment in the LR assets in the host country and damage the host growth rate both in the SR and in the LR. It is also shown that it takes time for some effects of FPI flows to surface and to appear on specific variables. The amount of time taken would depend on the speed of adjustment to the openness of FPI flows.

It is important to emphasize that the results are based on two key assumptions: (1) the role of the banks as central planners and (2) the interest rates being determined exogenously. When the two assumptions are relaxed, some results may be affected. The analysis which relaxes both assumptions will be discussed in Chapters 4, 5 and 6.

Notes

1 $\bar{k}_t = \pi(1-\beta)\bar{k}_t / \pi(1-\beta)$.

2 Note that the incentive constraint $ROR(k_t)r_{2t+2} > (1+i_t) > 0$ is a loosening constraint. The constraint works by assuming that the return from the SR loans would not be reinvested. One may also assume that the returns from SR loan would be reinvested. Then it will lead to a more strict incentive constraint: $ROR(k_t)r_{2t+2} > (1+i_t)^2 > 0$. At $\{\alpha_{1t+1}, \alpha_{2t+1}\} = \{1,0\}$, whether to reinvest would not affect the equilibrium allocation and the growth rates.

4 Capital flows, sudden stops and banking crises

Introduction: the facts and the issues

When there is a beginning, there is an end, just as an end is followed by a new beginning. Following the analysis of Chapter 3 on the openness of FPI flows, this chapter will focus on the sudden stops of FPI flows and the impacts on the banking systems and macroeconomic outcomes of both home and host countries in the SR and in the LR. As is well documented, the cessation of FPI flows has been considered one of the main causes of sudden stops, since FPI flows are more volatile and more sensitive to global economic conditions, as shown in Chapter 3.

The causes of sudden stops

Without the openness to capital flows, there would not be sudden stops, which are defined as the sudden slowdown of capital flows. Therefore, most studies on identifying the determinants of sudden stops have found foreign capital to be one crucial determinant. By investigating 20 emerging countries during 1880–1913, Bordo, Cavallo, and Meissner (2010) find that the countries which greatly rely on foreign capital would have the larger likelihood of triggering sudden stops. Along the line for foreign capital, Komulainen (2004) finds capital mobility as one of the causes of financial instability and could multiply the impacts of sudden stops by studying 31 emerging economies during 1980–2001. Similarly, de Mello, Padoan, and Rousova (2012) find that the position of capital flows in one country's external finance could be crucial to the magnitude of the impacts of sudden stops, which may lead to banking crises. However, Calvo et al (2003) find that it is the closedness of an economy that magnifies the effects of sudden stops, based on Argentina's experiences with convertibility (currency board). Looking at a different direction, Claessens and Kose (2013) argue that sudden stops are the adverse effects of crises rather than the causes of crises.

The literature in studying the causes of sudden stops raises several questions. First, what is the causality between sudden stops and instability/crises? Second, is the openness or the closedness to foreign capital more likely to cause the instability and magnify the impacts of sudden stops? Third, is Argentina's experience, studied by Calvo et al (2003), a special case due to its convertibility led by the crises?

Sudden stops and banking crises

Sudden stops would impact many macro variables. One stream has focused on the impacts on dollarization, and the other has focused on the impacts on the financial sectors, especially the links to banking crises. Being affected severely by sudden stops does not require dollarization, but the linkages of sudden stops to banking crises via financial sectors could affect the entire economy. Thus, it is the focus of this chapter to look into the linkages of sudden stops to the banking system and hence the impacts on macroeconomic variables and economic outcomes.

Not specifying the causality between sudden stops and banking crises, several studies find that it takes an external factor to link sudden stops and banking crises together. The external factors include the fall of currency board noted by Calvo et al (2003), large capital flows noted by Furceri, Guichard, and Rusticelli (2012) and credit boom noted by Mendoza and Terrones (2012). In particular, Calvo et al (2003) simply rationalize that banking crises accompanied the fall of currency board, which is vulnerable to sudden stops in capital flows. Using the panel data of developed and emerging economies during 1970–2007, Furceri et al (2012) argue that it is large capital flows that increase the probability of banking crises and sudden stops in the following 2 years. Mendoza and Terrones (2012) identify 70 credit booms in the data of 61 emerging and industrial countries during 1960–2010 and find that both sudden stops and banking crises follow credit booms.

Assuming that the banking crises would follow sudden stops, Joyce and Nabar (2009) take a broad sample of emerging markets during 1976–2002 and show that a strong banking sector is essential to sustain the negative impacts of sudden stops. Assuming the other way around, that sudden stops follow financial crisis, Gros and Alcidi (2015) take the European countries as their sample and show that the euro system serves as a protection for the countries experiencing sudden stops after global finance crises. For a study which could verify the order of the occurrences of sudden stops and banking crises, Fratzscher (2012) is the closest I could find. Fratzscher (2012) uses the dataset of 21 countries over the past 130 years since 1880 and find that the crashes/crises would depend on the composition of the flows which are subject to sudden stops risks. However, the order of occurrences as well as the causality of sudden stops and banking crises are still unclear and remained unanswered.

The effects of sudden stops on macro variables

Among the work studying the effects of sudden stops on macroeconomic variables, the results of the negative effects on the output level and hence economic growth are consistent across studies. For example, Bordo et al (2010) find that sudden stops have negative effects on growth. Moreover, when banking crises are preceded by sudden stops, the damage on economic growth would be even more severe. Similarly, Ratanamaneichat (2008) shows that the combination of sudden stops and banking crises would generate the most harmful *losses in output*. Using output to measure the costs as well, Vannapanich (2009) finds that banking crises would cost more than sudden stops. Interestingly, most studies have focused on the capital flows of the host countries. The impacts of sudden stops on the home countries have been neglected.

Suggested policies

As a recipient of FPI inflows, the host countries' role in capital flows tends to be passive. Therefore, it has been clear that sudden stops might not be controlled by the host countries. Thus, the policy suggestions to the host countries have focused on preventing banking crises. Joyce and Nabar (2009) suggest improving the strength of the banking sector in preventing banking crises followed by sudden stops. To be more specific for the policies for the banking sector, Vannapanich (2009) recommends accommodating policies rather than stricter policies. Ceh and Krznar (2008) show that foreign reserves may prevent crisis caused by sudden stops.

Theoretical framework

Depending on the circumstances, the occurrences of sudden stops and banking crises could be in a different order. The crises originating overseas could cause sudden stops on the inflows to the host country. Similarly, crises originating in the host country could drive inflows away and lead to sudden stops. In either case, depending on the economic conditions, especially the roles and the strength of the banking system, the sudden stops may or may not trigger banking crises and cause economic disruptions in the related countries. In other words, the role of the banking system is crucial in preventing banking crises as well as the possible damages to economic outcomes. Therefore, it is the aim of this chapter to examine the role of the banking system and its ability to prevent banking crises after sudden stops for both the home and the host countries in the SR and in the LR.

Following Chapter 3, the banking system is assumed to be fully funded. However, one assumption of exogenously determined interest rate is relaxed in this chapter. In this chapter, the interest rates of both the home and the host countries are endogenously determined and adjusted to the changes of FPI flows to the financial sector. As a result, it is shown that sudden stops would be stressful for the home banking system and would increase the probability of banking crises in the home country one period after sudden stops. Meanwhile, in response to sudden stops, a lower capital accumulation growth rate would damage future growth rate. Moreover, should a banking crisis occur, economic activities would be disrupted. The disrupted economic activities may have long-lasting effects on the economy. It is shown that even under a fully funded banking system, a relatively secure system, banking crises would occur after sudden stops. To prevent banking crises under the circumstance would require assistance from the authorities, either the central bank or international organizations, such as the IMF. Once the home country survives bank runs in the SR, the home country's growth rate would bounce back and become higher than the growth rate prior to sudden stops. The host country, however, would not have concerns for banking crises. The host growth rate would be higher in the SR but would decline in the LR after sudden stops.

The environment

The theoretical framework of this chapter inherits the three-period-lived overlapping-generations framework of Chapter 3 but with interest rates of both home and host countries endogenously determined. Moreover, while Chapter 3 moves from a closed economy to the openness of FPI, this chapter moves from an open economy with FPI flows to sudden stops which are assumed to occur unexpectedly to the open economy in period $t+1$.

Similar to Chapter 3, in the SR, the wage income has not yet adjusted to sudden stops and is assumed to remain the same as the wage income prior to sudden stops. In the LR, the wage income would adjust fully to the sudden stops.

To begin with, this chapter summarizes the basic framework and the key results of the equilibrium prior to sudden stops. It is assumed that every agent is born identical and is endowed with one unit of labour when young and nothing when middle aged and when old. The unit of labour would be supplied inelastically to produce output to earn wage income. The wage income would be paid in output goods, which would depreciate fully if not used or consumed within a period. However, the agent values only middle-aged consumption ($c_{2,t+1}$) and old consumption ($c_{3,t+2}$) and has the utility function in the form of:

$$u\left(c_{2,\,t+1}, c_{3,\,t+2}; \phi\right) = -\frac{\left(c_{2,t+1} + \phi c_{3,t+2}\right)^{-\gamma}}{\gamma}.$$

So the agents would have to find ways to store the value of their wage income. There are two assets: SR loans and LR assets. The SR loans would take one period to mature and provide interest rate $(1 + i_t)$ in output goods. The LR assets would take two periods to mature and would provide R in capital goods at maturity and χ in output goods if liquidated prematurely. It is assumed that only the banks have the access to these two assets. Therefore, the agents would deposit the entire wage income in the banks and withdraw in the later period after realizing their own types.

Each agent would learn its own type at the beginning of middle age. The type of an agent is exogenously determined and cannot be changed. There are three types: non-entrepreneurs with a probability $(1 - \pi)$, relocated entrepreneurs with a probability $(\pi\beta)$ and non-relocated entrepreneurs with a probability $(\pi(1 - \beta))$. The type of an agent is private information, while the distribution of types is public information. The non-entrepreneurs value only $c_{2,t+1}$ and would withdraw one period after deposits. The relocated entrepreneurs would invest in SR loans of the host country, so they would join the non-entrepreneurs to withdraw one period after deposits. When the incentive constraint holds, the non-relocated entrepreneurs would withdraw two periods after deposits to obtain capital goods to produce.

In order to start production, the entrepreneurs must borrow the amount $b_t = w_t L_t$ from the banks at the cost of $(1 + i_t)$, which must be repaid in the end of the period in order for the banks to pay for the returns of the withdrawals. To produce output goods would require both capital goods and labour. The production function is in the form of:

$$Y_t = A_t \bar{k}_t^{\delta} k_t^{\theta} L_t^{1-\theta}.$$

The capital gains of each entrepreneur would be:

$$\max_{L_t} \left\{ A_t \bar{k}_t^{\delta} k_t^{\theta} L_t^{1-\theta} - (1+i_t) w_t L_t \right\},$$

which gives the rate of return of capital:

$$ROR(k_t) = \frac{\left[A_t \bar{k}_t^{\delta} k_t^{\theta} L_t^{1-\theta} - (1+i_t) w_t L_t \right]}{k_t}, \tag{4.1}$$

The banks are assumed to be operating in a fully funded way and serving as a central planner to maximize the utility of the citizens of the country. So there would be no incentive or moral hazard problem of the banks, which earn zero profit. The problem faced by the banks would be:

$$\max \left\{ -\left(\frac{1-\pi}{\gamma}\right) \left(r_{1t,t+1} w_t \right)^{-\gamma} - \frac{\pi}{\gamma} \left[\begin{array}{c} ROR(k_t) r_{2t,t+2} w_t \\ + \tilde{r}_{2t,t+2} w_t \end{array} \right]^{-\gamma} \right\}, \tag{4.2}$$

subject to

$$\begin{aligned} &(1-\pi)(1+n)^2 r_{1t,t+1} = \alpha_{1t,t+1} z_t (1+i_t) + \alpha_{2t,t+1} q_{t+1} \chi, \\ &\pi (1+n)^2 r_{2t,t+2} = \left(1 - \alpha_{2t,t+1}\right) R q_t, \\ &\pi (1+n)^2 \tilde{r}_{2t,t+2} = \left(1 - \alpha_{1t,t+1}\right) z_t. \end{aligned} \tag{4.3}$$

The results

Similar to the previous chapters, this section will analyse the impacts of sudden stops on both the home and the host countries in the SR and in the LR. In the SR, the wage income has not yet adjusted to sudden stops, while in the LR, the wage income would have adjusted fully to sudden stops. Moreover, the interest rates of both the home and the host countries would be determined endogenously. It is assumed that sudden stops occur in period $t + 1$ unexpectedly and that it is until period $t + 3$ when the wage income would fully adjust to sudden stops, since some effects of sudden stops would take time to surface.

An open economy with FPI flows without sudden stops

To start with, I modify LR equilibrium to period t for both the home and the host countries in an open economy with FPI flows as derived in Chapter 3, which will be then be compared to the SR and LR equilibria of sudden stops which would occur in period $t+1$ in the later sections of the chapter.

The home country with FPI outflows

The equilibrium labour demand per entrepreneur would be:

$$L_t = k_t \left[\frac{(1-\theta) A_t \bar{k}_t^{\delta}}{(1+i_t) w_t} \right]^{1/\theta},$$

which can be combined with the equilibrium labour supply:

$$L_t = \frac{(1+n)^2}{\pi(1-\beta)}, \tag{4.4}$$

to derive the wage income

$$w_t = \left(\frac{\pi(1-\beta)}{(1+n)^2} \right)^{\theta} \frac{(1-\theta) A_t \bar{k}_t^{\delta} k_t^{\theta}}{(1+i_t)}. \tag{4.5}$$

The wage income w_t can then be plugged into equation (4.1) to derive $ROR(k_t)$:

$$ROR(k_t) = A_t \theta \left(\frac{(1+n)^2}{\pi(1-\beta)} \right)^{1-\theta} \bar{k}_t^{\delta} k_t^{\theta-1}. \tag{4.6}$$

When interest rates are endogenously determined, the home interest rate would be determined by loan supply $\left(LN_t^S\right)$ and loan demand $\left(LN_t^D\right)$:

$$LN_t^S = z_t (1+n)^2 w_t,$$
$$LN_t^D = \pi(1-\beta) w_t L_t,$$

which can be used to determine the home interest rate $(1 + i_t)$:

$$(1+i_t) = \frac{\pi(1-\beta) L_t}{z_t (1+n)^2}, \tag{4.7}$$

where $(1 + i_t)$ is decreasing in FPI factor β, implying that the lower the loan demand, the lower the $(1 + i_t)$ would be.

The FPI flows would modify the banks' problem to:

$$\max \left\{ -\left(\frac{1-\pi(1-\beta)}{\gamma} \right) \left(r_{1t,t+1} w_t \right)^{-\gamma} - \frac{\pi(1-\beta)}{\gamma} \left[ROR(k_t) r_{2t,t+2} w_t + \tilde{r}_{2t,t+2} w_t \right]^{-\gamma} \right\},$$

$$(1-\pi(1-\beta))(1+n)^2 r_{1t,t+1} = \alpha_{1t,t+1} z_t (1+i_t) + \alpha_{2t,t+2} q_t \chi, \tag{4.8}$$
$$\pi(1-\beta)(1+n)^2 \tilde{r}_{2t,t+2} = (1-\alpha_{1t,t+1})(1+i_t) z_t.$$
$$\pi(1-\beta)(1+n)^2 r_{2t,t+2} = (1-\alpha_{2t,t+1}) R q_t,$$

At the liquidation decision $\{\alpha_{1t,t+1}, \alpha_{2t,t+1}\} = \{1,0\}$, the returns to the withdrawals would be:

$$\begin{Bmatrix} r_{1t,t+1} \\ r_{2t,t+2} \\ \tilde{r}_{2t,t+2} \end{Bmatrix} = \begin{Bmatrix} \left(\dfrac{(1+i_{t+3})}{(1-\pi(1-\beta))(1+n)^2} \right)(1-q_t) \\ \left(\dfrac{R}{\pi(1-\beta)(1+n)^2} \right) q_t \\ 0 \end{Bmatrix}, \tag{4.9}$$

and the equilibrium portfolio allocation would be:

$$\{z_t, q_t\} = \left\{ \frac{1}{1+\Phi}, \frac{\Phi}{1+\Phi} \right\}, \text{ where } \Phi \equiv \left(\frac{\pi(1-\beta)}{1-\pi(1-\beta)} \right) \left[\frac{ROR(k_t)R}{(1+i_t)} \right]^{\frac{-\gamma}{1+\gamma}}, \tag{4.10}$$

which can be used to derive the equilibrium home growth rate:

$$\mu_{t+2} = \left(\frac{R}{\pi(1-\beta)(1+n)^2} \right) q_t \left(\frac{\pi(1-\beta)}{(1+n)^2} \right)^{\theta} \frac{(1-\theta) A_t \bar{k}_t^{\delta} k_t^{\theta-1}}{(1+i_t)}. \tag{4.11}$$

The host country with FPI inflows

As a recipient of FPI flows, the equilibrium wage income of the host country in an open economy would be

$$w_t^* = \left(\frac{\pi^*}{(1+n^*)^2} \right)^{\theta^*} \frac{(1-\theta^*) A_t^* (\bar{k}_t^*)^{\delta *} (k_t^*)^{\theta^*}}{(1+i_t^*)}, \tag{4.12}$$

which can be used to derive $ROR(k_t^*)$:

$$ROR(k_t^*) = A_t^* \theta^* \left(\frac{(1+n^*)^2}{\pi^*} \right)^{1-\theta^*} (\bar{k}_t^*)^{\delta *} (k_t^*)^{\theta^*-1}. \tag{4.13}$$

The loan supply and loan demand of the host country would be:

$$LN_t^{S*} = \pi\beta(1+n) r_{1t-1,t} w_{t-1} + z_t^* (1+n^*)^2 w_t^*,$$
$$LN_t^{D*} = \pi^* w_t^* L_t^*,$$

which give the host interest rate:

$$(1+i_t^*) = \frac{\pi^* w_t^* L_t^*}{\pi\beta(1+n) r_{1t-1,t} w_{t-1} + z_t^* (1+n^*)^2 w_t^*}. \tag{4.14}$$

where $(1+i_t^*)$ is also decreasing in β, similar to $(1 + i_t)$ [equation (4.7)]. The result shows that if FPI flows from the home to the host country continue after the adjustments of the interest rates, $(1+i_t) \le (1+i_t^*)$, one interpretation is that FPI outflows have severely damaged the loan demand of the home country and keep the home rate $(1 + i_t)$ lower than the host rate $(1+i_t^*)$.

The objective function faced by the host banks would be:

$$\max\left\{-\left(\frac{1-\pi^*}{\gamma^*}\right)\left(r_{1t,t+1}^* w_t^*\right)^{-\gamma^*} - \frac{\pi^*}{\gamma^*}\left[ROR\left(k_t^*\right) r_{2t,t+2}^* w_t + \tilde{r}_{2t,t+2}^* w_t^*\right]^{-\gamma^*}\right\},$$

with the SR budget constraint being modified to:

$$\left[\left(1-\pi^*\right)\left(1+n^*\right)^2 + \pi\beta(1+n)\right] r_{1t,t+1}^* = \alpha_{1t,t+1}^* z_t^* \left(1+i_t^*\right) + \alpha_{2t,t+1}^* q_t^* \chi.$$

At the liquidation decision $\left\{\alpha_{1t+3,t+4}^*, \alpha_{2t+3,t+4}^*\right\} = \{1,0\}$, the banks would provide the returns to the withdrawals:

$$\left\{r_{1t,t+1}^*, r_{2t,t+2}^*, \tilde{r}_{2t,t+2}^*\right\} = \left\{\frac{z_t^*\left(1+i_t^*\right)}{\left[\left(1-\pi^*\right)\left(1+n^*\right)^2 + \pi\beta(1+n)\right]}, \left(\frac{R}{\pi^*\left(1+n^*\right)^2}\right) q_t^*, 0\right\}. \tag{4.15}$$

The equilibrium portfolio allocation and the host growth rate would be:

$$\left\{z_t^*, q_t^*\right\} = \left\{\frac{1}{1+\Phi^*}, \frac{\Phi^*}{1+\Phi^*}\right\},$$

$$\Phi^* \equiv \left(\frac{\pi^*}{1-\pi^*}\right)^{\frac{1}{\gamma^*+1}} \left[\frac{ROR\left(k_t^*\right) R}{\pi^*\left(1+n^*\right)^2} \frac{\left[\left(1-\pi^*\right)\left(1+n^*\right)^2 + \pi\beta(1+n)\right]}{\left(1+i_t^*\right)}\right]^{\frac{-\gamma^*}{1+\gamma^*}} \tag{4.16}$$

$$\mu_{t+2}^* = \left(\frac{R}{\pi^*(1+n^*)^2}\right) q_t^* \left(\frac{\pi^*}{(1+n^*)^2}\right)^{\theta^*} \frac{(1-\theta^*) A_t^* (\bar{k}_t^*)^{\delta^*} (k_t^*)^{\theta^*-1}}{(1+i_t^*)}, \tag{4.17}$$

After sudden stops in the SR

In period $t+1$, sudden stops occur unexpectedly and would remain for a significant period of time. That implies that the middle-aged relocated home entrepreneurs (generation t) would not withdraw their deposits and invest in the host loans, $\beta_t = 0$, where $t \ge t$.[1] Since the banks operate in a fully funded way, the decisions of both the portfolio allocations and the returns to the withdrawals one period after deposit to generation t were already made in period t, prior to the realization of sudden stops. So the question now is whether the non-withdrawals from the home banks and non-reinvestment by the relocated home entrepreneurs into the host banks would be a concern for the home and the host banks.

Similar to the previous chapters, this section will analyse the impacts of sudden stops on the home and the host countries in the SR and in the LR. SR is for the period(s) when the wage income has not yet adjusted to sudden stops and will remain the same as period t, $w_{t+1}^{SR} = w_t$, while LR is the period when the wage income has fully adjusted to sudden stops. Since some effects will take time to surface, the analysis will focus on the time when sudden stops occur (period $t+1$) and the following period(s) ($t+2$, and $t+3$ if necessary) for the SR.

The home country in the SR after sudden stops

In period $t+1$, sudden stops occur. That is, the middle-aged relocated entrepreneurs (generation t) would not withdraw to invest in the host loans. Instead, they would join the non-relocated home entrepreneurs to withdraw their deposits in period $t+2$ to obtain the capital goods to start production. Meanwhile, the entrepreneurs who would start production in period $t+1$ would be the old non-relocated entrepreneurs (generation t–1) since the relocated entrepreneurs of generation t–1 had reinvested in host loans in period t. In the SR, the wage income has not yet adjusted to sudden stops, $w_{t+1}^{SR} = w_t$ [equation (4.5)],[2] and equilibrium labour per entrepreneur would remain the same, $L_{t+1} = L_t$ [equation (4.4)].

Since the banks operate in a fully funded way and as central planners, which earn zero profit, the non-withdrawals of the relocated entrepreneurs in period $t+1$ would be reinvested in home loans by the banks and provide returns to the entrepreneurs of generation t at the following period $t+2$. Therefore, the loan supply and demand in period $t+1$ would be:

$$LN_{t+1}^{S} = \pi\beta(1+n)^2 r_{1t,t+1} w_t + z_{t+1}(1+n)^3 w_{t+1}^{SR},$$
$$LN_{t+1}^{D} = \pi(1-\beta)(1+n) w_{t+1}^{SR} L_{t+1},$$

which gives $(1+i_{t+1})$

$$(1+i_{t+1}) = \frac{\pi(1-\beta)L_{t+1}}{\pi\beta(1+n)r_{1t,t+1} + z_{t+1}(1+n)^2}, \tag{4.18}$$

where $(1+i_{t+1})$ is decreasing in β and $(1+i_{t+1}) < (1+i_t)$ due to $LN_{t+1}^{S} > LN_t^{S}$, implying that sudden stops would reduce the home rate further $(1+i_{t+1})$. Based on $ROR(k_{t+1})$:

$$ROR(k_{t+1}) = A_{t+1}\bar{k}_{t+1}^{\delta} k_{t+1}^{\theta-1}\left[\frac{(1+n)^2}{\pi(1-\beta)}\right]^{1-\theta}\left[1-\left(\frac{1+i_{t+1}}{1+i_t}\right)(1-\theta)\right], \tag{4.19}$$

which shows that a lower $(1+i_{t+1})$ would increase $ROR(k_{t+1})$, $ROR(k_{t+1}) > ROR(k_t)$ [equation (4.6)].

After sudden stops, the relocated entrepreneurs would withdraw two periods after deposits, similar to the non-relocated entrepreneurs. The budget constraints faced by the banks would be as stated in equation (4.3). Therefore, at the liquidation decision $\{\alpha_{1t+1,t+3}, \alpha_{2t+1,t+3}\} = \{1,0\}$, the returns to the withdrawals to generation $t+1$ would be:

$$\begin{Bmatrix} r_{1t+1,t+2} \\ r_{2t+1,t+3} \\ \tilde{r}_{2t+1,t+3} \end{Bmatrix} = \begin{Bmatrix} \left(\frac{(1+i_{t+1})}{(1-\pi)(1+n)^3}\right)(1-q_{t+1}), \\ \left(\frac{R}{\pi(1+n)^3}\right)q_{t+1} \\ 0 \end{Bmatrix}, \tag{4.20}$$

and the portfolio allocation would become:

$$\{z_{t+1}, q_{t+1}\} = \left\{\frac{1}{1+\Phi}, \frac{\Phi}{1+\Phi}\right\}, \textit{ where } \Phi \equiv \left(\frac{\pi}{1-\pi}\right)\left[\frac{ROR(k_{t+1})R}{(1+i_{t+1})}\right]^{\frac{-\gamma}{1+\gamma}}, \tag{4.21}$$

where q_{t+1} is increasing in $(1 + i_{t+1})$. That is because a lower $(1 + i_{t+1})$ would cause the banks to compensate $r_{1t+1,t+2}$ by investing more in SR loans, which would crowd out investment in the LR assets. Meanwhile, a higher $ROR(k_{t+1})$ also implies that it does not require as much investment in LR assets to provide $r_{2t+1,t+3}$ the same returns. So the investment in LR assets would decrease (a decrease in q_{t+1}). Compared to q_t, sudden stops which remove FPI outflows $\beta_{t+1} = 0$ would increase q_{t+1} directly, while a lower $(1 + i_{t+1})$ would decrease q_{t+1}. Since the direct effects due to $\beta_{t+1} = 0$ dominate, $q_{t+1} > q_t$. Meanwhile, sudden stops, $\beta_{t+1} = 0$, would have direct negative effects on $r_{2t+1,t+3}$ [equation (4.9)]. Therefore, if the direct negative effects of $\beta_{t+1} = 0$ on $r_{2t+1,t+3}$ dominate the positive effects of q_{t+1} on $r_{2t+1,t+3}$, $r_{2t+1,t+3} < r_{2t,t+2}$. Given equations (4.20) and (4.21), the home growth rate would be:

$$\mu_{t+3} = \frac{r_{2t+1,t+3}w_{t+1}}{k_{t+1}} = \left(\frac{R}{\pi(1+n)^3}\right)q_{t+1}\left(\frac{\pi(1-\beta)}{(1+n)^2}\right)^{\theta}\frac{(1-\theta)A_t\bar{k}_t^{\delta}k_t^{\theta}}{(1+i_t)}, \tag{4.22}$$

where $\mu_{t+3} < \mu_{t+2}$ due to $r_{2t+1,t+3} < r_{2t,t+2}$ and $w_{t+1}^{SR} = w_t$. This is mainly because of the non-withdrawals by the relocated entrepreneurs, which reduce $(1 + i_{t+1})$ and $r_{1t+1,t+2}$. As central planners to maximize the expected utility of the agents, the banks would invest more in SR loans, which crowd out the investment in LR assets (a decrease in q_{t+1}) and hence lower the accumulation of capital goods and the economic growth rate.

In period $t+2$, the old relocated entrepreneurs (generation t) whose non-withdrawals causing sudden stops would withdraw their deposits to obtain capital goods to start production. In order to start production, the relocated entrepreneurs must borrow by applying for loans. Thus, the loan demand would increase to:

$$LN_{t+2}^{D} = \pi(1+n)^2 w_{t+2}L_{t+2}.$$

Because of the continuation of sudden stops, there would be no FPI flows conducted by the home entrepreneurs of generation $t+1$. The loan supply would be:

$$LN_{t+2}^{S} = z_{t+2}(1+n)^4 w_{t+2},$$

which gives $(1 + i_{t+2})$:

$$(1+i_{t+2}) = \frac{\pi L_{t+2}}{z_{t+2}(1+n)^2}, \tag{4.23}$$

where $(1 + i_t) > (1 + i_{t+2}) > (1 + i_{t+1})$ [equations (4.7) and (4.18)] due to a higher loan demand than periods t and $t+1$ and a lower loan supply than period $t+1$.

Given labour supply, the equilibrium labour per entrepreneur would be:

$$L_{t+2} = \frac{(1+n)^2}{\pi}, \tag{4.24}$$

where $L_{t+2} < L_t$. In the SR, $w_{t+2}^{SR} = w_t$, so $ROR(k_{t+2})$ would become:

$$ROR(k_{t+2}) = A_{t+2}\bar{k}_{t+2}^{\delta} k_{t+2}^{\theta-1}\left[\frac{(1+n)^2}{\pi}\right]^{1-\theta}\left[1-\left(\frac{1+i_{t+2}}{1+i_t}\right)(1-\theta)\right], \tag{4.25}$$

where $ROR(k_{t+2}) < ROR(k_t) < ROR(k_{t+1})$ [equation (4.19)] due to a higher $(1+i_{t+2})$ and sudden stops $\beta = 0$.

At the liquidation decision $\{\alpha_{1t,t+1}, \alpha_{2t,t+1}\} = \{1, 0\}$, the non-withdrawals of the old relocated entrepreneurs in period $t+1$ would change the banks' budget constraints for both $r_{2t,t+2}$ and $\tilde{r}_{2t,t+2}$ to:

$$\pi(1+n)^2 r_{2t,t+2} = Rq_t, \tag{4.26}$$

$$\pi(1+n)^2 \tilde{r}_{2t,t+2} = \pi\beta(1+n)^2(1+i_{t+1})r_{1t,t+1}w_t, \tag{4.27}$$

which would give:

$$\left\{\widehat{r_{2t,t+2}},\ \widehat{\tilde{r}_{2t,t+2}}\right\} = \left\{\left(\frac{R}{\pi(1+n)^2}\right)q_t,\ \beta(1+i_{t+1})r_{1t,t+1}w_t\right\}, \tag{4.28}$$

where $\widehat{r_{2t,t+2}}$ and $\widehat{\tilde{r}_{2t,t+2}}$ represent the actual returns to the entrepreneurs in capital goods and in output goods, respectively, and $\widehat{r_{2t,t+2}} < r_{2t,t+2}$, implying that the banks have failed demand deposits as stated in the deposit contracts at the time of deposits [equation (4.9)] and are subject to run in period $t+2$. This type of bank run is caused by failing demand deposits and is called a type I bank run.

Similar to Chapter 2, the fully funded banks would pay the returns to the entrepreneurs before going bankrupt, the so-called bank runs. This means that the entrepreneurs would still obtain the capital goods to start production. However, a lower $\widehat{r_{2t,t+2}}$, a lower $ROR(k_{t+2})$ and a higher $(1+i_{t+2})$ would shrink the gap of $\left[ROR(k_{t+2})R - r_{1t+1,t+2}\right]$, and make it difficult for the incentive constraints for the entrepreneurs, $ROR(k_{t+2})R > r_{1t+1,t+2}$, to hold. Should the incentive constraint fail to hold, the entrepreneurs would not want to produce and would have no incentive to withdraw in period $t+2$ for capital goods. Instead, they would withdraw in period $t+1$ to obtain output goods to consume and hence push bank runs to occur in period $t+1$. This type of bank run is caused by the lack of loan demand in period $t+2$ and is called a type II bank run. Meanwhile, when all entrepreneurs withdraw unexpectedly in period $t+1$, it would cause bank panic and reduce $r_{1t,t+1}$, and hence lead to bank runs, which would be also caused by failing demand deposits, the type I bank run. So it is a combination of type I and type II bank runs.

If the incentive constraint holds, the output level of the home country in period $t+2$ would be

$$TY_{t+2} = \pi(1+n)^2 Y_{t+2}, \tag{4.29}$$

where $Y_{t+2} < Y_t < Y_{t+1}$, implying that the output production per entrepreneur would be at the lowest level, compared to periods t and $t+1$, due to a lower $r_{2t,t+2}$ and a lower L_{t+2}. At $(1-\beta)(Y_t - Y_{t+2}) < \beta Y_{t+2}$, the output level of period $t+2$ would be less than that of both period t and $t+1$, $TY_{t+2} < TY_t < TY_{t+1}$, implying a negative growth rate for the home country in period $t+2$. The result of the negative effects of sudden stops on banking crises, output/growth, is similar to what has been described in Bordo et al (2010), Ratanamaneichat (2008) and Vannapanich (2009).

For the subsequent periods of $t+2$, zero output level would be the result because of bank runs. The result of the severe damage to the economy due to bank runs caused by sudden stops is an important message to the home country to pay attention to the sudden stops of outflows and to provide necessary assistance if possible. The necessary assistance would include but not be limited to the provision of the lending facilities to the banks to finance the liquidity shortages. Note that the liquidity shortages are not limited to the immediate shortage of output goods in period $t+1$ should all entrepreneurs withdraw in period $t+1$ but also the shortage of capital goods in period $t+2$ to satisfy the incentive constraint. The provision of lending facilities to the banks to finance liquidity shortages may prevent the type I bank runs but not the type II bank runs. That is because type II bank runs result from the lack of loan demand, which may have many causes. If it is due to failing of the incentive constraint, the provision of capital goods may need to be combined with the decrease in the home interest rate through various monetary tools. Other possible assistance, such as deposit insurance, will be discussed in Chapter 7.

The host country in the SR after sudden stops

In period $t+1$ and in the SR, the wage income has not yet adjusted to sudden stops, $w^*_{t+1} = w^*_t$ [equation (4.12)]. The sudden stops which cease FPI inflows would change the loan supply and the loan demand to:

$$LN^{S*}_{t+1} = z^*_{t+1}\left(1+n^*\right)^3 w^*_{t+1},$$
$$LN^{D}_{t+1} = \pi^*\left(1+n^*\right) w^*_{t+1} L^*_{t+1},$$

which would give:

$$\left(1+i_{t+1}^{*}\right)=\frac{\pi^{*}\left(1+n^{*}\right)w_{t+1}^{*}L_{t+1}^{*}}{z_{t+1}^{*}\left(1+n^{*}\right)^{3}w_{t+1}^{*}}, \tag{4.30}$$

where $\left(1+i_{t+1}^{*}\right)>\left(1+i_{t}^{*}\right)$ due to the decrease in the loan supply, $LN_{t+1}^{S*}<LN_{t}^{S*}$. A higher $\left(1+i_{t+1}^{*}\right)$ would change $ROR\left(k_{t+1}^{*}\right)$ to

$$ROR\left(k_{t+1}^{*}\right)=A_{t+1}^{*}\left(\bar{k}_{t+1}^{*}\right)^{\delta^{*}}\left(k_{t+1}^{*}\right)^{\theta^{*}-1}\left(\frac{\left(1+n^{*}\right)^{2}}{\pi^{*}}\right)^{1-\theta^{*}}\left[1-\left(\frac{1+i_{t+1}^{*}}{1+i_{t}^{*}}\right)\left(1-\theta^{*}\right)\right], \tag{4.31}$$

where $ROR\left(k_{t+1}^{*}\right)$ is decreasing in $\left(1+i_{t+1}^{*}\right)$ and $ROR\left(k_{t+1}^{*}\right)<ROR\left(k_{t}^{*}\right)$ due to $\left(1+i_{t+1}^{*}\right)>\left(1+i_{t}^{*}\right)$.

The sudden stops would lead the banks to revise their SR budget constraint for $r_{1t+1,t+2}^{*}$ to:

$$\left(1-\pi^{*}\right)\left(1+n^{*}\right)^{2}r_{1t+1,t+2}^{*}=\alpha_{1t+1,t+2}^{*}z_{t}^{*}\left(1+i_{t+1}^{*}\right)+\alpha_{2t+1,t+2}^{*}q_{t+1}^{*}\chi.$$

At $\left\{\alpha_{1t+1,t+2}^{*},\alpha_{2t+1,t+2}^{*}\right\}=\{1,0\}$, the returns to the withdrawals would change to:

$$\left\{r_{1t+1,t+2}^{*},r_{2t+1,t+3}^{*},\tilde{r}_{2t+1,t+3}^{*}\right\}=\left\{\frac{z_{t+1}^{*}\left(1+i_{t+1}^{*}\right)}{\left[\left(1-\pi^{*}\right)\left(1+n^{*}\right)^{2}\right]},\left(\frac{R}{\pi^{*}\left(1+n^{*}\right)^{2}}\right)q_{t+1}^{*},0\right\}, \tag{4.32}$$

where $r_{1t+1,t+2}^{*}>r_{1t,t+1}^{*}$. The host portfolio allocation would become:

$$\left\{z_{t+1}^{*},q_{t+1}^{*}\right\}=\left\{\frac{1}{1+\Phi^{*}},\frac{\Phi^{*}}{1+\Phi^{*}}\right\},$$

$$\text{where } \Phi^{*}\equiv\left(\frac{\pi^{*}}{1-\pi^{*}}\right)^{\frac{1}{\gamma^{*}+1}}\left[\frac{ROR\left(k_{t+1}^{*}\right)R}{\pi^{*}\left(1+n^{*}\right)^{2}}\frac{\left[\left(1-\pi^{*}\right)\left(1+n^{*}\right)^{2}\right]}{\left(1+i_{t+1}^{*}\right)}\right]^{\frac{-\gamma^{*}}{1+\gamma^{*}}}, \tag{4.33}$$

which would give a higher q_{t+1}^{*}, $q_{t+1}^{*}>q_{t}^{*}$ due to a lower $ROR\left(k_{t+1}^{*}\right)$ and a higher $\left(1+i_{t+1}^{*}\right)$. Accordingly, the host growth rate would be:

$$\mu_{t+3}^{*}=\left(\frac{R}{\pi^{*}\left(1+n^{*}\right)^{2}}\right)q_{t+1}^{*}\left(1-\theta^{*}\right)\left(\frac{\pi^{*}}{\left(1+n^{*}\right)^{2}}\right)^{\theta^{*}}\frac{A_{t+1}^{*}\left(\bar{k}_{t+1}^{*}\right)^{\delta^{*}}\left(k_{t+1}^{*}\right)^{\theta^{*}-1}}{\left(1+i_{t+1}^{*}\right)}, \tag{4.34}$$

where μ_{t+3}^{*} is increasing in q_{t+1}^{*} and $\mu_{t+3}^{*}>\mu_{t+2}^{*}$ due to $q_{t+1}^{*}>q_{t}^{*}$. The result shows that sudden stops would not cause unexpected withdrawals or non-withdrawals to the host country. Instead, sudden stops would increase $\left(1+i_{t+1}^{*}\right)$ and decrease

$ROR(k_{t+1}^{*})$, which would drive up investment in the LR assets q_{t+1}^{*} and hence promote the host growth rate μ_{t+3}^{*}. Moreover, the results of the subsequent periods in the SR, such as period $t+2$, when the wage income has not yet adjusted to sudden stops, would be similar to period $t+1$.

The result of positive effects on growth without possibility of bank runs is opposite to the findings of Bordo et al (2010), Ratanamaneichat (2008) and Vannapanich (2009) as described in the first section. This is because the theoretical result is based on the assumptions that the host banks operate in a fully funded way and that the host country would not lead SR FPI flows to investment other than SR loans. In reality, when either assumption does not hold, sudden stops may lead to bank runs and banking crises in the host countries and hence the disruption of economic activities and possible negative growth in the host country, as found in Bordo et al (2010), Ratanamaneichat (2008) and Vannapanich (2009). More details will be discussed in Chapter 7.

After sudden stops in the LR

In the LR, the wage income would adjust fully to sudden stops. It is assumed that it is not until period $t+3$ that the wage income has fully adjusted to sudden stops. Moreover, in order to discuss LR effects of sudden stops on the home country, it is assumed that the home country has survived the SR turmoil and possible economic disruptions.

The home country in the LR after sudden stops

In period $t+3$, in the LR after sudden stops, the equilibrium labour per entrepreneur would become:

$$L_{t+3}^{LR} = \frac{(1+n)^2}{\pi}, \tag{4.35}$$

where $L_{t+3}^{LR} = L_{t+2} < L_{t+1} = L_t$ [equation (4.4)]. The wage income would adjust to:

$$w_{t+3}^{LR} = \left(\frac{\pi}{(1+n)^2}\right)^{\theta} \frac{(1-\theta)A_{t+3}\bar{k}_{t+3}^{\delta}k_{t+3}^{\theta}}{(1+i_{t+3})}, \tag{4.36}$$

where $w_{t+3}^{LR} > w_t$ [equation (4.5)] due to an increase in labour demand and is the same as the level in a closed economy [equation (3.10)]. The rate of return of capital $ROR(k_{t+3}^{LR})$ would then become:

$$ROR\left(k_{t+3}^{LR}\right) = \theta A_{t+3}^{LR}\left(\bar{k}_{t+3}^{LR}\right)^{\delta}\left(k_{t+3}^{LR}\right)^{\theta-1}\left[\frac{(1+n)^2}{\pi}\right]^{1-\theta}, \tag{4.37}$$

where $ROR(k_{t+3}) < ROR(k_{t+2}) < ROR(k_{t+1})$ [equations (4.19) and (4.25)].

For the loan market, the loan demand and the loan supply would be similar to period $t+2$:

$$LN_{t+3}^{D} = \pi(1+n)^{3} w_{t+3} L_{t+3},$$
$$LN_{t+3}^{S} = z_{t+3}(1+n)^{5} w_{t+3},$$

which would give the interest rate:

$$\left(1+i_{t+3}^{LR}\right) = \frac{\pi L_{t+3}^{LR}}{z_{t+3}^{LR}(1+n)^{2}}, \tag{4.38}$$

where $(1+i_t) < \left(1+i_{t+3}^{LR}\right) = (1+i_{t+2}) < (1+i_{t+1})$ if $\left(L_{t+3}^{LR} / z_{t+3}^{LR}\right) > (1-\beta)(L_t / z_t)$.

At the liquidation decision $\{\alpha_{1t+3,t+4}, \alpha_{2t+3,t+4}\} = \{1, 0\}$, the returns to the withdrawals would be:

$$\begin{Bmatrix} r_{1t+3,t+4}^{LR} \\ r_{2t+3,t+5}^{LR} \\ \tilde{r}_{2t+3,t+5}^{LR} \end{Bmatrix} = \begin{Bmatrix} \left(\dfrac{\left(1+i_{t+3}^{LR}\right)}{(1-\pi)(1+n)^{2}}\right)\left(1-q_{t+3}^{LR}\right) \\ \left(\dfrac{R}{\pi(1+n)^{2}}\right) q_{t+3}^{LR} \\ 0 \end{Bmatrix}, \tag{4.39}$$

and the equilibrium portfolio allocation would be:

$$\left\{z_{t+3}^{LR}, q_{t+3}^{LR}\right\} = \left\{\frac{1}{1+\Phi}, \frac{\Phi}{1+\Phi}\right\}, \ \textit{where}\ \Phi \equiv \left(\frac{\pi}{1-\pi}\right)\left[\frac{ROR\left(k_{t+3}^{LR}\right)R}{\left(1+i_{t+3}^{LR}\right)}\right]^{\frac{-\gamma}{1+\gamma}}. \tag{4.40}$$

Based on equation (4.40), due to $ROR(k_{t+1}) > ROR(k_t) > ROR(k_{t+2}) > ROR\left(k_{t+3}^{LR}\right)$ and $(1+i_t) > (1+i_{t+2}) = \left(1+i_{t+3}^{LR}\right) > (1+i_{t+1})$, one can conclude $q_{t+3}^{LR} > q_{t+2} > q_{t+1} > q_t$. Note that the probability of bank runs in period $t+2$ in the home country is relatively high due to sudden stops. Should sudden stops occur, the bank runs at period $t+2$ imply that the banks would not have portfolio allocation decision to make, $q_{t+2} = 0$. According to equations (4.39) and (4.40), the home growth rate would be:

$$\mu_{t+5}^{LR} = \left(\frac{R}{\pi(1+n)^{2}}\right) q_{t+3}^{LR} \left(\frac{\pi}{(1+n)^{2}}\right)^{\theta} \frac{(1-\theta) A_{t+3}^{LR}\left(\bar{k}_{t+3}^{LR}\right)^{\delta}\left(k_{t+3}^{LR}\right)^{\theta-1}}{\left(1+i_{t+3}^{LR}\right)}, \tag{4.41}$$

where $\mu_{t+5} > \mu_{t+3}$ due to $q_{t+3}^{LR} > q_{t+1}$ and $w_{t+3}^{LR} > w_{t+1}$. The comparison to μ_{t+2} is more complicated. In the case without sudden stops, μ_{t+2} would be as shown in equation (4.11), which gives $\mu_{t+5}^{LR} > \mu_{t+2} > \mu_{t+3}$. However, sudden stops would cause the combination of type I and type II bank runs in period $t+2$ and cause negative home growth rate $\mu_{t+2} < 0$ as shown in equation (4.29). The result

Table 4.1 A comparison between SR and LR effects on the home country

Variables	*t*	*t + 1 (sudden stops)*	*t + 2*	*t + 3 (LR)*
$(1+i_t)$	$(1+i_t) > (1+i_{t+2}) = (1+i_{t+3}^{LR}) > (1+i_{t+1})\cdot$			
$ROR(k_t)$	$ROR(k_{t+1}) > ROR(k_t) > ROR(k_{t+2}) > ROR(k_{t+3}^{LR})$			
μ_{t+3}	$\mu_{t+5}^{LR} > \mu_{t+3} > 0 > \mu_{t+2}$			
Bank Runs IC holds*	No	No	Type I bank runs	No
Bank Runs IC fails*	No	Type I and type II bank runs	–	No

*IC represents incentive constraint for the entrepreneurs to produce.

indicates that sudden stops which cease capital outflows could promote the home growth rate in the LR through a higher wage income and more investment in LR assets. Before it is able to achieve a higher LR home growth rate, the home country must survive the instability of the banking system in the SR.

The host country in the LR after sudden stops

Since FPI flows would enter the loan market, the sudden stops of FPI flows would change the loan demand and the loan supply to:

$$LN_{t+3}^{S*} = z_{t+3}^{*}\left(1+n^{*}\right)^{3} w_{t+3}^{*},$$
$$LN_{t+3}^{D} = \pi^{*}\left(1+n^{*}\right) w_{t+3}^{*} L_{t+3}^{*},$$

which would give $\left(1+i_{t+3}^{LR*}\right)$:

$$\left(1+i_{t+3}^{LR*}\right) = \frac{\pi^{*} L_{t+3}^{*}}{z_{t+3}^{*}\left(1+n^{*}\right)^{2}}, \tag{4.42}$$

where $\left(1+i_{t+3}^{LR*}\right) = \left(1+i_{t+1}^{*}\right) > \left(1+i_{t}^{*}\right)$. Given $L_{t+3}^{*} = L_{t}^{*}$, the host wage income would become:

$$w_{t+3}^{LR*} = \left(\frac{\pi^{*}}{\left(1+n^{*}\right)^{2}}\right)^{\theta} \frac{(1-\theta) A_{t+3}^{LR*} \left(\bar{k}_{t+3}^{LR*}\right)^{\delta^{*}} \left(k_{t+3}^{LR*}\right)^{\theta^{*}}}{\left(1+i_{t+3}^{LR*}\right)}. \tag{4.43}$$

where $w_{t+3}^{LR*} < w_{t}^{*}$ due to $\left(1+i_{t+3}^{*}\right) > \left(1+i_{t}^{*}\right)$, and the value of $ROR\left(k_{t+3}^{*}\right)$ would change to:

$$ROR\left(k_{t+3}^{LR*}\right) = \theta^{*} A_{t+3}^{LR*} \left(\bar{k}_{t+3}^{LR*}\right)^{\delta^{*}} \left(k_{t+3}^{LR*}\right)^{\theta^{*}-1} \left(\frac{\left(1+n^{*}\right)^{2}}{\pi^{*}}\right)^{1-\theta^{*}}, \tag{4.44}$$

where $ROR\left(k_{t+3}^{LR*}\right) > ROR\left(k_{t}^{*}\right) > ROR\left(k_{t+1}^{*}\right)$ [equations (4.13) and (4.31)] due to $q_{t+3}^{LR*} > q_{t}^{*}$.

At $\left\{\alpha^{LR*}_{1t+3,t+4}, \alpha^{LR*}_{2t+3,t+4}\right\} = \{1,0\}$, the returns to the withdrawals would be:

$$\left\{r^{LR*}_{1t+3,t+4}, r^{LR*}_{2t+3,t+5}, \tilde{r}^{LR*}_{2t+3,t+5}\right\} = \left\{\frac{z^{LR*}_{t+3}\left(1+i^{LR*}_{t+3}\right)}{\left[\left(1-\pi^*\right)\left(1+n^*\right)^2\right]}, \left(\frac{R}{\pi^*\left(1+n^*\right)^2}\right) q^{LR*}_{t+3}, 0\right\}. \tag{4.45}$$

Accordingly, the equilibrium host portfolio allocation would be:

$$\left\{z^{LR*}_{t+3}, q^{LR*}_{t+3}\right\} = \left\{\frac{1}{1+\Phi^*}, \frac{\Phi^*}{1+\Phi^*}\right\},$$

$$\text{where } \Phi^* \equiv \left(\frac{\pi^*}{1-\pi^*}\right)^{\frac{1}{\gamma^*+1}} \left[\frac{ROR\left(k^{LR*}_{t+3}\right)R}{\pi^*\left(1+n^*\right)^2} \frac{\left[\left(1-\pi^*\right)\left(1+n^*\right)^2\right]}{\left(1+i^{LR*}_{t+3}\right)}\right]^{\frac{-\gamma^*}{1+\gamma^*}} \tag{4.46}$$

where q^{LR*}_{t+3} is decreasing in $ROR\left(k^*_{t+3}\right)$ but increasing in $\left(1+i^{LR*}_{t+3}\right)$. A higher $ROR\left(k^*_{t+3}\right)$ would reduce q^{LR*}_{t+3}, while a higher $\left(1+i^{LR*}_{t+3}\right)$ would increase q^{LR*}_{t+3}. Compared to the past periods, t and $t+1$, one can conclude that $q^{LR*}_{t+3} > q^*_t$ [equation (4.16)]; however, whether $q^{LR*}_{t+3} < q^*_{t+1}$ would depend on whether the negative effects via $ROR\left(k^*_{t+3}\right)$ would dominate the positive effects via $\left(1+i^{LR*}_{t+3}\right)$. If it does, then $q^{LR*}_{t+3} < q^*_{t+1}$. The host growth rate would be:

$$\mu^{LR*}_{t+5} = \left(\frac{R}{\pi^*\left(1+n^*\right)^2}\right) q^{LR*}_{t+3}\left(1-\theta^*\right)\left(\frac{\pi^*}{\left(1+n^*\right)^2}\right)^{\theta^*} \frac{A^{LR*}_{t+3}\left(\bar{k}^{LR*}_{t+3}\right)^{\delta^*}\left(k^{LR*}_{t+3}\right)^{\theta^*-1}}{\left(1+i^{LR*}_{t+3}\right)}, \tag{4.47}$$

where μ^{LR*}_{t+5} is increasing in both q^{LR*}_{t+3} and w^{LR*}_{t+3}. Although the overall effects of sudden stops on q^{LR*}_{t+3} are unclear, the negative impacts on w^{LR*}_{t+3} would reduce μ^{LR*}_{t+5} compared to the growth rate in period $t+1$, $\mu^{LR*}_{t+5} < \mu^*_{t+3}$. However, compared to μ^*_{t+2} prior to sudden stops, a lower w^{LR*}_{t+3} and a higher q^{LR*}_{t+3} would keep μ^{LR*}_{t+5} at a similar level to μ^*_{t+2}. The lower host growth rate in the LR due to sudden stops is consistent with the empirical findings of Bordo et al (2010), Ratanamaneichat (2008) and Vannapanich (2009), except that banking crises analysed in the empirical studies would not occur in the host country in the theoretical analysis. This implies that the fully funded banking system modelled in the theoretical framework has worked well in protecting the host country from bank runs and turmoil caused by sudden stops. Table 4.2 shows SR and LR results of the host country after sudden stops.

Table 4.2 A summary of SR and LR results for the host country after sudden stops

Variables	*t*	*t + 1 (sudden stops)*	*t + 2*	*t + 3 (LR)*
$\left(1+i^*_t\right)$		$\left(1+i^*_t\right) < \left(1+i^*_{t+1}\right) = \left(1+i^*_{t+2}\right) = \left(1+i^{LR*}_{t+3}\right)$		
$ROR\left(k^*_t\right)$		$ROR\left(k^*_{t+1}\right) = ROR\left(k^*_{t+2}\right) < ROR\left(k^*_t\right) < ROR\left(k^{LR*}_{t+3}\right)$		
μ^*_{t+2}		$\mu^*_{t+2} = \mu^{LR*}_{t+5} < \mu^*_{t+3} = \mu^*_{t+4}$		
Bank Runs	No	No	No	No

Conclusion

Following Chapter 3, which looks into the impacts of the openness to FPI flows, this chapter looks into the impacts when sudden stops of FPI flows occur. Extending the theoretical framework of Chapter 3 by allowing the interest rates endogenously determined, this chapter analyses the impacts of sudden stops on both the home and the host countries in the SR and in the LR. The sudden stops on FPI flows are assumed to occur unexpectedly and would continue for a significant period of time.

As a result, in the SR, when the incentive constraint for the entrepreneurs to produce is satisfied, the home country would have a positive but lower growth rate at the time when sudden stops occur but would experience a negative growth rate and bank runs in the following period due to failing demand deposits, the so-called type I bank runs. The output loss caused by sudden stops and banking crises is similar to the findings of Bordo et al (2010), Ratanamaneichat (2008) and Vannapanich (2009).

When the incentive constraint is failed, the entrepreneurs would join the non-entrepreneurs to withdraw in period $t+1$ and push bank runs to occur in period $t+1$, which would be the combination of both type I and type II bank runs. While type I bank runs are due to failing demand deposits, the type II bank runs are due to the lack of loan demand. For type I bank runs, the provision of lending facilities to the banks would be helpful in preventing bank runs. However, for type II bank runs, it would require the assistance which could satisfy the incentive constraint. Note that the banking system is assumed to be operating in a fully funded way and as a central planner, so it is a relative "secure" banking system without incentive problems or moral issues for the banks.

Without assistance, bank runs would be inevitable. When the bank runs occur, the home economy would experience the disruption of economic activities and could be difficult to recover, depending on economic conditions. After surviving or recovering from the SR turmoil caused by sudden stops, the home country would have a higher economic growth rate in the LR due to the increase in labour demand and more investment in LR assets.

For the host country, since FPI flows are assumed to be limited to the loan market, sudden stops of FPI flows would affect the host country via the interest rate, which is endogenously determined and would absorb the shocks caused by sudden stops. As a result, there would be no bank run for the host country either in the SR or in the LR. In addition to endogenously determined interest rate, another reason for the result of no bank run in the host country would be the fully funded banking system. The importance of the banking system in preventing bank runs is also highlighted in Joyce and Nabar (2009). Sudden stops would reduce the host loan supply and hence increase the host interest rate. The higher interest rate would reduce the rate of return of capital and increase the growth rate in the SR. In the LR, when the wage income would adjust fully to sudden stops, a lower wage income would reduce the host growth rate to a level similar to the growth rate during the time prior to sudden stops.

Notes

1 The subscript t of β in this expression represents generation t, who become middle aged at period $t+1$. Note that the probability of the types is based on the generations not the periods.

2 One may consider assuming w_{t+1}^{SR} would react to the endogenously determined $(1+i_{t+1})$ but not the factor representing sudden stops β. However, based on equation (4.18), the changes of $(1+i_{t+1})$ are to reflect the changes of β. Thus, it would be inconsistent to assume that w_{t+1}^{SR} would react to the changes of $(1+i_{t+1})$ but not β. This is why it is assumed that $w_{t+1}^{SR} = w_t$ [equation (4.5)].

5 Bank governance, bank runs and the effectiveness of liquidity provision

Introduction: the facts and the issues

In Chapters 2, 3 and 4, the banking system was considered fully funded and serving as a central planner that would maximize the expected welfare of the depositors, so the banks would have zero profit, and there would not be incentive problems or moral issues for banks. The zero-profit banking system assumption is similar to the way banks are modelled in the traditional frameworks, such as infinite-horizontal models, overlapping-generations models and financial development models. Moreover, these models tend to assume that the banks operate in a bank-selected fully funded (BSF) way. That is, the depositors are not offered various types of accounts, such as SR accounts and LR accounts. It is the bank's decision on portfolio allocations to invest deposits between the available assets. The term "fully funded" is similar to the concept used in social security literature. It implies that the returns from the investment for generation t would be returned to generation t in full, since it was generation t that provided the deposits for the investment. In other words, the new deposits would be invested in the assets rather than financing the withdrawals of other generations.

However, as mentioned in Chapter 1, the banks have become major players in the financial markets after the deregulations of banking systems, and the liberalization of capital accounts has expanded banking activities to an international level. As major players, the banks would answer to the shareholders, who would expect the banks to maximize the profits. So the traditional way to model banks as zero profit would no longer be suitable to the modern economy. Moreover, the policy implications which are based on the assumption of zero-profit banks must be revisited.

If we are not modelling the banks as zero profit, what are the alternative ways to model banks? Does bank governance matter to the economy? If so, what differences would bank governance make to economic outcome? How should we model banks to reflect bank governance in practice as closely as possible? To answer these questions, it is important to investigate the challenges and risks faced by the banks after the deregulation of the banking systems and the liberalization of capital accounts. Moreover, it is important to find out what the banks have developed in bank governance in adapting to their new roles as major players in the financial markets and to manage the risks and to overcome the challenges.

The role change of the banks to become major players in the financial markets has also brought challenges to the authorities. On one hand, the authorities must provide support to assist the banks to manage risks and to overcome challenges, as banking crises can easily cause the disruption of economic activities. On the other hand, the authorities must properly protect the depositors, whose rights to their deposits could be compromised by the banks' profit-seeking behaviours. The depositors whose deposits were threatened and whose rights to their deposits were compromised to a certain degree could cause bank panic and easily lead to banking crises. What assistance have the authorities provided to adapt to the role changes of the banks? How effective are these aids in preventing banking crises? This chapter will start by summarizing what has been found and addressed in the empirical studies to find the key features of bank governance which must be captured in the theoretical analysis.

Subjective bank governance

If one investigates banks worldwide, one sees that there is hardly a bank aiming for zero profit. One research stream on bank governance asserts that the banks are governed by the board members and shareholders, whose earnings are based on the banks' profits [De Jonghe, Disl, and Schoors (2012), Choudhry (2011), Hau and Marcel (2009)]. Hence, bank governance would depend on the ownership structure of the banks, namely, the board members and shareholders, who have the incentive to maximize banks' profits in order to maximize their own earnings. The banks' profits are based on their current and future values. While the current value is based on the types of assets and liabilities [Calomiris and Nissim (2014)], the future value is based on the trading costs, which depend on the current value [Calomiris and Nissim (2007)]. The banks' ownership structures are crucial in determining the banks' risk-taking behaviours and how the regulations would affect the banks' risk-taking behaviours [Laeven and Levine (2009)]. This is because the banks' risk-taking behaviours are conducted based on the best interests of the banks' ownership, namely, the board members and the shareholders of the banks. Stulz (2014) has addressed the goal of bank governance along this line clearly. Stulz (2014) shows that the purpose of bank governance is to maximize the wealth of the shareholders by identifying and managing the risks. La Porta et al (1998) find that the more concentrated the ownership is, the less protection for the investors there will be. In contrast, Fortin, Goldberg, and Roth (2010) argue that the risk-taking behaviours conducted by the banks would depend on how the CEOs have been paid by using a sample of US large bank holding companies. Note that most CEOs answer to the ownership of the banks rather than to the depositors. Unfortunately, by studying the experiences of failed banks, Choudhry (2011) finds that the boards may not have sufficient expertise in providing independent directions and long-term views for banks. So the regression shows that the compositions of boards on bank governance are not robust. Therefore, it is suggested that the measures related to (the expertise of) the board shall be implemented for regulation purposes. The fact that the ownership of the banks which does not have sufficient expertise in bank governance but aims to maximize profits would increase the possibility of looting and bankruptcy for profit, similar to what has been analysed in Akerlof and Romer (1993), has raised concerns about the fragility of the banking system.

Objective bank governance

Since bank governance provides an import base for the purposes of supervision, regulation and the provision of necessary assistance, it is important to have reliable measures which are more objective and can be applied to most banks' activities rather than the ownership of the banks, which tends to be subjective, non-robust and difficult to measure. Along the line of having objective and reliable measurements of bank governance, Dermine (2013) points out that the focus shall be on banks' ability to take and manage risks and the banks' adjustments of risk-taking behaviour in the face of shocks and changes of supervision and regulations.

There are at least two types of risks faced by the banks: banking systemic risks and one bank's individual risks. The two types of risks have different characteristics which would affect the impacts of the changes of economic conditions. Therefore, it is crucial that we develop methods that can differentiate the banking systemic risks from the banks' individual risks and measure various banks' individual risks and systemic risks. Hartmann, Straetmans, and Vries (2007) apply their new approach to assess banking system risks in the Euro area and in United States to assist bank supervision. Hovakimian, Kane, and Laeven (2015) propose a measure to estimate systemic risks of financial institutions and apply the measure to the data during 1974–2013. Studying Italian banks, Gambacorta (2008) discovers that the well-capitalized banks would react less to monetary shocks, regardless of the size of the banks. Peni and Vahamaa (2012) argue that strong bank governance has sustainable high stock returns after crises but may not have good stock market valuations. They conclude that good governance is not about good stock market valuations but about the ability to foresee the risks and to turn the crises into credibility. Although sounding reasonable, the argument does not seem to be supported by the test of the banks' loan performances during global finance crises [Peni, Smith, and Vahamaa (2013)].[1] Looking at bank governance in a different aspect, Williams (2014) suggests "national" governance, which could reduce banks' risk-taking behaviours and moral hazard problems of the banks, but such governance works only in the developed countries, not the developing countries.

Banks' roles and activities

The risk-taking behaviours of the banks have been of great concern, especially after the recent years in which banking crises have occurred more often. Will the concern lead the authorities to supervise and/or regulate banks' risk-taking behaviours? The answer is uncertain. On one hand, as shown by Calomiris

(2009), it is the government which introduced risk-inviting rules for the banks to produce prosperity and to release distress. On the other hand, as more and more financial innovations and tools are introduced and adopted by the banks, it is a challenge to supervise and/or to regulate various financial innovations and tools. Since the challenges result from the role changes of the banks to become the major players of the financial markets, it is important for us to return to the basic questions about the roles of the banks while deciding on suitable bank governance as well as supervision and regulations. The basic questions one must answer are the following.

1 What role(s) does the economy expect the banks to serve?
2 To serve the expected role(s), what activities are required?
3 Among all activities in which banks are involved, are there which could destabilize the economy? If so, under what circumstances?
4 What type of bank governance is more suitable than others to manage the activities without destabilizing the economy?
5 How effective are supervision and/or regulations in monitoring bank governance to prevent banking crises?

Although some specific roles of the banks are different across time and across eras, some roles of the banks expected by the economy are similar. The similarities include the roles as middlemen in the financial markets and as portfolio managers to reduce duplicated monitoring costs. The differences would depend on specific roles assigned to the banks by the countries during specific eras. For example, the banks were supposed to take corporate debt of the public companies as the debt of the banks in Japan prior to 1980, according to Hoshi, Kashyap, and Scharfstein (1993). After the deregulation, the banks changed their roles to become major players of the financial markets and would provide various financial products to the agents. The role change gave the banks space to seek higher profits. To seek higher profits, the banks are more motivated to leverage and to take more risks. As a result, there could be more incentive problems, moral problems as well as looting problems, as emphasized by Akerlof and Romer (1993). For example, Dang et al (2014) show that the banks would not reveal the information of the loans even though such opacity could affect allocation efficiency. Even though credit derivatives would expose the banks to credit risks and increase incentive problems, there are still bank holding companies using credit derivatives [Minton, Stulz, and Williamson (2009)].[2] In addition to the risky assets, such as credit derivatives, leverage would also increase risks. In the face of the risks, the banks would use specific tools of portfolio management, such as value at risk, to transfer risks. However, when specific tools become the pattern across banks, systemic risk is generated, and the banking system would be vulnerable to the shocks [Jorion (2007)].[3] Therefore, bank governance on portfolio management to transfer risks is crucial in preventing systemic risks which will destabilize the economy. Are risky assets and leverage the only two causes of bank failures which may lead to banking crises?

Possible causes of bank failure and banking crises

Based on the literature, the causes of bank failure and crises can be summarized in three categories. The three categories are risk taking, leverage/shadow banking and liquidity. Note that the three categories, although separate, are linked to each other closely. The categories of risk taking and leverage/shadow banking will be elaborated further with more evidence.

Risk taking/transferring

As mentioned, the risk-taking behaviours of the banks are encouraged by the governments, which have introduced risk-inviting micro rules to assist banks to release distress. The risk-taking behaviours taken by the banks include the use of credit derivatives [Minton et al (2009)], which would expose the banks to credit risks and actively offer high deposit rates, which would expose the banks to the risk of failure due to the increase of liability [Acharya and Mora (2012)]. Playing a crucial role and being one of the major players in both securities and derivative markets, the banks would use both securities and derivatives to trade and to transfer risks. Consequently, the banks are exposed to more risks, and the stability of the banking system will be shaken [Jorion (2007)]. To better understand the market risks led by risk-transferring behaviours, O'Brien and Berkowitz (2007) use proprietary daily trading revenues of six large bank dealers in a market factor model approach and find that at low market volatility, the banks would increase demand for risky assets simultaneously and generate systemic risks, which would increase instability. The result is similar to that of Allen and Gale (2007a), who find that risk-transferring activities, although improving the liquidity of bank assets, would increase the probability of instability and crises. The risk-taking behaviour of the banks certainly affects the banks' balance sheets and the value of the banks. Gertler and Kiyotaki (2015) have developed a theoretical model to demonstrate how bank balance sheets and the liquidation prices of banks may lead to bank runs.

Leverage

Leverage, according to the definition, serves at least two purposes: (1) to increase the returns and (2) to use the debt to finance asset purchases/investment. The amount of leverage done by the banks and the financial sector has increased dramatically during 1870–2008, based on the findings of Schularick and Taylor (2012), who use historical data of 14 countries. The increasing leverage would reduce the effectiveness of monetary policies. Moreover, Schularick and Taylor (2012) point out that a credit boom would encourage leverage, which would in turn have the banks overlook the risks and increase the instability. By identifying 147 banking crises during 1976–2011, Gamberger and Smuc (2013) also show that fast credit growth could lead to failures. This could explain why a credit boom is often shown as an indicator for crises. In addition to credit booms, another factor which would encourage leverage is shadow banking activities, which serve both purposes of leverage. By extending Diamond and Dybvig (1983), Kashyap, Tsomocos, and Vardoulakis (2014) show that a probability of bank runs is governed by the banks leverage and its mix of safe and risky assets. Through comparing both traditional and shadow banking activities, Hanson et al (2015) show that shadow banking activities would lead the banks subject to runs and to fire sale losses. By examining interbank repo, one of the major shadow banking activities, Chang (2015) shows that the banks which survive repo runs would be exposed to a high probability of bank runs and that repo runs could trigger contagious runs under certain circumstances.

Liquidity

Maintaining liquidity is an important task for the banks. The banks are expected to provide liquidity to both the borrowers and the depositors [Gatev, Schuermann, and Strahan (2007)]. Failing to maintain liquidity and failing to find the sources to finance the liquidity shortfalls are the main causes of the crises. The crises include the Great Depression [Bordo and Landon-Lane (2010)], the East Asian Crisis [Fukuda (2001)], and the recent crisis in Iceland [Baldursson and Portes (2013)]. Liquidity shortfalls can be led by the panic of the creditors, such as depositors, as demonstrated by Iyer, Puri, and Ryan (2013) and Diamond and Dybvig (1983), or by bank failure, which can be caused by incompetent bank governance and capital flows [Fukuda (2001)] as well as other factors. While maintaining the liquidity, the banks must maximize their profits. Unfortunately, under certain circumstances, maintaining liquidity could compromise banks' profits and vice versa. Therefore, in order to increase liquidity or to increase profits, the banks would conduct risk-taking and risk-transferring/trading behaviours through risky assets, leverage and shadow banking activities. As mentioned, risky assets, leverage and specific shadow banking activities would expose the banks and their trading partners to higher risks. When risk transferring becomes a pattern among banks, systemic risks are generated. As a result, the system becomes vulnerable to shocks and will increase instability and the probability of crises.

Remedies and their concerns

Proposed remedies

Since liquidity shortage is one of the main causes of bank failures which could lead to banking crises, it is natural for the authority to supervise and to regulate banks to maintain liquidity at a specific level. The related supervision and regulations include capital requirements [Pelizzon and Schaefer (2007)][4] and monetary tools, such as interest rates [Diamond and Rajan (2012)]. It is found that banks with more loans and liquidity and the countries with more strict capital requirements tend to perform better [Beltratti and Stulz (2012)]. At the time of financial disruption and crises, however, it is important for the authority to provide liquidity to assist the banks to finance the shortfalls to prevent financial disruption turning into crises and the crises becoming more severe. The reason to intervene in financial sectors, whether through the *ex ante* supervision and regulations or through *ex post* liquidity provision, is to reduce welfare loss caused by banking crises [Hart and Zingales (2014)]. The impacts of banking crises are not limited to the financial sector but to the whole economy. The disruption of economic activities caused by the crises could harm the economy severely [Gertler and Kiyotaki (2015)].

Supervision and regulations

There has been a broad discussion on both *ex ante* supervision [Masciandaro, Pansini, and Quintyn (2013), Masciandaro and Volpicella (2016)][5] and regulations [Freixas (2010), Kashyap, Tsomocos, and Vardoulakis (2014)][6] and *ex post* liquidity provision and their effectiveness in preventing banking crises. Although *ex post* liquidity may prevent the crises from being more severe, it might be better if *ex ante* supervision and regulations can prevent crises from occurring. However, the debates on *ex ante* supervision and regulations are still ongoing, and it will be difficult to reach an agreement at any time soon.

The studies that support regulations find that regulations could improve Pareto Optimality, which is defined as the allocation of resources which cannot make anyone better off without making others worse off [Kashyap et al (2014)]. Note that it has to be "proper" regulations. Improper regulations would instead lead to an inefficient banking industry [Freixas (2010)]. However, "proper" is difficult to determine, especially when economic conditions keep changing from time to time. The need to amend supervision and regulations to be more "proper" is often realized after the occurrences of the crises rather than prior to the crises. In other words, the effectiveness of supervision and regulations is in great doubt in preventing crises and even financial disruptions. Moreover, before adapting to economic conditions and becoming "proper", supervision and regulations tend to distort allocations away from efficiency and cause the banks to bear "unnecessary" costs and suffer profit loss [Tirole (2002, chapter 2)].[7] Note that profit loss is against the board members' objectives, which are to maximize the banks' profits and values in order to maximize the shareholders' wealth [Stulz (2014)]. Stulz (2014) argues further that detailed rules of regulation remove banks' flexibility in managing risks. In other words, supervision and regulations, although they serve the expectation of the economy to force the banks to maintain liquidity, could conflict with the banks' objectives in maximizing their own profits, especially during the period between the crises.

Moreover, in practice, it has been well known that the banks would seek all means to maximize profits. The means banks would take include leverage, shadow banking and risk-taking and risk-transferring activities to different fields and/or countries via various financial products and innovations. The extended activities involved by the banks imply that some activities of the banks may lie in the shadow and are not under supervision or regulations. When more activities are in the shadow and overseas, it becomes more difficult to supervise and regulate banking activities.

However, it does not mean not to supervise and/or to regulate. In response to the extended banking activities, the manuals of bank supervision and regulations have become thicker and thicker with legal terms so that only a few professionals would and could read and understand them. Unfortunately, such hard work and increasingly complicated supervision and regulations are still not effective in preventing crises. This implies that supervision and regulations require a thorough review of the roles of banks, both the ones currently played by the banks and those expected by the economy. One possibility is to have "motivation"-based supervision and regulations and to limit the financial products which can be adopted and purchased by the banks to a specific basket and to a specific amount. This is because more and more financial innovations and products have become too complicated for most people to understand the amount of risks involved. Although looking harmless during the boom time, the hidden risks of the financial products and innovations can be magnified and pull the trigger of financial disruption, which would lead to banking crises, such as the subprime mortgage crisis. There are a lot of fundamental work to do on supervision and regulations before they can be effective in preventing crises.

Liquidity provision

Before supervision and regulations become proper to obtain efficient outcomes and to prevent crises, liquidity provision, defined as the provision of lending facilities to assist the banks to finance liquidity shortfalls, is considered crucial in preventing the crises from getting worse. This is also why liquidity provision by the authorities has attracted broad attention in recent years. Liquidity provision can be in many forms, such as deposit insurance, lender as the last resort (LOLR) and short-term lending facilities (SRLF). The idea of liquidity provision is to prevent the creditors from panicking and joining the line to withdraw/liquidate their accounts and hence prevent bank runs and banking crises [Diamond and Dybvig (1983)]. However, liquidity provision has its downside. One well-documented negative effect of deposit insurance is the associated moral hazard problem of the banks, which have been shown in both theoretical and empirical studies [Demirgüç-Kunt et al (2014), Gropp and Vesala (2004), Hellmann et al (2000), Hooks and Robinson (2002), Kim, Kim, and Han (2014), Martin (2006), McCoy (2007), and Weinstein (1992)]. To overcome banks' moral hazard problems, Gropp and Vesala (2004) suggest being selective on the creditors insured by the deposit insurance, while Marin (2006) suggests more liquidity provision to the banks. The lender of last resort (LOLR) is also found to be associated with increasing leverage towards illiquid assets, which would lead to future liquidity shortfall and fire sales [Acharya and Tuckman (2014)]. SRLF, if not done properly, could trigger looting/moral hazard in banking [Chang (2013a)]. In short, if liquidity provision is not used properly, it would instead become the core problem which would trigger bank failure/crises. So although liquidity provision may stop financial disruption to a certain degree and prevent crises from getting worse, its associated downside problems shall not be ignored. Note that even without deposit insurance and its associated moral hazard problems, there are circumstances in which liquidity provision may or may not be sufficient in preventing financial disruptions/crises from getting worse. Therefore, it is the purpose of this chapter to develop a theoretical framework to examine various types of bank governance and their ability to prevent banking crises as well as the effectiveness of liquidity provision in preventing banking crises under various circumstances.

Theoretical background on bank governance

By extending the role of the banks in the BSF system, Diamond and Dybvig (1983) demonstrate the possibility of bank runs. Following their steps, there are studies using bank runs as one equilibrium to develop policies. Due to the setup of a BSF banking system, the focus of these studies is limited to the bank runs driven by the panic of the creditors. However, the setup of a BSF system is also a core problem of how bank runs occur in the framework [Wallace (1988, 1996)]. Under a BSF banking system, the zero-profit assumption for the banks when there is no uncertainty has left little space for the banks to deal with uncertainties. That is, the banks have little tolerance for unexpected withdrawals. When unexpected withdrawals reach a certain level, the banks would be out of resources and would be subject to runs. However, the banks have never operated in the way modelled in the BSF system. The policies which developed from the framework with a BSF system may raise more questions than answers.

Is a BSF system more likely to cause bank runs than other types of bank governance? To answer the question, two more types of bank governance, which are called systems in the model, are developed for examination. The examination will focus on the ability of the type of bank governance to absorb the shocks and their likelihood of bank runs in the face of the shocks as well the effectiveness of liquidity provision. There are two shocks introduced to the framework. One is the openness to FPI flows, and the other is sudden stops of FPI flows. The analysis would be for both home and host countries. To simplify the analysis, it is assumed that there is no deposit insurance.

In addition to the BSF banking system, the other two systems are called the depositor-selected fully funded (DSF) banking system and the depositor-selected leveraged (DSL) banking system. One distinguished feature of both DSF and DSL systems is that the depositors would decide the allocation of their income between the SR and the LR accounts offered by the banks. The difference between DSF and DSL systems is how the unexpected withdrawals would be financed. While DSF would finance the unexpected withdrawals based on the requests, DSL would finance via leverage.

Similar to what has been mentioned in Chapter 4, there are two types of bank runs which are defined based on the causes. The two types are called type I and type II bank runs. Type I bank runs are due to failing demand deposits, while type II bank runs are due to the lack of credible loans/liquid assets. Liquidity provision would be effective in preventing type I bank runs but not type II bank runs. It is found that at the time of the openness to FPI flows, the home countries in a DSL system are more vulnerable to experiencing both type I and type II bank runs, but not the host countries. At the time of sudden stops, it is also the home countries in both DSF and DSL systems that are more likely to experience bank runs. The host countries in a DSL system would experience bank runs if the banks invest excess illiquid assets as leverage. In other words, compared to a closed economy, an open economy exposes the home countries to a higher possibility of bank runs. Specific type(s) of bank governance would have larger likelihood of bank runs. Therefore, the banking system (bank governance) adopted in the economy is crucial in reducing the possibility of bank runs. Moreover, the effectiveness of liquidity provision is limited. There are circumstances in which liquidity provision cannot prevent crises from getting worse and may increase the possibility of looting/moral hazard in banking even in the absence of deposit insurance.

The theoretical framework

The agents

The basic framework is similar to that in Chapter 4 except for the banking system. Every agent is born identical, with one unit of labour endowment when young and nothing when middle aged and when old. Every agent would value only middle-aged consumption and old consumption. So the utility function of an agent would be in the form of:

$$u\left(c_{2,\,t+1}, c_{3,\,t+2}; \phi\right) = -\frac{\left(c_{2,t+1} + \phi c_{3,t+2}\right)^{-\gamma}}{\gamma}. \tag{5.1}$$

The banks have exclusive access to asset investment in the financial markets. Thus, the agents would deposit the entire income in the banks when young. At middle age, every agent would learn his/her own type, which is exogenously determined and is private information to the agent. There are three types: non-entrepreneurs with a probability of $(1-\pi)$, relocated entrepreneurs with a probability of $\pi\beta$ and non-relocated entrepreneurs with a probability of $\pi(1-\beta)$. The distribution of the types, however, is public information.

Under bank governance of both depositor-selected fully funded (DSF) and depositor-selected leveraged (DSL) banking systems, the depositors would allocate their income between the two types of accounts, SR and LR accounts, offered by the banks, and the banks would maximize their profits by using all available resources to meet demand deposits and to defer bank runs.

For the two accounts offered to the depositors to allocate their income, the SR accounts take one period to mature and are offered a return rate $\left(1+i_t^D\right)$ at maturity. The LR accounts take two periods to mature and are offered a return rate $\left(1+i_t^{LRD}\right)$ at maturity and a return rate $\left(1+i_t^{EL}\right)$ for any premature liquidation,

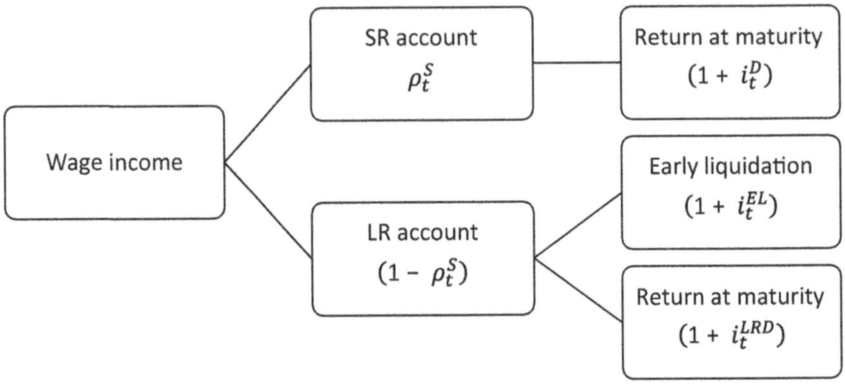

Figure 5.1 An agent's portfolio allocation and the return rates

where $\left(1+i_t^{EL}\right)<\left(1+i_t^D\right)$ and $\left(1+i_t^D\right)^2<\left(1+i_t^{LRD}\right)$. Let ρ_t^s denote the fraction of income placed in the SR accounts, and let $\left(1-\rho_t^s\right)$ denote the fraction placed in the LR accounts. An agent's portfolio allocation and the return rates would be as depicted in Figure 5.1.

According to the portfolio allocation, a middle-aged agent (of generation t) in period $t+1$ would expect to receive W_{t+1}^M, the returns of the SR accounts:

$$W_{t+1}^M \equiv \left(1+i_t^D\right)\rho_t^s w_t. \tag{5.2}$$

Meanwhile, after learning his/her own type, the middle-aged non-entrepreneur would liquidate all of their LR accounts to consume. The relocated entrepreneurs would liquidate all of their LR accounts and invest both W_{t+1}^M and the returns to the premature liquidation of their LR accounts in the SR accounts in the host banks. The middle-aged non-relocated entrepreneurs would redeposit W_{t+1}^M into SR accounts in the home banks.

The non-relocated entrepreneurs and production

In period $t+2$, the old non-relocated entrepreneurs (of generation t) would withdraw their matured LR accounts and obtain capital goods for production. To start production, a non-relocated entrepreneur must borrow $b_{t+2}=w_{t+2}L_{t+2}$ in output goods from the domestic banks in order to start production. By doing so, the rate of return of capital $ROR\left(k_{t+2}\right)$ would be:

$$ROR\left(k_{t+2}\right)=\frac{\left[A_{t+2}\bar{k}_{t+2}^{\delta}k_{t+2}^{\theta}L_{t+2}^{1-\theta}-\left(1+i_{t+2}\right)b_{t+2}\right]}{k_{t+2}}. \tag{5.3}$$

The banks

There are two types of assets: SR loans and LR assets. The access to invest in both assets is limited to the banks only. The returns of the assets will be returned to the banks. The SR loans take one period to mature with a return rate $\left(1+i_t^{loan}\right)$ in output goods, while the LR assets take two periods to mature with a return rate R in capital goods at maturity and with a return rate χ in output goods if liquidated prematurely, where $\chi < \left(1+i_t^{loan}\right)$ and $\left(1+i_t^{loan}\right)^2 < R$. To maximize the profits, the banks under DSF and DSL systems would prefer not to liquidate LR assets prematurely unless it is necessary. One source of the banks' profits is the margin between the returns of the assets and the returns to the withdrawals for both types of accounts – that is, $\left[\left(1+i_t^{loan}\right)-\left(1+i_t^{D}\right)\right]$ in output goods for SR accounts, $\left[R-\left(1+i_t^{LRD}\right)\right]$ in capital goods for mature LR accounts and $\left[\chi-\left(1+i_t^{EL}\right)\right]$ in output goods for premature liquidated LR accounts. It is assumed that it is costless for the banks to convert the capital goods into output goods as their profits; however, it is costly for the agents to convert the capital goods into output goods. The conversion cost is assumed to be too high for the agents, so the agents would liquidate the LR accounts prematurely as soon as they realize they will not start production.

After gathering the deposits, it is assumed that both DSF and DSL systems would allocate the assets as the portfolio selected by the depositors. That is, a fraction ρ_t^s of total deposits would be invested in SR loans and a fraction $\left(1-\rho_t^s\right)$ would be invested in LR assets, with one exception. The exception is that the expected premature liquidation, such as the premature liquidation by the non-entrepreneurs, would be pulled out to invest in SR loans. So for the expected premature liquidation, the margin earned by the bank would be $\left[\left(1+i_t^{loan}\right)-\left(1+i_{t+1}^{EL}\right)\right] > \left[\chi-\left(1+i_{t+1}^{EL}\right)\right]$. By preparing for expected premature liquidation, the banks would earn higher profits. The portfolio allocation of the banks is as depicted in Figure 5.2.

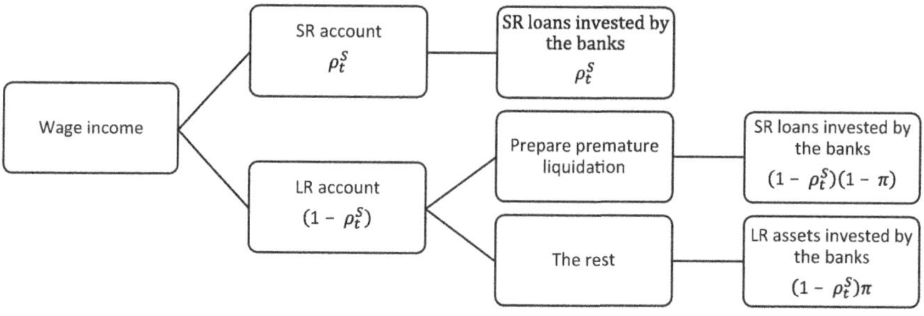

Figure 5.2 The depositors' portfolio allocation versus the banks' portfolio allocation

Without uncertainty, the unexpected withdrawals, both DSF and DSL systems would function in a fully funded way. That is, when generation t withdraw in period $t+1$ and/or $t+2$, the returns to their withdrawals are from the returns to the investment which came from the deposits of generation t in period t. Moreover, the returns of SR loans would be used to pay for SR accounts, while the returns of LR assets would be used to pay for LR accounts. As for unexpected withdrawals, it depends on bank governance to decide the resources to be used to pay for the unexpected withdrawals. To be more specific, the DSF would liquidate LR assets as requested by the depositors to pay for the unexpected withdrawals, while the DSL system would use the new deposits, the liability of the banks, to pay for the unexpected withdrawals.

According to Table 5.1, the banks' profits in period $t+2$ would be:

$$\Pi^{B}_{t+2} = \left(\Pi^{B,SR}_{t+2}\right) + \left(\Pi^{B,LR}_{t+2}\right), \tag{5.4}$$

Table 5.1 The balance sheet of a bank in a closed economy at period $t+2$

	Assets	*Liabilities*
SR	AS1. Due Loan repayments $\left(1+i^{loan}_{t+1}\right)\pi(1+n)b_{t+1}$	LS1. Due mature SR accounts $\left(1+i^{D}_{t+1}\right)\rho^{s}_{t+1}w_{t+1}(1+n)^{3}+\pi(1+n)^{2}\left(1+i^{D}_{t+1}\right)W^{M}_{t+1}$
	New Loans $\pi(1+n)^{2}b_{t+2}$	LS2. Due expected premature liquidation $\left(1+i^{EL}_{t+1}\right)(1+n)^{3}(1-\pi)\rho^{L}_{t+1}w_{t+1}$
		SR profits $\left(\Pi^{B,SR}_{t+2}\right)$ AS1-(LS1 + LS2)
		Expected premature liquidation $(1+n)^{4}(1-\pi)\rho^{L}_{t+2}w_{t+2}$
		New SR accounts $\rho^{s}_{t+2}w_{t+2}(1+n)^{4}$
LR	AL1. Due asset returns $R\left(1-\xi^{B}_{t+1}\right)\pi\rho^{L}_{t}w_{t}(1+n)^{2}$	LL1. Due mature LR accounts $\left(1+i^{LRD}_{t}\right)\left(1-\xi_{t+1}\right)\rho^{L}_{t}w_{t}\pi(1+n)^{2}$
	AL2. Unexpected premature liquidation returns $\chi(1+n)^{3}\rho^{L}_{t+1}w_{t+1}\pi\xi^{B}_{t+2}$	LL2. Unexpected premature Liquidation $\left(1+i^{EL}_{t+1}\right)(1+n)^{3}\rho^{L}_{t+1}w_{t+1}\pi\xi_{t+2}$
	Immature LR assets $\pi(1+n)^{3}\left(1-\xi^{B}_{t+2}\right)\rho^{L}_{t+1}w_{t+1}$	LR profits $\left(\Pi^{B,LR}_{t+2}\right)$ AL1 + AL2-(LL1 + LL2)
	New LR Asset investment $\rho^{L}_{t+2}w_{t+2}\pi(1+n)^{4}$	Immature LR accounts $\pi(1+n)^{3}\left(1-\xi_{t+2}\right)\rho^{L}_{t+1}w_{t+1}$
		New LR accounts $\rho^{L}_{t+2}w_{t+2}(1+n)^{4}$

where

$$\Pi_{t+2}^{B,SR} = \left(1+i_{t+1}^{loan}\right)\pi(1+n)b_{t+1} - \Big[\left(1+i_{t+1}^{D}\right)\rho_{t+1}^{s}w_{t+1}(1+n)^3 + \pi(1+n)^2\left(1+i_{t+1}^{D}\right)$$
$$W_{t+1}^{M}\Big] - \left(1+i_{t+1}^{EL}\right)(1+n)^3(1-\pi)\rho_{t+1}^{L}w_{t+1},$$
$$\Pi_{t+2}^{B,LR} = R\left(1-\xi_{t+1}^{B}\right)\pi\rho_t^{L}w_t(1+n)^2 + \chi(1+n)^3\rho_{t+1}^{L}w_{t+1}\pi\xi_{t+2}^{B} - \left(1+i_t^{LRD}\right)\left(1-\xi_{t+1}\right)$$
$$\rho_t^{L}w_t\pi(1+n)^2 - \left(1+i_{t+1}^{EL}\right)(1+n)^3\rho_{t+1}^{L}w_{t+1}\pi\xi_{t+2}$$

The banks would earn the profits as shown in equation (5.4) if the banks meet the budget constraints in period $t+2$. As shown in what follows, the banks would have three budget constraints: one constraint for SR accounts [equation (5.5a)] and two constraints for LR accounts – one for capital goods [equation (5.5b)] and the other for output goods [equation (5.5c)]:

$$\left(1+i_{t+1}^{loan}\right)\pi(1+n)b_{t+1} \geq \left(1+i_{t+1}^{D}\right)\rho_{t+1}^{s}w_{t+1}(1+n)^3 + \pi(1+n)^2\left(1+i_{t+1}^{D}\right)W_{t+1}^{M}$$
$$+\left(1+i_{t+1}^{EL}\right)(1+n)^3(1-\pi)\rho_{t+1}^{L}w_{t+1}, \tag{5.5a}$$
$$R\left(1-\xi_{t+1}^{B}\right)\pi\rho_t^{L}w_t(1+n)^2 \geq \left(1+i_t^{LRD}\right)\left(1-\xi_{t+1}\right)\rho_t^{L}w_t\pi(1+n)^2, \tag{5.5b}$$
$$\chi(1+n)^3\rho_{t+1}^{L}w_{t+1}\pi\xi_{t+2}^{B} \geq \left(1+i_{t+1}^{EL}\right)(1+n)^3\rho_{t+1}^{L}w_{t+1}\pi\xi_{t+2}. \tag{5.5c}$$

The results

In this section, the analysis will start from the result of a closed economy before moving to the results of an open economy under both DSF and DSL systems, followed by the discussions of the effectiveness of liquidity provision in preventing banking crises should there be any possibility of bank runs. As demonstrated in Chapter 4, under a BSF system in which banks are assumed to have zero profit, the openness to FPI flows would result in banking crises for the home country in the SR. The examination in this chapter turns to operations under other types of bank governance, namely, the DSF and DSL systems in which the banks maximize their own profits, and whether the openness of FPI would reduce the possibility of banking crises.

A closed economy

In a closed economy in which there is no capital flow, the equilibrium labour would be:

$$L_{t+2} = k_t\left[\frac{(1-\theta)A_{t+2}\bar{k}_{t+2}^{\delta}}{\left(1+i_{t+2}^{loan}\right)w_{t+2}}\right]^{1/\theta} \tag{5.6}$$

Under full employment, the equilibrium wage income would be:

$$w_{t+2} = \left(\frac{\pi}{(1+n)^2}\right)^{\theta} \frac{(1-\theta) A_{t+2} \bar{k}_{t+2}^{\delta} k_{t+2}^{\theta}}{\left(1+i_{t+2}^{loan}\right)}, \tag{5.7}$$

which can be plugged into equation (5.3) to derive $ROR(k_{t+2})$:

$$ROR(k_{t+2}) = A_{t+2}\theta \left(\frac{(1+n)^2}{\pi}\right)^{1-\theta} \bar{k}_{t+2}^{\delta} k_{t+2}^{\theta-1}, \tag{5.8}$$

In the loan market, given the loan supply $\left(\mathrm{LN}_{t+2}^{S}\right)$ and the loan demand $\left(\mathrm{LN}_{t+2}^{D}\right)$:

$$\begin{aligned} \mathrm{LN}_{t+2}^{S} &= \rho_{t+2}^{s} w_{t+2} (1+n)^4 + \pi(1+n)^3 W_{t+2}^{M} + (1+n)^4 (1-\pi) \rho_{t+2}^{L} w_{t+2}, \\ \mathrm{LN}_{t+2}^{D} &= \pi(1+n)^2 b_{t+2}, \end{aligned} \tag{5.9}$$

the equilibrium loan rate would be:

$$\left(1+i_{t+2}^{loan}\right) = \frac{\pi w_{t+2} L_{t+2}}{(1+n)^2 w_{t+2}\left[\rho_{t+2}^{s} + (1-\pi)\rho_{t+2}^{L}\right] + (1+n)\pi W_{t+2}^{M}}, \tag{5.10}$$

where $\left(1+i_{t+2}^{loan}\right)$ is increasing in L_{t+2} but is decreasing in $(1+n)$, $\left(1+i_{t+1}^{D}\right)$, ρ_{t+2}^{s}, and ρ_{t+2}^{L}.

In order to maximize the profits, the banks must set the rates such that $\left(1+i_{t+1}^{loan}\right) > \left(1+i_{t+1}^{D}\right)$, $\chi > \left(1+i_{t+2}^{EL}\right)$, and $R > \left(1+i_{t}^{LRD}\right)$, subject to the budget constraints [equations (5.5a)–(5.5c)]. In a closed economy, when there are no unexpected withdrawals, $\xi_{t+1}^{B} = \xi_{t+2}^{B} = \xi_{t+1} = \xi_{t+2} = 0$, and the banks' profits $\left(\Pi_{t+2}^{B,closed}\right)$ would be the same under both DSF and DSL systems. When the budget constraints are satisfied, based on equation (5.4), the value of $\Pi_{t+2}^{B,closed}$ would be:

$$\begin{aligned} \Pi_{t+2}^{B,closed} &= \Pi_{t+2}^{B,SR,closed} + \Pi_{t+2}^{B,LR,closed}, \\ \Pi_{t+2}^{B,SR} &= \left(1+i_{t+1}^{loan}\right)\pi(1+n) b_{t+1} - \left(1+i_{t+1}^{D}\right)\left[\rho_{t+1}^{s} w_{t+1} (1+n)^3 + \pi(1+n)^2 W_{t+1}^{M}\right] \\ &\quad - \left(1+i_{t+1}^{EL}\right)(1+n)^3 (1-\pi) \rho_{t+1}^{L} w_{t+1}, \\ \Pi_{t+2}^{B,LR} &= R\pi\rho_t^{L} w_t (1+n)^2 - \left(1+i_t^{LRD}\right)\rho_t^{L} w_t \pi (1+n)^2. \end{aligned} \tag{5.11}$$

The gross returns to the withdrawals in period $t+2$ would be:

$$\begin{Bmatrix} r_{1t+1,t+2} w_{t+1} \\ r_{2t,t+2} w_t \\ \widehat{r_{2t,t+2}} w_t \end{Bmatrix} = \begin{Bmatrix} \left(1+i_{t+1}^{D}\right)\rho_{t+1}^{s} w_{t+1} + \left(1+i_{t+2}^{EL}\right)\rho_{t+1}^{L} w_{t+1} \\ \left(1+i_t^{LRD}\right)\rho_t^{L} w_t \\ \left(1+i_{t+1}^{D}\right) W_{t+1}^{M} \end{Bmatrix}, \tag{5.12}$$

where $r_{2t,t+2}$ is in capital goods, and both $r_{1t+1,t+2}$ and $\widehat{r_{2t,t+2}}$ are in output goods.

In equilibrium, the portfolio allocation by the young would be based on the distribution of the types:

$$\{\rho^{s}_{t+2}, \rho^{L}_{t+2}\} = \{\pi, (1-\pi)\}. \tag{5.13}$$

The incentive constraint for the entrepreneur to produce is $ROR(k_{t+2})r_{2t,t+2} > (1+i_t^D)$. When the incentive constraint holds, the growth rate would be:

$$\mu_{t+2}^{DSF/DSL} = \frac{r_{2t,t+2}w_t}{k_t} = \left(1+i_{t+2}^{LRD}\right)\rho_t^L\left(\frac{\pi}{(1+n)^2}\right)^{\theta}\frac{(1-\theta)A_t\bar{k}_t^{\delta}k_t^{\theta-1}}{\left(1+i_t^{loan}\right)}, \tag{5.14}$$

where $\mu_{t+2}^{DSF,closed}$ is increasing in $\left(1+i_t^{LRD}\right)$ and ρ_t^L but decreasing in $\left(1+i_t^{loan}\right)$. The higher return rate to the matured LR accounts would stimulate the growth rate, while a higher $\left(1+i_t^{loan}\right)$ would damage the growth rate.

Compared to a BSF system in which the zero-profit banks select portfolios for the depositors, both DSF and DSL systems would make all agents worse off due to lower returns to the withdrawals. There are two reasons for the lower returns to the withdrawals in both DSF and DSL systems. One is that when depositors decide portfolios, it is also the depositors who bear the uncertainty cost of the individual type. Another reason is that the banks maximize profits which would be from the margins of the investment and would crowd out the return rates to the depositors. According to equation (5.14), in a closed economy, the growth rate in both DSF and DSL systems would be lower than that in a BSF system, $\mu_{t+2}^{DSF,closed} = \mu_{t+2}^{DSL,closed} < \mu_{t+2}^{BSF,closed}$.

An open economy (SR): the home country

Following Chapters 3 and 4, it is assumed that it is in period *t* when the economy is open to FPI flows in both the home and the host coutries and that FPI would flow from the home to the host country. The openness to FPI would lead the relocated entrepreneurs to liquidate prematurely all LR accounts to invest in the host country, $\xi_t = \beta$, and cause unexpected withdrawals:

$$UEL_t = (1+n)\pi\beta\rho_{t-1}^L w_{t-1}. \tag{5.15}$$

To maintain the profits, it is assumed that the banks would not spend their existing profits to finance the unexpected withdrawals. How the banks would use the available resources to finance the unexpected withdrawals would depend on bank governance, namely, whether a DSF or DSL banking system is adopted by the home country.

Depositor-selected fully funded (DSF) banking system: $\xi_t^B > 0, \xi_t > 0$

In a DSF system, the banks would liquidate LR assets to finance the unexpected withdrawals by the relocated entrepreneurs (of generation *t*–1). The budget constraints related to the unexpected withdrawals would be the LR accounts of generation $t-1$, which would become:

$$R\left(1-\xi_t^{\xi B}\right)\pi\rho_{t-1}^L w_{t-1}\left(1+n\right)\ge\left(1+i_{t-1}^{LRD}\right)\left(1-\xi_t\right)\rho_{t-1}^L w_{t-1}\pi\left(1+n\right), \tag{5.16a}$$

$$\chi\left(1+n\right)\rho_{t-1}^L w_{t-1}\pi\xi_t^{\xi B}\ge\left(1+i_{t-1}^{EL}\right)\left(1+n\right)\rho_{t-1}^L w_{t-1}\pi\xi_t, \tag{5.16b}$$

where equation (5.16a) is for period $t+1$ in capital goods, and equation (5.16b) is for period t in output goods. The two budget constraints [equations (5.16a) and (5.16b)] show that the banks in a DSF system would have two options. Option one is to have $\xi_t^{\xi B}=\xi_t$. Option two is to have $\xi_t^{\xi B}<\xi_t$. The option chosen by the banks would affect the banks' profits. Meanwhile, in response to the openness to FPI flows, the banks would start preparing the premature liquidation by the relocated entrepreneurs of generation t in period t.

OPTION ONE (DSF): $\xi_t^{\xi B}=\xi_t=\beta$

In period t. The liquidation $\xi_t^{\xi B}=\xi_t$ would change the banks' profits to:

$$\Pi_t^{B,DSF}=\Pi_t^{B,SR,DSF}+\Pi_t^{B,LR,DSF}, \tag{5.17}$$

where $\Pi_t^{B,SR,DSF}=\Pi_{t-1}^{B,SR,closed}$

$$\Pi_t^{B,LR,DSF}=\left[R-\left(1+i_{t-2}^{LRD}\right)\right]\rho_{t-2}^L w_{t-2}\pi+\left[\chi-\left(1+i_{t-1}^{EL}\right)\right]\beta\pi\left(1+n\right)\rho_{t-1}^L w_{t-1},$$

where the second term of $\Pi_t^{B,LR,DSF}$ is the extra profits from the premature liquidation of the relocated entrepreneurs. So the banks would earn higher profits in period t when the economy is open to FPI flows, $\Pi_t^{B,DSF}>\Pi_{t-1}^{B,DSF,closed}$.

In preparing for the premature liquidation of the relocated entrepreneurs of generation t, the banks would take the expected amount to invest in SR loans. Meanwhile, the relocated entrepreneurs of generation $t-1$ would not reinvest their mature SR account returns into the home banks. The loan supply would become

$$LN_t^{S,DSF}=\rho_t^s w_t\left(1+n\right)^2+\pi\left(1-\beta\right)\left(1+n\right)W_t^M+\left(1+n\right)^2\left[1-\pi\left(1-\beta\right)\right]\rho_t^L w_t, \tag{5.18}$$

where $LN_t^{S,DSF}>LN_{t-1}^{S,closed}$ if $\left(1+n\right)\rho_t^L w_t>W_t^M$. Since the loan demand would remain the same [equation (5.9)], the loan rate would become:

$$\left(1+i_t^{loan,DSF}\right)=\frac{\pi w_t L_t}{\pi\left(1-\beta\right)\left(1+n\right)W_t^M+\left(1+n\right)^2 w_t\left\{\rho_t^s+\left[1-\pi\left(1-\beta\right)\right]\rho_t^L\right\}}, \tag{5.19}$$

where $\left(1+i_t^{loan,DSF}\right)<\left(1+i_{t-1}^{loan,closed}\right)$ due to $LN_t^{S,DSF}>LN_{t-1}^{S,closed}$.

In period $t+1$. The preparation of the premature liquidation by the relocated entrepreneurs of generation t would change the banks' profits to:

$$\Pi_{t+1}^{B,DSF} = \Pi_{t+1}^{B,SR,DSF} + \Pi_{t+1}^{B,LR,DSF}, \tag{5.20}$$

where

$$\Pi_{t+1}^{B,SR,DSF} = \left[\left(1+i_t^{loan,DSF}\right)-\left(1+i_t^{D}\right)\right]\left[\rho_t^s w_t (1+n)^2 + \pi(1-\beta)(1+n)W_t^M\right]$$
$$+\left[\left(1+i_t^{loan,DSF}\right)-\left(1+i_t^{EL}\right)\right](1+n)^2\left[1-\pi(1-\beta)\right]\rho_t^L w_t,$$
$$\Pi_{t+1}^{B,LR,DSF} = \left[R-\left(1+i_{t-1}^{LRD}\right)\right]\pi(1-\beta)\rho_{t-1}^L w_{t-1}(1+n).$$

Equation (5.20) shows that the banks' total profits in period $t+1$ would be lower than the profits in period t, $\Pi_{t+1}^{B,DSF} < \Pi_t^{B,DSF}$, if the effects on the LR account profits dominate $\left|\Pi_{t+1}^{B,LR,DSF} - \Pi_t^{B,LR,DSF}\right| > \left|\Pi_{t+1}^{B,SR,DSF} - \Pi_t^{B,SR,DSF}\right|$. This is because $\Pi_{t+1}^{B,LR,DSF} < \Pi_t^{B,LR,DSF}$, but the effects of the openness of FPI on $\Pi_{t+1,SR}^{B,SR,DSF}$ is ambiguous. On one hand, a lower $\left(1+i_t^{loan,DSF}\right)$ would reduce the margins of both SR accounts and premature liquidation earned by the banks and lower $\Pi_{t+1,SR}^{B,SR,DSF}$. On the other hand, a higher $LN_t^{S,DSF}$ would increase $\Pi_{t+1}^{B,SR,DSF}$. So the overall effect on $\Pi_{t+1}^{B,SR,DSF}$ is ambiguous.

For the loan market, the loan supply would be the same as period t [equation (5.18)], while the relocated entrepreneurs of generation t would reduce the loan demand to:

$$LN_{t+1}^{D} = \pi(1-\beta)(1+n)b_{t+1}. \tag{5.21}$$

So the loan rate would become:

$$\left(1+i_{t+1}^{loan,DSF}\right) = \frac{(1+n)\pi(1-\beta)w_{t+1}}{(1+n)^3 w_{t+1}\left\{\rho_{t+1}^s + \left[1-\pi(1-\beta)\right]\rho_{t+1}^L\right\} + \pi(1-\beta)(1+n)^2 W_{t+1}^M}, \tag{5.22}$$

where $\left(1+i_{t+1}^{loan,DSF}\right) < \left(1+i_t^{loan,DSF}\right) < \left(1+i_{t-1}^{loan,closed}\right)$.

In period $t+2$. The lower $\left(1+i_{t+1}^{loan,DSF}\right)$ would then change the banks' profits to:

$$\Pi_{t+2}^{B,DSF} = \Pi_{t+2}^{B,SR,DSF} + \Pi_{t+2}^{B,LR,DSF}, \tag{5.23}$$

where

$$\Pi_{t+2}^{B,SR,DSF} = \left[\left(1+i_{t+1}^{loan,DSF}\right)-\left(1+i_{t+1}^{D}\right)\right]\left[\rho_{t+1}^s w_{t+1}(1+n)^3 + \pi(1-\beta)(1+n)^2 W_{t+1}^M\right]$$
$$+\left[\left(1+i_{t+1}^{loan,DSF}\right)-\left(1+i_{t+1}^{EL}\right)\right](1+n)^3\left[1-\pi(1-\beta)\right]\rho_{t+1}^L w_{t+1},$$
$$\Pi_{t+2}^{B,LR,DSF} = \left[R-\left(1+i_t^{LRD}\right)\right](1-\beta)\rho_t^L w_t \pi(1+n)^2,$$

where at no population growth ($n = 0$), banks' profits in period $t+2$ would be even lower than the profits in period $t+1$, $\Pi_{t+2}^{B,\,DSF} < \Pi_{t+1}^{B,DSF}$. This is mainly because a lower $\left(1+i_{t+1}^{loan,DSF}\right)$ would reduce $\Pi_{t+2}^{B,SR,DSF}$, while $\Pi_{t+2}^{B,LR,DSF}$ remains the same given $\left(1+i_{t}^{LRD}\right)$.

OPTION TWO (DSF): $\xi_t^{B} = \xi_t = \beta$

In period *t*. Although the liquidation decision is different from option one, the loan market conditions would remain the same. So the loan rates in option two would be the same as in option one. The fraction to liquidate by the banks must be sufficient to finance the unexpected withdrawals: $\xi_t^{B}\,\chi\pi(1+n)\rho_{t-1}^{L}w_{t-1} \geq \left(1+i_{t-1}^{EL}\right)UEL_t$ [equation (5.15)], which gives

$$\xi_t^{B} \geq \frac{\left(1+i_{t-1}^{EL}\right)\beta}{\chi} \equiv \check{\xi}_t^{B}, \tag{5.24}$$

where $\check{\xi}_t^{B}$ is increasing in β and $\left(1+i_{t-1}^{EL}\right)$ but decreasing in χ. At $\xi_t^{B} = \check{\xi}_t^{B}$, the banks' profits would be:

$$\left(\Pi_t^{B,DSF}\right)' = \left(\Pi_t^{B,SR}\right)' + \left(\Pi_t^{B,LR}\right)', \tag{5.25}$$

where $\left(\Pi_t^{B,SR}\right)' = \Pi_{t-1}^{B,SR,closed}$

$$\left(\Pi_t^{B,LR}\right)' = \left[R-\left(1+i_{t-2}^{LRD}\right)\right]\rho_{t-2}^{L}w_{t-2}\pi = \Pi_t^{B,LR,closed},$$

where $\left(\Pi_t^{B,DSF}\right)' = \Pi_{t-1}^{B,closed}$ [equation (5.11)].

In period *t*+ 1. As derived in equation (5.19), the lower $\left(1+i_t^{loan,DSF}\right)$ would change the banks' profits to:

$$\left(\Pi_{t+1}^{B,DSF}\right)' = \left(\Pi_{t+1}^{B,SR,DSF}\right)' + \left(\Pi_{t+1}^{B,LR,DSF}\right)', \tag{5.26}$$

where

$$\left(\Pi_{t+1}^{B,SR,DSF}\right)' = \left[\left(1+i_t^{loan,DSF}\right)-\left(1+i_t^{D}\right)\right]\left[\rho_t^{s}w_t(1+n)^2 + \pi(1-\beta)(1+n)W_t^{M}\right]$$
$$+\left[\left(1+i_t^{loan,DSF}\right)-\left(1+i_t^{EL}\right)\right](1+n)^2\left[1-\pi(1-\beta)\right]\rho_t^{L}w_t,$$

$$\left(\Pi_{t+1}^{B,LR,DSF}\right)' = \left[R-\left(1+i_{t-1}^{LRD}\right)\right](1-\beta)\rho_{t-1}^{L}w_{t-1}\pi(1+n) + R\left(\beta-\xi_t^{B}\right)\pi(1+n)\rho_{t-1}^{L}w_{t-1},$$

where the second term in $\left(\Pi_{t+1}^{B,LR,DSF}\right)'$ is the extra profits due to $\xi_t^{B} < \xi_t = \beta$, and would increase the LR account profits, $\left(\Pi_{t+1}^{B,LR,DSF}\right)' > \left(\Pi_t^{B,LR,DSF}\right)'$. Similar to option one, the effect of the openness to FPI flows on $\left(\Pi_{t+1}^{B,SR,DSF}\right)'$ is ambiguous. Therefore, when the effects on $\left(\Pi_{t+1}^{B,LR,DSF}\right)'$ dominate, $\left|\left(\Pi_{t+1}^{B,LR,DSF}\right)' - \left(\Pi_t^{B,LR,DSF}\right)'\right| > \left|\left(\Pi_{t+1}^{B,SR,DSF}\right)' - \left(\Pi_t^{B,SR,DSF}\right)'\right|$, the total banks' profits in period $t+1$ would be higher than the profits in period t, $\left(\Pi_{t+1}^{B,DSF}\right)' > \left(\Pi_t^{B,DSF}\right)'$.

In period $t+2$. As derived in equation (5.22), the lower $\left(1+i_{t+1}^{loan,DSF}\right)$ would change the banks' profits to:

$$\left(\Pi_{t+2}^{B,DSF}\right)' = \left(\Pi_{t+2}^{B,SR,DSF}\right)' + \left(\Pi_{t+2}^{B,LR,DSF}\right)', \tag{5.27}$$

where

$$\left(\Pi_{t+2}^{B,SR,DSF}\right)' = \left[\left(1+i_{t+1}^{loan,DSF}\right)-\left(1+i_{t+1}^{D}\right)\right]\left[\rho_{t+1}^{s}w_{t+1}\left(1+n\right)^{3}+\pi\left(1-\beta\right)\left(1+n\right)^{2}W_{t+1}^{M}\right]$$
$$+\left[\left(1+i_{t+1}^{loan,DSF}\right)-\left(1+i_{t+1}^{EL}\right)\right]\left(1+n\right)^{3}\left[1-\pi\left(1-\beta\right)\right]\rho_{t+1}^{L}w_{t+1},$$
$$\left(\Pi_{t+2}^{B,LR,DSF}\right)' = \left[R-\left(1+i_{t}^{LRD}\right)\right]\left(1-\beta\right)\rho_{t}^{L}w_{t}\pi\left(1+n\right)^{2},$$

where at $n=0, \left(\Pi_{t+2}^{B,DSF}\right)' < \left(\Pi_{t+1}^{B,DSF}\right)'$ since $\left(\Pi_{t+2}^{B,LR,DSF}\right)' < \left(\Pi_{t+1}^{B,LR,DSF}\right)'$ and $\left(\Pi_{t+2}^{B,SR,DSF}\right)' <$ $\left(\Pi_{t+1}^{B,SR,DSF}\right)'$ due to $\left(1+i_{t+1}^{loan,DSF}\right) < \left(1+i_{t}^{loan,DSF}\right)$.

PRODUCTION SECTOR

In the SR, when the wage income has not adjusted, the rate of return of capital $ROR\left(k_{t}\right)$ would be:

$$ROR\left(k_{t}\right) = A_{t}\bar{k}_{t}^{\delta}k_{t}^{\theta-1}\left[\frac{\left(1+n\right)^{2}}{\pi\left(1-\beta\right)}\right]^{1-\theta}\left[1-\left(\frac{1+i_{t}^{loan}}{1+i_{t-1}^{loan}}\right)\left(1-\theta\right)\right], \tag{5.28}$$

where $ROR\left(k_{t}\right)$ is decreasing in $\left(1+i_{t}^{loan,DSF}\right)$. Since the openness of FPI flows, the loan rate has decreased over time, $\left(1+i_{t+1}^{loan,DSF}\right) < \left(1+i_{t}^{loan,DSF}\right) < \left(1+i_{t-1}^{loan,DSF}\right)$. The over-time decreasing loan rates would then increase $ROR\left(k_{t}\right)$ over time, $ROR\left(k_{t+1}\right) > ROR\left(k_{t}\right) > ROR\left(k_{t-1}\right)$, according to equation (5.28).

The increasing $ROR\left(k_{t}\right)$ would make the incentive constraint $ROR\left(k_{t}\right)r_{2t-2,t} >$ $\left(1+i_{t-2}^{D}\right)$ easier to hold, since it widens the gap between $ROR\left(k_{t}\right)r_{2t-2,t}w_{t-2}$ and $\left(1+i_{t-2}^{D}\right)$. Meanwhile, given $\left(1+i_{t}^{LRD}\right)$, the increasing $ROR\left(k_{t}\right)$ would make the non-relocated entrepreneurs better off over time in a DSF system after the openness of FPI flows.

COMPARING THE TWO OPTIONS IN A *DSF* SYSTEM

The difference between option one and option two is the profits earned in period t and in period $t+1$. Option one gives higher profits in period t and lower profits in period $t+1$, while option two is the opposite. Given the banks' intertemporal profits across periods t and $t+1$, $\Pi_{t,SR}^{B,DSF} + \phi^{B}\Pi_{t+1,SR}^{B,DSF}$. Which option the banks would choose would depend on the banks' discount factor ϕ^{B}, where $0 \leq \phi^{B} \leq 1$. A higher ϕ^{B} means that future profits would carry a higher weight for the bank, so the banks are more likely to choose option two. Otherwise, the first option would be preferable. In either option one or option two, the banks can manage

Table 5.2 DSF (SR): from a closed to an open economy

Period		*t*	*t+ 1*	*t+ 2*
$\left(1+i_t^{loan,DSF}\right)$			$\left(1+i_{t-1}^{loan,DSF}\right)>\left(1+i_t^{loan,DSF}\right)>\left(1+i_{t+1}^{loan,DSF}\right)$	
$ROR\left(k_t^{DSF}\right)$			$ROR\left(k_{t-1}\right)<ROR\left(k_t\right)<ROR\left(k_{t+1}\right)$	
$\Pi_{t,SR}^{B,DSF}$	1 $\xi_t^B=\xi_t$	$\Pi_{t-1,SR}^{B,DSF}<\Pi_{t,SR}^{B,DSF}$	$\Pi_{t,SR}^{B,DSF}>\Pi_{t+1,SR}^{B,DSF}$	$\Pi_{t+1,SR}^{B,DSF}>\Pi_{t+2,SR}^{B,\ DSF}$
	2 $\xi_t^B<\xi_t$	$\left(\Pi_{t,SR}^{B,DSF}\right)'=\Pi_{t-1}^{B,DSF}$	$\left(\Pi_{t,SR}^{B,DSF}\right)'<\left(\Pi_{t+1,SR}^{B,DSF}\right)'$	$\left(\Pi_{t+1,SR}^{B,DSF}\right)'>\left(\Pi_{t+2,SR}^{B,DSF}\right)'$
Bank runs		No	No	No

the unexpected withdrawals, so they are less likely to have bank runs in a DSF system after the openness to FPI flows. This is mainly because the depositors take the costs of uncertainty of the individual type.

Depositor-selected leveraged (DSL) system

In a DSL system, the banks would use the liability, the new accounts, to finance the unexpected withdrawals of the relocated entrepreneurs in period *t*, UEL_t. To simplify the analysis, it is assumed that the banks would use either the new SR accounts or the new LR accounts but not both. So the banks would have two options in a DSL system. Option one is to use the new SR accounts, and option two is to use the new LR accounts to finance UEL_t. The budget constraints which would be affected by the unexpected withdrawals caused by the openness of FPI flows would depend on the type of new accounts used by the banks to finance UEL_t. In response to the openness of FPI flows, the banks in a DSL system would also start preparing for the premature liquidation of relocated entrepreneurs of generation *t* in period *t*.

OPTION ONE (DSL): USE NEW SR ACCOUNTS

In period *t*. The budget constraint for using the new SR accounts to finance UEL_t would be:

$$\rho_t^s w_t(1+n)^2+\pi(1-\beta)(1+n)W_t^M\geq\left(1+i_{t-1}^{EL}\right)UEL_t.$$

After paying for UEL_t, the amount of loan supply would change to:

$$\begin{aligned}\mathrm{LN}_t^{S,DSL}&=\rho_t^s w_t(1+n)^2+\pi(1-\beta)(1+n)W_t^M-\left(1+i_{t-1}^{EL}\right)UEL_t\\&\quad+(1+n)^2\left[1-\pi(1-\beta)\right]\rho_t^L w_t,\end{aligned}\tag{5.29}$$

where $\mathrm{LN}_t^{S,DSL}<\mathrm{LN}_{t-1}^{S,DSL}$ because $W_t^M+\left(1+i_{t-1}^{EL}\right)\rho_{t-1}^L w_{t-1}>(1+n)\rho_t^L w_t$. So the loan rate would become:

$$\left(1+i_t^{loan,DSL}\right)=\frac{\pi w_t L_t}{\begin{Bmatrix}w_t(1+n)^2\left\{\rho_t^s+\left[1-\pi(1-\beta)\right]\rho_t^L\right\}\\+\pi(1-\beta)(1+n)W_t^M-\left(1+i_{t-1}^{EL}\right)UEL_t\end{Bmatrix}},\tag{5.30}$$

where $\left(1+i_t^{loan,DSL}\right)$ is increasing in β and $\left(1+i_t^{loan,DSL}\right)>\left(1+i_{t-1}^{loan}\right)$, since $\mathrm{LN}_t^{S,DSL}<\mathrm{LN}_{t-1}^{S,DSL}$. The higher $\left(1+i_t^{loan,DSL}\right)$ would then reduce $ROR\left(k_t^{DSL}\right)$ to:

$$ROR\left(k_t^{DSL}\right)=A_t\bar{k}_t^{\delta}k_t^{\theta-1}\left[\frac{(1+n)^2}{\pi(1-\beta)}\right]^{1-\theta}\left[1-\left(\frac{1+i_t^{loan,DSL}}{1+i_{t-1}^{loan}}\right)(1-\theta)\right], \tag{5.31}$$

where $ROR\left(k_t^{DSL}\right)$ is decreasing in $\left(1+i_t^{loan,DSL}\right)$, and $ROR\left(k_t^{DSL}\right)<ROR\left(k_{t-1}\right)$. Given $\left(1+i_t^D\right)$, a lower $ROR\left(k_t^{DSL}\right)$ would shrink the gap between $ROR\left(k_t\right)r_{2t,t+2}$ and $\left(1+i_t^D\right)$ and make it difficult for the incentive constraint for the non-relocated entrepreneurs to produce, $ROR\left(k_t\right)R\geq\left(1+i_t^D\right)$, to hold. When the incentive constraint fails, the entrepreneurs of generation t would not demand the loans to produce. Thus, to satisfy the incentive constraint, the loan rate must be sufficiently low:

$$\left(1+i_t^{loan,DSL}\right)<\frac{\left(1+i_{t-1}^{loan}\right)}{(1-\theta)}\left\{1-\frac{\left(1+i_t^D\right)}{RA_t\bar{k}_t^{\delta}k_t^{\theta-1}\left[\frac{(1+n)^2}{\pi(1-\beta)}\right]^{1-\theta}}\right\}\equiv\overline{\left(1+i_t^{loan,DSL}\right)}, \tag{5.32}$$

where $\overline{\left(1+i_t^{loan,DSL}\right)}$ is the upper bound of $\left(1+i_t^{loan,DSL}\right)$. By substituting $\overline{\left(1+i_t^{loan,DSL}\right)}$ into equation (5.30), one can find that to keep $\left(1+i_t^{loan,DSL}\right)$ within the range for the entrepreneurs to demand loans would require $\xi_t=\beta$ to be sufficiently low:

$$\begin{aligned}\xi_t=\beta<\frac{1}{\left(1+i_{t-1}^{EL}\right)(1+n)\rho_{t-1}^{L}w_{t-1}\pi}&\left\{(1+n)w_t\left\{\rho_t^s+\left[1-\pi(1-\beta)\right]\rho_t^L\right\}\right.\\&\left.+\pi(1-\beta)\left(1+i_{t-1}^D\right)\rho_{t-1}^s w_{t-1}-\frac{(1+n)\pi w_t}{\overline{\left(1+i_t^{loan,DSL}\right)}}\right\}\equiv\bar{\xi}_t.\end{aligned} \tag{5.33}$$

where $\bar{\xi}_t$ represents the upper bound of premature liquidation by the relocated entrepreneurs.

At $\xi_t>\bar{\xi}_t$, $\left(1+i_t^{loan,DSL}\right)>\overline{\left(1+i_t^{loan,DSL}\right)}$, the incentive constraint fails, and there would be no demand for loans. Without loan demand, there would be no loan repayment to the banks to pay for $\left(1+i_t^D\right)$ in period $t+1$. As a result, bank runs in period $t+1$ would be inevitable. The bank runs in period $t+1$ would be both type I and type II bank runs. Type I bank runs are due to failing demand deposits, while type II bank runs are due to the lack of loan demand.

At $\beta<\bar{\xi}_t$, $\left(1+i_t^{loan,DSL}\right)<\overline{\left(1+i_t^{loan,DSL}\right)}$, the entrepreneurs would demand loans to produce in period t and provide loan repayments for the banks to pay for $\left(1+i_t^D\right)$ in period $t+1$. So the banks are less likely to have runs in the current period t. The banks' profits would be:

$$\Pi_t^{B,DSL}=\Pi_t^{B,SR,DSL}+\Pi_t^{B,LR,DSL}, \tag{5.34}$$

where

$$\Pi_t^{B,SR,DSL} = \left[\left(1+i_{t-1}^{loan}\right)-\left(1+i_{t-1}^{D}\right)\right]\left[\rho_{t-1}^{s} w_{t-1}(1+n)+\pi W_{t-1}^{M}\right]+\left[\left(1+i_{t-1}^{loan}\right)\right.$$
$$\left.-\left(1+i_{t-1}^{EL}\right)\right](1+n)\left[1-\pi(1-\beta)\right]\rho_{t-1}^{L} w_{t-1},$$
$$\Pi_t^{B,LR,DSL} = \left[R-\left(1+i_{t-2}^{LRD}\right)\right]\rho_{t-2}^{L} w_{t-2}\pi,$$

where $\Pi_t^{B,DSL} > \Pi_{t-1}^{B,DSL}$ since $\Pi_{t,SR}^{B,LR,DSL} = \Pi_{t-1}^{B,LR}$ and $\Pi_{t,SR}^{B,SR,DSL} > \Pi_{t-1,SR}^{B,SR,DSL}$ if $(1+n)\rho_{t-1}^{L}$ $w_{t-1} > \left(1+i_{t-2}^{D}\right)\rho_{t-2}^{s} w_{t-2}$.

In period $t+1$. Without the liquidation of LR assets, the banks' budget constraint for the LR accounts of generation t–1 would change to:

$$R\pi\rho_{t-1}^{L} w_{t-1} \geq \left(1+i_{t-1}^{LRD}\right)\rho_{t-1}^{L} w_{t-1}\pi(1-\beta). \tag{3.35a}$$

Due to the preparation of relocated entrepreneurs and the payments to UEL_t, the banks' budget constraint for due SR accounts would be:

$$\left(1+i_t^{loan,DSL}\right)\pi b_t \geq \left(1+i_t^{D}\right)\rho_t^{s} w_t (1+n)^2 + \left(1+i_t^{D}\right)\pi(1-\beta)(1+n)W_t^{M}$$
$$+\left(1+i_t^{EL}\right)(1+n)^2\left[1-\pi(1-\beta)\right]\rho_t^{L} w_t, \tag{5.35b}$$

which gives the lower bound loan rate $\left(1+\check{i}_t^{loan,DSL}\right)$:

$$\left(1+i_t^{loan,DSL}\right) \geq \frac{1}{\pi b_t}\left\{\begin{array}{c}\left(1+i_t^{D}\right)\rho_t^{s} w_t (1+n)^2 \\ +\left(1+i_t^{D}\right)\pi(1-\beta)(1+n)W_t^{M} \\ +\left(1+i_t^{EL}\right)(1+n)^2\left[1-\pi(1-\beta)\right]\rho_t^{L} w_t\end{array}\right\} \equiv \left(1+\check{i}_t^{loan,DSL}\right), \tag{5.36}$$

where $\left(1+\check{i}_t^{loan,DSL}\right)$ is the minimum loan rate to fulfil demand deposits.

At $\left(1+i_t^{loan,DSL}\right) < \left(1+\check{i}_t^{loan,DSL}\right)$, the banks fail to satisfy the SR budget constraint [equation (5.35b)] and need to find resources to finance the liquidity shortfalls. If, as assumed, the banks would not compromise their profits to finance the liquidity shortages,[8] type I bank runs in period $t+1$ would be inevitable, since they are caused by the banks failing demand deposits. The banks in this case would run voluntarily with their existing profits and leave the liquidity shortage unpaid. Note that the resources which banks could use to finance the liquidity shortfalls include their profits from the LR accounts and the liquidation of LR assets.

If one combines equations (5.32) and (5.36), the loan rate must be kept within the range $\left(1+\check{i}_t^{loan,DSL}\right) \leq \left(1+i_t^{loan,DSL}\right) \leq \overline{\left(1+i_t^{loan,DSL}\right)}$ to prevent bank runs in periods t and $t+1$. When there is no bank run, the banks' profits in period $t+1$ would be:

$$\Pi_{t+1}^{B,DSL} = \Pi_{t+1}^{B,SR,DSL} + \Pi_{t+1}^{B,LR,DSL}, \tag{5.37}$$

where

$$\Pi_{t+1}^{B,SR,DSL} = \left[\left(1+i_t^{loan,DSL}\right)-\left(1+i_t^{D}\right)\right]\left[\rho_t^s w_t (1+n)^2 + \pi(1-\beta)(1+n)W_t^M\right] + \left[\left(1+i_t^{loan,DSL}\right)-\left(1+i_t^{EL}\right)\right](1+n)^2\left[1-\pi(1-\beta)\right]\rho_t^L w_t,$$

$$\Pi_{t+1}^{B,LR,DSL} = \left[R-\left(1+i_{t-1}^{LRD}\right)\right]\rho_{t-1}^L w_{t-1}\pi(1-\beta)(1+n) + R\rho_{t-1}^L w_{t-1}\pi\beta(1+n),$$

where the second term of $\Pi_{t+1}^{B,LR,DSL}$ is the extra profits by not liquidating the LR assets to finance UEL_t, and $\Pi_{t+1}^{B,LR,DSL} > \Pi_t^{B,LR,DSL}$. The total bank profits in period $t+1$ would be higher than the profits in period t, $\Pi_{t+1,SR}^{B,DSL} > \Pi_{t,SR}^{B,DSL}$, if the effects on the LR account profits dominate, $\Pi_{t+1,SR}^{B,LR,DSL} - \Pi_{t,SR}^{B,LR,DSL} > \left|\Pi_{t+1,SR}^{B,SR,DSL} - \Pi_{t,SR}^{B,SR,DSL}\right|$.

In period $t+1$, when there is no bank run, the loan supply and the loan demand would change to:

$$LN_{t+1}^{S,DSL} = \left[\rho_{t+1}^s w_{t+1}(1+n)^3 + \pi(1-\beta)(1+n)^2 W_{t+1}^M\right] + (1+n)^3\left[1-\pi(1-\beta)\right]\rho_{t+1}^L w_{t+1}, \tag{5.38}$$

$$LN_{t+1}^{D,DSL} = \pi(1-\beta)b_{t+1}.$$

The loan rate in period $t+1$ would be:

$$\left(1+i_{t+1}^{loan,DSL}\right) = \frac{\pi(1-\beta)b_{t+1}}{\left\{\begin{array}{c}\rho_{t+1}^s w_{t+1}(1+n)^3 + \pi(1-\beta)(1+n)^2\left(1+i_t^D\right)\rho_t^s w_t \\ +(1+n)^3\left[1-\pi(1-\beta)\right]\rho_{t+1}^L w_{t+1}\end{array}\right\}}, \tag{5.39}$$

where $\left(1+i_{t+1}^{loan,DSL}\right) < \left(1+i_{t-1}^{loan}\right) < \left(1+i_t^{loan,DSL}\right)$ due to a higher loan supply and a lower loan demand.

The lower $\left(1+i_{t+1}^{loan,DSL}\right)$ would give a higher $ROR\left(k_{t+1}^{DSL}\right)$, $ROR\left(k_{t+1}^{DSL}\right) > ROR\left(k_{t-1}\right) > ROR\left(k_t^{DSL}\right)$ [equation (5.31)] and would make it easier to satisfy the incentive constraint, $ROR\left(k_{t+1}^{DSL}\right) r_{2t-1,t+1} w_{t-1} > \left(1+i_{t-1}^D\right)$, for the entrepreneurs to produce.

In period $t+2$. Due to the changes of loan demand and loan supply in period $t+1$ and the preparation for the premature liquidation of the relocated entrepreneurs, the banks' budget constraints for due SR accounts and LR accounts in period $t+2$ would change to:

$$\left(1+i_{t+1}^{loan,DSL}\right)\pi b_t \geq \left(1+i_{t+1}^D\right)\rho_{t+1}^s w_{t+1}(1+n)^3 + \left(1+i_{t+1}^D\right)\pi(1+n)^2 W_{t+1}^M + \left(1+i_{t+1}^{EL}\right)(1+n)^3\left[1-\pi(1-\beta)\right]\rho_{t+1}^L w_{t+1}, \tag{5.40a}$$

$$R\pi(1-\beta)\rho_t^L w_t \geq \left(1+i_t^{LRD}\right)\rho_t^L w_t \pi(1-\beta), \tag{5.40b}$$

where equation (5.40b) holds due to $R > \left(1 + i_t^{LRD}\right)$. To satisfy equation (5.40a) would require $\left(1 + i_{t+1}^{loan,DSL}\right)$ to be sufficiently high:

$$\left(1 + i_{t+1}^{loan,DSL}\right) \geq \frac{1}{\pi b_t} \left\{ \begin{array}{c} \left(1 + i_{t+1}^{D}\right) \rho_{t+1}^{s} w_{t+1} \left(1 + n\right)^3 \\ + \left(1 + i_{t+1}^{D}\right) \pi \left(1 + n\right)^2 W_{t+1}^{M} \\ + \left(1 + i_{t+1}^{EL}\right) \left(1 + n\right)^3 \left[1 - \pi\left(1 - \beta\right)\right] \rho_{t+1}^{L} w_{t+1} \end{array} \right\} \equiv \left(1 + \check{i}_{t+1}^{loan,DSL}\right), \tag{5.41}$$

where $\left(1 + \check{i}_{t+1}^{loan,DSL}\right)$ is the minimum value of the loan rate to fulfil demand deposits of the LR accounts. At $\left(1 + i_{t+1}^{loan,DSL}\right) < \left(1 + \check{i}_{t+1}^{loan,DSL}\right)$, the liquidity shortfalls for LR accounts would occur. If the banks would not compromise their profits to finance the shortfalls, type I bank runs in period $t + 2$ would be inevitable.

At $\left(1 + i_{t+1}^{loan,DSL}\right) > \left(1 + \check{i}_{t+1}^{loan,DSL}\right)$, bank runs are less likely, and the banks' profits would be:

$$\Pi_{t+2}^{B,DSL} = \Pi_{t+2}^{B,SR,DSL} + \Pi_{t+2}^{B,LR,DSL}, \tag{5.42}$$

where

$$\begin{aligned} \Pi_{t+2}^{B,SR,DSL} &= \left[\left(1 + i_{t+1}^{loan,DSL}\right) - \left(1 + i_{t+1}^{D}\right)\right]\left[\rho_{t+1}^{s} w_{t+1} \left(1 + n\right)^3 + \pi\left(1 - \beta\right)\left(1 + n\right)^2 W_{t+1}^{M}\right] \\ &\quad + \left[\left(1 + i_{t+1}^{loan,DSL}\right) - \left(1 + i_{t+1}^{EL}\right)\right]\left(1 + n\right)^3 \left[1 - \pi\left(1 - \beta\right)\right] \rho_{t+1}^{L} w_{t+1}, \\ \Pi_{t+2,SR}^{B,LR,DSL} &= \left[R - \left(1 + i_t^{LRD}\right)\right] \rho_t^{L} w_t \pi \left(1 - \beta\right)\left(1 + n\right)^2, \end{aligned}$$

where $\Pi_{t+2,SR}^{B,DSL} < \Pi_{t+1,SR}^{B,\ DSL}$ due to $\Pi_{t+2}^{B,LR,DSL} < \Pi_{t+1}^{B,LR,DSL}$ and $\Pi_{t+2}^{B,SR,DSL} < \Pi_{t+1}^{B,SR,DSL}$ since $\left(1 + i_{t+1}^{loan,DSL}\right) < \left(1 + i_t^{loan,DSL}\right)$.

Table 5.3 Home country – DSL – use new SR accounts to finance $\boldsymbol{UEL_t}$

Period	*t*	*t + 1*	*t + 2*
$\left(1 + i_t^{loan,DSL}\right)$		$\left(1 + i_{t+1}^{loan,DSL}\right) < \left(1 + i_{t-1}^{loan}\right) < \left(1 + i_t^{loan,DSL}\right)$	
$ROR\left(k_t^{DSL}\right)$		$ROR\left(k_{t+1}^{DSL}\right) > ROR\left(k_{t-1}\right) > ROR\left(k_t^{DSL}\right)$	
$\Pi_{t,SR}^{B,DSL}$	$\Pi_{t-1}^{B,DSL} < \Pi_t^{B,DSL}$	$\Pi_t^{B,DSL} < \Pi_{t+1}^{B,DSL}$	$\Pi_{t+1}^{B,\ DSL} > \Pi_{t+2}^{B,DSL}$
Bank runs	Fail IC- Types I + II runs at $t + 1$ IC holds – no run.	SR BC fails- Type I runs at $t + 1$ SR BC holds – no run.	SR BC fails- Type I runs at $t + 2$ SR BC holds – no run.

where IC is the abbreviation of incentive constraint and BC is the abbreviation of budget constraint

OPTION TWO (DSL): USE LR ACCOUNTS

In period t. The banks would prepare for the premature liquidation of the relocated entrepreneurs of generation t, so the budget constraint for UEL_t would be:

$$\pi(1-\beta)\rho_t^L w_t(1+n)^2 \geq (1+i_{t-1}^{EL})(1+n)\rho_{t-1}^L w_{t-1}\pi\xi_t. \tag{5.43}$$

When equation (5.43) is satisfied, bank runs are less likely in period t. The banks' profits would be:

$$(\Pi_t^{B,DSL})' = (\Pi_t^{B,SR,DSL})' + (\Pi_t^{B,LR,DSL})', \tag{5.44}$$

where

$$(\Pi_t^{B,SR,DSL})' = [(1+i_{t-1}^{loan}) - (1+i_{t-1}^D)][\rho_{t-1}^s w_{t-1}(1+n) + \pi W_{t-1}^M] + [(1+i_{t-1}^{loan})$$
$$- (1+i_{t-1}^{EL})](1+n)[1-\pi(1-\beta)]\rho_{t-1}^L w_{t-1},$$
$$(\Pi_t^{B,LR,DSL})' = [R - (1+i_{t-2}^{LRD})]\rho_{t-2}^L w_{t-2}\pi,$$

where $(\Pi_t^{B,DSL})' > \Pi_{t-1}^B$ since $(\Pi_{t,SR}^{B,LR,DSL})' = \Pi_{t,SR}^{B,LR,DSL}$ and $(\Pi_{t,SR}^{B,SR,DSL})' > (\Pi_{t-1,SR}^{B,SR,DSL})'$.

Meanwhile, the preparation of the relocated entrepreneurs of generation t would change the loan supply to:

$$(LN_t^{S,DSL})' = \rho_t^s w_t(1+n)^2 + \pi(1-\beta)(1+n)W_t^M + (1+n)^2[1-\pi(1-\beta)]\rho_t^L w_t, \tag{5.45}$$

where $(LN_t^{S,DSL})' > LN_{t-1}^S$ if $(1+n)\rho_t^L w_t > W_t^M$, and the loan rate would become:

$$(1+i_t^{loan,DSL})' = \frac{\pi w_t L_t}{\{(1+n)^2 w_t\{\rho_t^s + [1-\pi(1-\beta)]\rho_t^L\} + \pi(1-\beta)(1+n)W_t^M\}}, \tag{5.46}$$

where $(1+i_t^{loan,DSL})' < (1+i_{t-1}^{loan})$ due to a higher $(LN_t^{S,DSL})'$. A lower $(1+i_t^{loan,DSL})'$ would increase $(ROR(k_t^{DSL}))$ to:

$$(ROR(k_t^{DSL}))' = A_t\bar{k}_t^{\delta}k_t^{\theta-1}\left[\frac{(1+n)^2}{\pi(1-\beta)}\right]^{1-\theta}\left\{1-\left[\frac{(1+i_t^{loan,DSL})'}{1+i_{t-1}^{loan}}\right](1-\theta)\right\}, \tag{5.47}$$

where $(ROR(k_t^{DSL}))' > ROR(k_{t-1})$. A higher $(ROR(k_t^{DSL}))'$ would make it easier to satisfy the inventive constraint for the entrepreneurs to produce, $(ROR(k_t^{DSL}))'$ $r_{2t-2,t}w_{t-2} > (1+i_{t-2}^D)$.

In period $t+1$. The lower $\left(1+i_t^{loan,DSL}\right)'$ must satisfy the banks' budget constraint for the due SR accounts:

$$\left(1+i_t^{loan,DSL}\right)'\pi b_t \ge \left(1+i_t^{D}\right)\left[\rho_t^s w_t (1+n)^2 + \pi(1-\beta)(1+n)W_t^M\right] + \left(1+i_t^{EL}\right)$$
$$(1+n)^2\left[1-\pi(1-\beta)\right]\rho_t^L w_t, \tag{5.48}$$

which requires $\left(1+i_t^{loan,DSL}\right)'$ to be sufficiently high:

$$\left(1+i_t^{loan,DSL}\right)' \ge \frac{1}{\pi b_t}\left\{\begin{array}{c}\left(1+i_t^{D}\right)\rho_t^s w_t (1+n)^2 \\ +\left(1+i_t^{D}\right)\pi(1-\beta)(1+n)W_t^M \\ +\left(1+i_t^{EL}\right)(1+n)^2\left[1-\pi(1-\beta)\right]\rho_t^L w_t\end{array}\right\} \equiv \overset{\vee}{\left(1+i_t^{loan,DSL}\right)}', \tag{5.49}$$

where $\overset{\vee}{\left(1+i_t^{loan,DSL}\right)}'$ is the minimum value of the loan rate to fulfil demand deposits. At $\left(1+i_t^{loan,DSL}\right)' < \overset{\vee}{\left(1+i_t^{loan,DSL}\right)}'$, the liquidity shortfalls for SR accounts would occur. If the banks would not compromise their profits to finance the shortfalls, type I bank runs would be inevitable in period $t+1$.

At $\left(1+i_t^{loan,DSL}\right)' \ge \overset{\vee}{\left(1+i_t^{loan,DSL}\right)}'$, bank runs are less likely in period $t+1$. The banks' profits would be:

$$\left(\Pi_{t+1}^{B,DSL}\right)' = \left(\Pi_{t+1}^{B,SR,DSL}\right)' + \left(\Pi_{t+1}^{B,LR,DSL}\right)', \tag{5.50}$$

where

$$\left(\Pi_{t+1}^{B,SR,DSL}\right)' = \left[\left(1+i_t^{loan,DSL}\right)' - \left(1+i_t^{D}\right)\right]\left[\rho_t^s w_t (1+n)^2 + \pi(1-\beta)(1+n)W_t^M\right]$$
$$+\left[\left(1+i_t^{loan,DSL}\right)' - \left(1+i_t^{EL}\right)\right](1+n)^2\left[1-\pi(1-\beta)\right]\rho_t^L w_t,$$
$$\left(\Pi_{t+1}^{B,LR,DSL}\right)' = \left[R-\left(1+i_{t-1}^{LRD}\right)\right]\rho_{t-1}^L w_{t-1}\pi(1-\beta)(1+n) + R\beta\pi(1+n)\rho_{t-1}^L w_{t-1},$$

where the second term of $\left(\Pi_{t+1}^{B,LR,DSL}\right)'$ is the extra profits by not liquidating LR accounts prematurely to finance UEL_t, and would give a higher LR account profits, $\left(\Pi_{t+1}^{B,LR,DSL}\right)' > \left(\Pi_{t}^{B,LR,DSL}\right)$. The SR account profits, however, would be lower, $\left(\Pi_{t+1}^{B,SR,DSL}\right)' < \left(\Pi_{t}^{B,SR,DSL}\right)$, due to a lower $\left(1+i_t^{loan,DSL}\right)'$ and fewer renewed SR accounts because of FPI outflows by the relocated entrepreneurs. As a result, the total banks' profits would be higher, $\left(\Pi_{t+1,SR}^{B,DSL}\right)' > \left(\Pi_{t,SR}^{B,DSL}\right)$, if the effects of the LR account profits dominate, $\left(\Pi_{t+1,SR}^{B,LR,DSL}\right)' - \left(\Pi_{t,SR}^{B,LR,DSL}\right) > \left|\left(\Pi_{t+1,SR}^{B,SR,DSL}\right)' - \left(\Pi_{t,SR}^{B,SR,DSL}\right)\right|$.

While the loan supply would be similar to $\left(LN_t^{S,DSL}\right)'$ [equation (5.45)], the loan demand would change to:

$$\left(LN_{t+1}^{D,DSL}\right)' = (1+n)\pi(1-\beta)w_{t-1}. \tag{5.51}$$

So the loan rate would become

$$\left(1+i_{t+1}^{loan,DSL}\right)' = \frac{\pi(1-\beta)w_{t+1}L_{t+1}}{\left\{(1+n)^2 w_{t+1}\left\{\rho_{t+1}^{s}+\left[1-\pi(1-\beta)\right]\rho_{t+1}^{L}\right\}+\pi(1-\beta)W_{t+1}^{M}\right\}}, \tag{5.52}$$

where $\left(1+i_{t+1}^{loan,DSL}\right)' < \left(1+i_{t}^{loan,DSL}\right)$ due to a lower loan demand. A lower $\left(1+i_{t+1}^{loan,DSL}\right)'$ would increase $\left(ROR\left(k_{t+1}^{DSL}\right)\right)'$ and make it easier to satisfy the incentive constraint for the entrepreneurs to produce, $\left(ROR\left(k_{t+1}^{DSL}\right)\right)' r_{2t-1,t+1}w_{t-1} > \left(1+i_{t-1}^{D}\right)$, to hold.

In period $t+2$. The lower $\left(1+i_{t+1}^{loan,DSL}\right)'$ would tighten the budget constraint for the due SR accounts:

$$\left(1+i_{t+1}^{loan,DSL}\right)' \pi b_{t+1} \geq \left(1+i_{t+1}^{D}\right)\rho_{t+1}^{s}w_{t+1}(1+n)^3 + \left(1+i_{t}^{D}\right)\pi(1-\beta)(1+n)^2 W_{t}^{M} + \left(1+i_{t+1}^{EL}\right)(1+n)^3\left[1-\pi(1-\beta)\right]\rho_{t+1}^{L}w_{t+1}. \tag{5.53}$$

In order to satisfy the due SR account budget constraint [equation (5.33)], $\left(1+i_{t+1}^{loan,DSL}\right)'$ must be sufficiently high:

$$\left(1+i_{t+1}^{loan,DSL}\right)' \geq \frac{1}{\pi b_{t+1}}\left\{\begin{array}{c}\left(1+i_{t+1}^{D}\right)\rho_{t+1}^{s}w_{t+1}(1+n)^3 \\ +\left(1+i_{t}^{D}\right)\pi(1-\beta)(1+n)^2 W_{t}^{M} \\ +\left(1+i_{t+1}^{EL}\right)(1+n)^3\left[1-\pi(1-\beta)\right]\rho_{t+1}^{L}w_{t+1}\end{array}\right\} \equiv \left(1+\check{i}_{t+1}^{loan,DSL}\right)', \tag{5.54}$$

where $\left(1+\check{i}_{t+1}^{loan,DSL}\right)'$ is the minimum value of $\left(1+i_{t+1}^{loan,DSL}\right)'$ to fulfil demand deposits. At $\left(1+i_{t+1}^{loan,DSL}\right)' < \left(1+\check{i}_{t+1}^{loan,DSL}\right)'$, the liquidity shortfalls would occur. If the banks would not compromise their profits to finance the liquidity shortfalls, type I bank runs would be inevitable in period $t+2$.

After using the new LR accounts to finance UEL_t in period t, the budget constraint for the due LR accounts faced by the banks in period $t+2$ would be:

$$R\left[\rho_{t}^{L}w_{t}(1+n)^2 - \left(1+i_{t-1}^{EL}\right)UEL_{t}\right] \geq \left(1+i_{t}^{LRD}\right)\rho_{t}^{L}w_{t}\pi(1-\beta). \tag{5.55}$$

In order to satisfy the LR budget constraint [equation (5.65)], $\left(1+i_{t}^{LRD}\right)$ must be sufficiently low:

$$\left(1+i_{t}^{LRD}\right)' \leq \frac{R\left[\rho_{t}^{L}w_{t}(1+n)^2 - \left(1+i_{t-1}^{EL}\right)UEL_{t}\right]}{\rho_{t}^{L}w_{t}\pi(1-\beta)} \equiv \overline{\left(1+i_{t}^{LRD}\right)'}, \tag{5.56}$$

where $\overline{\left(1+i_{t}^{LRD}\right)'}$ represents the maximum value of $\left(1+i_{t}^{LRD}\right)$ to fulfil demand deposits of LR accounts. At $\left(1+i_{t}^{LRD}\right) > \overline{\left(1+i_{t}^{LRD}\right)'}$, the liquidity shortfalls for

LR accounts would occur. Note that $\left(1+i_t^{LRD}\right)'$ is paid in capital goods which cannot be replaced by the returns of other assets. Moreover, if the banks would not compromise their profits to finance the liquidity shortfalls, type I bank runs would be inevitable in period $t+2$.

Meanwhile, $\left(1+i_t^{LRD}\right)'$ in capital goods paid to the non-relocated entrepreneurs are the required inputs for production, $k_{t+2} = \left(1+i_t^{LRD}\right)' \rho_t^L w_t$. A lower $\left(1+i_t^{LRD}\right)'$ would reduce k_{t+2} and hence reduce $\left(ROR\left(k_{t+2}^{DSL}\right)\right)'$, $\left(ROR\left(k_{t+2}^{DSL}\right)\right)' < \left(ROR\left(k_{t+1}^{DSL}\right)\right)$. A lower $\left(ROR\left(k_{t+2}^{DSL}\right)\right)'$ would tighten the incentive constraint for the entrepreneurs to produce $\left(ROR\left(k_{t+2}^{DSL}\right)\right)' r_{2t,t+2}{}' w_t > \left(1+i_{t+1}^D\right)$. To satisfy the incentive constraint would require $\left(1+i_t^{LRD}\right)'$ to be sufficiently high:

$$\left(1+i_t^{LRD}\right)' \ge \overset{\vee}{\left(1+i_t^{LRD}\right)}' \equiv \frac{\overset{\vee}{k}{}_{t+2}^{DSL}}{\rho_t^L w_t}, \textit{where} \left(ROR\left(\overset{\vee}{k}{}_{t+2}^{DSL}\right)\right)' R = \left(1+i_{t+1}^D\right). \tag{5.57}$$

If the actual $\left(1+i_t^{LRD}\right)'$ provided in period $t+2$ is less than $\left(1+i_t^{LRD}\right)$ promised in period t and $\left(1+i_t^{LRD}\right)' < \overset{\vee}{\left(1+i_t^{LRD}\right)}'$, the incentive constraint fails, and the non-relocated entrepreneurs would not demand loans to produce in period $t+2$. Without loan demand, the banks would not have returns to pay for SR account at the following period, $t+3$, and type I and II bank runs would be inevitable in period $t+3$.

However, if $\left(1+i_t^{LRD}\right)'$ was realized in period t and $\left(1+i_t^{LRD}\right)' < \overset{\vee}{\left(1+i_t^{LRD}\right)}'$, the non-relocated entrepreneurs would join the line to liquidate their LR accounts prematurely in period $t+1$, and type I bank runs in period $t+1$ would be inevitable.

By combining equations (5.56) and (5.57), it requires $\overset{\vee}{\left(1+i_t^{LRD}\right)}' \le \left(1+i_t^{LRD}\right)' \le \overline{\left(1+i_t^{LRD}\right)}$ to reduce the possibility of bank runs. When there is no bank run, the banks' profits would be:

$$\left(\Pi_{t+2}^{B,DSL}\right)' = \left(\Pi_{t+2}^{B,SR,DSL}\right)' + \left(\Pi_{t+2}^{B,LR,DSL}\right)', \tag{5.58}$$

where

$$\left(\Pi_{t+2}^{B,SR,DSL}\right)' = \left[\left(1+i_{t+1}^{loan,DSL}\right)' - \left(1+i_{t+1}^D\right)\right]\left[\rho_{t+1}^s w_{t+1}(1+n)^3 + \pi(1-\beta)(1+n)^2 W_{t+1}^M\right]$$
$$+\left[\left(1+i_{t+1}^{loan,DSL}\right)' - \left(1+i_{t+1}^{EL}\right)\right](1+n)^3\left[1-\pi(1-\beta)\right]\rho_{t+1}^L w_{t+1},$$

$$\left(\Pi_{t+2}^{B,LR,DSL}\right)' = \left[R - \left(1+i_t^{LRD}\right)'\right]\rho_t^L w_t \pi(1-\beta)(1+n)^2,$$

where $\left(\Pi_{t+2}^{B,LR,DSL}\right)' < \left(\Pi_{t+1}^{B,LR,DSL}\right)$ and $\left(\Pi_{t+2}^{B,SR,DSL}\right)' < \left(\Pi_{t+1}^{B,SR,DSL}\right)$ due to $\left(1+i_{t+1}^{loan,DSL}\right)' < \left(1+i_t^{loan,DSL}\right)$, so the total banks' profits would be lower in period $t+2$ than the profits in period $t+1$, $\left(\Pi_{t+2}^{B,DSL}\right)' < \left(\Pi_{t+1}^{B,DSL}\right)$.

Table 5.4 Home country – DSL – use new LR accounts to finance UEL_t

Period	t	t + *1*	t + *2*
$\left(1+i_t^{loan,DSL}\right)'$		$\left(1+i_{t-1}^{loan}\right)>\left(1+i_t^{loan,DSL}\right)'>\left(1+i_{t+1}^{loan,DSL}\right)'$	
$\left(ROR\left(k_t^{DSL}\right)\right)'$		$ROR\left(k_{t-1}\right)<\left(ROR\left(k_t^{DSL}\right)\right)'<\left(ROR\left(k_{t+1}^{DSL}\right)\right)'$	
$\left(\Pi_{t,SR}^{B,DSL}\right)'$	$\Pi_{t-1}^{B}<\left(\Pi_{t,SR}^{B,DSL}\right)'$	$\left(\Pi_{t,SR}^{B,DSL}\right)'<\left(\Pi_{t+1,SR}^{B,DSL}\right)'$	$\left(\Pi_{t+1,SR}^{B,DSL}\right)'>\left(\Pi_{t+2,SR}^{B,DSL}\right)'$
Bank runs	**No run.**	**SRBC fails – Type I runs at $t+1$** **SR BC holds, no run**	**SRBC fails or LRBC fails- Type I runs at $t+2$** **IC fails – Type I runs at $t+1$ or Type I + II runs at $t+3$** **SRBC, LRBC and IC holds, no run**

where SRBC is the abbreviation of the short-run budget constraint, LRBC is the abbreviation of long-run budget constraint and IC is the abbreviation of incentive constraint

COMPARISON OF THE TWO OPTIONS OF THE DSL SYSTEM

Comparing Tables 5.3 and 5.4, one can find that option one (use new SR account) would increase the probability of bank runs for periods t, $t+1$ and $t+2$. Option two (use LR accounts), although preventing bank runs in period t, would increase the probability of bank runs for periods $t+1$, $t+2$ and $t+3$. Moreover, type II bank runs due to the lack of loan demand would occur in period t in option one but would occur in period $t+2$ in option two. In other words, option two simply defers bank runs to the later period, and the banking system would become very vulnerable in period $t+2$, as the banks can easily fail three constraints: the budget constraints for both SR and LR accounts and the incentive constraint. The fail of either constraint could lead to bank runs. Either option one or option two of the DSL system is less stable than the DSF system, in which bank runs are less likely to occur.

When the bank runs are caused by failing demand deposits, the liquidity provision, either by the lender of last resort (LOLR) or by lending facilities, would be effective in preventing bank runs. However, when the bank runs are caused by the lack of loan demand, the liquidity provision may not hold the incentive constraint and hence prevent bank runs. Moreover, in order to protect the existing profits, the banks would have the incentive to loot and conduct moral hazard in banking. So the ability of the liquidity provision to prevent type I bank runs would be effective, but the ability to prevent type II bank runs would be limited.

An open economy (SR): the host country (DSF and DSL)

As a recipient of FPI flows, the host country would not have unexpected withdrawals. Without unexpected withdrawals, the operations of both DSF and DSL systems would be similar after the openness of FPI flows, and bank runs are less likely to occur in period *t*. The FPI flows, however, would affect the loan rate in the host country through the effects on the loan supply.

In period t. The banks' profits in period *t* would be:

$$\Pi_t^{B*} = \Pi_t^{B*,SR} + \Pi_t^{B*,LR}, \tag{5.59}$$

where

$$\Pi_t^{B*,SR} = \left[\left(1+i_{t-1}^{loan*}\right)-\left(1+i_{t-1}^{D*}\right)\right]\left[\rho_{t-1}^{s*}w_{t-1}^{*}\left(1+n^{*}\right)+\pi^{*}W_{t-1}^{M*}\right]+\left[\left(1+i_{t-1}^{loan*}\right)\right.$$
$$\left.-\left(1+i_{t-1}^{EL*}\right)\right]\left(1+n^{*}\right)\left(1-\pi^{*}\right)\rho_{t-1}^{L*}w_{t-1}^{*},.$$
$$\Pi_t^{B*,LR} = \left[R-\left(1+i_{t-2}^{LRD*}\right)\right]\rho_{t-2}^{L*}w_{t-2}^{*}\pi^{*},$$

where $\Pi_{t,SR}^{B*} = \Pi_{t-1,SR}^{B*}$.

The openness of FPI flows would result in the relocated home entrepreneurs investing in the loan market of the host country. Since the FPI flows would not affect the loan demand, the loan supply and the loan demand would be:

$$\mathrm{LN}_t^{S*} = \left[\rho_t^{s*}w_t^{*}\left(1+n^{*}\right)^2+\pi^{*}\left(1+n^{*}\right)W_t^{M*}\right]+\left(1+n^{*}\right)^2\left(1-\pi^{*}\right)\rho_t^{L*}w_t^{*}$$
$$+\pi\beta(1+n)W_t^{M}+\left(1+i_{t-1}^{EL}\right)\pi\beta(1+n)\rho_{t-1}^{L}w_{t-1},$$
$$\mathrm{LN}_t^{D*} = \pi^{*}b_t^{*}. \tag{5.60}$$

So the host loan rate would change to:

$$\left(1+i_t^{loan*}\right) = \frac{\pi^{*}w_t^{*}L_t^{*}}{\left\{\begin{array}{c}\left[\rho_t^{s*}w_t^{*}\left(1+n^{*}\right)^2+\pi^{*}\left(1+n^{*}\right)W_t^{M*}\right]+\left(1+n^{*}\right)^2\left(1-\pi^{*}\right)\rho_t^{L*}w_t^{*}\\+\pi\beta(1+n)W_t^{M}+\left(1+i_{t-1}^{EL}\right)\pi\beta(1+n)\rho_{t-1}^{L}w_{t-1}\end{array}\right\}}, \tag{5.61}$$

where $\left(1+i_t^{loan*}\right)<\left(1+i_{t-1}^{loan*}\right)$ due to a higher loan supply. The lower $\left(1+i_t^{loan*}\right)$ would increase $ROR\left(k_t^{*}\right)$ to:

$$ROR\left(k_t^{*}\right) = A_t^{*}\bar{k}_t^{\delta*}k_t^{\theta*-1}\left[\frac{\left(1+n^{*}\right)^2}{\pi^{*}}\right]^{1-\theta}\left[1-\left(\frac{1+i_t^{loan*}}{1+i_{t-1}^{loan*}}\right)\left(1-\theta^{*}\right)\right], \tag{5.62}$$

where $ROR\left(k_t^{*}\right) > ROR\left(k_{t-1}^{*}\right)$. A higher $ROR\left(k_t^{*}\right)$ would increase the gap between $ROR\left(k_t^{*}\right)r_{t-2,t}^{*}$ and $\left(1+i_{t-2}^{D*}\right)$ and make it easier to satisfy the incentive constraint for the entrepreneurs to produce, $ROR\left(k_t^{*}\right)r_{t-2,t}^{*} > \left(1+i_{t-1}^{D*}\right)$.

In period t + 1 and period t + 2. Provided $\left(1+i_t^{loan*}\right)$ [equation (5.61)], the banks' profits would be:

$$\Pi_{t+1}^{B*} = \Pi_{t+1}^{B*,SR} + \Pi_{t+1}^{B*,LR}, \tag{5.63}$$

Table 5.5 Host country – DSF and DSL

Period	t	t + *1*	t + *2*
$\left(1+i_t^{loan*,DSL}\right)$		$\left(1+i_{t-1}^{loan*}\right)>\left(1+i_t^{loan*}\right)=\left(1+i_{t+1}^{loan*}\right)$	
$ROR\left(k_t^{DSL*}\right)$		$ROR\left(k_{t-1}^{*}\right)<ROR\left(k_t^{*}\right)=ROR\left(k_{t+1}^{*}\right)$	
$\Pi_{t,SR}^{B*,DSL}$		$\Pi_{t,SR}^{B*}<\Pi_{t+1,SR}^{B*}=\Pi_{t+2,SR}^{B*}$	
Bank runs	No run.		

where

$$\Pi_{t+1}^{B*,SR}=\left[\left(1+i_t^{loan*}\right)-\left(1+i_t^{D*}\right)\right]\left[\rho_t^{s*}w_t^{*}\left(1+n^{*}\right)^2+\pi^{*}W_t^{M*}\right]+\left[\left(1+i_t^{loan*}\right)-\left(1+i_t^{EL*}\right)\right]$$
$$\left(1+n^{*}\right)^2\left(1-\pi^{*}\right)\rho_t^{L*}w_t^{*}+\left[\left(1+i_t^{loan*}\right)-\left(1+i_t^{D*}\right)\right]\left[\pi\beta(1+n)W_t^{M}+\left(1+i_{t-1}^{EL}\right)\right.$$
$$\left.\pi\beta(1+n)\rho_{t-1}^{L}w_{t-1}\right],$$
$$\Pi_{t+1}^{B*,LR}=\left[R-\left(1+i_{t-1}^{LRD*}\right)\right]\rho_{t-1}^{L*}w_{t-1}^{*}\pi^{*},$$

where the third term of $\Pi_{t+1}^{B*,SR}$ is the extra profits from FPI flows, and would increase $\Pi_{t+1}^{B*,SR}$, $\Pi_{t+1}^{B*,SR}>\Pi_t^{B*,SR}$. Given $\Pi_{t+1}^{B*,LR}=\Pi_t^{B*,LR}$, the banks' total profits in period $t+1$ would be higher than the profits in period t, $\Pi_{t+1}^{B*}>\Pi_t^{B*}$.

When FPI inflows continue to arrive in the same way, the host country's loan rate would be the same as $\left(1+i_t^{loan*}\right)$, $\left(1+i_{t+2}^{loan*}\right)=\left(1+i_{t+1}^{loan*}\right)=\left(1+i_t^{loan*}\right)$, and hence $ROR\left(k_{t+2}^{*}\right)=ROR\left(k_{t+1}^{*}\right)=ROR\left(k_t^{*}\right)>ROR\left(k_{t-1}^{*}\right)$. So the incentive constraint would hold, and bank runs are less likely to occur in the host country after the openness to FPI flows.

Compared to the home country, after the openness to FPI flows, the host country would not have unexpected withdrawals. As the recipient of FPI flows, the increase in the loan supply would reduce the host loan rate $\left(1+i_t^{loan*}\right)$ and stimulate $ROR\left(k_t^{*}\right)$ and make the incentive constraint easier to hold. So the probability of type II bank runs is reduced. Meanwhile, without unexpected withdrawals, liquidity shortfalls and bank runs are less likely to occur in the host country. So the probability of type I bank runs is also reduced. As a result, the host banks would also obtain higher profits after the openness to FPI. The openness to FPI would not affect the stability of the host banking system regardless of DSF or DSL system.

Sudden stops and banking crises

Sudden stops are defined as sudden slowdowns of private capital flows. That is, the relocated home entrepreneurs stop to conduct FPI flows. To analyse sudden stops, it is important to assume that the home countries in a DSL system, which have a higher probability of bank runs, have survived the SR turmoil. Since some effects of the openness of FPI flows would take place in period $t+3$, to avoid complications, it is assumed that sudden stops arrive after all the effects of the openness to FPI flows take place. That is, sudden stops are assumed to occur in period $t+4$ unexpectedly and would continue for a significant period of time.

The home country: both DSF and DSL systems

In period $t+4$, the middle-aged relocated home entrepreneurs (of generation $t+3$) would stop liquidating their LR accounts. Instead, they would renew their SR accounts with the home banks in period $t+4$ and withdraw their LR accounts at maturity in period $t+5$. However, because of the openness of FPI flows, the home banks will have prepared for the premature liquidation by the relocated entrepreneurs in period $t+3$. So the withdrawals of the LR accounts at maturity would be unexpected by the home banks and could cause liquidity shortfalls in LR accounts. This would be the challenge faced by the home banks at the time of sudden stops. Since the returns to the withdrawals of LR accounts at maturity would be paid in capital goods, either the new accounts or the returns, by liquidating existing LR accounts, cannot be used to finance the liquidity shortfalls, as they are all in output goods. Therefore, the home country, whether it is in a DSF system or in a DSL system, would face similar situations.

In period $t+4$. When sudden stops occur, the relocated entrepreneurs would not liquidate LR accounts, $\xi^{B}_{t+4} = \xi_{t+4} = 0$. So the budget constraints for both SR and LR accounts in period $t+4$ would be:

$$\begin{aligned}\left(1+i^{loan}_{t+3}\right)\pi(1+n)^3 b_{t+3} \geq \left(1+i^{D}_{t+3}\right)\left[\rho^{s}_{t+3}w_{t+3}(1+n)^5 + \pi(1+n)^4 W^{M}_{t+3}\right]\\ +\left(1+i^{EL}_{t+3}\right)(1+n)^5(1-\pi)\rho^{L}_{t+3}w_{t+3},\end{aligned} \tag{5.64a}$$

$$R\pi(1-\beta)(1+n)^4\rho^{L}_{t+2}w_{t+2} \geq \left(1+i^{LRD}_{t+2}\right)\rho^{L}_{t+2}w_{t+2}\pi(1-\beta)(1+n)^4, \tag{5.64b}$$

where both equations (5.64a) and (5.64b) are satisfied due to $R > \left(1+i^{LRD}_{t+2}\right)$, $\left(1+i^{loan}_{t+3}\right) > \left(1+i^{D}_{t+3}\right)$, and $\left(1+i^{loan}_{t+3}\right) > \left(1+i^{EL}_{t+3}\right)$. Bank runs are less likely to occur. The banks' profits in period $t+4$ would be:

$$\Pi^{B}_{t+4} = \Pi^{B,SR}_{t+4} + \Pi^{B,LR}_{t+4}, \tag{5.65}$$

where

$$\begin{aligned}\Pi^{B,SR}_{t+4} = &\left[\left(1+i^{loan}_{t+3}\right)-\left(1+i^{D}_{t+3}\right)\right]\left[\rho^{s}_{t+3}w_{t+3}(1+n)^5 + \pi(1-\beta)(1+n)^4 W^{M}_{t+3}\right] + \left[\left(1+i^{loan}_{t+3}\right)\right.\\ &\left.-\left(1+i^{EL}_{t+3}\right)\right](1+n)^5(1-\pi)\rho^{L}_{t+3}w_{t+3} + \left(1+i^{loan}_{t+3}\right)(1+n)^5\pi\beta\rho^{L}_{t+3}w_{t+3},\\ \Pi^{B,LR}_{t+4} = &\left[R-\left(1+i^{LRD}_{t+2}\right)\right]\pi(1-\beta)(1+n)^4\rho^{L}_{t+2}w_{t+2},\end{aligned}$$

where the third term of $\Pi^{B,SR}_{t+4}$ is the extra profits from the preparation of the premature liquidation by the relocated entrepreneurs and would increase $\Pi^{B,SR}_{t+4}, \Pi^{B,SR}_{t+4} > \Pi^{B,SR}_{t+3}$. Given $\Pi^{B,LR}_{t+4} = \Pi^{B,LR}_{t+3}$, the banks' total profits in period $t+4$ would be higher than the profits in period $t+3, \Pi^{B}_{t+4} > \Pi^{B}_{t+3}$.

Sudden stops would affect the loan supply but not the loan demand. The loan supply would change to:

$$LN^S_{t+4} = \rho^s_{t+4} w_{t+4} (1+n)^6 + \pi(1+n)^5 W^M_{t+4} + (1+n)^6 (1-\pi) \rho^L_{t+4} w_{t+4}, \tag{5.66}$$

where $LN^S_{t+4} = LN^{S,closed}_{t-1} < LN^S_{t+2}$, since $(1+n)\rho^L_{t+4} w_{t+4} > W^M_{t+4}$. So the loan rate would change to:

$$\left(1+i^{loan}_{t+4}\right) = \frac{\pi(1-\beta) w_{t+4} L_{t+4}}{(1+n)^2 w_{t+4}\left[\rho^s_{t+4} + (1-\pi)\rho^L_{t+4}\right] + \pi(1+n) W^M_{t+4}}, \tag{5.67}$$

where $\left(1+i^{loan,closed}_{t-1}\right) > \left(1+i^{loan}_{t+4}\right) > \left(1+i^{loan}_{t+2}\right)$. A higher $\left(1+i^{loan,DSF}_{t+4}\right)$ would reduce $ROR(k_{t+4})$:

$$ROR(k_{t+4}) = A_{t+4} \bar{k}^{\delta}_{t+4} k^{\theta-1}_{t+4} \left[\frac{(1+n)^2}{\pi(1-\beta)}\right]^{1-\theta} \left[1 - \left(\frac{1+i^{loan}_{t+4}}{1+i^{loan}_{t+2}}\right)(1-\theta)\right],$$

where $ROR(k_{t+4}) < ROR\left(k^{DSF}_{t+2}\right)$. A lower $ROR(k_{t+4})$ would make it more difficult to satisfy the incentive constraint for the entrepreneurs to produce. To satisfy the incentive constraint $ROR\left(\overline{k_{t+4}}\right) r_{t+2,t+4} > \left(1+i^D_{t+2}\right)$ would require $\left(1+i^{loan}_{t+4}\right)$ to be sufficiently low:

$$\left(1+i^{loan}_{t+4}\right) \leq \overline{\left(1+i^{loan}_{t+4}\right)}, \tag{5.68}$$

where $\overline{\left(1+i^{loan,DSF}_{t+4}\right)}$ is defined such that $ROR\left(\overline{k_{t+4}}\right) R = \left(1+i^D_{t+2}\right)$.

At $\left(1+i^{loan}_{t+4}\right) > \overline{\left(1+i^{loan}_{t+4}\right)}$, the incentive constraint fails, and the entrepreneurs would not demand loans. Without loan repayments, the banks would fail demand deposits in period $t+5$, and both type I and II bank runs in period $t+5$ would be inevitable.

In period $t+5$. The unexpected withdrawals of the LR accounts by the relocated entrepreneurs (of generation $t+3$) would change the budget constraint for the LR account in period $t+5$ to:

$$R\pi(1-\beta)(1+n)^5 \rho^L_{t+3} w_{t+3} \geq \left(1+i^{LRD}_{t+3}\right) \rho^L_{t+3} w_{t+3} \pi (1+n)^5. \tag{5.69}$$

To satisfy equation (5.69) would require $\left(1+i^{LRD}_{t+3}\right)$ to be sufficiently low:

$$\left(1+i^{LRD}_{t+3}\right) \leq R(1-\beta) \equiv \overline{\left(1+i^{LRD}_{t+3}\right)}, \tag{5.70}$$

where $\overline{\left(1+i^{LRD}_{t+3}\right)}$ represents the maximum value of $\left(1+i^{LRD}_{t+3}\right)$. At $\left(1+i^{LRD}_{t+3}\right) > \overline{\left(1+i^{LRD}_{t+3}\right)}$, the budget constraint fails, and the liquidity shortfalls for the LR accounts would occur. Since LR accounts are paid in capital goods, the new accounts or the liquidation of the existing LR accounts which are in output goods cannot be used to finance the liquidity shortfalls of the matured LR accounts. If the banks would not compromise their profits in capital goods to finance the shortfalls, type I bank runs in period t + 5 would be inevitable.

Meanwhile, as the budget constraint for the LR accounts [equation (5.69)] gets tighter, the returns to the mature LR accounts $r_{t+3,t+5}$ would be lower. A lower $r_{t+3,t+5}$ would make it more difficult to satisfy the incentive constraint for the entrepreneurs to produce, $ROR(k_{t+5})r_{t+3,t+5} > (1+i^{D}_{t+3})$. In order to hold the incentive constraint, $(1+i^{LRD}_{t+3})$ must be sufficiently high:

$$(1+i^{LRD}_{t+3}) \geq (1+\check{i}^{LRD}_{t+3}) \equiv \frac{\check{k}_{t+5}}{\rho^{L}_{t+3}w_{t+3}}, \; where\left(ROR\left(\check{k}_{t+5}\right)\right)' R = (1+i^{D}_{t+3}), \quad (5.71)$$

where $(1+\check{i}^{LRD}_{t+3})$ represents the minimum value of $(1+i^{LRD}_{t+3})$ to satisfy the incentive constraint. At $(1+i^{LRD}_{t+3}) < (1+\check{i}^{LRD}_{t+3})$, the entrepreneurs would not demand loans to produce. Without loan demand, the banks would fail to pay for the due SR accounts at the following period $t+6$, and type I and type II bank runs in period $t+6$ would be inevitable.

For the loan market, the loan demand would increase to:

$$\mathrm{LN}^{D}_{t+5} = \pi(1+n)^{5} b_{t+5}. \quad (5.72)$$

Provided the loan supply [equation (5.67)], the loan rate would become:

$$(1+i^{loan}_{t+5}) = \frac{\pi w_{t+5} L_{t+5}}{(1+n)^{2} w_{t+5}\left[\rho^{s}_{t+5} + (1-\pi)\rho^{L}_{t+5}\right] + \pi(1+n)W^{M}_{t+5}}, \quad (5.73)$$

where $(1+i^{loan}_{t+5}) = (1+i^{loan,closed}_{t-1}) > (1+i^{loan}_{t+4}) > (1+i^{loan,DSF}_{t+2})$, implying that the home loan rate would increase after sudden stops occur. A higher $(1+i^{loan}_{t+5})$ would reduce $ROR(k_{t+5})$ and would make it more difficult to satisfy the incentive constraint: $ROR(k_{t+5})r_{t+3,t+5} > (1+i^{D}_{t+3})$. To satisfy the incentive constraint would require $(1+i^{loan}_{t+5})$ to be sufficiently low:

$$(1+i^{loan}_{t+5}) \leq \overline{(1+i^{loan}_{t+5})}, \quad (5.74)$$

where $\overline{(1+i^{loan}_{t+5})}$ represents the minimum value of $(1+i^{loan}_{t+5})$ to hold the incentive constraint, and is defined such that $ROR(\overline{k_{t+5}})r_{t+3,t+5} = (1+i^{D}_{t+3})$. At $(1+i^{loan}_{t+5}) \leq \overline{(1+i^{loan}_{t+5})}$, the incentive constraint fails, and the entrepreneurs would not demand loans to produce. As a result, type I and type II bank runs in period $t+6$ would be inevitable. Combining equations (5.71) and (5.74), in order to prevent type I and type II bank runs caused by failing the incentive constraint, two conditions must be satisfied: $(1+i^{LRD}_{t+3}) \geq (1+\check{i}^{LRD}_{t+3})$ and $(1+i^{loan}_{t+5}) \leq \overline{(1+i^{loan}_{t+5})}$.

Table 5.6 Sudden stops – home country DSF and DSL

Period	t + 2	t + 4	t + 5
$\left(1+i_{t+4}^{loan,DSF}\right)$	$\left(1+i_{t+5}^{loan}\right)=\left(1+i_{t-1}^{loan,closed}\right)>\left(1+i_{t+4}^{loan}\right)>\left(1+i_{t+2}^{loan,DSF}\right)$		
$ROR\left(k_{t+4}^{DSF}\right)$	$ROR\left(k_{t+2}\right)>ROR\left(k_{t+4}\right)>ROR\left(k_{t+5}\right)$		
$\Pi_{t+4,SR}^{B}$		$\Pi_{t+5}^{B}<\Pi_{t+2}^{B}<\Pi_{t+4}^{B}$	
Bank runs		IC fails- Type I + II runs at $t+5$	LR BC fails Type I runs at $t+5$ IC fails Type I and II runs at period $t+6$
		IC holds, no run	IC hold and LRBC holds (need 2 conditions) – -no run

When equations (5.70), (5.71) and (5.74) are satisfied, bank runs are less likely to occur. The banks' profits would be:

$$\Pi_{t+5}^{B}=\Pi_{t+5}^{B,SR}+\Pi_{t+5}^{B,LR}, \tag{5.75}$$

where

$$\Pi_{t+5}^{B,SR}=\left[\left(1+i_{t+4}^{loan}\right)-\left(1+i_{t+4}^{D}\right)\right]\left[\rho_{t+4}^{s}w_{t+4}\left(1+n\right)^{6}+\pi\left(1+n\right)^{4}W_{t+4}^{M}\right]+\left[\left(1+i_{t+4}^{loan}\right)-\left(1+i_{t+4}^{EL}\right)\right]\left(1+n\right)^{6}\left(1-\pi\right)\rho_{t+4}^{L}w_{t+4},$$

$$\Pi_{t+5}^{B,LR}=\left[R-\left(1+i_{t+3}^{LRD}\right)\right]\left(1-\beta\right)\rho_{t+3}^{L}w_{t+3}\pi\left(1+n\right)^{5}-\left(1+i_{t+3}^{LRD}\right)\pi\beta\left(1+n\right)^{5}\rho_{t+3}^{L}w_{t+3},$$

where $\Pi_{t+5}^{B,LR}<\Pi_{t+2}^{B}<\Pi_{t+4}^{B,LR}$, while $\Pi_{t+5}^{B,SR}=\Pi_{t+4}^{B,SR}$, so $\Pi_{t+5,SR}^{B}<\Pi_{t+4,SR}^{B}$.

As shown in Table 5.6, sudden stops would make the incentive constraint difficult to hold for the home country. When the incentive constraint fails, the lack of loan demand would cause type I and type II bank runs for the home country. The situation in period $t+5$, one period after sudden stops occur, faced by the home country would be even more severe, since the home country would face possible failures of LR budget constraint as well as the incentive constraint. Moreover, the incentive constraint in period $t+5$ would require two conditions to hold. This situation shows that the banking system of the home country one period after sudden stops would be very vulnerable to shocks, regardless of whether it used a DSF or a DSL system. The type II bank runs resulting from the failure of the incentive constraint might not be prevented by the liquidity provision.

The host country: DSF and DSL

When sudden stops occur in period $t+4$, the host country would still have the due SR accounts of the relocated home entrepreneurs (of generation $t+2$) to pay but would not have the new SR accounts opened by the relocated home entrepreneurs (of generation $t+2$) and would have no unexpected withdrawals. Without unexpected withdrawals, the banks in both DSF and DSL would operate similarly.

In period $t+4$. The banks' profits would be:

$$\Pi_{t+4}^{B*} = \Pi_{t+4}^{B*,SR} + \Pi_{t+4}^{B*,LR}, \tag{5.76}$$

where

$$\Pi_{t+4}^{B*,SR} = \left[\left(1+i_{t+3}^{loan*}\right)-\left(1+i_{t+3}^{D*}\right)\right]\left[\rho_{t+3}^{s*}w_{t+3}^{*}\left(1+n^{*}\right)^{5}+\pi^{*}\left(1+n^{*}\right)^{4}W_{t+3}^{M*}\right]$$
$$\left[\left(1+i_{t+3}^{loan*}\right)-\left(1+i_{t+3}^{EL*}\right)\right]\left(1+n^{*}\right)^{5}\left(1-\pi^{*}\right)\rho_{t+3}^{L*}w_{t+3}^{*}+\left[\left(1+i_{t+3}^{loan*}\right)-\left(1+i_{t+3}^{D*}\right)\right]$$
$$\left[\pi\beta(1+n)^{3}W_{t+3}^{M}+\left(1+i_{t+2}^{EL}\right)\pi\beta(1+n)^{4}\rho_{t+2}^{L}w_{t+2}\right],$$

$$\Pi_{t+3}^{B*,LR} = \left[R-\left(1+i_{t+2}^{LRD*}\right)\right]\rho_{t+2}^{L*}w_{t+2}^{*}\pi^{*},$$

where $\Pi_{t+4}^{B*} = \Pi_{t+2}^{B*}$.

Meanwhile, sudden stops would change the loan supply to:

$$\mathrm{LN}_{t+4}^{S*} = w_{t+4}^{*}\left(1+n^{*}\right)^{6}\left[\rho_{t+4}^{s*}+\left(1-\pi^{*}\right)\rho_{t+4}^{L*}w_{t+4}^{*}\right]+\pi^{*}\left(1+n^{*}\right)^{5}W_{t+4}^{M*}, \tag{5.77}$$

where $\mathrm{LN}_{t+4}^{S*} < \mathrm{LN}_{t+2}^{S*}$. Given the loan demand [equation (5.60)], the host loan rate would be:

$$\left(1+i_{t+4}^{loan*}\right) = \frac{\pi^{*}w_{t+4}^{*}L_{t+4}^{*}}{w_{t+4}^{*}\left(1+n^{*}\right)^{2}\left[\rho_{t+4}^{s*}+\left(1-\pi^{*}\right)\rho_{t+4}^{L*}w_{t+4}^{*}\right]+\pi^{*}\left(1+n^{*}\right)W_{t+4}^{M*}}, \tag{5.78}$$

where $\left(1+i_{t+4}^{loan*}\right) > \left(1+i_{t+2}^{loan*}\right)$. A higher $\left(1+i_{t+4}^{loan*}\right)$ would reduce $ROR\left(k_{t+4}^{*}\right)$, $ROR\left(k_{t+4}^{*}\right) < ROR\left(k_{t+2}^{*}\right)$. A lower $ROR\left(k_{t+4}^{*}\right)$ would make it more difficult to satisfy the incentive constraint: $ROR\left(k_{t+4}^{*}\right)r_{t+2,t+4}^{*} > \left(1+i_{t+4}^{D*}\right)$. To satisfy the incentive constraint would require $\left(1+i_{t+4}^{loan*}\right)$ to be sufficiently low:

$$\left(1+i_{t+4}^{loan*}\right) \le \overline{\left(1+i_{t+4}^{loan*}\right)}, \tag{5.79}$$

where $\overline{\left(1+i_{t+4}^{loan*}\right)}$ represents the maximum value of $\left(1+i_{t+4}^{loan*}\right)$ to hold the incentive constraint, and is defined such that $ROR\overline{\left(k_{t+4}^{*}\right)}r_{t+2,t+4}^{*} = \left(1+i_{t+4}^{D*}\right)$. At $\left(1+i_{t+4}^{loan*}\right) > \overline{\left(1+i_{t+4}^{loan*}\right)}$, the incentive constraint fails, and the entrepreneurs would not demand loans to produce. Without loan demand, the host banks could not pay for the SR accounts in the following period $t+5$, and type I and type II bank runs would be inevitable in period $t+5$.

In period $t+5$. When the incentive constraint holds, bank runs are less likely to occur. The banks' profits would be:

$$\Pi_{t+5}^{B*} = \Pi_{t+5}^{B*,SR} + \Pi_{t+5}^{B*,LR}, \tag{5.80}$$

Table 5.7 Sudden stops – host country DSF and DSL

Period	t + 2	t + 4	t + 5
$\left(1+i_{t+4}^{loan*}\right)$		$\left(1+i_{t+2}^{loan*}\right)<\left(1+i_{t+4}^{loan*}\right)=\left(1+i_{t+5}^{loan*}\right)$	
$\boldsymbol{ROR\left(k_{t+4}^{*}\right)}$		$ROR\left(k_{t+2}^{*}\right)>ROR\left(k_{t+4}^{*}\right)=ROR\left(k_{t+5}^{*}\right)$	
Π_{t+4}^{B*}		$\Pi_{t+2}^{B*}=\Pi_{t+4}^{B*}>\Pi_{t+5}^{B*}$	
Bank runs		IC fails, Types I + II runs at $t+5$ IC holds, no run	No run

where

$$\Pi_{t+5}^{B*,SR}=\left[\left(1+i_{t+4}^{loan*}\right)-\left(1+i_{t+4}^{D*}\right)\right]\left[\rho_{t+4}^{s*}w_{t+4}^{*}\left(1+n^{*}\right)^{6}+\pi^{*}\left(1+n^{*}\right)^{5}W_{t+4}^{M*}\right]+\left[\left(1+i_{t+4}^{loan*}\right)\right.$$
$$\left.-\left(1+i_{t+4}^{EL*}\right)\right]\left(1+n^{*}\right)^{6}\left(1-\pi^{*}\right)\rho_{t+4}^{L*}w_{t+4}^{*},$$
$$\Pi_{t+5}^{B*,LR}=\left[R-\left(1+i_{t+3}^{LRD*}\right)\right]\rho_{t+3}^{L*}w_{t+3}^{*}\pi^{*},$$

where $\Pi_{t+5}^{B*}<\Pi_{t+4}^{B*}=\Pi_{t+2}^{B*}$, since $\Pi_{t+4,SR}^{B*,SR}<\Pi_{t+3,SR}^{B*,SR}=\Pi_{t+2,SR}^{B*,SR}$.

Conclusion

This chapter examines how various types of bank governance would react to the openness of FPI flows and sudden stops. Since banking crises are more likely to occur in the SR, the analysis has focused on the SR impacts for both the home and the host countries. The two bank governance systems examined are the DSF (depositor-selected fully funded) and DSL (depositor-selected leveraged) systems. Different from the traditional zero-profit banks in the BSF (bank-selected fully funded) system, the banks would maximize their own profits in both DSF and DSL systems. In both DSF and DSL systems, the depositors who choose their portfolios would bear the costs involved into the uncertainties of their own types. Therefore, as the banks would take the margins of the two types of accounts as their profits, the agents would be worse off in both DSF and DSL systems compared to the BSF system.

The difference between DSF and DSL systems is in how the systems finance unexpected withdrawals. While the DSF system would liquidate LR assets as requested by the depositors, the DSL system would use the bank liability, the new SR or LR accounts, to finance the unexpected withdrawals. Therefore, when the openness of FPI occurs unexpectedly, the unexpected withdrawals would lead to different outcomes for the DSF and DSL systems. In a DSF system, the openness of FPI flows would not increase the possibility of bank runs for the home country, although the banks' profits might fluctuate. In a DSL system, however, the possibility of bank runs would increase after the openness of FPI flows, regardless of whether they are using the new SR or LR accounts to finance the unexpected withdrawals. Compared to using the new SR accounts to finance the unexpected withdrawals, using the new LR accounts would defer bank runs by one period but would damage the stability of the home banking system more severely. The openness of FPI flows, however, would increase the host banks' profits without affecting the stability of the host banking system, whether it is in a DSF or a DSL system.

Sudden stops would lead to unexpected withdrawals of mature LR accounts for the home banks. The unexpected withdrawals would increase the possibility of both type I and type II bank runs for three consecutive periods for the home country in both DSF and DSL systems. Although without unexpected withdrawals, the host country would also be affected by sudden stops via the loan market. As a result, sudden stops would also increase the possibility of bank runs in the host country at the time when sudden stops occur, but the host banks would not have the same long-lasting effects as the home country.

It has been shown that bank governance plays a crucial role in reacting to the shocks. The reactions of the banks to the shocks could prevent the bank runs or put the banks into a situation in which bank runs would be inevitable. As demonstrated in the chapter, due to the causes, there are various types of bank runs. The liquidity provision would be effective in preventing type I bank runs; however, its effectiveness in preventing type II bank runs is limited.

Notes

1 When applying the arguments to the loan performances of the banks during global finance crises, Peni et al (2013) find mixed results which show that the banks with strong governance lost less in real estate loans during 2006–2008 but had larger losses in 2009.
2 Minton et al (2009) use the database of the Federal Reserve Bank of Chicago on 345 bank holding companies during 1999–2003. These bank holding companies are the ones with high percentages of commercial and industrial loans in banks' loan portfolios. They find that although only 19 bank holding companies use credit derivatives, the assets of these few banks represent two thirds of the assets of all bank holding companies.
3 The findings of Jorion (2007) are based on the investigation of US commercial banks' quarterly reports during 1995–2003. To detect commonalities, Jorion (2007) uses segment information to break down into fixed income, currencies, equities and commodities categories.
4 Pelizzon and Schaefer (2007) use Basel to examine capital requirements and other regulations.
5 Masciandaro and Volpicella (2016) use micro supervision independence to examine central banks' role in macro prudential, while Masciandaro et al (2013) test supervision and supervisory governance by using the data of 102 countries.
6 Freixas (2010) argues that regulations are important regardless of whether crises would occur. Non-proper regulations would lead to an inefficient banking industry.
7 The costs and profit loss are considered unnecessary when the banks believe that the possibility of bank runs is low and financial crises are based on speculations.
8 As is well documented in the literature, the banks answer to the shareholders and board members, who are less likely to compromise their profits for liquidity shortfalls. To prevent runs, the banks can certainly use other financial methods to finance the shortfalls in the boom time. However, when most banks follow similar patterns, systemic risks are generated, and the financial tools may not work as well as expected. As a result, to protect the shareholders' profits, bank runs can be the result.

6 Capital controls and banking crises

Introduction: facts and evidence

The concerns of financial crises contagious through the openness to capital flows have led more and more countries to implement capital controls. Depending on the directions and the formats, there are many ways to divide controls into many types. A relatively simple way is to differentiate controls by direction: controls on inflows and controls on outflows. Depending on the economic conditions at the time of implementation of controls, the country may react differently via different channels. Moreover, the deregulation of the banking system has changed the roles of the banks and caused the banks to react differently to the impacts of the shocks. How the banks react to the shocks depends not only on the changes of the regulations of the banking system but also on bank governance, as shown in Chapter 5. However, it has been challenging for empirics to study the impacts of shocks via banking channels, especially in an open economy. This is mainly because of the difficulties in obtaining the data of banks and because the data of banks often do not reveal bank governance, as some information is considered confidential. Therefore, it is the purpose of this chapter to develop a theoretical framework which incorporates the banking system to examine the impacts of capital controls to the economy and the effectiveness of capital controls, especially the ability of controls to prevent/to increase banking crises. While Chapter 5 analyses how bank governance affect the banks' responses to the shocks and hence the possibility of banking crises, this chapter will analyse the linkages between the implementation of capital controls and the stability of the banking system. The capital controls to be analysed include symmetric and asymmetric controls. The banking system to be analysed in this chapter is the DSF banking system since the DSF banking system is less likely to have bank runs in an open economy [see Table 5.2], compared to the traditional zero-profit BSF system. Also, a DSF system is less likely to have looting/moral hazard problems in banking compared to a DSL system. By reducing the possibility of bank runs to a lower level, we can better understand the impacts driven by capital controls to the economy.

To understand the current state of capital controls, we cannot ignore the history of capital controls, which have been switched on and off from time to time. Prior to the 1970s, capital controls were adopted broadly. Gradually, capital controls were removed, and free capital mobility was promoted until the 1990s, when more countries started to implement capital controls [Edwards (2009a), Johnson et al (2007)]. Before the 1997 Asian Financial Crisis (AFC), most capital controls implemented were inflow controls, such as those in Thailand, Malaysia, Philippines, Indonesia, the Czech Republic, Colombia and Brazil. One exception was Spain, which implemented outflow controls. Post–AFC in 1998, more Latin American countries, such as Argentina, joined the group to control capital flows. Meanwhile, the countries with inflow controls added outflow controls, such as Thailand, Malaysia and Brazil. Moreover, in 2012, four years after the Global Financial Crisis (GFC) in 2008, the International Monetary Fund (IMF) joined the institutional view by pointing out that free capital flows, in spite of their benefits, carry risks which would increase challenges on policies and must be managed [IMF (2012)]. This is one of the reasons why capital controls are considered as part of macro-prudential regulations in some studies.

The determinants of capital flows

Since capital controls aim to control capital flows, it is important to understand what determines capital flows. Based on recent studies, the main determinants of capital flows include interest rate differential [Ahmed and Zlate (2014), Amin and Annamalah (2013), Garcia and Barcinski (1998)], economic output/growth [Ahmed and Zlate (2014), Edwards (2007a, 2007b), Kinda (2012)] and other factors, such as excessive credit provision [Kinda (2012)], the degree of capital mobility and current account deficit [Edwards (2004, 2007a, 2007b)] and income level [Ding and Jinjarak (2012)]. By identifying extreme capital flow movements, Forbes and Warnock (2012) find that contagion through trade, banking and geography often occur in the episodes of stop and retrenchment. Therefore, preventing contagion without capital controls would occur through the determinants of capital flows, either interest rate differential or outputs. Unfortunately, neither outputs nor interest rate differentials are fully controlled by the domestic policy makers. While output level is endogenously determined by the economy, the interest rate differentials would depend on the interest rate level of the partner country. Moreover, interest rate level is crucial to many macroeconomic variables, especially exports, imports and investment. Using interest rate level as a tool to control capital flows may easily cause complex effects on the economy which may not be expected by the policy makers. Compared to the complications caused by interest rate differentials, capital controls are considered a more direct way to manage capital flows.

The facts and effects of capital flows

What impacts have capital flows caused that are required to be managed? Verdier (2008) uses foreign debt data in 1970–1998 and finds that domestic saving serves as a complement to capital flows, which usually go to the countries with scarce resources. Extending an overlapping-generations framework, Alfaro (2004) finds that opening capital inflows are often found in the capital import countries, while closing capital inflows are often found in capital export countries, and Alfaro and Kanczuk (2004) find that the countries in intermediate development are the ones with cycles between open and closed for capital flows. These discoveries show that capital flows would affect domestic macro variables. From time to time, depending on the development of specific sector(s), one country may need to manage capital flows in specific directions. Such management of capital flows has been disagreed upon by the conventional arguments, which promote free capital flows and assert that free capital flows would increase international financial integration. However, the study of Damasceno (2011), which uses the data of 105 countries during 1980–2004, shows that capital flows do not increase international financial integration and external savings as asserted in conventional arguments in supporting free capital flows. Moreover, based on the literature, it seems there have been more negative effects than positive effects associated with capital flows.

On one hand, a positive effect is found by Hartwell (2014), who shows that capital openness is strongly correlated with new firm entry by using the datasets of 112 countries during 2001–2011. On the other hand, there are several negative effects supported by empirical studies. Wong and Eng (2015) find that capital outflows tighten credit availability and lead to financial fragility and possibly economic downturn. Park (2013) finds that it is portfolio debt outflows accompanied by portfolio equity flows that destabilize foreign exchange markets. Using the panel data for 43 advanced and emerging countries, Frost and van Tilburg (2014) find that gross capital inflows often occur prior to credit growth and that both gross inflows and high private domestic credit often occur before banking crises. Based on the findings of Wong and Eng (2015), Park (2013) and Frost and van Tilburg (2014), it seems reasonable to manage capital flows to a certain degree to reduce the negative effects and, if possible, to prevent banking crises.

Instead of analysing capital flows in general, some research approaches capital flows by looking at the composition of flows and the linkages to financial stability. Using three indices of financial integration of multiple countries during 1970–2004 in probit equation, Edwards (2007a) shows that although higher capital mobility and current account deficit would increase the probability of contraction in capital flows, a high ratio of FDI to GDP would reduce the probability. As discussed in Chapter 2, FDI flows are LR flows and tend to be more stable. Defining the composition of capital flows as the ratio of SR capital to LR FDI, Montiel and Reinhart (1999) show that the composition of capital flows is often associated with financial stability and should be managed properly. Furthermore, Magud and Reinhart (2007) point out that the effects on the composition of flows shall be one of the main goals to be achieved by capital controls. By using SR debt to reserve ratio as the predictor of financial crises, Rodrik and Velasco (2000) find that high levels of M2/GDP and per capital income are correlated with SR maturities of external debt but not trade credit.

The forms and the types of controls

There are many ways to manage capital flows and to implement capital controls. In terms of the directions of flows, the controls can be on either inflows or outflows or both [Pasricha (2012)]. In terms of the types of flows, the controls can be implemented on bond flows, credit flows or debt flows [Molnar, Tateno, and Supornsinchai (2013), Tamirisa (2006)]. In terms of forms, the controls can be in the form of prudential tax [Wong and Eng (2015)] and/or taxes on financial transactions [Neely (1999), Wibaut (2014)]. In addition to direct controls as mentioned earlier, there are indirect controls to affect capital flows, such as interest rates, reserves [Jeanne (2016), Steiner (2013), Vithessonthi and Tongurai (2013)], the restrictions on the right of capital owners [Sigurgeirsdottir and Wade (2015)] and exchange rate intervention [Blanchard, Adler, and Filho (2015)]. What types controls are needed would depend on economic conditions of one country, such as exchange rate [Ding and Jinjarak (2012), Pandey et al (2015)], credit market tightness indicators [Cheung and Herrala (2014)] and growth, as well as global financial conditions [Ding and Jinjarak (2012)]. Different types of controls might cause different impacts to the economy via different channels. Moreover, the same type(s) of controls, when implemented in different periods of time, might have different impacts due to the changes of economic conditions and global financial conditions. This is why it has been challenging for the empirical studies to analyse the impacts of capital controls, especially when grouping many countries together. This is exactly where a theoretical analysis can assist us to focus on specific types of controls to analyse their impacts to the economy and their linkages to the stability of the banking system. It is the goal of this chapter to focus on the direct controls in the form of tax in either and both directions of flows. As the world is interdependent, the effects of capital controls of one country would also depend on the controls or non-controls of the other country. This chapter will analyse the impacts of symmetric and asymmetric controls. Such controls are called bilateral and unilateral controls in some research work.

Capital controls and perfect capital mobility

To conclude whether one country should implement/liberalize capital controls, one must compare the outcome with capital controls to the outcome with perfect capital mobility. Interestingly, most comparisons have focused on either efficiency or welfare/social optima, and most studies find that the economy with capital controls can improve market efficiency and can be welfare improving compared to the economy with free capital mobility. To be more specific, in terms of *market efficiency*, Acharya and Bengui (2016) find that free capital flows cannot support demand and expenditure reallocation during a liquidity trap. So they suggest that capital management can be necessary but must be coordinated across countries. Approaching misallocation from a different direction, El-Shagi (2012a, 2012b) finds that although capital controls might distort international capital allocations, capital controls would protect the countries from future crises, and it is important that they be implemented. Meanwhile, Forbes (2005) argues that the costs of capital controls are sustainable and would lead distortions which would decrease market efficiency. However, through the examination of the market efficiency of Iceland, Graham, Peltomaki, and Sturludottir (2015) find that the stock market of Iceland was more efficient under capital controls compared to the periods with free capital flows.

In terms of *welfare analysis*, it has been well documented that capital controls are welfare improving under many circumstances. The circumstances include the periods during crises [Benigno et al (2014)], when the government may default on behalf of all residents and lead to inefficient private lending [Wright (2006)], when there are prolonged controls and in the debt level below the threshold [Singh and Subramanian (2008)],[1] when externality is sufficiently small [Korinek (2011), Michaud and Rothert (2014)], when the financial system is less efficient and costly [Kitano (2011)], when the outcome is inefficient due to externalities [Brunnermeier and Sannikov (2015)] and when the economy has a financial accelerator and a fixed exchange rate regime [Kitano and Takaku (2015)]. Note that the approaches used by these studies are various. Benigno et al (2014) use *ex ante* and *ex post* optimal design. Kitano (2011) uses tax as the form of capital controls on foreign borrowing. Theoretically, Michaud and Rothert (2014) learn from China's experience and develop a theory of capital controls to use international borrowing constraint as a tool to correct externality. Kitano and Takaku (2015) use a new Keynesian model, while Brunnermeier and Sannikov (2015) use a neo-classical model with incomplete market.

The reasons capital controls can be welfare improving have been shown by many studies. For example, Liu and Spiegel (2015) find that it is because capital controls serve as a complement to sterilization to improve welfare by using a dynamic stochastic general equilibrium (DSGE) model to examine tax on capital inflows. Korinek (2011) concludes that it is because capital controls could internalize externalities and improve welfare by examining emerging markets. Dooley (2002) uses an insurance model and finds that it is because capital controls would limit gains and losses generated by the financial intermediaries during crises. Gu and Sheng (2010) find that it is because capital controls would reduce speculative SR flows when accounting for volatility. Callen and Cashin (2002) use the experiences of India and find that it is because capital controls would support optimality of external borrowing. Moreover, according to Michaud and Rothert (2014), the welfare level achieved by capital controls can be closest to the first best outcome. Similarly, Gu and Sheng (2010) find that the outcomes achieved by capital controls would be Pareto optimal for both capital-importing and -exporting countries.

The effects of capital controls

What are the effects of capital controls that can be welfare improving? Four main effects are expected to be achieved by capital controls: (1) financial stability, (2) monetary autonomy, (3) macroeconomic outcome and (4) others. Moreover, Magud and Reinhart (2007) have stated that effective capital controls must (1) reduce the volumes of flows, (2) alter the composition of flows, (3) reduce real exchange rate pressure and (4) allow for more independent monetary policy. As one can observe, while the goal of independent monetary policy is related monetary autonomy, the goals of affecting the pressure of exchange rate and of affecting the volumes and the compositions of flows are related to the effects on financial stability and macroeconomic outcomes. Although the main effects are expected to be achieved by implementing capital controls, the effects and the effectiveness of capital controls would depend strongly on the types of implemented controls as well as on the economic conditions and global financial conditions. Meanwhile, the sensitivity of results to both the methods and dataset adopted has increased the complexity of analysing the empirical results and of finding the causes, which lead mixed results. This is where the theoretical analysis can be helpful in examining possible causes which drive the results. Before doing so, it is important to summarize what has been found in each expected effect.

On the volumes and the composition of capital flows

There are studies finding that capital controls do achieve the goal of reducing the volumes of flows [Goh (2005), Inoguchi (2009), Neumann (2006)], especially of banking debt flows [Dell'Erba, Salvatore, and Reinhardt (2015)] and portfolio debt investment inflows [Park (2013)]. Through affecting the volumes of specific flows, capital controls then affect the composition of flows. Moreover, it has been found that capital controls could affect the volatility of LR FDI flows [Li and Rajan (2015)] and SR flows [Ferreira and Jose Luis da Costa (2008)].

To be more specific, Dell'Erba, Salvatore, and Reinhardt (2015) show that capital controls would reduce banking debt flows but increase FDI flows in the financial sector. Taking the experiences of Malaysia, Amin and Annamalah (2013) find that capital controls can divert SR flows to LR flows without jeopardizing LR investment. Focusing on the experiences of Brazil, da Silva and Resende (2010) find that capital controls would reduce capital flight in Brazil during the period of large financial instability. Learning from South Africa, Ahmed, Arezki, and Funke (2007) find that capital controls can increase FDI and affect the composition of capital flows. The result of affecting the composition of flows is also found in Campion and Neumann (2003), who use the panel data of Latin America, while Cardoso and Goldfajn (1998) study the controls in Brazil, as well as other studies, such as Binici, Hutchison, and Schindler (2010), Dell'Erba, Salvatore, and Reinhardt (2015), Gu and Sheng (2010), Montiel and Reinhart (1999). As Molnar et al (2013) have pointed out, it is through limiting portfolio flows that capital controls are able to reduce lending booms and hence reduce the impacts on the macro economy.

However, there are also studies finding that capital controls are ineffective or insignificant in affecting the volumes and/or the volatility of capital flows [Concha, Galindo, and Vasquez (2011), Esaka and Takagi (2013), Forbes and Klein (2015) and Montiel and Reinhart (1999)]. In particular, Wibaut (2014) finds that controls cannot control volatility, while Chung and Ni (2002) find that controls would instead increase both inflows and outflows. Similar results are also found in El-Shagi (2012b), which find that controls would in fact increase a surge caused by a financial crisis.

On financial stability (including asset prices, exchange rate and credit)

Da Silva and Resende (2010) have found, by studying the experiences of Brazil, that through obstructing capital flight, capital controls have increased financial stabilities. Ramos-Tallada (2013) shows that capital controls in the recipient countries serve better in increasing the stability. Capital controls are capable of increasing stability through limiting the risks of globalization [Bibow (2008–2009)] and reducing financial crises [Mishkin (2001)] and/or preventing banking/financial crises [El-Shagi (2012a), Frost and van Tilburg (2014)].

Practically, India used controls to insulate the country from the Eastern Asian Financial Crisis, as shown in Joshi (2001), and Brazil used capital controls to reduce capital flight and increase financial stability [da Silva and Resende (2010)]. It has been well documented that how capital controls would increase stability is through reducing exchange rate volatility [Ahmed et al (2007), Altinkemer (2005), Chen and Chang (2015), Concha et al (2011), Fernando de Paula and Magalhaes Prates (2015), Concha et al (2011)] to affect the real exchange rates [David (2009), Michaud and Rothert (2014)] and hence stabilizing asset prices [Korinek and Sandri (2016)]. However, not all types of capital controls would have the effect of increasing financial stability. Andreasen, Schindler, and Valenetzuela (2015) point out that inflow controls are effective in producing international corporate bonds in both advanced and emerging economies, especially during periods of financial distress.

Meanwhile, there are also studies finding capital controls have limited and/or negative effects on increasing financial stability. De Roure, Furnagiev, and Reitz (2015) find that capital controls have no direct price impacts on financial flows. Chamon and Garcia (2016) find that the effects of capital controls on exchange rate appreciation are limited.

On monetary and other autonomy

It has been shown in several studies that capital controls can gain the country space for monetary autonomy [Goh (2005), Grabel (2015), Han and Wei (2014), Kawai and Liu (2015), Kim and Yang (2012a, 2012b), Ma and McCauley (2008), Schaling (2009), You, Kim, and Ren (2014)] and other autonomies [Altinkemer (2005), David (2008), Felix (2003), Garcia and Valpassos (2000)]. Other autonomies include fiscal policy autonomy [Boucekkine, Pommeret, and Prieur (2013)] and the autonomy of time to apply remedies to the economy [Athukorala and Jongwanich (2012)].

However, there are studies finding that capital controls are not effective in gaining monetary independence for the nation [Jongwanich and Kohpaiboon (2012), Mitchener and Wandschneider (2015), Straetmans et al (2013), Tamirisa (2006)]. Since interest rate is one of the monetary tools, Forbes et al (2015) and Edwards (2012) focus on the interest rates when examining monetary autonomy of nations. Forbes et al (2015) find that capital controls do not affect interest rate differentials significantly. Edwards (2012) finds that controls cannot isolate emerging countries from interest rate disturbances.

On macroeconomic outcome

Through managing capital flows, increasing financial stability and gaining monetary and other policy autonomies, capital controls could produce a more promising future macroeconomic outcome [Aguirre Carmona (2014)], especially for the recipient countries [Ramos-Tallada (2013)]. As a result, fluctuations are reduced [Mishkin (2001)], more output is produced [Hsu (2005)] and economic growth is greater [Mishkin (2001)] and faster [Costinot et al (2014)]. Because of capital controls, the decrease in fluctuation and volatility is not limited to the exchange rates but also to the macroeconomic variables, such as consumption, investment and employment [Chen and Chang (2015)]. The reduction in fluctuations would then stabilize the macro economy [Korinek (2011), Liu and Spiegel (2015)]. Moreover, it has been shown that how capital controls could produce better macroeconomic outcomes is through reducing global risks carried by capital inflow bonanzas and their cumulative impacts on the economy [Molnar et al (2013)]. The reduction in global risks would then decrease both the overseas spillover effects [Buss (2013)] and the impacts of external shocks [Chang, Liu, and Spiegel (2015), Forssbaeck and Oxelheim (2006), Han and Wei (2014), Ibrahim (2006)].

However, there are also studies finding that capital controls do not have positive effects on macroeconomic outcomes. For example, Darku (2010) finds that capital controls would limit the use of international financial markets to smooth consumption. Duasa and Mosley (2006) find that capital controls do not affect economic productivity and GDP across a sample of 30 developing countries during 1980–2003. Klein (2012) finds that the countries with long-standing controls tend to be poor on average and that there is little evidence of capital controls affecting GDP. Moreover, Forbes and Klein (2015) find that capital controls would have significant effects in decreasing GDP growth. Mitchener and Wandschneider (2015) find that capital controls would not accelerate macroeconomic recovery.

Other effects

Other effects of capital controls include affecting market participants' behaviours [de Roure et al (2015)], providing a stronger correlation between savings and investment [Raza, Zoega, and Kinsella (2015)], weakening currencies [Akram and Byrne (2015)], causing conflicts on the obligations of trade and investment treaties [Feibelman (2015)] and decreasing portfolio allocation in both bonds and equities, based on Brazil's experiences [Forbes et al (2016)]. Also, based on the experiences of Chile, Forbes (2007) finds that capital controls would not lead to significant financial constraints for smaller firms.

The factors crucial to the effects of capital controls

Many factors would influence the effects of capital controls on capital flows. One factor is that the datasets adopted would affect the analytical results. David (2007) points out the importance in differentiating net flows from gross (total) flows. By using the data of transactions of Brazil, David (2007) finds that capital controls would affect net capital income flows and gross portfolio flows. Ahmed and Zlate (2014) find that capital controls would discourage net inflows.

Additional to the adopted datasets, the effects of controls on flows would also be affected by the economic conditions of a country. When examining Chile and Colombia, David (2009) finds that controls would reduce SR net flows but not LR flows of Chile but would affect total flows and LR flows of Colombia. In Malaysia, Goh (2005) finds that controls would reduce total flows. Comparing the controls in Thailand and Malaysia during 2000–2010 in a vector autoregression (VAR) model, Jongwanich et al (2011) find that controls are effective on outflows but not on inflows of Thailand. However, in Malaysia, it is the liberalization of controls that has the impacts on both FDI and FPI flows. In both countries, the controls have no effect on the exchange rates.

Note that some economic conditions are not only specific to one country but also are specific to a period of time. The specific economic conditions during a specific period of time would also affect the effects of controls on the flows, and so does the extensiveness of capital controls. As shown in Yepez Albornoz (2012), when the macroeconomic position is strong, controls (liberalization) on outflows would reduce net outflows (inflows). By studying 17 countries during 2001–2011, Bijsterbosch et al (2015) find that controls are effective prior to the crises and the effectiveness is weakened in the aftermath of crises in the emerging markets. Park (2013) shows that the effects of controls would diminish in the LR by using regression analysis. However, Eichengreen and Rose (2014) find that the effects of controls on financial capital can be highly durable. Klein and Shambaugh (2015) show that controls have to be extensive to be effective.

The value of the exchange rate and its associated current account deficits are also important factors in affecting the effects of capital controls on flows. By examining optimal controls to manage surges, Ostry et al (2011) find that controls would be useful in managing flows when the exchange rate is not undervalued and when the flows are likely to be transitory. However, Fratzscher (2012) shows that capital controls are usually associated with countries which have undervalued exchange rates and fixed exchange rate regimes and with countries which have concerns about capital inflows triggering an overheating economy. Ghosh and Qureshi (2016) find that controls are often with the countries which have current account deficits.

Not surprisingly, the types of controls are crucial in affecting the effects of controls on flows. Some types of controls target specific types of assets and the direction(s) of flows. So we need empirical studies to understand the types of controls and to select the correct types of assets and/or the direction(s) of flows to analyse the actual effects of the controls on the flows. This is shown by You et al (2014), who examine the datasets of 88 countries during 1995–2010 and find that the types of assets and the direction of capital flows selected are crucial in affecting the effects of the controls on the flows. By using weighted capital control datasets and panel VAR to study emerging markets during 2001–2011, Pasricha et al (2015) find that outflow controls have no strong effect on the variables of their model, but inflow controls may increase domestic monetary autonomy. In other words, if the types of assets targeted by the controls were not included in the analysis or not essential to the flows, the studies would tend to conclude that the controls are ineffective, regardless of the effectiveness being evaluated based on the volumes or on the compositions of the flows. This may explain why Jongwanich and Kohpaiboon (2012) find that the effects of controls depend on the composition of flows.

For the controls targeting specific flows and/or assets, Tamirisa (2006) shows that the controls on portfolio inflows, together with the restrictions on banks, foreign exchange and stock market operations, would be effective in affecting interest rate differentials but not the controls on portfolio outflows and international transaction, based on the experiences of Malaysia. By investigating 74 countries during 1995–2005, Binici et al (2010) show that the controls on debt and equity flows would be effective in affecting outflows but not inflows and that outflow controls are more effective for high-income countries.

The examination of direct controls is straightforward, but the examination of indirect controls is not. For example, Garcia and Barcinski (1998) use interest rate differential as a control on flows and conclude that effectiveness of controls depends on whether capital flows are affected. However, it is controversial to use interest rate differential to examine the effects of capital flows for two reasons. First, the interest rate differential depends on the interest rate of other countries. The change of domestic interest rate may or may not affect the interest rate differential and hence the capital flows. Second, interest rate itself would affect many macroeconomic variables that may or may not move in the same direction and may offset (or magnify) the effects on the capital flows. Then it raises a question of whether the effects which offset each other shall be called "no effect".

Liberalizing capital controls

The implemented controls can also be liberalized. What are the effects of the liberalization of the controls? Would it be simply the opposite of the implementation of controls? Similar to the effects of the implemented capital controls, the effects of the liberalization of controls can be summarized into the areas of the volumes and the compositions of capital flows, financial stability, monetary autonomy, macroeconomic outcomes and others.

Depending on the types of controls being liberalized, it has been found that the liberalization of controls would encourage both FDI and FPI flows [Jongwanich et al (2011)]. Inoguchi (2009) finds that this is especially true for capital outflows, while Edison and Warnock (2008) find that this is true for short-lived inflows for a longer time. Unexpectedly, it seems that the liberalization of controls is also used for other purposes. For example, Pasricha (2012) points out that outflow liberalization was used as a tool to reduce net inflows prior to crisis. Jinjarak, Noy, and Zheng (2013) find that liberalization would prevent inflows from declining further.

For financial stability, it has been found that liberalization would provide wage–price exchange rate flexibility [Bahmani (2012)], reduce exchange rate appreciation [Forbes et al (2015)] and increase the role of banks and financial institutions [Grittersova (2014)] but might increase financial volatility [Orlov (2005)].[2] For monetary autonomy, it is found that the liberalization would increase foreign exchange holdings (foreign reserves) by the central banks [Steiner (2013)]. For macroeconomic outcomes, it has been found that the liberalization of capital accounts and/or controls would integrate onshore and offshore markets [Hutchison et al (2012)],[3] smooth consumption [Darku (2010)] and accelerate output and productivity growth [Romero-Avila (2009), Song, Storesletten, and Zilibotti (2014)]. However, Benzing (2001) also finds that financial liberalization would increase inefficiency in emerging markets. For other effects, Boucekkine et al (2013) find that full liberalization would be optimal to switch to from capital controls only when the country has wealth reaching a threshold and when the country does not seek a large amount of public expenditure.

The literature of the liberalization of capital controls has raised two questions. First, in order to obtain the benefits of the liberalization of controls, shouldn't the countries implement controls in the first place so that they would have controls to liberalize? Second, in order for the liberalization of controls to be effective, wouldn't it be assumed that capital controls have been effective? Otherwise, how could the liberalization of ineffective capital controls be effective? This is followed by another question: If capital controls have been effective, why liberalize the effective controls? The answers to these questions seem to point in the same direction. That is, in order for liberalization of controls to be effective, capital controls must be effective in the first place. Therefore, this chapter will focus on the impacts of capital controls and their effectiveness.

The theoretical framework and the results

As shown, the empirical results of capital controls are mixed. Some results are sensitive to the adopted datasets and/or the methodologies. Moreover, the definitions and measurements of capital accounts and flows may be different across datasets, countries and the periods of time. Without consistent definitions and measurements, the debates over the mixed empirical results of capital controls are similar to comparing apples to oranges. It is challenging to reach an agreement and to understand the true impacts of capital controls and the causes which lead to various results in different countries in different periods of time. The inadequate datasets have led Fernandez et al (2015) to create a new dataset with asset categories of 100 countries and a longer period during 1995–2003. However, the problems of inconsistent definitions and measurements of capital account–related variables remain for the countries, the periods and the assets not covered in the new dataset. This is why Magud and Reinhart (2007) suggest that it is crucial to have a unified theoretical analysis to study capital controls. It is the goal of this chapter to develop a theoretical framework which incorporates the features of capital flows and controls to analyse the effects of capital controls and their effectiveness. Through the theoretical analysis, we may find the factors which have been neglected and identify the causes which lead to inconsistent results in empirical studies.

The theoretical framework extends the model of Chapters 3 to 5 with a DSF banking system to analyse the impacts of symmetric and asymmetric controls on the home and the host countries. The effectiveness of capital controls would be evaluated on whether the controls have achieved the goals of (1) the volumes and the compositions of flows and (2) the decrease in the possibility of bank runs, both type I and type II bank runs, as defined in Chapters 4 and 5.

As a result, it is found that the inflow controls would be effective for the country which implements controls (country X) and would have negative impacts on the other country (country Y) by increasing the possibility of type I bank runs in country Y. Meanwhile, outflow controls would be ineffective for the country which implements the controls (country X) by increasing the possibility of type I bank runs but would benefit the other country (country Y) by decreasing the possibility of type I bank runs in country Y. Therefore, depending on the direction of capital flows of the countries in a pair, the countries would be benefitted or damaged by the controls implemented in the home and/or the partner country.

The rest of the chapter is organized as follows. The second section describes the environment of the theoretical framework, while the third section discusses the results of the basic framework, including the directions of flows. The fourth section analyses the results of capital controls in different cases. A conclusion will be provided in the fifth section.

The theoretical framework

The theoretical framework is based on Chang (2013b) and extends the models of Chapters 2 to 5 in a DSF banking system, which has a lower probability of bank runs than BSF and DSL banking systems in an open economy. The benchmark framework is when both countries are opened to capital flows. To analyse capital controls of either or both directions, it is assumed that the home and the foreign countries can be either the source or the destination country of capital flows, depending on the return rate to the SR accounts.[4] This is because the SR flows have been found to have stronger connections to financial stability compared to LR FDI flows, as mentioned in Chapters 3 and 4. The volumes of capital flows would depend on the relative interest rates and the risk premiums of foreign investment, the so-called home bias. In response to the volumes of capital flows, the countries would implement capital controls to manage either inflows or outflows or both. Depending on the related capital controls of the other country, the impacts of controls on one country could be different.

Agents

Without the access to asset investment, the agents would deposit their income in the banks when young. At middle age, each agent would learn his/her own type. The type of each agent is assumed to be exogenously determined and is private information to the agent only, while the distribution of the types is public information. To simplify the model, it is assumed that there are two types of agents: investors with a probability $(1 - \pi)$ and entrepreneurs with a probability π. Both types are assumed to value only old consumption. So the utility function of an agent would be in the form of:

$$u\left(c_{3,t+2}\right) = -\frac{\left(c_{3,t+2}\right)^{-\gamma}}{\gamma}. \tag{6.1}$$

In a DSF system, two types of accounts are offered to the depositors: SR and LR accounts. The SR accounts would take one period to mature and are offered a return rate $\left(1+i_t^D\right)$ at maturity, while the LR accounts would take two periods to mature and are offered a return rate $\left(1+i_t^{LRD}\right)$ at maturity, but the return rate would reduce to $\left(1+i_t^{EL}\right)$ for premature liquidation, where $\left(1+i_t^{EL}\right) < \left(1+i_t^D\right)$ and $\left(1+i_t^D\right)^2 < \left(1+i_t^{LRD}\right)$. Based on the offered return rates, the depositors would allocate their income between the SR and LR accounts. Let ρ_t^s denote the fraction of income placed into the SR accounts and $\left(1-\rho_t^s\right)$ denote the fraction of income placed into the LR accounts. Accordingly, a middle-aged agent in period $t+1$ would expect to receive the returns of the matured SR accounts:

$$W_{t+1}^M \equiv \left(1+i_t^D\right)\rho_t^s w_t. \tag{6.2}$$

After receiving W_{t+1}^M, the entrepreneurs would reinvest W_{t+1}^M in the SR accounts of their home banks; the investors, however, would liquidate all their LR accounts and re-invest in the SR accounts of a country of their choice.

Entrepreneurs and production

In period $t + 2$, the old entrepreneurs would obtain capital goods from their matured LR accounts for production. To start production, the entrepreneurs must also borrow $b_{t+2} = w_{t+2}L_{t+2}$ in the beginning of the period to pay for wage income. The production would be completed in the end of the period. After the completion of production, the entrepreneurs would repay the loan and obtain capital gains $KG_{t+2} = \max_{L_{t+2}}\left\{A_{t+2}\bar{k}_{t+2}^{\delta}k_{t+2}^{\theta}L_{t+2}^{1-\theta} - \left(1+i_{t+2}^{loan}\right)b_{t+2}\right\}$, which would give the rate of return of capital $ROR(k_{t+2})$:

$$ROR\left(k_{t+2}\right) = \frac{\left[A_{t+2}\bar{k}_{t+2}^{\delta}k_{t+2}^{\theta}L_{t+2}^{1-\theta} - \left(1+i_{t+2}^{loan}\right)b_{t+2}\right]}{k_{t+2}}. \tag{6.3}$$

It requires $ROR(k_{t+2})$ to be sufficiently high to satisfy the incentive constraint for the entrepreneurs to produce in order to prevent type II bank runs. More details will be analysed in the next section(s).

Investors

Different from the entrepreneurs, the investors do not have the skills to operate production. It is assumed that it is costly for the agents of all types to convert capital goods into output goods if not using capital goods for production. The conversion cost is assumed to be sufficiently high so that the agents would liquidate their LR accounts prematurely as soon as learning that they would not start production. For the investors, the capital goods from the matured LR accounts would not be useful. So the investors would liquidate their LR accounts after learning their types. Therefore, the investors would liquidate all of their LR accounts after learning their types and gather information to decide in which country to invest their wealth. It is assumed that the transaction cost to invest in one country is constant. The constant transaction cost means that the more the investment is, the higher the rate of return would be since the transaction cost is decreasing in the amount of investment. So the investors would prefer selecting one country in which to invest their wealth rather than diversifying the investment between two countries.

After liquidating the LR accounts, a middle-aged investor would have the amount I_{t+1} in period $t+1$ to reinvest, where

$$I_{t+1} = W_{t+1}^{M} + \left(1 + i_t^{EL}\right)\left(1 - \rho_t^{s}\right) w_t. \tag{6.4}$$

The investment targets of the investors would be the SR accounts. In period $t+1$, the return rate of home SR accounts would be $\left(1 + i_{t+1}^{D}\right)$, while the return rate of foreign SR accounts would be $(1 + i_{t+1}^{D*})$. Due to asymmetric information, the investors would know better the economic conditions of their home countries than that of the foreign country. Therefore, it would require a risk premium for the home investors to invest in the foreign country and vice versa. This is the so-called home bias. Let ξ_t^{H} denote the risk premium for the home investors to invest in the foreign SR accounts, and let ξ_t^{H} denote the risk premium of the foreign investors to invest in the home SR accounts. At $\left(1 + i_{t+1}^{D*}\right) = \left(1 + i_{t+1}^{D}\right) + \xi_t^{H}$, the home investors would be indifferent in investing in either the home or the foreign country. It is assumed that the indifference would have a fraction ψ_{t+1} of home investors invest in the home SR accounts, while a fraction $(1 - \psi_{t+1})$ of home investors would invest in the foreign SR accounts. Accordingly, a home investor's wealth in period $t+2$ would be:

$$W_{t+2}^{M} = \begin{cases} \left(1 + i_{t+1}^{D}\right) I_{t+1}, \text{at} \left(1 + i_{t+1}^{D*}\right) \leq \left(1 + i_{t+1}^{D}\right) + \xi_t^{H} \\ \left(1 + i_{t+1}^{D*}\right) I_{t+1}, \text{at} \left(1 + i_{t+1}^{D*}\right) \geq \left(1 + i_{t+1}^{D}\right) + \xi_t^{H} \end{cases}. \tag{6.5}$$

The banks and capital flows

In a DSF banking system, the depositors would choose their portfolios, and the banks would invest and liquidate as requested while earning the banks' profits which are from the margins of the accounts.[5] The margins of the accounts are as follows. For the SR investment, the return rate of loans at maturity would be $\left(1+i_t^{loan}\right)$, while the return rate to the matured SR accounts would be $\left(1+i_t^{D}\right)$. For the LR investment, the return rate received by the banks from the LR assets at maturity would be R, while the return rate offered by the banks to the matured LR accounts would be $\left(1+i_{t+1}^{LRD}\right)$. The return rate received by the banks from the premature liquidation of the LR assets would be χ, while the return rate offered by the banks to the premature liquidation of LR accounts would be $\left(1+i_t^{EL}\right)$. Therefore, the marginal rates earned by the banks would be $\left[\left(1+i_t^{loan}\right)-\left(1+i_t^{D}\right)\right]$ for matured SR accounts, $\left[\mathrm{R}-\left(1+i_{t+1}^{LRD}\right)\right]$ for matured LR accounts and $\left[\chi-\left(1+i_t^{EL}\right)\right]$ for the premature liquidation of LR accounts. Based on the distribution of the types of agents, the banks would invest a fraction $(1-\pi)$ of LR accounts in the loans to prepare for the investors' premature liquidation. The preparation for the investors' premature liquidation would earn the banks an extra marginal rate: $\left[\left(1+i_t^{loan}\right)-\left(1+i_t^{EL}\right)\right]$, where $\left[\left(1+i_t^{loan}\right)-\left(1+i_t^{EL}\right)\right]>\left[\left(1+i_t^{loan}\right)-\left(1+i_t^{D}\right)\right]$.

Since the investors would choose one country's SR accounts to reinvest, the banks would have extra new SR accounts of the middle-aged investors. These new SR accounts are additional to the new SR accounts of the young and the middle-aged entrepreneurs. Depending on the return rates of the SR accounts in the home and the foreign countries, a fraction $\left(\alpha_t^H\right)$ of home investors would invest in the homeland, where $\alpha_t^H\in\left[0,\psi_t,1\right]$, and so do the foreign investors. When home banks have new SR accounts of the foreign investors, the home country has capital inflows. Let $CI_t^H\left(CO_t^H\right)$ denote the capital inflows (outflows) of the home country, and let $\alpha_t^F\in\left[0,\psi_t^*,1\right]$ denote the fraction of foreign investors reinvesting in the foreign country. One can write that the amount of capital inflows (outflows) to (from) the home country in period t would be:

$$\begin{aligned}CI_t^H&=\left(1-\alpha_t^F\right)I_t^*\left(1+n^*\right),\\CO_t^H&=\left(1-\alpha_t^H\right)I_t\left(1+n\right).\end{aligned}\tag{6.6}$$

Accordingly, the banks' profits in the following period would be:

$$\begin{aligned}\Pi_{t+1}^B=&\left[\left(1+i_t^{loan}\right)-\left(1+i_t^{D}\right)\right]\left[\rho_t^s w_t\left(1+n\right)^2+\left(1+n\right)\pi W_t^M+CI_t^H+\alpha_t^H I_t\left(1+n\right)\right]\\&+\left[\mathrm{R}-\left(1+i_{t+1}^{LRD}\right)\right]\left(1-\rho_{t-1}^s\right)w_{t-1}\left(\pi\right)\left(1+n\right)\\&+\left[\left(1+i_t^{loan}\right)-\left(1+i_t^{EL}\right)\right]\left(1-\pi\right)\left(1-\rho_t^s\right)w_t,\end{aligned}\tag{6.7}$$

where the first term is the earnings from the matured SR accounts, the second term from the matured LR accounts and the third term from the premature liquidation of the LR accounts by the investors. The banks' budget constraints for SR and LR accounts would be:

$$\begin{aligned}
&\left(1+i_t^{loan}\right)\pi b_t \\
&\qquad \geq \left(1+i_t^D\right)\left[\rho_t^s w_t (1+n)^2 + \pi(1+n)W_t^M + CI_t^H + \alpha_t^H I_t (1+n)\right] \\
&\qquad + \left(1+i_t^{EL}\right)(1+n)^2(1-\pi)\left(1-\rho_t^s\right)w_t, \\
&R\pi\left(1-\rho_{t-1}^s\right)w_{t-1}(1+n) \geq \left(1+i_{t-1}^{LRD}\right)\left(1-\rho_{t-1}^s\right)w_{t-1}\pi(1+n).
\end{aligned} \tag{6.8}$$

The loan market

The reinvestment of both the home and the foreign investors would change the home loan supply (LS_t^H) and the home loan demand (LD_t^H) to:

$$\begin{aligned}
LS_t^H &= \rho_t^s w_t (1+n)^2 + \pi(1+n)W_t^M + CI_t^H + \alpha_t^H I_t (1+n) \\
&\quad + (1+n)^2(1-\pi)\left(1-\rho_t^s\right)w_t\ . \\
LD_t^H &= \pi b_t,
\end{aligned} \tag{6.9}$$

which would give the loan rate:

$$\left(1+i_t^{loan}\right) = \frac{\pi b_t}{\left\{\begin{matrix}\rho_t^s w_t (1+n)^2 + \pi(1+n)W_t^M \\ +CI_t^H + \alpha_t^H I_t(1+n) + (1+n)^2(1-\pi)\left(1-\rho_t^s\right)w_t\end{matrix}\right\}}. \tag{6.10}$$

Both equations (6.9) and (6.10) show that there is no credit rationing, regardless of whether it is type I or type II.[6] The endogenously determined $\left(1+i_t^{loan}\right)$ would adjust to the relative changes of the loan demand and the loan supply.

Given $\left(1+i_t^{loan}\right)$ [equation (6.10)], it would require $\left(1+i_t^D\right)$ to be sufficiently small to satisfy the budget constraint of the SR accounts [equation (6.8)]:

$$\begin{aligned}
\left(1+i_t^D\right) &\leq \frac{\left(1+i_t^{loan}\right)^2 LS_t^H - \left(1+i_t^{EL}\right)(1+n)^2(1-\pi)\left(1-\rho_t^s\right)w_t}{\left[\rho_t^s w_t (1+n)^2 + \pi(1+n)W_t^M + CI_t^H + \alpha_t^H I_t(1+n)\right]} \\
&\equiv \overline{\left(1+i_t^D\right)}.
\end{aligned} \tag{6.11}$$

At $\left(1+i_t^D\right) > \overline{\left(1+i_t^D\right)}$, the budget constraint of SR accounts fails, and type I bank runs would occur, similar to what has been analysed in Chapters 4 and 5.

The results

In this section, the results of the benchmark will be derived for both the home and the foreign countries without controls. The cases with controls will be analysed in

Table 6.1 The countries in which the investors would invest

Case	Relative rates and risk premium	Home	Foreign
A	$\left(1+i_t^{D*}\right) = \left(1+i_t^{D}\right) + \xi_t^{H}$	H,F (net outflows)	F
B	$\left(1+i_t^{D}\right) = \left(1+i_t^{D*}\right) + \xi_t^{F}$	H (net inflows)	H,F
C	$\left(1+i_t^{D*}\right) > \left(1+i_t^{D}\right) + \xi_t^{H}$	F (net outflows)	F
D	$\left(1+i_t^{D}\right) > \left(1+i_t^{D*}\right) + \xi_t^{F}$	H (net inflows)	H
E	$\left(1+i_t^{D}\right) \leq \left(1+i_t^{D*}\right) < \left(1+i_t^{D}\right) + \xi_t^{H}$	H (no flow)	F
F	$\left(1+i_t^{D*}\right) \leq \left(1+i_t^{D}\right) < \left(1+i_t^{D*}\right) + \xi_t^{F}$	H (no flow)	F

the next section. Given labour demand and labour supply, the equilibrium labour per entrepreneur would be:

$$L_{t+2} = k_{t+2}\left[\frac{(1-\theta)A_{t+2}\bar{k}_{t+2}^{\delta}}{\left(1+i_{t+2}^{loan}\right)w_{t+2}}\right]^{1/\theta}. \tag{6.12}$$

Under full employment, the equilibrium wage income would be:

$$w_{t+2} = \left(\frac{\pi}{\left(1+n\right)^{2}}\right)^{\theta}\frac{(1-\theta)A_{t+2}\bar{k}_{t+2}^{\delta}k_{t+2}^{\theta}}{\left(1+i_{t+2}^{loan}\right)}. \tag{6.13}$$

So the rate of return of capital in a general form would be:

$$ROR\left(k_{t+2}\right) = A_{t+2}\bar{k}_{t+2}^{\delta}k_{t+2}^{\theta-1}\left[\frac{\left(1+n\right)^{2}}{\pi}\right]^{1-\theta}\left[1-\left(\frac{1+i_{t+2}^{loan}}{1+i_{t+1}^{loan}}\right)(1-\theta)\right], \tag{6.14}$$

where $ROR(k_{t+2})$ must be sufficiently high to satisfy the incentive constraint: $ROR\left(k_{t+2}\right)\rho_t^{L}\left(1+i_t^{LRD}\right) \geq \left(1+i_t^{D}\right)\rho_t^{i}$ and to prevent type II bank runs.

Depending on the home and the foreign return rates of the SR accounts and the risk premiums, the investors would decide the country in which to reinvest their wealth, as shown in Table 6.1.

In cases A and C, the home country would have net capital outflows, while in cases B and D, the home country would have net capital inflows. In cases E and F, there would be no capital inflow or outflow between the home and the foreign countries due to home bias.

As shown in Table 6.1, the volumes of capital inflows to the home country in case D is higher than in case B, $CI_t^{H,D} > CI_t^{H,B}$. The volume of capital outflows from the home country in case C is higher than in case A, $CO_t^{H,C} > CO_t^{H,A}$. Based on equation (6.9), the loan supply of the home country can be ranked as:

$$LS_t^{H}: D > B > E = F > A > C. \tag{6.15}$$

According to equation (6.11), $\left(1+i_t^{loan}\right)$ can be ranked as:

$$\left(1+i_t^{loan}\right): D < B < E = F < A < C. \tag{6.16}$$

According to equation (6.10), $\left(1+i_t^{loan}\right)$ is endogenously determined by the loan demand and the loan supply, which would depend on $\left(1+i_t^{D}\right)$. So $\left(1+i_t^{D}\right)$ would be determined prior to $\left(1+i_t^{loan}\right)$ and would determine the volumes and the compositions of capital flows. The composition of flows is defined as the proportion of SR flows to LR flows. The flows in this model are for SR assets and would be classified as SR flows. Therefore, given LR flows, the change of SR flows would affect the composition of flows.

At $\left(1+i_t^{D}\right) \geq \left(1+i_t^{D*}\right)+\xi_t^F$ *(Net inflows to home: Cases B and D)*

The loan rate would be

$$\left(1+i_t^{loan,i}\right)=\frac{\pi b_t}{\left\{\begin{array}{c}\rho_t^s w_t(1+n)^2+\pi(1+n)W_t^M \\ +CI_t^H\big|_{\alpha_t^F}+\alpha_t^H I_t(1+n)+(1+n)^2(1-\pi)\left(1-\rho_t^s\right)w_t\end{array}\right\}},$$

where $i = D$, B and $\alpha_t^H = 1$, $\alpha_t^F = \begin{cases} 0, & i = D \\ \psi_t^*, & i = B \end{cases}$,

where $\left(1+i_t^{loan,D}\right)<\left(1+i_t^{loan,B}\right)<\left(1+i_t^{loan,E/F}\right)$. A lower $\left(1+i_t^{loan}\right)$, compared to cases E and F, would give a higher $ROR\left(k_t^H\right)$ [equation (6.14)] and would be more likely to satisfy the incentive constraint for the entrepreneurs to produce.

The next step is to check whether the budget constraints hold. Based on equation (6.11), at $\left(1+i_t^{D}\right) \leq \overline{\left(1+i_t^{D,D}\right)} \leq \overline{\left(1+i_t^{D,B}\right)}$, the budget constraints are satisfied, and there would be no bank run in both cases B and D. At $\overline{\left(1+i_t^{D,D}\right)} < \left(1+i_t^{D}\right) < \overline{\left(1+i_t^{D,B}\right)}$, there would be type I bank runs in case D but not in case B. At $\left(1+i_t^{D}\right) > \overline{\left(1+i_t^{D,B}\right)}$, the budget constraints for SR accounts fail, and there would be type I bank runs in cases B and D.[7] In other words, bank runs are more likely to occur in the home country in case D, where there are more capital inflows to the home country than in case B.

At $\left(1+i_t^{D*}\right) \geq \left(1+i_t^{D}\right)+\xi_t^H$ *(Net outflows from home: Cases A and C)*

The loan rate would be:

$$\left(1+i_t^{loan,i}\right)=\frac{\pi b_t}{\left\{\begin{array}{c}\rho_t^s w_t(1+n)^2+\pi(1+n)W_t^M \\ +\alpha_t^H I_t(1+n)+(1+n)^2(1-\pi)\left(1-\rho_t^s\right)w_t\end{array}\right\}},$$

where $i = A, C$, and $\alpha_t^H = \begin{cases} 0, & i = C \\ \psi_t, & i = A \end{cases}$,

where $(1+i_t^{loan,C}) > (1+i_t^{loan,A}) > (1+i_t^{loan,E/F})$ due to the lower loan supply. The higher $(1+i_t^{loan})$ would reduce $ROR(k_t^H)$ and make it more difficult to satisfy the incentive constraint. To satisfy the incentive constraint would require a sufficiently low $(1+i_t^{loan})$:

$$(1+i_t^{loan}) \le \widehat{(1+i_t^{loan})}, \tag{6.17}$$

where $\widehat{(1+i_t^{loan})}$: *such that* $ROR(\widehat{k_t^H})(1+i_{t-2}^{LRD})\rho_{t-2}^L = (1+i_{t-2}^D)\rho_{t-2}^S$.

At $(1+i_t^{loan}) > \widehat{(1+i_t^{loan})}$, the incentive constraint fails, and no entrepreneur would demand loans. Without loan demand, there would be no loan repayment for the banks to pay for the SR accounts. So both type I and type II bank runs would be inevitable in the home country. When expecting the failure of the incentive constraint, the entrepreneurs would join the investors to invest in the SR assets of either country and would speed up home bank runs.

At $(1+i_t^{loan}) \le \widehat{(1+i_t^{loan})}$, there would be no type II bank run. However, whether to have type I bank runs would depend on $(1+i_t^D)$. At $(1+i_t^D) \le \overline{(1+i_t^{D,A})} \le \overline{(1+i_t^{D,C})}$, the budget constraints are satisfied, and there would be no type I bank run in both cases A and C. At $\overline{(1+i_t^{D,A})} < (1+i_t^D) < \overline{(1+i_t^{D,C})}$, type I bank runs would occur in case A but not in case C. At $(1+i_t^D) > \overline{(1+i_t^{D,C})}$, type I bank runs would occur in both cases A and C. In other words, case A, in which there is less capital outflow, would be more likely to experience type I bank runs in the home country than case C.

At $\boldsymbol{(1+i_t^D) \le (1+i_t^{D*}) < (1+i_t^D) + \xi_t^H}$ ***&*** $\boldsymbol{(1+i_t^{D*}) \le (1+i_t^D) < (1+i_t^{D*}) + \xi_t^F}$ ***(No flow between home and foreign: Cases E & F)***

The loan rate would be:

$$(1+i_t^{loan,i}) = \frac{\pi b_t}{\left\{\begin{array}{l} \rho_t^S w_t(1+n)^2 + \pi(1+n)W_t^M \\ +\alpha_t^H I_t(1+n) + (1+n)^2(1-\pi)(1-\rho_t^S)w_t \end{array}\right\}}, \quad \textit{where } \alpha_t^H = 1,\ i = E, F$$

Without capital flows, $(1+i_t^{loan,E}) = (1+i_t^{loan,F})$ would be similar to that in a closed economy. The higher risk premiums of both countries (ξ_t^H and ξ_t^F) imply that the flows between the home and the foreign countries are less likely to occur. Capital controls implemented in both cases E and F would tend to be ineffective. The volumes of capital flows and the possibilities of all cases are summarized in Table 6.2.

Table 6.2 Equilibrium capital flows and the possibility of bank runs

Case	*Home capital flows*	*Home bank runs*	*Foreign capital flows*	*Foreign bank runs*
A	$CO_t^H\|_{\alpha_t^H=\psi_t} = (1-\alpha_t^H)I_t(1+n)$	Type I & II runs	$CI_t^F = CO_t^H\|_{\alpha_t^H=\psi_t}$	Type I runs
B	$CI_t^H\|_{\alpha_t^F=\psi_t^*} = (1-\alpha_t^F)I_t^*(1+n^*)$	Type I runs	$CO_t^F = CI_t^H\|_{\alpha_t^F=\psi_t^*}$	Type I & II runs
C	$CO_t^H\|_{\alpha_t^H=0} = (1-\alpha_t^H)I_t(1+n)$	Type I & II runs	$CI_t^F = CO_t^H\|_{\alpha_t^H=0}$	Type I runs
D	$CI_t^H\|_{\alpha_t^F=0} = (1-\alpha_t^F)I_t^*(1+n^*)$	Type I runs	$CO_t^F = CI_t^H\|_{\alpha_t^F=0}$	Type I & II runs
E	–	–	–	–
F	–	–	–	–

Capital controls

Capital controls can be implemented in both the home and the foreign countries and could affect the capital flows of both countries, depending on the types of controls being implemented. This section would analyse the impacts of capital controls and their effectiveness. The effectiveness would be evaluated based on whether the controls have achieved the following goals: (1) affecting the volumes and the composition of capital flows and (2) reducing the possibility of bank runs and hence banking crises.

Controls on capital inflows

Taking the home country as an example, depending on the level of controls to be implemented, the volumes and the composition of capital inflows in both cases B and D might be affected, regardless of the controls of the foreign country. The inflow controls of the home country might affect the outflows of the foreign country. Similarly, the inflow controls of the foreign country could affect the inflows to the foreign country in both cases A and C, in which the outflows from the home country could be affected. Therefore, inflow controls could affect the capital flows between the two countries in cases A, B, C and D.

It is assumed that controls on inflows would be to set an upper limit for capital inflows $\left(\overline{1-\alpha_t^{F,CI}}\right)$, where $\left(\overline{1-\alpha_t^{F,CI}}\right) < (1-\psi_t^*)$, implying that the volumes of capital inflows in both cases B and D would be reduce to:

$$\overline{CI_t^{H,CI}} = \left(\overline{1-\alpha_t^F}\right) I_t^* \left(1+n^*\right), \tag{6.18}$$

where $\widetilde{CI_t^{H,CI}} < CI_t^{H,B}|_{\alpha_t^F=\psi_t} < CI_t^{H,D}|_{\alpha_t^F=0}$. Since the capital flows are SR flows, given LR flows, a decrease in SR flows would reduce the ratio of the SR to LR flow, which is defined as the composition of flows.

A lower volume of capital inflows would reduce the loan supply and increase the home loan rate to:

$$\widetilde{\left(1+i_t^{loan,CI}\right)} = \frac{\pi b_t}{\left[\begin{array}{c}\rho_t^s w_t (1+n)^2 + \pi(1+n) W_t^M \\ +\widetilde{CI_t^{H,CI}} + I_t(1+n) + (1+n)^2(1-\pi)(1-\rho_t^s) w_t\end{array}\right]}, \tag{6.19}$$

where $\widetilde{\left(1+i_t^{loan,CI}\right)} > \left(1+i_t^{loan,B}\right) > \left(1+i_t^{loan,D}\right)$. The higher $\widetilde{\left(1+i_t^{loan,CI}\right)}$ would reduce $ROR\left(\widetilde{k_t^{H,CI}}\right)$ and tighten the incentive constraint for the entrepreneurs to produce. However, the positive capital inflows $\widetilde{CI_t^H} > 0$ imply $\widetilde{\left(1+i_t^{loan,CI}\right)} < \left(1+i_t^{loan,E}\right) = \left(1+i_t^{loan,F}\right)$. So the incentive constraint would still hold and would not affect the possibility of type II bank runs. A higher $\left(1+i_t^{loan,CI}\right)$ would give a higher $\left(1+i_t^D\right)$. Therefore, it would be easier to satisfy the budget constraints and reduce the possibility of type I bank runs. So the inflow controls of the home country would reduce the volume and the composition of capital inflows and would reduce the possibility of type I bank runs while not affecting the possibility of type II bank runs. Therefore, the inflow controls of the home country can be concluded as semi-effective in both cases B and D.

Asymmetric controls: home inflows versus foreign no control (AHIFN)

When the foreign country has no control, the volumes of outflows from the foreign country would be as set by the home inflow controls, $\widetilde{CO_t^F} = \widetilde{CI_t^{H,CI}}$ [equation (6.18)] in cases B and D. The effects on the home country would be as described earlier. As for the foreign country in the two-country model, lower outflows would increase the loan supply in the foreign country and decrease $\left(1+i_t^{loan*}\right)$. The lower $\left(1+i_t^{loan*}\right)$ would increase $ROR\left(k_t^{F*}\right)$, which would make it easier to satisfy the incentive constraint and reduce the possibility of type II bank runs in the foreign country. The lower $\widetilde{\left(1+i_t^{loan*}\right)}$, however, would decrease $\widetilde{\left(1+i_t^{D*}\right)}$, which would tighten the budget constraints, $\left(1+i_t^D\right) \leq \widetilde{\left(1+i_t^{D*}\right)}$, and increase the possibility of type I bank runs in the foreign country. Therefore, in cases B and D, although having no capital control, the foreign country would be affected by the home inflow controls. The effects of the home inflow controls on the foreign country are both positive and negative.

Symmetric controls: home inflows versus foreign inflows (SHIFI)

The symmetric inflow controls of the home and the foreign countries would affect the capital flows between the two countries in cases A, B, C and D. Since cases B and D have been analysed already, this subsection would focus on cases A and C.

The inflow controls of the foreign country would affect the volumes and composition of capital flows of the foreign country in cases A and C. The inflow controls of the foreign country set an upper limit for capital inflows $\overbrace{(1-\alpha_t^{H,CI})} < (1-\psi_t)$ and would reduce the volumes of inflows to the foreign country to:

$$\overbrace{CI_t^{F,CI}} = \overbrace{(1-\alpha_t^{H,CI})} I_t(1+n). \tag{6.20}$$

A lower volume of inflows would reduce the ratio of SR to LR flows, the composition of inflows. The lower capital inflows would increase $\overbrace{(1+i_t^{loan*,CI})} > (1+i_t^{loan*,A}) > (1+i_t^{loan*,C})$. However, a higher $\overbrace{(1+i_t^{loan*,CI})}$ would reduce $ROR\left(\overbrace{k_t^F}\right)$. The positive $\overbrace{CI_t^{F,CI}} > 0$ implies that $\overbrace{(1+i_t^{loan*,CI})} < (1+i_t^{loan*,E/F})$ and would not affect the possibility of type II bank runs. Meanwhile, the higher $\overbrace{(1+i_t^{loan*,CI})}$ would loosen the SR budget constraint $(1+i_t^{D*}) \leq \overbrace{(1+i_t^{loan*,CI})}^{2}$ and hence reduce the possibility of type I bank runs in cases A and C in the foreign country.

Similarly, in cases A and C, the lower outflows from the home country would be due to the inflow controls of the foreign country and would increase the loan supply in the home country and hence decrease the home loan rate $\overbrace{(1+i_t^{loan})} < (1+i_t^{loan,A}) < (1+i_t^{loan,C})$. The lower $\overbrace{(1+i_t^{loan})}$ would increase $ROR\left(\overbrace{k_t^H}\right)$ and make it easier to satisfy the incentive constraint for the entrepreneurs to produce and decrease the possibility of type II bank runs. Meanwhile, the lower $\overbrace{(1+i_t^{loan})}$ would tighten the budget constraints and increase the possibility of type I bank runs in the home country. This is to show that in cases A and C, capital flows of the home country would be affected by the inflow controls of the foreign country, not the home country.

When inflow controls are implemented by both the home and the foreign countries, capital flows between the two countries would be affected in cases A, B, C and D. Moreover, the stability of the banking system of both countries would be affected, either actively by the inflow controls of the home country or passively by the inflow controls of the foreign country, and vice versa.

Asymmetric controls: home inflows versus foreign outflows (AHIFO)

The outflow controls of the foreign country would affect the volumes and the compositions of capital outflows in cases B and D. The outflow controls would be to set an upper limit $\overbrace{(1-\alpha_t^F)} < (1-\psi_t^*)$ on outflows and would reduce the volumes of outflows to:

$$\overbrace{CO_t^F} = \overbrace{(1-\alpha_t^F)} I_t^*(1+n^*), \tag{6.21}$$

$$\overbrace{CI_t^H} = \overbrace{(1-\alpha_t^F)}I_t^*(1+n^*), \tag{6.22}$$

where $\overbrace{CO_t^F} < CO_t^{F,B} < CO_t^{F,D}$. The decrease in SR flows would reduce the ratio of SR to LR flows, the composition of outflows from the foreign country.

The decrease in outflows would increase the loan supply in the foreign country and change the loan rate to $\overbrace{\left(1+i_t^{loan*,CO}\right)}$:

$$\overbrace{\left(1+i_t^{loan*,CO}\right)} = \frac{\pi^* b_t^*}{\left\{\begin{array}{c} \rho_t^{s*} w_t^* \left(1+n^*\right)^2 + \pi^*\left(1+n^*\right)W_t^{M*} \\ + \overbrace{\alpha_t^F} I_t^*\left(1+n^*\right) + \left(1+n^*\right)^2\left(1-\pi^*\right)\left(1-\rho_t^{s*}\right)w_t^* \end{array}\right\}}, \tag{6.23}$$

where $\overbrace{\left(1+i_t^{loan*,CO}\right)} < \left(1+i_t^{loan*,B}\right) < \left(1+i_t^{loan*,D}\right)$. The lower $\overbrace{\left(1+i_t^{loan*,CO}\right)}$ would increase $ROR\left(\mathrm{k}_t^{F*,CO}\right)$ and make it easier to satisfy the incentive constraint and hence decrease the possibility of type II bank runs in the foreign country.

The lower $\overbrace{\left(1+i_t^{loan*,CO}\right)}$, however, would tighten the SR budget constraint. At $\left(1+i_t^{D*}\right) \le \overbrace{\left(1+i_t^{D*,CO}\right)}$, the budget constraint would be satisfied, and it would not affect the possibility of type I bank runs in the foreign country in cases B and D. At $\overbrace{\left(1+i_t^{D*,CO}\right)} < \left(1+i_t^{D*}\right) \le \overline{\left(1+i_t^{D*,B}\right)}$, the outflow controls would cause type I bank runs, which would not occur in cases B and D. At $\overbrace{\left(1+i_t^{D*,CO}\right)} < \overline{\left(1+i_t^{D*,B}\right)} < \left(1+i_t^{D*}\right) \le \overline{\left(1+i_t^{D*,D}\right)}$, the foreign outflow controls would cause type I bank runs, which would also occur in case B but not in case D. At $\overbrace{\left(1+i_t^{D*,CO}\right)} < \overline{\left(1+i_t^{D*,B}\right)} < \overline{\left(1+i_t^{D*,D}\right)} < \left(1+i_t^{D*}\right)$, type I bank runs, which occur in cases B and D, would still occur. The foreign outflow controls fail to reduce the possibility of type I bank runs in both cases B and D for the foreign country. Overall, in both cases B and D, although the outflow controls would reduce type II bank runs, they would increase the possibility of type I bank runs for the foreign country. Therefore, the effectiveness of the controls on outflows would be limited.

Combining the controls of both countries, the actual effects on the flows in cases B and D would depend on the relative levels of the controls. When home inflow controls $\widetilde{\left(1-\alpha_t^F\right)}$ are the same as foreign outflow controls $\overbrace{\left(1-\alpha_t^F\right)}$, $\widetilde{\left(1-\alpha_t^F\right)} = \overbrace{\left(1-\alpha_t^F\right)}$, the results would be the same as what has been analysed previously.

At $\widetilde{\left(1-\alpha_t^F\right)} > \overbrace{\left(1-\alpha_t^F\right)}$, the stricter foreign outflow controls would have stronger effects than the home inflow controls. The capital inflows to the home country would be lower than expected: $\widehat{CI_t^H} = \overbrace{\left(1-\alpha_t^F\right)} I_t^*(1+\mathrm{n}^*) < \widetilde{CI_t^H}$. The lower capital flows means a lower loan supply, which would increase $\overline{\left(1+i_t^{loan,CI}\right)} > \left(1+i_t^{loan,CI}\right)$. The positive capital inflows, $\widehat{CI_t^H} > 0$ give $\overline{\left(1+i_t^{loan,CI}\right)} < \left(1+i_t^{loan,E/F}\right)$, implying that the higher $\overline{\left(1+i_t^{loan,CI}\right)}$ would still be manageable and would satisfy the incentive constraint for the entrepreneurs to produce. Therefore, the possibility of type II bank runs would not be affected. Meanwhile, the higher $\overline{\left(1+i_t^{loan,CI}\right)}$ would loosen the SR budget constraint $\left(1+i_t^D\right) \leq \overline{\left(1+i_t^{D,CI}\right)}$ and reduce the possibility of type I bank runs in the home country even further compared to the case with home inflow controls alone.

At $\overline{\left(1-\alpha_t^F\right)} < \overbrace{\left(1-\alpha_t^F\right)}$, the home inflow controls would be stricter than the foreign outflow controls. The foreign country would have capital outflows lower than expected: $\check{CO}_t^F = \overline{\left(1-\alpha_t^F\right)} I_t^*\left(1+n^*\right) < \overbrace{CO_t^F}$ [equation (6.21)]. The lower capital outflows would increase the loan supply in the foreign country and would reduce $\left(1+\check{i}_t^{loan^*,CO}\right)$ further, $\left(1+\check{i}_t^{loan^*,CO}\right) < \overbrace{\left(1+i_t^{loan^*,CO}\right)}$. The lower loan rate would increase $ROR\left(\check{k}_t^{F^*,CO}\right)$, which would make it easier to satisfy the incentive constraint and reduce the possibility of type II bank runs further. The lower $\left(1+\check{i}_t^{loan^*,CO}\right)$, however, would tighten the SR budget constraint, $\left(1+i_t^{D^*}\right) \leq \left(1+\check{i}_t^{D^*,CO}\right)$, and increase the possibility of type I bank runs further in the foreign country.

Controls on capital outflows

The home outflow controls would directly affect the volumes of outflows from the home country in cases A and C, while the foreign outflow controls would directly affect the outflows from the foreign country in cases B and D.

Take the home country's outflow control as an example. The home outflow controls would set an upper limit for the outflows from the home country, $\overline{\left(1-\alpha_t^H\right)} < \left(1-\psi_t\right)$, which would reduce capital outflows to:

$$\overline{CO_t^{H,CO}} = \overline{\left(1-\alpha_t^H\right)} I_t\left(1+n\right), \tag{6.24}$$

where $\overline{CO_t^{H,CO}} < CO_t^{H,A} < CO_t^{H,C}$. Lower capital outflows mean a higher loan supply, which would reduce $\overline{\left(1+i_t^{loan,CO}\right)}$ to:

$$\overline{\left(1+i_t^{loan,CO}\right)} = \frac{\pi b_t}{\left\{\begin{array}{c} \rho_t^s w_t\left(1+n\right)^2 + \pi\left(1+n\right)W_t^M \\ +\alpha_t^H I_t\left(1+n\right) + \left(1+n\right)^2\left(1-\pi\right)\left(1-\rho_t^s\right)w_t \end{array}\right\}},$$

where $\overline{(1+i_t^{loan,CO})} < (1+i_t^{loan,A}) < (1+i_t^{loan,C})$. The lower $\overline{(1+i_t^{loan,CO})}$ would increase $ROR\left(\overline{k_t^{H,CO}}\right)$. A higher $ROR\left(\overline{k_t^{H,CO}}\right)$ would then make it easier to satisfy the incentive constraint for the entrepreneurs to produce and reduce the possibility of type II bank runs in the home country.

The lower $\overline{(1+i_t^{loan,CO})}$, however, would tighten the SR budget constraint. At $(1+i_t^{D}) \le \overline{(1+i_t^{D,CO})}$, there would not be type I bank runs in cases A and C. At $\overline{(1+i_t^{D,CO})} < (1+i_t^{D}) \le \overline{(1+i_t^{D,A})}$, the home outflow controls would cause type I bank runs, which would not occur in cases A and C. At $\overline{(1+i_t^{D,CO})} \le \overline{(1+i_t^{D,A})} < (1+i_t^{D}) < \overline{(1+i_t^{D,C})}$, type I bank runs in case A would still occur but not the ones in case C. At $(1+i_t^{D}) > \overline{(1+i_t^{D,C})}$, type I bank runs in cases A and C would still occur, and the home outflow controls would not prevent type I bank runs in cases A and C. Overall, the home outflow controls would increase the possibility of type I bank runs in the home country.

Asymmetric controls: home outflows versus foreign no control (AHOFN)

Without control in the foreign country, the home outflow controls would affect the volumes and the composition of capital flows in cases A and C. As analysed in AHIFO for the home country, the home outflow controls would reduce the possibility of type II bank runs but would increase the possibility of type I bank runs. As for the foreign country, a lower volume of inflows due to the controls of the home country would reduce the possibility of type I bank runs while not affecting the possibility of type II bank runs in cases A and C.

Symmetric controls: home outflows versus foreign outflows (SHOFO)

While the home outflow controls would reduce outflows from the home country in cases A and C, the foreign outflow controls would reduce outflows from the foreign country in cases B and D. So in symmetric controls on outflows, the flows would be affected in cases A, B, C and D.

In cases A and C, the home outflow controls would lower the possibility of type II bank runs but would increase the possibility of type I bank runs in the home country. Meanwhile, it would reduce the possibility of type I bank runs while not affecting the possibility of type II bank runs in the foreign country. In cases B and D, the foreign outflow controls would lower the possibility of type II bank runs but would increase the possibility of type I bank runs in the foreign country while reducing the possibility of type I bank runs without affecting the possibility of type II bank runs in the home country.

Asymmetric controls: home outflows versus foreign inflows (AHOFI)

Both home outflow controls $\overline{(1-\alpha_t^{H})}$ and foreign inflow controls $\widehat{(1-\alpha_t^{H})}$ would affect capital flows in cases A and C. Combining the home and the foreign controls, the size of the effects would be dominated by the stricter controls. When the levels of the home and the foreign controls are the same, $\overline{(1-\alpha_t^H)} = \widehat{(1-\alpha_t^H)}$, the results would be similar to what has been analysed earlier. That is, the controls would reduce the possibility of type II bank runs but would increase the possibility of type I bank runs in the home country while reducing the possibility of type I bank runs without affecting the possibility of type II bank runs in the foreign country.

At $\overline{(1-\alpha_t^H)} < \widehat{(1-\alpha_t^H)}$, the home outflow controls are stricter. The inflows to the foreign country would be lower than expected:

$$\check{CI}_t^{F,CI} = \overline{(1-\alpha_t^H)} I_t (1+n), \tag{6.25}$$

where $\check{CI}_t^{F,CI} < \widehat{CI}_t^{F,CI}$ [equation (6.20)], which gives $(1+\check{i}_t^{loan*,CO}) > \widehat{(1+i_t^{loan*,CO})}$. The higher $(1+\check{i}_t^{loan*,CO})$ would reduce $ROR(\check{k}_t^{F*,CO})$, but since $\check{CI}_t^F > 0$, it would still satisfy the incentive constraint for the entrepreneurs to produce and would not affect the possibility of type II bank runs in the foreign country.

At $\overline{(1-\alpha_t^H)} > \widehat{(1-\alpha_t^H)}$, the foreign inflow controls are stricter. In the two-country model, the outflows from the home country would be lower than expected:

$$\overset{\frown}{CO}_t^H = \widehat{(1-\alpha_t^H)} I_t (1+n), \tag{6.26}$$

where $\overset{\frown}{CO}_t^{H,CO} < \widehat{CO}_t^{H,CO}$ [equation (6.24)]. The lower outflows would increase the loan supply in the home country and reduce $\overline{(1+i_t^{loan,CO})}$, $\overline{(1+i_t^{loan,CO})} < \widehat{(1+i_t^{loan,CO})}$. The lower $\overline{(1+i_t^{loan,CO})}$ would increase $ROR\left(\overline{k_t^{H,CO}}\right)$ and make it easier to satisfy the incentive constraint and hence reduce the possibility of the type II bank runs in the home country. However, the lower $\overline{(1+i_t^{loan,CO})}$ would make it more difficult to meet the demand deposits, $\overline{(1+i_t^{D,CO})} > \overline{(1+i_t^D)}$, and increase the possibility of type I bank runs in the home country.

No controls

The results when both countries have no controls are analysed in the previous section. The next two subsections discuss the cases when the home country has no controls, while the foreign country has either inflow or outflow controls.

Asymmetric controls: home no control versus foreign inflows (AHNFI)

The foreign inflow controls $\widehat{(1-\alpha_t^H)} < (1-\psi_t)$ would reduce the flows from the home country in cases A and C. The lower outflows would increase the loan supply in the home country and reduce $\overline{(1+i_t^{loan,N})}$, $\overline{(1+i_t^{loan,N})} < \widehat{(1+i_t^{loan,A})} < \widehat{(1+i_t^{loan,C})}$.

The lower $\widehat{\left(1+i_t^{loan,N}\right)}$ would increase $ROR\left(\widehat{k_t^{H,N}}\right)$, which would make it easier to satisfy the incentive constraint and to reduce the possibility of type II bank runs in the home country. The lower $\widehat{\left(1+i_t^{loan,N}\right)}$, however, would make it more difficult to satisfy the SR budget constraint, $\left(1+i_t^{D}\right) \leq \widehat{\left(1+i_t^{D,N}\right)}$, and hence increase the possibility of type I bank runs in the home country. This is an example of how the countries without controls would be affected by the controls of the other country. The effects of the controls of other countries can be both costly and beneficial. The results may raise the doubts on the studies which find no control would be welfare improving, as such welfare improving may be due to the controls of other countries instead of the no control of the home country.

Asymmetric controls: home no control versus foreign outflows (AHNFO)

The foreign outflow controls $\widehat{\left(1-\alpha_t^{F}\right)} < \left(1-\psi_t^{*}\right)$ would reduce the inflows to the home country in cases B and D. The lower inflows to the home country would increase $\widehat{\left(1+i_t^{loan,N}\right)}, \widehat{\left(1+i_t^{loan,N}\right)} > \left(1+i_t^{loan,B}\right) > \left(1+i_t^{loan,D}\right)$. Although a higher $\widehat{\left(1+i_t^{loan,N}\right)}$ would reduce $ROR\left(\widehat{k_t^{H,N}}\right)$ and tighten the incentive constraint, the positive inflows, $\widehat{CI_t^{H,N}} > 0$, would keep $\widehat{\left(1+i_t^{loan,N}\right)} < \left(1+i_t^{loan,E/F}\right)$ and would not affect the possibility of type II bank runs. Meanwhile, the higher $\widehat{\left(1+i_t^{loan,N}\right)}$ would loosen the SR budget constraint and hence reduce the possibility of type I bank runs. Note that in this case, even without control, the home country is benefitted by the foreign outflow controls.

The comparison of the effectiveness of the controls in all cases

The effectiveness and ineffectiveness of capital controls and no control analysed in all cases are summarised in Table 6.3.

Table 6.3 The effectiveness of capital controls

Controls	*Home*				*Foreign*			
	Case(s)	*V & C*	*Type I*	*Type II*	*Case(s)*	*V & C*	*Type I*	*Type II*
HNFN	–	–	–	–	–	–	–	–
SHIFI	BD	Y	↓	–	–	–	↑	↓
	–	–	↑	↓	AC	Y	↓	–
AHIFO	BD	Y	↓	–	BD	Y	↑	↓
AHIFN	BD	Y	↓	–	–	Y	↑	↓
SHOFO	AC	Y	↑	↓	–	Y	↓	–
	–	Y	↓	–	BD	Y	↑	↓
AHOFI	AC	Y	↑	↓	AC	Y	↓	–
AHOFN	AC	Y	↑	↓	–	Y	↓	–
AHNFI	–	Y	↑	↓	AC	Y	↓	–
AHNFO	–	Y	↓	–	BD	Y	↑	↓

Several implications of Table 6.3 are very interesting. First, inflow controls seem effective for the countries which implement the controls (country X) by reducing the possibility of type I bank runs without affecting the possibility of type II bank runs in country X. Second, the inflow controls, however, would have negative effects on the other country (country Y), as the controls would increase the possibility of type I bank runs while reducing the possibility of type II bank runs of the other country (country Y). Third, the outflow controls do not seem effective for the countries which implement the controls (country X), since the outflow controls would increase the possibility of type I bank runs while leaving the possibility of type II bank runs unaffected in country X. Fourth, the outflow controls, however, would benefit the other countries (country Y) by decreasing the possibility of type I bank runs without affecting the possibility of type II bank runs in country Y.

Conclusion

In this chapter, by incorporating interest rate differentials, the direction as well as the volumes and the composition of capital flows can be determined to discuss the effectiveness of capital controls. The effectiveness of capital controls is determined by achieving three goals: (1) affecting the volumes of capital flows, (2) affecting the composition of capital flows and (3) decreasing the possibility of either or both type I and type II bank runs (details are discussed in Chapter 5). The results show that inflow controls would be effective for the country which implements controls but would have negative side impacts on the partner country by increasing type I bank runs in the partner country. Meanwhile, outflow controls would be ineffective for the country which implements controls by increasing the possibility of type I bank runs but would benefit the partner country by decreasing the possibility of type I bank runs in the partner country. Therefore, depending on the directions of capital flows, the countries would be benefitted or damaged by the controls implemented in the home or the partner country. Taking the aspect of banking crises, the results suggest that coordination of capital controls across countries is crucial for the countries to benefit from the controls, similar to the suggestion by Acharya and Bengui (2016), who take the aspect of liquidity trap. Moreover, the results show that as the role of banks and financial institutions has increased since 1990 [Grittersova (2014)], it has become urgent and important to manage controls with caution, especially the types of controls which would increase the probability of bank runs.

Notes

1 Singh and Subramanian (2008) find that although temporary controls can be worse than perfect capital mobility in terms of welfare, prolonged capital controls can be welfare improving if the debt level is below the threshold
2 The finding of Orlov (2005) is based on the experience of Chile, which liberalized capital controls in 1998.
3 The finding of Hutchison, Pasricha, and Singh (2012) is based on the liberalization of capital accounts in India by using the dataset of the non-deliverable forward market in the self-exciting threshold autoregressive (SETAR) model.

4 Note that the term "host country" has been changed to "foreign country" to reflect the fact that the foreign country can be either the source or the destination of capital flows.
5 More details of how the DSF system operates can be found in Chapter 4.
6 According to Stiglitz and Weiss (1981), among identical borrowers, type I rationing is when some borrowers get partial loans, while type II rationing is when some get full loans but others don't.
7 The details about type I and II bank runs have been analysed in both Chapters 4 and 5.

7 Theoretical and empirical analysis

Practical lessons and policy implications

Introduction

Based on the theoretical analysis in Chapters 2 to 6, the goal of this chapter is to map the theoretical results to the existing empirical findings in the literature and to identify what has been overlooked in each analysis. Each analysis has its strengths and weaknesses, regardless of theoretical or empirical analysis. Also, blind spots may arise for specific analysis, especially when specific methods have been taken as given without further examination. Therefore, it is crucial to keep learning and examining various analyses.

In the literature on capital flows and the connections to banking crises, the results have been mixed. The mixed results have brought about many puzzles and debates. It has been well documented that many puzzles and debates have resulted from the use of various definitions and measurements of datasets across countries and across time. Although there have been many methods developed in empirical studies, the methods which have been applied to analyse capital flows are actually quite limited. Among the specific methods adopted to analyse capital flows, the characteristics of these specific methods tend to drive similar results [Forbes (2012)]. Moreover, specific treatments of the data may affect the results but are hardly explained in the empirical studies. We will require the professionals with expertise in constructing various datasets across countries and in methodologies to provide specific comments and to point out what future work will be needed. Because I am not an expert on various datasets and econometric methodologies, I will focus on the lessons learned from the theoretical and empirical analysis regarding the possible causes of these inconsistent results and the policy implications as well as the most fruitful directions for future work.

The chapter is organized as follows. The second section will discuss general issues in empirical studies. The third and fourth sections will look at the impacts of FDI and FPI flows on economic growth, respectively. The fifth section will be on sudden stops and banking crises, while the sixth will be on bank governance and banking crises. The seventh section will focus on capital controls. The eighth section will provide the conclusion.

Lessons in general for empirical studies on capital flows

Home and host

In a theoretical framework, it is simple to differentiate the home countries from the host countries and to analyse the impacts to the home and to the host countries. However, in practice, one country is often both a home and a host country. To be more specific, one country can be a home country of a group of countries while being a host country of another group of countries. Or one country can be a home country of specific industries while being a host country of other specific industries to the same group of countries.

Reflecting on the data, if one does not investigate the interconnections between countries carefully, the empirical results can easily be dominated by the directions of flows and specific countries or industries during specific periods of time. For example, even for the studies focusing on relatively steady LR FDI flows in Italy, the results of Federico and Minerva (2008) and Imbriani, Pittiglio and Reganati (2001) are inconsistent. As a result, most empirical results are country, period, industry and region dependent. The interpretation of the empirical results for one country is already difficult and becomes even more difficult when studying a group of countries. Therefore, not being able to differentiate one country's role as a home and a host country to a specific other country or industry can be one of the causes for inconsistent empirical findings in capital flows. One suggestion for future empirical studies on capital flows is to clarify the sources or the destinations of capital flows and to analyse the data and the interconnections between the two countries before moving on to a group of countries.

The selection of time and industries

In a theoretical framework, it is simple to specify the time when one country opens to capital flows and to analyse the impacts on the macro variables. However, in practice, each country can open itself up to capital flows at its own time. The openness to capital flows can be limited to specific industries for FDI flows and limited to specific types of flows for FPI flows. Meanwhile, the controls or the closedness on capital flows, either in general or in specific industries or on specific types of flows, can be imposed by the countries at their own time and pace. Therefore, the selection of the time periods and specific industries to analyse becomes crucial. One suggestion for the future empirical work is to study the details of the capital flows of specific countries prior to choosing the time period and industries/types of flows to analyse. I suggest researchers go country by country rather than picking a group of countries when investigating the impacts of capital flows.

Economic conditions: individual and global economy

Capital flows have their impacts on the economy. How each economy reacts to the openness to capital flows and would be affected by the flows would depend on the economic conditions of the specific country and of the global economy as well as the connections the country has to the global economy. In theory, the economic conditions of a specific country and the global economy as well as their interconnectedness can be specified to analyse the impacts on the economy. However, in practice, the economic conditions and the connections between different economies change from time to time.

Capital flows have brought all countries closer and made them more interdependent. So one country's economic conditions have become more sensitive to the economic conditions of other countries and to the global economy. The direct impacts of dynamic economic conditions are that the same type and format of capital flows may be effective during a specific period for a specific country but become ineffective when implemented in the same country during another period of time. Or, the same type and format of controls are effective in one country but not effective in another country at the same development stage during the same period of time. Or even a country that does not have capital controls would be affected by other countries' policies related to capital flows, as shown in the theoretical analysis in Chapter 6.

For example, economic conditions are found to be crucial to the effects of FDI flows on home growth [Choi (2004) and Fortanier (2007)].[1] Although both are developed countries, Driffield, Love, and Taylor (2009) find positive effects of FDI flows on the productivity for the United Kingdom over the period 1978–1994, while Braconier et al (2001) find negative effects for Sweden over the period 1978–1994. Focusing on both national and multinational firms (MNFs) during the period of 1993–2000, Barba Navaretti, Castellani, and Disdier (2010) find that in Italy, outward FDI has positive effects on home productivity, employment and output, while in France, outward FDI has positive effects on home employment and output but no effect on productivity. Meanwhile, economic conditions are also found to be crucial to the effects of FDI flows on the host countries. The economic conditions include policies [Barclay (2004), Kotrajaras, Tubtimtong, and Wiboonchutikula (2011)],[2] the stage of development [Solomon (2011), Suliman and Elian (2014), Wang and Wong (2009a, 2009b)][3] and other characteristics of the country [Doytch and Uctum (2011), Forte and Moura (2013), Kasibhatla et al (2008), Mayer-Foulkes and Nunnenkamp (2009)].[4]

Not being able to identify the features of specific economic conditions of individual and global economies and the interconnections/interdependence between countries would raise doubt about studies on the impacts of capital flows and related policies. For example, the implementation/liberalization of capital controls which appear to be effective can be due to the development of the markets and the economy or the changes in the economic conditions of other countries rather than the policies. Therefore, one suggestion for future empirical work is to develop methods with which identify specific features of the economic conditions and interdependence between countries. When the economic conditions and interdependence between countries can be controlled, it is possible to have more consistent findings.

The development of financial/capital markets

Capital flows are related to capital accounts. The purpose of capital flows is to seek investment opportunities, whether direct investment or portfolio investment. The investment opportunities have direct impacts on the financial markets of the countries involved. Therefore, the development of financial markets/capital markets has been an important component in the literature on capital flows, especially on FPI flows. The development of financial/capital markets is one of the essential aspects of an economy. There are various definitions as to what constitutes of the development of financial/capital markets, including the openness, the integration, the number of sectors, and so forth.

In a theoretical framework, one can set up an environment which incorporates the development of the financial/capital markets to analyse the impacts of capital flows on the economy at different stages of the development of the financial/capital markets. However, in practice, it is challenging to identify the different development stages of the financial/capital markets. The financial and the capital markets can be defined differently across countries. As the financial markets may have various sectors, different regulations and controls in different sectors increase the complications in analysing the development of one country's financial/capital markets. Moreover, various financial frictions in the financial markets/capital markets and their associated risks have made it more difficult to analyse the effects of the development of the financial markets on the economy and the influences of the development of these financial markets on the effects of capital flows.

It is especially interesting when pulling together all the empirical studies on capital flows and financial markets. On one hand, the development of the financial/capital markets may encourage capital flows, especially FPI flows, and improve their effects [Abid and Bahloul (2011), Agbloyor et al (2014), Errunza (2001), Osazee and Idolor (2014)]. On the other hand, the openness and the integration of financial/capital markets may expose one country's financial markets to more risks and higher risks and hence increase contagion effects across markets and across countries [Brink and Viviers (2003), Lee, Park, and Byun (2013), Uctum and Uctum (2011)]. As a result, on closer look, it is not surprising to see various terms on the development of financial markets used in empirical studies, such as the openness of financial markets [Bartokova (2011), Popov (2014)], the openness of capital markets [Errunza (2001)], financial integration [Gur (2015)], the development of the financial sector [Choong et al (2010a, 2010b)] and financial development [Agbloyor et al (2014)]. Without clear definitions in the studies, it is difficult to compare the results. Note that even the slightest difference in definitions may affect the selection of variables and data adopted for analysis and hence affect the results. The suggestions are to unify the definitions and terms on the development of financial/capital markets and to develop methodologies with which to analyse the data and to identify the economy at various development stages of the financial/capital markets.

Financial frictions and risks

In addition to accounting for the development stages of the financial markets, we need to deal with financial frictions in the financial/capital markets, which have direct impacts on the production sectors. In a theoretical framework, there are various ways to model financial frictions through matching functions and to model risks through probabilities and then to analyse the impacts of capital flows in the presence of financial frictions and risks at various degrees. However, in practice, due to limited information, it is difficult to measure financial frictions and risks. This is mainly because, depending on the size and the financial position of the firms, the access to various financial sectors is different. Moreover, the regulations and controls are different across financial sectors, across countries and across time. For example, not every firm is eligible to issue equities/corporate bonds in the financial markets.

The introduction of capital flows, especially FPI flows, may not improve financial frictions of one country. In fact, FPI flows may have complicated the analysis of financial frictions and risks. On one hand, FPI flows can reach out to the small firms via banking channels [Knill (2013)] and reduce financial frictions. On the other hand, the highly volatile FPI flows would restrict the access of small firms to finance [Knill and Lee (2014)] and increase financial frictions and risks. As a result, FPI favoured/dependent equities would require higher premiums at the time of crises [Hsu (2013) and Hsu et al (2013)]. Note that the required premium is one of the key indicators of riskiness and would affect the performances of the firms. Therefore, it will be important for empirical studies to develop methodologies to measure such financial frictions and risks. By controlling for financial frictions and risks, empirical studies would be able to evaluate the connections between financial frictions and capital flows and their impacts on macro performances and the stability of the financial markets and banking systems.

Short-run (SR) effects and long-run (LR) effects

In response to shocks or the changes in economic conditions/policies, the macro variables will adjust accordingly. However, depending on elasticity and sensitivity, some variables adjust quickly, while some adjust slowly. Therefore, some effects can be seen during a short period of time, while other effects may not appear until several periods later. In a theoretical framework, one can set up a clear definition to differentiate SR and LR effects. For example, in Chapters 2 to 4, it is assumed that SR is when wage income has not yet adjusted to the openness to flows or sudden stops, while LR is when wage income has fully adjusted to the changes. Also, in an overlapping-generations framework, one can analyse the effects period by period and find the length of time required for specific effects to appear.

However, in practice, it is challenging to differentiate SR effects from LR effects for several reasons. First, it is difficult to use the adjustment of a single variable to differentiate SR from LR. For example, wage income can be different across industries. Moreover, the segmentation of the labour market and the characteristics of positions and the payment systems would increase the difficulties in analysing the data on wage income. The adjustments of wage income may be due to the changes of the contracts, regulations, labour law or the formations of the labour market instead of to capital flows. Therefore, if empirical studies plan to use the adjustments of one variable, such as wage income, to differentiate SR effects from LR effects, one suggestion is to control the factors that have their influences on wage income. Similar arguments apply to other variables which will be used to differentiate SR effects from LR effects.

Second, it is difficult to identify the length of time required for the effects to appear. Depending on the industries/types of flows which are opened to capital flows, the elasticity and the sensitivities of macro variables would be different across time and across countries. Therefore, the speed of adjustment would be different. Some variables may take a few months, while other variables may take several years or up to a decade or so, especially for capital flows which would stimulate technological innovations/diffusion. This is because technological innovations/diffusion would affect one country broadly and in a complex way. Moreover, specific innovations and technology diffusion may take longer to develop and to replace the old technology, so their effects on the economy may take longer to appear. When the effects appear several years later, the economic conditions and policies may have changed. Therefore, the appearing effects may be counted as the effects of the changes of economic conditions and/or policies rather than the effects of capital flows. One suggestion for the future work is to utilize the data of the industries/types of flows which are opened to capital flows, which may be affected by the openness to capital flows and which has the information of the investment in research and development (R&D) to analyse the effects of capital flows prior to using the aggregate variables, such as gross domestic product (GDP). Moreover, it is important to develop methodologies to measure the elasticity and sensitivities of macro variables to the openness to various types of capital flows. I also suggest that it is crucial to control for the changes in economic conditions and policies while analysing the effects of capital flows.

Equilibrium output

For research aiming to analyse the effects on economic growth, output is a key variable, since economic growth is based on the changes of output. In economics, output is defined as final goods, which exclude intermediate goods. Economic growth is defined as the change of output goods between two periods. So the concept of output is a flow variable rather than a stock variable. In a theoretical framework, one can easily differentiate intermediate goods from final goods by using different sectors and using tradeable and nontradeable goods. The final goods produced within a period and the assumption of full depreciation after the period if not used allow the output, in theoretical analysis, to fit into the concept of a flow variable. Moreover, except for the literature on inventory and the literature on durable goods, most theoretical studies have assumed no inventory and no durable goods, so output demand often equals output supply, and equilibrium output can be determined.

However, in practice, the measurement of economic output, so-called gross domestic product (GDP), can be very complicated in several ways. First, the differentiation of intermediate goods and final goods can be difficult, especially for goods that have been recycled and reproduced, and for recycled energy that has been used for production and for consumption. Second, the presence of durable goods and inventories may generate gaps between output demand and output supply. Both durable goods and some inventories are the concept of stock variables, as they can be consumed for a longer period of time. To count the durables and inventories as part of economic output requires methods to convert to flow variables. Note that there are various depreciation rates to the durable goods and inventories. The actual depreciation rates may differ from accounting depreciation rates. While durable goods are part of output demand and output supply, inventories are on the side of output supply only. Depending on the frequency of usage and the quality of the goods, the depreciation rates of durable goods as consumption/investment (output demand) may differ from the depreciation as production (output supply). As a result, the gap between output demand and output supply is generated, and equilibrium output may be redefined or adjusted.[5] Third, it requires inflation to find real GDP. However, the methods used to select the baskets of goods to measure GDP and the methods used to calculate inflation rates are debatable. These issues have raised concerns about how well GDP can truly reflect the output and the growth rate of a nation. Therefore, future empirical studies must develop methods which can measure the demand and the supply of economic output more consistently and which can better reflect the changes and the sustainability of one country's output, as pointed out by Stiglitz, Sen, and Fitoussi (2010).

Economic growth

While most empirical analyses use economic "growth", most theoretical analyses use economic "growth rate" or "output level". There are gaps between these terms, so one has to be careful when comparing theoretical and empirical results. The terms "growth" and "growth rate" regard the change of the output level. A growth rate is the rate of change of the output levels between two consecutive periods, while growth "may be" the level of change.[6] To have an increase in growth rate would require the output level to grow at an increasing rate. However, to have an increase in growth only requires an increase in output level. Therefore, it is possible that one economy could have an increase in growth but a decrease in the growth rate. One country which has an increase in its economic growth rate would have an increase in economic growth but not vice versa. So any comparison of the theoretical analyses which use growth rate to the empirical analyses which use growth must be nuanced. In the comparison in terms of economic growth in this chapter, the word "similar" is used rather than "consistent".

For example, regarding the effects of FDI flows on economic growth of the home country, the empirical findings of Zhang (2013) on 59 countries during 1980–2010, Herzer (2008) on 14 industrial countries over the period 1971–2005 and Herzer (2012) on Germany are similar to the theoretical result of positive effects on SR home growth rate but are opposite to the theoretical result of negative effects on LR home growth rate in the absence of scale effects. The theoretical results on economic growth are also different from the findings of Lee (2010), which concludes that the causality between outward FDI and home growth is positive in the LR but non-positive in the SR.

Regarding the effects of FDI flows on economic growth of the host country, the theoretical result of negative effects on the SR host growth rate is similar to the findings of Mencinger (2003) on eight EU transition countries in 1994–2001, of Azman-Saini et al (2010) on 85 countries during 1976–2004 and of Nunnenkamp (2004) on the developing countries. The theoretical result of positive effects on the LR host growth rate is similar to many empirical studies which focus on either one country or a group of countries, regardless of the development stage, the region and the relations to origins of FDI, such as Asiedu (2004), Bengoa and Sancgez-Eobles (2003), Borenszrein et al (1998), Campos and Kinoshita (2002), Cipollina et al (2012), Kim et al (2003), Kornecki (2008), Moudatsou (2003), Razin (2003), Poon and Thompson (1998), Sghaier et al (2013), Stehrer and Woerz (2009) and Wang (2009).

FDI and growth

Chapter 2 analyses the impacts of FDI flows on the economic growth rate in the home and in the host countries in the SR and in the LR. It is shown that through investment portfolios of the banks, in the SR, the home country would have an increase in unemployment and in the growth rate but a decrease in the rate of return of capital, while the host country would have an increase in the rate of return of capital but a decrease in the growth rate. In the LR, the home country would have a decrease in wage income due to the lack of labour demand, while the host country would have an increase in wage income. The effects on both the rates of return of capital and the growth rates, however, would depend on the presence of the scale effects for both the home and the host countries.

Possible future work for empirical studies

Employment and wage income

Among capital flows, FDI flows have more direct impacts on the production sector than FPI flows. The effects on the production sector would affect both employment and wage income. In a theoretical framework, one can assume full employment and identical firms. So wage income can be solved via the labour market clearing condition. Since wage income is the same and the firms are identical, there would not be labour mobility across firms.

However, in practice, countries are not under full employment; wage income can be different across firms, industries and positions. There is labour mobility between firms and industries and countries. The openness to FDI can be limited to specific industries. The specific industries may use specific type(s) of labour, such as unskilled or skilled labour. The change of labour demand would then affect wage income, wage gap and employment of the country.[7] Therefore, it is important to identify the specific industries opened to FDI flows, the types of labour demand affected by the openness of FDI flows, the labour market frictions and the labour mobility across industries and across countries. However, most empirical studies do not do so. As a result, it is not surprising to have mixed results in empirical studies on FDI flows. The mixed results mean that the theoretical results would be consistent with some but inconsistent with others.

The theoretical result that FDI outflows would reduce labour demand, which would lower the employment level in the home country, is consistent with the findings of Marin (2004) on Germany and Austria, Debaere et al (2010) on multinational corporations, Elia et al (2009) on Italy and Lee et al (2009) on four Asian Tigers. Meanwhile, although Masso et al (2008) on Estonia and Federico and Minerva (2008) on Italy have found positive/non-negative effects on home employment, their results depend on the selection of sectors [Masso et al (2008)], the industries [Federico and Minerva (2008)] and the periods of time [Federico and Minerva (2008), Masso et al (2008)]. By using firm-level data on Italy during different periods of time, Imbriani, Pittiglio and Reganati (2011) find negative effects on home employment. The comparison shows that although the empirical findings appear to be mixed, the negative effects on home employment seem most robust, while the non-negative effects would depend on the selection of the variables and datasets. Therefore, I suggest that the future empirical research must study the openness of FDI in details prior to the selection of industries, datasets and periods of time.

In addition to the selection of specific industries, datasets and periods of time, economic conditions of the countries are also crucial to the results, as mentioned in the second section. As shown in Molnar et al (2008), through the investigation of multinational enterprises (MNEs) of OECD countries, they conclude that the effect of FDI on home employment can be country dependent. To be more specific, they show that outward FDI flows, although having negative effects on Japan's home employment, have positive effects on the United States' home employment. Lipsey (2004) finds that the country-dependent effects of FDI on home employment would be based on whether the parent firms in the home country have been reallocated to capital-intensive production. The country going through the reallocation would tend to find positive effects of FDI on home employment, such as in the United States. It is suggested that the future empirical studies aiming to analyse the effects of FDI flows on home employment must identify and control specific economic conditions, such as the reallocation of specific types of firms.

Regarding datasets, many empirical studies tend to adopt the data of MNEs to analyse the impacts of FDI on the economy. It is important to emphasize that the performances of MNEs represent part of the economy in specific industries but not the whole economy. As shown in Nachum et al (2001), there exists a gap between the performances of MNEs and the economy as a whole and as a country. Since the openness to FDI flows of specific industries may crowd out or complement other industries, it is important to have a thorough investigation of the industries which would be affected prior to drawing policy implications based on the studies adopting data of MNEs only.

Technology changes, scale effects and productivity

Pioneered by Aghion and Howitt (1998), Jones (1999) and Young (1998), it has been found that technological progress could generate scale effects and increasing returns and hence improve productivity and economic growth. It has been raised in several empirical studies that technological progress plays an important role in FDI flows, but the causes of technological progress in the home and in the host countries are different. The cause of technological progress in the home countries is more likely to be innovations, while the cause in the host countries is more likely to be imitations. Either cause of technological progress would generate the scale effects in the SR and would affect both productivity and economic growth positively. Note that even without FDI flows, technological progress in one country would generate the scale effects and increase both its productivity and economic growth. When the effects of technological progress are strong enough, it could overwrite or magnify the effects of FDI flows on both productivity and economic growth. Therefore, it is important to identify the likelihood of technological progress associated with FDI flows and separate the effects of technological progress from the effects of FDI flows.

In a theoretical framework, one can extend an endogenous growth model to discuss the technological progress and the scale effects, as shown in Aghion and Howitt (1998), Jones (1999) and Young (1998). Alternatively, one can extend an overlapping-generations framework to analyse the effects of technological progress and the scale effects, as shown in Chapter 2. While an endogenous growth model can determine the elasticity of economic growth to technological progress, the overlapping-generations model can show the weights of technological progress, the scale effects and FDI flows on productivity and economic growth. Through theoretical analysis, it is possible to identify the effects of technological progress and the scale effects on productivity and economic growth separately from the effects of FDI flows.

The theoretical result of positive effects on the SR home productivity is consistent with the empirical findings of Herzer (2010, 2012), while the theoretical result of negative effects on the LR home productivity is consistent with the empirical findings of Braconier et al (2001), Bitzer and Gorg (2009) and Hijzen et al (2011). For the host country, the empirical findings of Bodman and Le (2013), Narula and Driffield (2012) and Lee (2007) are consistent with the theoretical result of positive effects on the SR host productivity but opposite to the theoretical results of negative effects on the LR host productivity.

However, in practice, it takes time to replace the old technology and to train labour to use the new technology. Whether one country can take the new technology and the length of time it will take for the scale effects to appear and to disappear may depend on the capacity of the industries, the regulations and related policies as well as the development of more advanced technologies. If we do not know the amount of time it takes for technological progress and the scale effects to appear, it becomes a challenge to select the period of time to reflect the effects of technological progress. Because we are unable to identify the effects of technological progress alone, it is difficult to separate the effects of technological progress from the effects of FDI flows.

Moreover, technological progress and the scale effects can hardly be analysed from the data. The changes in productivity and economic growth often mix the effects of FDI flows and technological progress. Consequently, the overall effects on productivity and economic growth can be dominated by the effects of FDI flows for the countries' lack of technological progress, or dominated by the effects of technological progress and provide mixed results in the literature. This may be one of the reasons why some empirical studies would use technological progress as an interpretation but with no evidence to prove the arguments. One suggestion for future empirical studies is to analyse the balance sheets of the firms of specific industries opened to FDI flows in order to identify the changes of technological progress and the changes of investment in research and development before and after the openness to FDI and to analyze how the changes would affect the production and the profits prior to moving to the aggregate data, which has been affected by many factors other than FDI.

Investment portfolios

As mentioned earlier, the investment of firms is crucial to the technological progress, which would affect the productivity and the performances of the firms. It is also shown in Chapter 2 that the investment portfolios play a crucial role in affecting both the productivity and economic growth rate. The differences are that in the theoretical analysis of Chapter 2, the investment portfolios are determined by the banks, while in practice, the firms have their own investment portfolios.

Moreover, the investment portfolios of the firms are more complicated, as they may involve leverage, debts and cash flows. Depending on the industries, the investment portfolios can be complicated, especially for multinational enterprises (MNEs). Firms are also connected in specific ways, either horizontally or vertically. So the investment portfolios may affect and be affected by the portfolios of other firms. When one country is opened to FDI flows for specific industries, the investment portfolios of the specific industries would be adjusted accordingly, and so would the investment portfolios of the related industries and firms. The change of the investment portfolios would, in turn, affect one country's technological progress, productivity and economic growth. Therefore, it is important to investigate the effects of FDI flows on investment portfolios of the firms. The related investigation should be a focus of future empirical studies.

Possible theoretical extensions

Several limitations of the theoretical analysis give possible extensions.

Economic conditions

Because economic conditions are crucial in affecting the outcome of FDI flows, it is important to extend the current analysis to incorporate specific economic conditions, such as the development stage and the development in the financial markets and banking systems to examine how specific economic conditions may affect FDI flows and the effects associated with FDI flows.

Investment portfolios

As found in Chapter 2, investment portfolios play a crucial role in affecting the effects of FDI flows on productivity and economic growth. The investment portfolios can be divided into the portfolios of the banks and the portfolios of the firms. Different portfolios would have different impacts on economic outcome. While the portfolios of the banks would be more related to the financial sectors and affect the financial stability, the portfolios of the firms would be more related to the production sector and affect the technological progress and productivity. Both portfolios may have their mutual effects with FDI flows and are crucial in affecting the effects of FDI flows. So an extension to examine the mutual effects of both types of investment portfolios and FDI flows would be important.

Market frictions

The connections of FDI flows and the production sector have led the impacts of FDI flows on employment and wage income. Meanwhile, the effects of FDI flows on employment and wage income are also affected by labour market frictions, which could also affect productivity and growth. Meanwhile, the mutual effects of FDI flows and investment portfolios are affected by financial market frictions. Both labour market frictions and financial market frictions play a crucial role in affecting FDI flows and the effects of FDI flows. Therefore, it is important to have an extension to incorporate market frictions to examine the impacts of friction on the effects of FDI flows.

Heterogeneity of firms

The openness to FDI flows can be limited to specific industries, so the impacts of FDI flows would be different in different industries. The extensions to examine the impacts in different industries will need to incorporate firms with heterogeneity, which can be either horizontally or vertically related to the firms directly affected by the openness to FDI flows. Moreover, firms with heterogeneity may provide different wage income and cause labor mobility, which is one crucial factor in affecting FDI flows and the effects of FDI.

Human capital

The specific industries which are opened to FDI flows may require specific types of human capital, which, in some cases, is the driving force of FDI flows. The labour demand for specific types of human capital may affect labour market frictions and generate a wage gap, which would affect economic productivity and growth. Therefore, an extension to incorporate human capital to examine the mutual effects of FDI flows and the levels of human capital would be important to clarify the connections of FDI flows and the labour markets.

International trade

FDI flows would affect output production, which may affect the trading sector of one country and hence its economic growth. Therefore, one extension would be to examine the linkages between FDI flows and the trading sectors and the connections to economic growth.

Demographic issues

As shown in Chapter 2, countries with large populations could attract FDI flows which seek cheap labour costs. Currently, there have been increasing issues in the demographics which may affect capital flows and the effects of flows, such as aging society and demographic cliff [Inagaki (2016)].[8] These issues have affected the composition of the labour force and would have impacts on FDI flows. Therefore, it has become urgent and important to conduct research to analyse the connections between demographic issues and capital flows.

Policy implications

As demonstrated in the theoretical analysis in Chapter 2, the investment portfolios endogenously determined by the banks which serve as central planners play a crucial role in affecting the effects of FDI on productivity and economic growth in both the home and the host countries. Empirically, the importance of the governance and development of financial markets and institutions in affecting the impacts of FDI is also found in Kotrajaras et al (2011). Therefore, the policies which would affect the investment portfolios, either the investment portfolios of the banks or of the firms, would be crucial in affecting the effects of FDI flows. The policies which would affect the investment portfolios of the banks include capital requirements, macro-prudential policies and supervision. The policies which would affect the investment portfolios of the firms include encouraging innovations and reducing financial frictions.

There is no doubt that FDI flows have linked the home and the host countries more closely and more interdependently. FDI flows would affect not only the host countries but also the home countries. Among many factors, economic conditions are crucial in affecting the effects of FDI flows on the macro variables in both the home and the host countries. Moreover, economic conditions would affect the ability of the host countries to attract FDI inflows and the ability of the home countries to control FDI outflows limited to specific industries. Also, economic conditions of the host countries could affect the home countries via FDI flows [Lipsey (2004), Molnar et al (2008)] and vice versa [Choi (2004) and Fortanier (2007)]. Therefore, the policies which would improve economic conditions and affect the interdependence between countries can be effective in affecting FDI flows, both inflows and outflows.[9] Note that policies and regulations [Barclay (2004), Kotrajaras et al (2011)] are part of economic conditions and are crucial in affecting FDI flows as well as the effects of FDI flows.

As shown in Chapter 2, the presence of return flows would improve the home country's growth rate in the SR. The return flows would depend on the barriers of the host country on capital flows. Therefore, in a home country, the policies which can discourage FDI flows to the countries with high barriers on capital flows may be effective in affecting the home growth rate.

FPI flows

Chapter 3 examines the impacts of FPI flows and the possibility of banking crises associated with FPI flows. It is found that FPI flows would affect the growth rates negatively in both the home and the host countries. The theoretical result of negative effects on macro performances is similar to the empirical findings of Agbloyor et al (2014), Popov (2014) and Shen et al (2010). The result of the causality of FPI flows on growth is similar to the findings of Bhattacharya and Bhattacharya (2012).

Also, the openness to FPI flows would lead to unexpected withdrawals in the home country. In a bank-selected fully funded (BSF) banking system in which the banks serve as central planners with zero profit, a relatively secure banking system without incentive problems, bank runs in the home country would be inevitable. The BSF system, however, has protected the host country from banking crises. The importance of banking systems in preventing banking crises is consistent with the suggestion of Joyce and Nabar (2009).

A country must have openness to capital flows in order to have sudden stops of the flows. Without capital flows, there are no flows to be stopped suddenly. Since FPI flows are volatile SR flows, it is often FPI flows being suddenly stopped. When FPI flows have increased one country's dependency on foreign capital, sudden stops are more likely to occur [Bordo et al (2010)], and the impacts of sudden stops are stronger. As a result, instability in the financial markets and in the banking systems would increase [de Mello, Padoan and Rousova (2012), Komulainen (2004)]. Chapter 4 examines the impacts of sudden stops and the effects on the possibility of banking crises. In a BSF banking system with interest rates endogenously determined, it is found that sudden stops could cause bank runs in the home country but not in the host country. The bank runs would cause output loss in the home country and reduce the home growth rate to negative. If the system in the host country does not use FPI inflows for purposes other than SR investment, the host growth rate could be higher in the SR but lower in the LR.

The theoretical result of the effects of sudden stops on incentive constraint of the entrepreneurs to produce is similar to the empirical findings of firms becoming vulnerable and sensitive to FPI flows [Hsu (2013), Hsu et al (2013), Knill (2013), Knill and Lee (2014)]. The theoretical result of the effects of sudden stops on increasing banking crises confirms the empirical findings of de Mello, Padoan and Rousova (2012), Komulainen (2004), Lee et al (2013), Uctum and Uctum (2011) and Brink and Viviers (2003). The theoretical result of the negative effects on economic growth is similar to the findings of Bordo et al (2010). The theoretical result of the loss of output caused by sudden stops and banking crises is similar to the findings of Ratanamaneichat (2008) and Vannapanich (2009).

Possible future work for empirical studies

The causes of banking crises in the home countries

Aiming for SR investment, FPI flows tend to be more volatile and more sensitive to the shocks and the changes in economic conditions [Bohn and Tesar (1996), Goldstein and Razin (2006), Levchenko and Mauro (2007)] compared to FDI flows. The sensitivity of FPI flows could expose one country to higher risks, increasing financial instability and a higher possibility of banking crises [Brink and Viviers (2003), Lee et al (2013) and Uctum and Uctum (2011)]. In the worse case scenario, the volatility of FPI flows may trigger crises and disrupt economic activities [de Mello, Padoan and Rousova (2012)]. In a theoretical framework, one can set up an environment with an explicit banking sector to analyse FPI flows and the possibility of bank runs and banking crises. Moreover, the theoretical analysis can focus on a relatively secure bank governance to discuss type I and type II bank runs caused by FPI flows. While type I bank runs are caused by the failure to meet demand deposits, type II bank runs are caused by the failure to hold incentive constraint.

However, in practice, the deregulations of banking systems and the liberalization of capital markets have led the banks to expand their activities to an international level and increase the banks' activities in taking risks. That is, FPI flows would include the banks' international activities. The banks' activities in taking and transferring risks are tasks for bank governance. When bank governance fails to manage risks well, bank failure would be the result, and bank runs and banking crises will be inevitable. Moreover, in practice, the banks maximize profits and may have both moral hazard and adverse selection problems, which would cause bank runs and banking crises. These various causes of banking crises may not be due to the openness to FPI flows. Therefore, to identify banking crises caused by FPI flows, it is important for empirical studies to develop methodologies with which to identify various causes of banking crises. As many banks' activities do not appear in the balance sheets or reports, it is crucial to have policies and regulations that require transparency in bank activities.

Another challenge in practice is the various ways to handle bank failures, such as mergers, government loans and take overs by the government (nationalization), in addition to liquidation. Therefore, the actual bank runs and banking crises observed in the data would be less than in the theoretical analysis, since some bank failures have been handled in a different way. Future empirical studies should include bank failures, and the way they have been handled differently, in the analysis before developing methodologies to identify the causes of banking crises.

FPI flows in the host countries

The purpose of FPI inflows is to invest in SR investment to obtain the returns. How FPI flows are invested and how the returns are provided to FPI are crucial in affecting the effects of FPI flows in the host country. In a theoretical framework as shown in Chapter 3, it is assumed that FPI inflows are invested in SR loans in a collective way and will not be used for other purposes, so there would not be any banking crises in the host countries.

However, in practice, SR FPI flows may be redirected to invest in LR assets and generate mismatch in maturity. That is, when FPI flows require their returns to be provided, the returns of the LR assets are not yet available. The mismatch would increase the instability in the financial markets and in the banking system in the host country and may lead to banking crises. Therefore, one future topic for empirical studies would be to investigate the proportion of FPI flows that is invested in the LR assets in the host countries so that it is possible to differentiate whether the banking crises in the host countries are caused by maturity mismatch or FPI flows.

The causes of sudden stops

The possibility that sudden stops may increase instability in the financial markets and banking systems would make it important to find the causes of sudden stops. The causes of sudden stops may be due to the changes in economic conditions of an individual economy and/or the global economy and due to the changes in the investors' financial conditions.

In empirical studies, it has been found that dependency on foreign capital may trigger sudden stops [Bordo et al (2010)]. However, it is unclear whether all types of foreign capital would trigger sudden stops or only specific types of foreign capital. Moreover, it is unclear whether specific assets/capital invested mainly by FPI flows matters to sudden stops. Note that the foreign capital refers to the capital of the source country, while the assets/capital invested by FPI flows are the assets of the destination country. Therefore, future empirical studies could investigate further following from Bordo et al (2010)'s work to better understand the type(s) of FPI flows and the investment of FPI flows.

Possible theoretical extensions

To simplify the analysis, the theoretical framework in Chapters 2 and 3 assumes that interest rates are exogenously determined and that bank governance is a BSF system. Three immediate extensions would be to allow for the interest rate to be endogenously determined and to incorporate different types of bank governance, as addressed in Chapters 4 and 5, respectively. If FPI inflows were spent on financing liquidity shortfalls or investment in LR assets/risky assets by the banks, bank governance in the host country would be similar to a depositor-selected leveraged (DSL) system. The maturity mismatch could increase the possibility of bank runs and banking crises in the host country, as demonstrated in Chapter 5. Also, another immediate extension worth examining the effects of capital controls on FPI flows, as shown in Kinda (2012), Lajuni et al (2008) and Jongwanich et al (2011), and addressed in Chapter 6. Other possible extensions are as follows.

The causality of growth on FPI flows

The economic conditions of one country may determine FPI flows. The economic conditions include economic growth [Baek (2006), Duasa and Kassim (2009) and Garg and Dua (2014)] and the conditions of financial markets, which can be the investors' protection [Poshakwale and Thapa (2011)], investment barriers and riskiness [Liljeblom and Loflund (2005), Tabova (2013)] and market entry costs/geographical distance [Araujo et al (2015), Sarisoy Guerin (2006)]. The extensions would be to examine the effects of various economic conditions on FPI flows and whether specific economic conditions would have stronger effects on the volatility of FPI and the impacts of FPI flows to the economy.

Dependency on foreign capital

In some host countries, FPI flows could target specific equities and affect the production of the firms via stock markets [Knill (2005), Knill (2013), Knill and Lee (2014)]. When more and more firms' production depends on FPI flows, the host country would become more dependent on foreign capital and more vulnerable to the volatility of FPI flows. Therefore, it is crucial to have an extension to examine the factors which may affect firms' dependence on foreign capital by incorporating heterogeneous firms and/or by incorporating the firms' various financial methods as well as financial frictions.

The cause of sudden stops

There are many causes of sudden stops. Some of the causes are dependency on foreign capital, as shown in Bordo et al (2010), and the position of FPI flows in one country's external finance. Moreover, there are factors which might trigger both sudden stops and banking crises, such as credit booms [Mendoza and Terrones (2012)] or large capital flows [Furceri et al (2012)]. Meanwhile, although sudden stops might increase the instability of financial markets and banking systems [Komulainen (2004)], and financial crises might cause sudden stops [Claessens and Kose (2013)], there might be ways, such as the Euro system, as shown in Gros and Alcidi (2015), to protect the countries from experiencing sudden stops after global financial crises. Above all, there is still a lot to learn regarding the linkages between sudden stops and financial crises as well as possible causes of both sudden stops and banking crises. Theoretical frameworks would be helpful in analysing the linkages, which might still be challenging for empirical studies.

Policies

In the face of the possibility of bank runs, it has been found that lending facilities would be helpful in preventing type I bank runs but not type II bank runs. As there are other causes of bank runs which have not yet been identified in this book, it would be important to examine various policies and their ability to prevent various causes of bank runs, such as foreign reserves [Ceh and Krznar (2008)] and other regulations.

Policy implications

Liquidity provision and policies to prevent crises

Based on the theoretical results of Chapters 3 and 4 and empirical findings, the openness to FPI flows and the associated sudden stops would increase the possibility of bank runs and banking crises and increase financial instability. Depending on the causes, there are various types of bank runs. The type of bank runs, such as type I bank runs, which are caused by liquidity shortfalls, can be prevented by liquidity provision. Liquidity provision can be considered as *ex post* since lending facilities provided by the central banks may prevent financial disruptions from getting worse and as *ex ante* since deposit insurance may prevent the panicking of the creditors. However, compared to other *ex ante* policies, liquidity provision is often grouped in *ex post* remedy to the banking crises. The *ex ante* remedy to crises often refers to the policies, supervision and regulations which can encourage banks to hold liquidity for unexpected incidences, such as liquidity requirements, and may also be helpful in preventing this type of bank runs. However, some policies, such as capital requirements, may instead lead to more bank activities in taking and transferring risks, as shown in Chang (2015), and require more investigation prior to the implementation.

Other types of bank runs, such as type II bank runs, involve the incentive constraints and would require policies and regulations for the financial sector and the production sector to cooperate and to produce the conditions to stimulate loan demand. One way to hold the incentive constraint is to increase the rate of return of capital. To increase the rate of return of capital, interest rate policies or policies that would encourage research and development and productivity would be helpful.

Bank governance

As shown in Chapters 3 and 4, one reason the theoretical analysis does not show the increasing possibility of bank runs/banking crises in the host country is proper bank governance. However, based on the empirical findings, the increasing possibility of crises due to FPI flows would also happen in the host countries. Joyce and Nabar (2009) have also pointed out the importance in strengthening banking systems in preventing crises. Combining both the theoretical and empirical findings, one can conclude that contagion effects/banking crises can be prevented if bank governance has managed the risks well. Determining what policies/regulations would assist the banks to have proper bank governance to manage risks well and to prevent crises would be an important task for the policy makers.

Economic growth

The theoretical result of negative impacts of FPI flows on both the home and the host economic growth rates is similar to the empirical findings of Agbloyor et al (2014), Popov (2014) and Shen et al (2010).[10] The empirical findings of negative impacts of FPI flows on growth seem robust in the studies focusing on either one country or a group of countries. It is important to emphasize that the theoretical framework in Chapter 3 assumes that the banks serve as central planners and would maximize welfare via adjusting investment portfolios. It has been shown that the investment portfolios are crucial in affecting macro-economic variables and economic growth. In practice, the banks are not central planners but would have their own investment portfolios to maximize their profits. Therefore, the policies which would affect the investment portfolios of the banks could matter to economic growth, and the policies which could improve the stability of the banking system and the financial markets would be crucial to have sustainable growth without being disrupted by the crises.

The empirical studies on FPI flows with findings of positive [Debbiche and Rahmouni (2015)] or non-negative effects [Boero et al (2015)] on growth have included LR FDI flows. As shown in the theoretical analysis in Chapter 2, depending on SR/LR effects and the home/host country, FDI flows could affect growth rate positively. Therefore, mixing FDI flows into FPI flows would raise doubts as to whether the positive/non-negative effects on economic growth are dominated by FDI rather than FPI flows. Knowing the different effects FPI flows and FDI flows have, it is important to be cautious when drawing policy implications on FPI flows from specific research work.

The development of financial markets

As mentioned in Chapter 3 and the earlier subsections, several empirical studies have suggested that the openness/development of financial markets and integration to promote FPI flows might possibly turn the effects of FPI flows from negative to positive [Abid and Bahloul (2011), Agbloyor et al (2014), Bartokova (2011), Bartram and Dufey (2001), Choong et al (2010a, 2010b), Errunza (2001), Gur (2015), Popov (2014)]. However, one should be careful that the development of financial markets and the improvement of financial integration would reduce financial frictions of one economy and promote economic growth, regardless of whether the economy is opened to FPI flows. As summarized, the negative effects of FPI flows are caused by bank governance and the volatility of FPI flows [Brink and Vivers (2003), Lee et al (2013), Uctum and Uctum (2011)]. Therefore, the policies aiming to improve the negative effects of FPI flows should focus on creating economic conditions to reduce the volatility of FPI flows and on macro-prudential policies and bank supervision to stabilize the banking system and the financial markets to prevent banking crises.

Dependence on foreign capital

It has been shown that dependency on foreign capital could raise several issues. It would trigger sudden stops [Bordo et al (2010)]. It would make FPI favoured firms more vulnerable and sensitive to the volatility of FPI flows [Hsu (2013), Hsu et al (2013), Knill (2013), Knill and Lee (2014)]. It would also increase the position of FPI flows in one country's external finance [de Mello, Padoan and Rousova (2012)]. Therefore, to stabilize the economy, it is important to have policies that would reduce the position of FPI flows of one country's external finance and reduce firms' dependency on foreign capital. This may include policies to reduce financial frictions in the financial markets and to assist the firms to obtain external finance of domestic capital. Other policies that have been implemented are capital controls, whose effectiveness would also depend on the policies of other countries. More analysis regarding capital controls is analysed in Chapter 6.

Bank governance

As shown in Chapters 3 and 4, the bank governance in a BSF system could prevent banking crises in the host country. The importance of strengthening banking systems to prevent banking crises is also suggested by Joyce and Nabar (2009). The assumptions about banks in a BSF system such as acting as central planners and taking zero profit do not match how banks operate. Therefore, Chapter 5 examines alternative bank governance which is closer to bank governance in practice and the ability to prevent banking crises. The two types of bank governance examined are depositor-selected-fully-funded (DSF) and depositor-selected-leverage (DSL) banking systems. It is found that a DSF system, not a DSL system, may prevent the banking crises that might occur in a BSF system.

Challenges for empirical studies

The discussions of bank governance can be divided into two categories. One is subjective and the other is objective. Subjective bank governance regards the ownership and the board members of the banks, while objective bank governance regards the banks' ability to managing risks. The focus of the book is objective bank governance.

Objective bank governance and measurements

As mentioned in [Dermine (2013)], objective bank governance is related to banks' ability to manage risks and to adjust risk taking and transferring behaviours in the face of the shocks and the changes of regulations. There have been increasing types of banks, non-bank financial institutions and non-financial institutions that engage in financial activities. Some are regulated and some are not. As they all involve financial activities, the banks face increasing competition and are willing to take more and higher risks in order to maximize their profits, including taking shadow banking activities, credit derivatives and swaps. To measure the banks' ability in managing risks, it is crucial to know the activities undertaken by the banks.

However, the deregulation of the banking systems has expanded banking activities to an international level, and some banks have become multinational enterprises. Moreover, different regulations and policies across countries have made it even more challenging to monitor bank activities. As a result, often only selected bank activities are reported to meet the regulations. Measures of the risks based on selected bank activities can be misleading. Therefore, it is important for the countries to cooperate and to unify the accounting rules as well as regulations and policies to have bank activities become transparent. Transparent bank activities would allow the authorities to monitor and to supervise banks more effectively and to detect crises at an early stage and mitigate them. At the current stage, one important task for empirical studies would be to cross-reference banks' reports and balance sheets in details from period to period and to investigate the accounting rules which would allow specific activities to be hidden so that the risk measurements can be adjusted accordingly.

Banks' risks and systemic risks

It has been well documented that the banks' risk-taking, leveraging and liquidity problems are the main causes of bank failure. It has been known that banks taking credit derivatives would expose the banks to credit risks [Minton et al (2009)]. The banks which offer high deposit rates would increase the banks' liability and increase banks' risk of failure [Acharya and Mora (2012)]. The more and higher risks to which the banks are exposed would make the banking system more fragile and unstable. One important task for future empirical studies is to monitor and to analyse the share of risky assets held by the banks relative to other assets. Another important job is to analyse the deposit rate offered by the banks relative to the profits and the investment portfolios of the banks in order to develop the methodologies to measure the risks of individual banks.

When the banks take/transfer risks by using similar tools, the patterns of the banks would generate systemic risks and make the banking system vulnerable to shocks [Jorion (2007)]. Having the features of being difficult to detect and easy to trade, shadow banking activities have become more popular tools used by the banks and have raised great concerns [Hanson et al (2015)]. One of the shadow banking activities, repurchase agreement (repo) and its reverse, has been highlighted regularly by the former chair of the Federal Reserve Bank, Professor Bernanke, in his speeches in 2008a, 2008b, 2009, and 2014 regarding its cause on systemic risks. As shown in Chang (2015), interbank repo would lead to repo runs and trigger contagion effects. Therefore, an important future empirical study would be to investigate the patterns of bank activities, especially the activities in transferring risks, leverage and shadow banking.

Ex post *liquidity provision versus* ex ante *policies*

To prevent banking crises, there are *ex post* liquidity provisions and *ex ante* policies which include macro-prudential policies, regulations and requirements. Liquidity provision might assist bank failure caused by liquidity problems, while other causes of bank failure, such as risk taking and transferring and leverage, would require policies to increase the banks' abilities in managing the risks.

On one hand, liquidity provision and policies might be able to prevent banking crises under certain circumstances. On the other hand, their associated problems might increase bank failure. For example, it has been well documented that liquidity provision, such as deposit insurance, would lead the banks to overlook the risks and overtake risky activities and increase moral hazard problems [Demirgüç-Kunt et al (2014), Diamond and Dybvig (1983) Gropp and Vesala (2004), Hellmann et al (2000), Hooks and Robinson (2002), Kim et al (2014), Martin (2006), McCoy (2007), Weinstein (1992)]. Capital requirement, as a macro-prudential policy and supervision, has been implemented to reduce the risks taken by the banks and to reduce the liquidity problems. However, Hellmann, Murdock and Stiglitz (2000) show that capital requirements would lead to inefficient outcome and increase gambling behaviours of the banks to increase bank values. Therefore, one important task for empirical study is to investigate the changes in bank activities in order to meet the requirements or the changes of policies as well as to obtain liquidity provision.

Possible theoretical extensions

The theoretical framework has been simplified in several ways to focus on the analysis of the possibility of bank runs under different bank governance. For the extensions, specific assumptions may be relaxed to analyse different issues related to bank governance.

The reallocation of FPI flows and the removal of the restrictions

The theoretical framework of Chapter 5 has assumed that the host country would restrict FPI flows to invest in SR assets only. The assumption of the restrictions is crucial in preventing the host country from experiencing unexpected withdrawals caused by sudden stops. In practice, most host countries do not have such restrictions, and FPI inflows could be reallocated to invest in LR assets via the financial markets of the host country. Therefore, one extension would be to examine the effects on the possibility of bank runs when FPI flows are reallocated to invest in LR assets and when the restrictions to invest in LR assets are removed in the host country.

Risk taking and transferring activities

As mentioned by Calomiris (2009), the government's risk-inviting rules have encouraged the banks to take risks. In order to maximize the profits, the banks would take risky activities which would shake the stability of the banking system [Jorion (2007)]. These risky activities include using credit derivatives to expose the banks to credit risks [Minton et al (2009)] and offering high deposit rate to increase liability and expose the banks to failure [Acharya and Mora (2012)]. Meanwhile, leverage would increase risk-taking activities and cause bank runs [Kashyap et al (2014)], and so would shadow banking activities [Chang (2015), Hanson et al (2015)]. At the time of a credit boom, banks would overlook the risks and take more leverage. Then bank failure and instability would be the result [Gamberger and Smuc (2013), Schularick and Taylor (2012)]. The risk-taking activities can be overtaken when leverage and shadow banking activities are allowed and available. The risk-taking and then risk transferring activities would then generate systemic risks and increase instability further [Allen and Gale (2007a), O'Brien and Berkowitz (2007)]. The banks' risk-taking and transferring activities are large areas in bank governance. Therefore, it is important to have an extension to examine the impacts of the risk-taking and transferring activities thoroughly.

Incentive problems/looting problems

The profit-maximizing goal of the banks can easily generate incentive problems of the banks. In more serious cases, the possibility of moral hazard in banking and looting problems, as emphasized by Akerlof and Romer (1993), cannot be ruled out. Therefore, it is important to have an extension to analyse the incentive problems, looting and moral hazard in banking.

Heterogeneous banks

The setup of the framework assumes identical banks. The identical banks tend to share debts and assets with similar maturity and generate similar patterns and hence systemic risks [Jorion (2007)]. Therefore, one extension is to incorporate heterogeneous banks that have debts and assets with different maturities and to examine the contagion effects across banks of heterogeneity, the effects on systemic risks and the possibility of bank runs.

Contagion effects

The banks' activities of taking and transferring risks can easily cause contagion effects. The contagion effects may be revealed in the balance sheets, as pointed out by Kiyotaki and Moore (1997, 2002), or in other ways, such as shadow banking activities [Chang (2015)]. The contagion effects may not be limited to one country. The banks' activities have expanded to an international level due to the deregulation of the banking system and the liberalization of the capital markets. Therefore, it is important and urgent to have an extension to examine the impacts of the risk taking and transferring on an international level and the possibility of this in affecting the contagion effects via the banking channel across countries.

Liquidity, policies and supervision

To prevent banking crises, both the *ex post* provision of liquidity and the *ex ante* policies have been suggested. However, the effectiveness of the liquidity provision and related policies is limited to certain circumstances and may have their own associated costs/negative impacts to the economy. Therefore, an extension to examine various policies on liquidity provision, supervision and regulations and their impacts on banking crises and stability is very important. Moreover, as shown in Kashyap et al (2014) and Freixas (2010), only proper regulations can improve Pareto Optimal. It is the task of theoretical analysis to find those "proper" regulations.

Policy implications

Restrict leveraging/shadow banking activities

As pointed out by Allen and Gale (2007a), Jorion (2007), O'Brien and Berkowitz (2007) and Gertler and Kiyotaki (2015), the risk-taking and transferring activities of the banks can cause bank failure, which can generate systemic risks and increase instability. Moreover, the increasing amount of leverage and shadow banking activities conducted by the banks and financial sectors is of great concern since leverage would have the banks overlook risks and increase risk-taking and transferring activities, which would increase instability and crises [Chang (2015), Hanson et al (2015), Kashyap et al (2014), Schularick and Taylor (2012)]. Since managing risks is one main focus of bank governance [Dermine (2013)], the policies which encourage the banks to improve bank governance would be a large improvement. Meanwhile, the policies that would restrict the banks from taking specific high-risk activities, such as leveraging and shadow banking, are also important. Note that the policies should not be simply to restrict specific activities but to understand the reasons the activities are taken and have the policies to find alternative ways to help the banks resolve the problems by taking safer steps/activities.

Reduce systemic risks

When banks' activities of taking and transferring risks become a pattern, systemic risks are generated, and the banking system would be vulnerable to shocks [Jorion (2007)]. When systemic risks are detected, it is important to have the policies to manage the risks. For example, repurchase agreement (repo) and reverse, as one major shadow banking activity which has been widely adopted by the banks, has been referred to as one main cause of systemic risks. Bernanke [2008a, 2008b, 2009, 2014], the chairperson of the Federal Reserve Bank during the period, has pointed this out and suggested facilitating reverse to reduce systemic risks.

Accounting rules and transparent banking activities

When the banks' activities have expanded to an international level, the risk-taking and transferring activities are also taken to an international level. The activities at the international level, on one hand, could earn the banks more profits. On the other hand, the banks are taking and exposing themselves to more risks. The banking channel becomes open to contagion effects via balance sheets [Kiyotaki and Moore (2002)] or other ways, such as shadow banking activities [Chang (2015)]. Unfortunately, it is well known that the accounting rules in making banks' balance sheets are very complicated, especially for banks involved in international activities. The complicated accounting rules make it difficult to detect specific activities which involve high risks and might shake the stability of the banking system and the financial markets. Being incapable of detecting high-risk activities would handicap macro-prudential policies, supervision and regulation. Therefore, one important step to detect high-risk activities of the banks is to unify the accounting rules at an international level. Moreover, the accounting rules should be simple and should reveal the bank activities clearly and transparently.

Encourage heterogeneity in banks

As discussed, identical banks can easily generate the same pattern and hence systemic risks. One possible remedy is to have heterogeneous banks, which tend to hold different types of assets and liabilities that may reduce systemic risks. Moreover, the policies which restrict specific risks transferring across banks may prevent contagion effects of bank runs.

Liquidity and policies

As analysed in Chapters 3 and 4, even in a relatively secure bank governance in a BSF system, bank runs can be inevitable. Therefore, proper liquidity assistance would be effective in preventing type I bank runs and preventing economic activities from being disrupted. The importance of liquidity assistance in preventing banking crises is also found in Baldursson and Portes (2013), Bordo and

Landon-Lane (2010) and Fukuda (2001). However, liquidity provision, such as deposit insurance, could lead to moral hazards in banking [Demirgüç-Kunt et al (2014), Diamond and Dybvig (1983), Gropp and Vesala (2004), Hellmann et al (2000), Hooks and Robinson (2002), Kim et al (2014), Martin (2006), McCoy (2007), Weinstein (1992)]. Therefore, policies to improve bank governance to manage risks are important.

Many policies, including macro-prudential policies, supervision and regulations, have been broadly discussed concerning their effectiveness in improving bank governance [Freixas (2010), Kashyap et al (2014), Masciandaro and Volpicella (2016), Masciandaro et al (2013)]. One of the most popular policies which has been implemented is capital requirement. However, due to the banks' main goal of maximizing profits, it has been found that capital requirements would cause inefficient outcome and encourage gambling behaviour by the banks [Hellmann et al (2000)]. The analysis of Hellmann et al (2000) shows that there might be problems associated with policies. Therefore, it is crucial for the authorities to examine the policies thoroughly prior to their implementation in the economy. Moreover, having simple and easy-to-understand accounting rules to show the activities and transactions transparently would improve the effectiveness of policies.

Capital controls

According to the theoretical results of Chapter 3 and the empirical findings of Lee et al (2013), Uctum and Uctum (2011) and Brink and Viviers (2003), the openness to FPI would expose the country to high risks and a higher possibility of banking crises. Moreover, FPI flows would increase dependency on foreign capital and would trigger sudden stops [Bordo et al (2010)], which would then cause financial instability and banking crises [Komulainen (2004), de Mello, Padoan and Rousova (2012)], as shown in the theoretical analysis of Chapter 4. Therefore, there have been an increasing number of countries implementing capital controls, especially after the 1990s [Edwards (2009a), Johnson et al (2007)]. The implementation of capital controls has been supported by the IMF [IMF (2012)] since 2012 even though the results of the effectiveness of capital controls are mixed in empirical studies. By summarizing the empirical studies, one can identify the challenges to empirics in studying capital controls. These challenges have contributed to the mixed results of capital controls.

Challenges for empirical studies

The formats of controls

Controls can be implemented in different formats and can be direct and indirect. The direct controls can be in terms of directions [Pasricha (2012)], in terms of the types, such as bond flows, credit flows or debt flows [Molnar et al (2013), Tamirisa (2006)] or in terms of forms such as taxes [Neely (1999), Wibaut (2014),

Wong and Eng (2015)]. The indirect controls include interest rate, reserves [Jeanne (2016), Steiner (2013), Vithessonthi and Tongurai (2013)], the restrictions on the right of capital owners [Sigurgeirsdottir and Wade (2015)] and exchange rate intervention [Blanchard et al (2015)]. Depending on the characteristics, one country would implement specific format(s) of controls but not others. Depending on the specific economic conditions of the countries, some controls may work more effectively than others. Therefore, empirical studies are needed to tease out more details as to the formats of the controls and the economic conditions of the countries needed to analyse whether the controls are in/effective under certain circumstances only. Unfortunately, only a few empirical studies focus on specific formats of controls for analysis. Empirical studies which take a sample of countries during a specific period of time to analyse capital controls can easily mislead the understanding of the effects of capital controls, especially when there is no investigation of the timing and the formats of the controls which have been implemented in each country included in the analysis.

On and off capital controls

Capital controls are not universal policies. The countries can decide whether to implement or to remove the controls, depending on what suits the countries best at the time. After the removal of capital controls during the 1970s to 1990, more countries have started to implement controls. These countries are Thailand, Malaysia, Philippines and Indonesia in Asia, Czech Republic and Spain in Europe and Colombia, Brazil and Argentina in South America. The removal and the re-implementation of capital controls would increase the challenges in analysing the impacts of controls, especially when some effects take time to surface, as shown in the theoretical analysis in Chapters 3 to 5. Before the effects surface, the changes related to the policies would mix the effects of the initial policies and the changes of the policies. Unfortunately, it is difficult to understand the length of time for specific effects to surface, and most countries simply implement or change policies when they need to. Therefore, it has been a challenge for empirical studies to analyse the effects of controls and the related policies accurately. Moreover, since there are several formats of controls, the countries may implement several controls together and then add/remove some controls. Therefore, the empirical studies which select a period of time to examine the effects of controls without knowing the formats and the time when the controls are amended could easily have mixed results, which can mislead policy makers and must be interpreted with caution. This may be one of the reasons empirical studies of capital controls are sensitive not only to the data and methodologies but also to the selected time, formats and countries.

Financial markets and banking systems

As discussed in Chapter 3, despite various terms and definitions, several empirical studies have stated that FPI flows are connected to the financial markets [Abid and Bahloul (2011), Agbloyor et al (2014), Bartokova (2011), Choong et al

(2010a, 2010b), Errunza (2001), Gur (2015), Popov (2014)], whether it is the openness or the integration of the financial markets. Regarding the restrictions of financial openness and integration, both Kinda (2012) and Lajuni et al (2008) refer to it as capital controls. However, it is important to acknowledge that the financial markets which are less developed may not be as open and as integrated as expected. The concepts which consider controls as restrictions of the openness and the integration of financial markets are appliable only to the financial markets which are relatively developed and have the ability to open and to be integrated or integrate other markets but choose not to do so. Unfortunately, it is difficult for empirical studies to differentiate the financial markets at different development stages and to identify whether it is the controls or the under/development of the financial markets that have affected capital flows and their effects.

Moreover, to develop and stabilize the financial markets, the stability of the banking system is very important [Joyce and Nabar (2009)]. To improve the stability of the banking system, bank governance to manage the risks well is crucial, as analysed in Chapter 5 and pointed out by Dermine (2013). Regarding the risks of the banking system, there are systemic risks and the risks of each individual bank. It is crucial to differentiate systemic risks from the risks of each individual bank so that proper policies can be applied, whether macro-prudential policies, supervision or regulations. Several studies have taken the first step to make the differentiations. For example, Hartmann et al (2007) and Hovakimian et al (2015) have developed methodologies to assess system risks. Gambacorta (2008) and Williams (2014) examine the performances of the banks and find that capital structures and national governance may help the banks to manage risks and reduce the risks of the individual banks.

The controls of other countries

Capital controls are not limited to one country. When more countries have implemented controls, the impacts of the controls of other countries would affect the effects of the controls of the domestic country. Between two countries, when one country controls inflows while the other country controls outflows, the impacts of the controls would depend on the size of the controls in each of the two countries. When one country does not implement controls while the other countries have controls on either inflows or outflows, then the country without controls would be affected by the controls of other countries. Moreover, among multiple countries, the changes in the volumes and the composition of one country's FPI flows may be due to the implementation/liberalization of some countries' controls, not because of one country's economic conditions, such as the openness or integration of financial markets. This is because the outflows/inflows to/from specific countries can be substitutes or complements, depending on the motives for different types of flows. The analysis accounting for the controls on different types of flows would be even more complicated. Furthermore, it is difficult for empirical studies to verify whether the changes of flows are due to the controls of the countries or other economic conditions. Researchers who are not able to verify the causes of the changes of the volumes and the compositions of flows could easily misinterpret the findings of the empirical studies, especially when the results are mixed. This is why Chapter 6 has conducted a theoretical analysis on the effects of relative controls of both the home and the foreign countries.

Possible theoretical extensions

To examine the effectiveness of capital controls, following the foci of the empirical studies, the theoretical analysis in Chapter 6 focuses on three areas: (1) the volumes of capital flows, (2) the composition of capital flows and (3) the decrease on the possibility of bank runs/banking crises. Following Montiel and Reinhart (1999), the composition of capital flows is defined as the ratio of SR capital to LR FDI. It is shown that in a two-country model, the inflow controls would be effective for the country which implements controls and would have negative impacts on the partner country by increasing the possibility of type I bank runs in the partner country. Meanwhile, outflow controls would be ineffective for the country which implements the controls by increasing the possibility of type I bank runs but would benefit the partner country by decreasing the possibility of type I bank runs in the partner country. Therefore, depending on the directions of capital flows of the countries between countries, the countries would be benefitted or damaged by the controls implemented in the home and/or the partner country.

Controls of multiple countries

The current framework in Chapter 6 is a two-country model that cannot assess the characteristics of flows to and from different countries, which may be substitutes or complements. Therefore, the controls of one country on a specific type of flows could affect the flows of a country that has no direct connection to the country with controls.

The overlapping effects of the changes of policies

Due to the changes of economic conditions and global financial conditions, countries can change controls by adding more or removing some. Depending on the economic conditions, it may take longer for some countries to absorb the changes of the policies. Therefore, the frequent changes in the policies would make it difficult to analyse the effects of the controls, especially when various types of controls are involved. Therefore, one possible extension is to examine the effects of frequent changes in policies. This extension may help identify causes for the mixed results of empirical studies.

The development of financial markets

The development of financial markets could affect FPI flows and the effects of flows, as well as the effects of controls. Meanwhile, capital controls could restrict specific financial activities and affect FPI flows. Chapter 6 analyses the effects of capital controls on FPI flows. One extension would be to analyse the effects of the financial markets at different development stages on the effects of capital controls.

The formats of controls and economic conditions

Various formats of controls would have different impacts on the economy. When one country implements more than one format of controls, the impacts could be offset or magnified, depending on the formats of the controls as well as the economic conditions of the country and global financial conditions. Therefore, it would be important to have an extension to analyse the effects caused by various formats of controls to identify possible causes for the mixed results in empirical studies.

Policy implications

The increasing possibility of banking crises and financial instability associated with the openness to FPI flows and sudden stops has led many countries to implement policies to manage the risks, especially after the 1990s and the suggestion of the IMF in 2012 [IMF (2012)]. Capital controls have been among the policies that have been broadly implemented by countries to manage these risks, despite the findings of some studies that instead suggest promoting free capital mobility.

The goals of controls

It is important to understand that not every policy serves the same goal. Some policies aim to improve market efficiency, and some policies aim to manage risks. While implementing policies with various goals, it is crucial to analyse and understand the effects of each policy so that the goals/effects of some policies do not compromise others. While free capital mobility is among the former policies aiming to improve market efficiency, capital controls are the latter policies aiming to manage risks. Even though free capital mobility aims to improve market efficiency, Benzing (2001) finds that financial liberalization would increase inefficiency in emerging markets. According to Acharya and Bengui (2016), it is important for capital management to be in place, since free capital flows may not always achieve market efficiency. At the time when free capital mobility fails to improve market efficiency, it is important to examine the causes which prevent the liberalization of controls from achieving the goal to improve market efficiency rather than requiring the policies, such as capital controls, which aim to manage risks to improve market efficiency.

Although it is not the main goal for capital controls to improve market efficiency, it is wonderful when the controls have managed risks and improved market efficiency simultaneously, as shown in Graham et al (2015)'s study on Iceland. If not, it is important for controls to focus on a goal of managing risks even though it might distort international capital allocations, as shown in El-Shagi (2012a, 2012b). Therefore, the effectiveness of capital controls should be evaluated in terms of their effects on affecting the volumes and the compositions of capital flows and on affecting the possibility of banking crises.

Liberalization and implementation

It has been a struggle for many countries to decide whether to implement/liberalize capital controls, especially when the results of capital controls are mixed. The mixed results of capital controls result from two research streams, one on capital control implementation and the other on capital control liberalization. While capital control implementation is about the effects of implementing controls in the countries which have not yet implemented such controls, capital control liberalization is about the effects of taking controls away from the countries which have implemented them. If capital controls were not effective in affecting the volumes and the compositions of capital flows, it is more likely that the liberalization of the controls would not affect much of the volumes and the compositions of the flows. Therefore, in order for capital control liberalization to be effective, the implementation of capital controls would be effective, or the change of economic conditions/global financial conditions would have increased the effectiveness of the implementation/liberalization of capital controls. If this is not the case, then it is important for research claiming the effectiveness of liberalization to clarify what may have been overlooked in this argument and whether there is evidence to support that the effectiveness of liberalization can stand alone without the effectiveness of controls and/or the changes of economic conditions/global financial conditions.

Economic conditions of countries and global financial conditions

Economic conditions and the connections to global financial conditions are crucial in affecting the effects of the implementation/liberalization of capital controls, including the magnitude and the length of the effects. In general, several economic conditions are found to be crucial in affecting the effects of capital controls. The economic conditions include macroeconomic positions [Yepez Albornoz (2012)], exchange rate positions [Fratzscher (2012), Ostry et al (2011)], current account deficits [Ghosh and Qureshi (2016)], income levels [Binici et al (2010)], the policies of the banks and financial markets [Tamirisa (2006)] and the period time prior to or during the aftermath of crises [Bijsterbosch et al (2015)], which would affect the effectiveness of capital controls. Depending on the countries, David (2009) finds that the controls have different effects on the SR and LR flows in Chile and Colombia, while Jongwanich et al (2011) find that controls have different effects on inflows and outflows in Thailand and in Malaysia.

The length of effectiveness

Depending on economic conditions, it may take some countries longer than others to adjust fully to the changes in policies. After economic variables have fully adjusted to the changes in the policies, the SR effects would be replaced by the

LR effects, which may be different from the SR effects. Therefore, it is crucial to understand both the SR and the LR effects of policies and the factors which would influence the SR and/LR effects of policies, such as the type(s) of controls [Eichengreen and Rose (2014)] and the length of controls [Klein and Shambaugh (2015)].

Similar to most empirical studies on capital flows, most research on the liberalization of controls does not specify whether the effects are for SR or for LR. Based on the effects found in the empirical studies, such as increasing FDI and FPI flows [Jongwanich et al (2011)] and reducing exchange rate appreciation [Forbes et al (2015)], it seems that these effects tend to be for SR not for LR. This is because it is less likely to keep reducing the exchange rate, and it is less likely for one country to have continuously growing capital inflows or outflows over time, due to the limit of capital one country has.

If the effects of liberalization were not for LR, the benefits associated with the liberalization would disappear gradually, and economic variables would adjust accordingly. When all controls were liberalized, the LR effects of the liberalization would be similar to the case of an open economy without controls. This may explain why Grittersova (2014) and Orlov (2005) find that the liberalization would increase the roles of banks and financial institutions and increase financial volatility. The increase in the role of the banks, as analysed in the previous section and in Chapter 5, would increase risk-taking and transferring activities of the banks and increase instability in the banking system and in the financial markets. The increase in volatility would expose one country to more financial risks and contagion effects [Brink and Viviers (2003), Lee et al (2013)]. Moreover, the increase in dependency on foreign capital would trigger sudden stops [Bordo et al (2010)], and the increasing capital mobility would increase financial instability [Komulainen (2004)] and lead to banking crises [de Mello, Padoan, and Rousova (2012)].

As discussed in the previous section, the goal served by the liberalization of controls is to improve market efficiency, which can be at the costs of exposing the economy to financial risks and hence increase financial instability and the possibility of banking crises. Meanwhile, the goal served by the implementation of capital controls is to manage risks, which can be at the cost of distorting capital allocation. Therefore, it is important to understand which goal is more important and urgent to achieve for the economy under the current economic conditions of the country and global financial conditions.

The compositions of flows and the formats/types of controls

Depending on the economic conditions of the countries, global financial conditions and policies, the compositions and the volumes of capital flows may change accordingly. Depending on the compositions of flows, the implementation/liberalization of some controls may be more effective than others [Jongwanich and Kohpaiboon (2012)]. To simplify the analysis, most studies follow Montiel and Reinhart (1999) to define the composition of flows as the ratio of SR capital to LR FDI. However, it is important to keep in mind that the composition of controls is not only regarding the proportion of SR capital to LR capital but also regarding the proportion of type A flows to type B flows, such as banking debt flows to portfolio investment flows, and the proportion of flows from country A to country B as well as the flows from/to different countries.

Various types/formats of controls can be implemented for different countries and different types of flows. Different types/formats of controls would have different impacts on different flows/variables [Pasricha et al (2015), You et al (2014)]. To find the suitable controls to implement would require thorough investigations and analysis of economic conditions of countries, including their related policies and the connections to global financial conditions. Note that the conditions are dynamic, so the investigations and analysis should adjust accordingly, and so do the changes in policies, in order for it to benefit the countries the most. For example, wealth and the level of public expenditure are two economic conditions of a country. Accordingly to Boucekkine et al (2013), depending on the level of public expenditure, capital controls and liberalization have their suitable wealth level. That is, within a specific range of wealth, controls would be more suitable than liberalization, while outside the range, liberalization would be more suitable than controls.

Conclusion

This chapter revisits the empirical findings and theoretical results of each topic in order to identify the factors that might contribute to the inconsistency in results between theoretical and empirical analysis and the causes which may have led to mixed results in empirical findings in the literature. Moreover, the chapter discusses possible theoretical extensions and policy implications that may be useful for future studies if we wish to understand capital flows better.

It is challenging to conduct empirical studies in international economics on capital flows. One of the reasons is associated with the various definitions and measurements across countries and across time. The characteristics of some methodologies also tend to lead to specific results. Therefore, it has been well documented that the results of capital flows are sensitive to the datasets and methodologies adopted for empirical analysis. This chapter goes further to discuss the complications which are involved in capital flows, such as the changes of economic conditions and global financial conditions, as well as other factors which are crucial in affecting the effects of capital flows and their related policies. It is possible that the chapter may have overlooked some factors which may affect capital flows, and I will leave it to future studies to provide evidence and to investigate/analyze further.

Notes

1 Fortanier (2007) uses the dataset of bilateral investment stock of six major outward investor countries in 71 host countries for the period 1989–2002 and finds that the FDI effects on growth would depend on both the home countries and the

characteristics of the host countries. Choi (2004) investigates OECD from 1982 to 1997 and finds that an increase in bilateral FDI would narrow the growth gap between the home and the host countries. Moreover, Choi (2004) finds that it is geographical closedness and common language which contribute to the growth and income convergence between the home and the host countries.

2 Barclay (2004) finds that intervention policies to improve technology capacity are crucial to the effects of FDI on growth when studying less developed countries. Kotrajaras et al (2011), when studying 15 Asian countries, find that the FDI effects on growth would depend on the macro policies as well as the governance and development of financial markets and institutions of the host countries.

3 Solomon (2011) finds that the levels of economic development, human capital and quality of the political environment have significant impacts on the FDI effects on growth when studying the panel data of 111 countries from 1981 to 2005. The importance of human capital level is supported by Wang and Wong (2009a, 2009b). Wang and Wong (2009a) find that obtaining positive FDI effects on host growth would require a specific level of human capital and financial development in the host country. Meanwhile, the effects would also depend on the type of investment [Wang and Wong (2009b)] and the quality of education [Wang and Wong (2011)]. Moreover, Wang and Wong (2009b) study 84 countries during 1987 to 2001 and find that the effects also depend on the type of investment. To be more specific, greenfield investment promotes economic growth, while cross-border mergers and acquisitions would require an adequate level of human capital in order to have positive effects. Wang and Wong (2011) re-examine the schooling data of Borensztein, De Gregori, and Lee (1998) and find that the positive effects of FDI would depend on the quality of education.

4 Doytch and Uctum (2011) study middle- to low-income countries and the economies with a large industry share, including countries in Latin America-Caribbean and in Europe and central Asia, and find that the effects of FDI vary in industries and can be affected by the regions and the location of the host countries. Extending the study to include high-income countries by using the World Bank's classification, Kasibhatla, Stewart, and Khojasteh (2008) find that among the five countries studied (China, India, Mexico, the UK and the US), only India shows FDI–led growth as a host country. The result does not apply to the other four (China, Mexico, the UK and the US). However, whether it is India's location or other characteristics which lead to positive effects is not explained in their work. Another work focusing on the income level of the countries is Mayer-Foulkes and Nunnenkamp (2009). By accounting for both positive and negative effects of FDI on host countries, Mayer-Foulkes and Nunnenkamp (2009) find that the convergence would accelerate only for high-income countries but would slow down for other countries. By summarizing many theoretical and empirical works, Forte and Moura (2013) also conclude that the effects of FDI would depend on the economic conditions of the host countries.

5 More issues related to the mismatch between output demand and output supply and mismeasurement of GDP can be found in Stiglitz, Sen, and Fitoussi (2010).

6 The term "may be" is used here because most studies do not define the word "growth".

7 As mentioned in the second section, in practice, it is difficult to select one single variable and use the adjustments of the variable to differentiate SR from LR, so most empirical studies do not specify whether their results are for SR or for LR. Therefore, the comparison of empirical findings would focus on the general results rather than on SR or LR results.

8 Inagaki (2016) uses the data of G7 countries to analyse the effects of population aging on capital flows and current account reversals.

9 Regarding to policies in affecting the interdependence between countries, one can start with the research of Fortanier (2007) and Choi (2004). Fortanier (2007) uses the bilateral investment stock dataset to study the interdependence between the home and the host countries, and Choi (2004) investigates bilateral FDI between the home and the host countries and the impacts on the growth gap.

10 Agbloyor et al (2014) focuses on economic growth in Africa during the period 1990–2007 when using a panel instrumental variable generalized method of moments (IV-GMM) to estimate the empirical relations. Popov (2014) focuses on 93 countries during the 1973–2009 period when using panel analysis for both aggregate and sector-level data by controlling time-varying and country-specific factors across countries. Shen et al (2010) focus on the panel data for 80 countries during 1976–2007 when using OLS, the fixed-effect and random-effect models.

8 Conclusion

Introduction

Capital flows connect countries and change what has happened in a closed economy. The capital flows have tied the financial markets and the production sectors across countries together, and they become more interdependent. Through capital flows, both their volumes and their compositions, one can analyse the development of one country's markets and exposure to the contagion effects of other countries as well as one country's sensitivity to the changes of global financial conditions. The interdependence and closedness of the markets and sectors across countries have increased challenges for empirical studies. Moreover, various definitions and measurements of datasets across countries and across time have made it more difficult to analyse the data prior to applying methodologies, and some methodologies tend to lead to specific results due to their characteristics. Therefore, most empirical studies on capital flows tend to have mixed results. The results which are achieved without thorough examination of datasets, methodologies, the economic conditions of the countries and global financial conditions can easily mislead related policy implications and generate more puzzles and endless debates. These are debates which are difficult to find common ground or agreement to move the debates forward and continue to be endless if we keep taking datasets and specific methodologies as granted without further examination of their suitability in analyzing capital flows and if we keep neglecting the practical lessons from theoretical analysis.

Empirical and theoretical work cannot be separated from each other. We require empirical work to show more realities for the theoretical framework so we know what to simplify and to focus on in the analysis. We require theoretical analysis of the empirical works to know what factors have been overlooked and to understand better the causality and the changes of variables as well as the possible impacts of shocks and policies. Through theoretical analysis, we are more likely to identify the possible causes of the inconsistency in the empirical findings and to build up the bridge between arguments.

It is the goal of this book to construct a theoretical framework to analyse capital flows and their linkages to economic growth and banking systems. There are various types of capital flows. The two main types of flows are foreign direct investment (FDI) flows and foreign portfolio investment (FPI) flows, which are the focuses of this book. Each type of flow has characteristics which can impact the economy in different ways. Depending on how data is collected and measured and how the datasets are constructed, it is difficult to conduct empirical studies to identify the different impacts caused by different types of flows and to analyse them for some countries during specific periods of time. This is where the theoretical analyses can help. Throughout the book, a theoretical framework of three-period-lived overlapping generations in an open economy with two countries is constructed. To start with, the theoretical framework is incorporated with an explicit banking sector in which the banks serve as portfolio managers for the depositors, as is the traditional setup of banks, to analyse the effects on growth. The model is then modified accordingly to analyse the issues of each topic. Chapters 2 and 3 analyse the impacts of FDI and FPI flows on economic growth, respectively. FPI flows are closely connected to sudden stops, which raise concerns about the stability of the financial system and banking system. The analysis of the impacts of sudden stops and their relations to the banking system is provided in Chapter 4. In addition to capital flows, bank governance is also crucial to the stability of the banking system. Therefore, Chapter 5 examines various forms of bank governance and their connections to the possibility of banking crises as well as the effectiveness of liquidity provisions. In response to capital flows and the associated financial risks, an increasing number of countries have implemented capital controls even though the empirical results have been mixed. Due to interdependence, every country is connected to other countries, which may or may not have controls. Chapter 6 examines the interdependence and mutual effects of the controls and their effectiveness. Chapter 7 maps the theoretical results of the previous chapters to the empirical findings in the literature and provides practical lessons for both theoretical and empirical analyses. Note that the possible causes of mixed empirical results are based on the lessons learned from the theoretical analysis. I don't rule out the possibility that the causes of the mixed empirical results can be due to datasets and methodologies, which will be left to the experts in those areas to comment on.

FDI and growth

FDI flows are LR flows and are connected to the production sectors. Depending on wage income, it is assumed that the firms would conduct FDI flows to take advantage of the labour supply with lower wage income. The FDI flows modelled are similar to the FDI flows from the developed to the developing countries. Moreover, following the traditional literature, the banks are assumed to have zero profit and to serve as central planners without incentive problems, so there would be no bank run. Therefore, the analysis can focus on the impacts of FDI flows on economic growth in the home and the host countries in the SR and in the LR. SR is defined as when wage income has not yet adjusted to the openness to FDI flows, while LR is defined as when wage income has fully adjusted to the openness to FDI flows.

Through investment portfolio adjustments of the banks to maximize the welfare of the depositors, it is found that the home countries with FDI outflows are more likely to experience an increase in unemployment and a higher growth rate in the SR. Meanwhile, the adjustments of the portfolios would lead to an increase in the rate of return of capital but a decrease in the growth rate in the host country in the SR. In the LR, the home country would have a decrease in wage income resulting from a decrease in labour demand. A host country would have an increase in wage income in the LR due to FDI inflows, which increase labour demand. The impacts of FDI flows on the rate of return of capital and the growth rates in both home and host countries would depend on the presence of the scale effects.

FPI and growth

FPI flows, in contrast to FDI flows, are the SR flows and tend to be more volatile. The volatile FPI flows have raised great concern about increasing financial instability and banking crises. This is mainly because the volatility of FPI flows would increase the volatility of the performances of the firms which depend on FPI flows and hence the volatility of the financial markets. Interestingly, most empirical studies find that FPI flows have negative impacts on economic growth. However, it is still a challenge for empirical work to connect FPI flows and crises.

Note that some effects take time to appear. The causes of the crises and the crises may not occur in the same period. Similarly, an incident may have SR and LR impacts. The SR and LR impacts may take time to appear and to be reflected in the data. The overlapping-generations theoretical framework is especially helpful in analysing the shocks which have both SR and LR impacts, and the impacts would take time to appear.

The theoretical framework has been modified to incorporate FPI flowing into the financial markets to invest in SR assets. Similar to Chapter 2, the banking system is assumed to be serving as a central planner and a portfolio manager for the depositors, called a bank-selected fully funded (BSF) system, in which there is no incentive problem, looting problem or moral hazard in banking. Consistent with most empirical findings, the theoretical analysis finds that FPI flows would reduce the growth rates of both home and host countries. Even under relatively secure bank governance, the BSF system, the banks would have liquidity shortfalls, which would lead to bank runs and banking crises if they were not being assisted properly. The bank runs which are caused by the failure to meet demand deposits are called type I bank runs, which might be prevented by proper liquidity provision.

Sudden stops and banking crises

As shown in several empirical studies, the increasing dependency on foreign capital could trigger sudden stops and increase financial instability and banking crises [Bordo et al (2007), de Mello, Padoan and Rousova (2012), Komulainen (2004)]. Sudden stops often refer to sudden slowdown of capital inflows from the viewpoint of the host countries. The impact of sudden stops on outflows has been neglected. In the modern economy, most countries are not only the home but also the host countries of FPI flows. The impacts of FPI flows on the home and the host countries are different and can be opposite under certain circumstances. Therefore, it is important to clarify whether the positive/negative impacts of FPI flows are from the role as a home or a host country.

The theoretical framework analyses the impacts of sudden stops in the home and in the host countries and incorporates endogenously determined interest rates in the SR and in the LR. Following Chapters 2 and 3, a BSF banking system is assumed. As a result, it is found that sudden stops would increase the probability of bank runs and banking crises in the home country but not in the host country. In response to sudden stops, a lower capital accumulation growth rate would damage future growth rate in the home country. Moreover, should bank runs and banking crises occur, economic activities would be disrupted, and the negative impacts on the economy would be long-lasting. Note that sudden stops could fail the incentive constraint and cause type II bank runs, which cannot be prevented by liquidity provision.

In the LR, after the home country survives turmoil in the SR, the home country's growth rate would bounce back and become higher than the growth rate prior to sudden stops. The host country, without the concerns of banking crises, would have a higher growth rate in the SR and a lower growth rate in the LR.

Bank governance and banking crises

There are several causes of bank runs and banking crises. One of the main causes is bank governance. Proper bank governance would manage risks well and have the ability to prevent bank runs and banking crises. Learning from bank governance in practice, the theoretical framework examines alternative bank governance, which assumes that the banks would maximize their profits rather than serving as central planners with zero profit, as in the traditional setup. The two alternative forms of bank governance examined in this topic are depositor-selected-fully-funded (DSF) and depositor-selected-leveraged (DSL) banking systems.

Different from the BSF system, the banks using DSF and DSL systems maximize their profits and do not take the costs which can be taken by the depositors. As a result, both DSF and DSL systems have more space to react to unexpected withdrawals. One major difference between DSF and DSL systems is how the system reacts to unexpected withdrawals. The DSF system would liquidate the LR assets as requested, while the DSL system would leverage by using the new accounts (the liability of the banks) to finance the liquidity shortfalls (the debt). Comparing the DSF and DSL systems, we find that the DSF system might lead to bank runs in the case of sudden stops but not the case of the openness to FPI flows, while the DSL system would cause bank runs and banking crises in the home country in both cases of the openness to FPI flows and of sudden stops. Since the bank runs are either or both type I and type II bank runs, the ability of liquidity provision to prevent bank runs and banking crises is limited.

The assumption that the host country would not reallocate FPI flows for LR investment has prevented unexpected withdrawals in the banking system and hence prevented bank runs and banking crises in the host country in either a DSF or a DSL system. The result implies that for the host countries to prevent banking crises, it is crucial to have proper bank governance and not to reallocate FPI flows for LR investment.

Capital controls and their effectiveness

The increasing instability in the financial and banking system associated with capital flows has led more countries to implement capital controls. There are various types and formats of capital controls which would impact the economy differently and via different channels. Meanwhile, the empirical findings give mixed results regarding the effectiveness of capital controls.

The interdependence between countries means that every country is connected to the countries with and without controls. Regardless of whether one country has its own control, the country is affected by the controls and non-controls of other countries. The theoretical analysis focuses on the interdependence and examines how one country is affected by its own controls and the controls of other countries. The effectiveness of the controls is evaluated by whether the controls would affect the volumes and the compositions of flows and whether the controls would reduce the possibility of bank runs and banking crises.

As a result, it is found that the inflow controls would be effective for the country which implements the controls and would have negative impacts on the other country by increasing the possibility of type I bank runs in the other country. Meanwhile, outflow controls would be ineffective for the country which implements the controls by increasing the possibility of type I bank runs but would benefit the other country by decreasing the possibility of type I bank runs in the other country. Therefore, depending on the directions of capital flows between the countries, the countries would be benefitted or damaged by the controls implemented in the home and/or the other country.

The lessons

By reviewing and comparing the theoretical results to empirical findings, we identify several possible causes on the inconsistent results. These are the causes in addition to the well-documented issues related to definitions and measurements of datasets and the characteristics of specific methodologies.

As one may realize, the data contains various frictions which can hardly be isolated and identified. The issues are more complicated in aggregate data which include many industries of a country. In contrast to LR FDI flows, SR FPI flows have more types and are more volatile. While the openness to FDI flows can be limited to specific industries, the openness to FPI flows can be limited to specific types of flows. Therefore, the impacts of the limited openness to capital flows would impact the industries differently and may be in opposite directions.

Depending on the speed of the responses to the openness, the data of a selected period tend to be dominated by specific industries. Therefore, the empirical findings tend to be sensitive to many factors, including the selected periods of time, even for the same country. The attempt to understand the empirical studies on a group of countries is even more difficult, since the openness time and industries/types of flows are different across countries. However, most of these causes seem neglected in many empirical studies. Therefore, inconsistent results in capital flows and the related controls become common, and debates are endless.

There is no doubt that there have been few theoretical frameworks developed to analyse capital flows and the connections to banking crises. The complications of analysing the data of capital flows and of analysing banking crises empirically make it more important to have theoretical analysis which can analyse the connections between capital flows and crises in a more comprehensive way. The theoretical analysis, in order to focus on specific issues, would simplify the economy to isolate specific factors to analyse the effects. Through comprehensive analysis, the theoretical framework is able to identify possible causes of inconsistent results. It is crucial for theoretical and empirical analysis not to separate from each other. Each analysis has its strengths and weaknesses. The theoretical and empirical analysis together are more complements rather than substitutes.

To learn lessons from both theoretical and empirical analysis is especially important for the studies which plan to draw policy implications. As pointed out throughout the book, the datasets, the methodologies, the countries and the selected periods of time would affect the policy implications drawn from specific empirical studies. Meanwhile, the simplifications made in theoretical analysis may also affect the policy implications. Therefore, it is crucial for policy makers to understand the issues related to specific research work prior to implementing/changing policies to regulate/liberalize capital flows.

There are many lessons one analysis can learn from another. All the existing research makes a contribution to future research. What this book has done is to construct a theoretical framework by incorporating the features learned from the empirical studies and to identify possible causes for the inconsistent empirical findings in order to move the debates forward and to draw the attention of policy makers to be cautious when considering policies based on specific research work. There are factors and connections which might be overlooked in this book. It would require future research to investigate and to analyse further to help us understand better the linkages between capital flows, financial markets and the banking system and their related issues.

References

Abbott, Andrew, and Glauco De Vita (2003), "Another Piece in the Feldstein-Horioka Puzzle", *Scottish Journal of Political Economics*, Vol. 50(1), pp. 69–89.

Abid, Fathi, and Slah Bahloul (2011), "Selected MENA Countries' Attractiveness to G7 Investors", *Economic Modelling*, September, Vol. 28(5), pp. 2197–207.

Acemoglu, Daron (2009), *Introduction to Modern Economic Growth*, Princeton University Press, Princeton, NJ.

Acharya, Sushant, and Julien Bengui (2016), "Liquidity Traps, Capital Flows", *Federal Reserve Bank of New York staff reports* 765.

Acharya, Viral V. and Bruce Tuckman (2014), "Unintended Consequences of LOLR Facilities: The Case of Illiquid Leverage", *IMF Economic Review*, Vol. 62, pp. 606–55.

Acharya, Viral V., and Nada Mora (2012), "Are Banks Passive Liquidity Backstops? Deposit Rates and Flows during the 2007–2009 Crisis", *NBER Working Paper 17838*, National Bureau of Economic Research.Cambridge, MA.

Agbloyor, Elikplimi Komla, Joshua Yindenaba Abor, Charles Komla Delali Adjasi, and Alfred Yawson (2014), "Private Capital Flows and Economic Growth in Africa: The Role of Domestic Financial Markets", *Journal of International Financial Markets, Institutions and Money*, May, Vol. 30, pp. 137–52.

Aggarwal, Raj, Colm Kearney, and Brian Lucey (2012), "Gravity and Culture in Foreign Portfolio Investment", *Journal of Banking and Finance*, Vol. 36(2), pp. 525–38.

Aghion, Philippe, and Peter Howitt (1998), *Endogenous Growth Theory*, MIT Press, Cambridge, MA.

Aguirre Carmona, Pablo (2014), "Capital Account Regulation in Iceland: Does Anybody Know What Is Going to Happen?", *Journal of Post Keynesian Economics*, Spring, Vol. 36(3), pp. 491–511.

Ahmed, Faisal, Rabah Arezki, and Norbert Funke (2007), "The Composition of Capital Flows to South Africa", *Journal of International Development*, March, Vol. 19(2), pp. 275–94.

Ahmed, Shaghil, and Andrei Zlate (2014), "Capital Flows to Emerging Market Economies: A Brave New World?", *Journal of International Money and Finance*, November, Vol. 48, pp. 221–48.

Akerlof, George, and Paul Romer (1993), "Looting: The Economic Underworld of Bankruptcy for Profit", *Brooking Papers on Economic Activity*, Vol. 1993(2), pp. 1–73.

Akram, Gilal Muhammad, and Joseph P. Byrne (2015), "Foreign Exchange Market Pressure and Capital Controls", *Journal of International Financial Markets, Institutions and Money*, July, Vol. 37, pp. 42–53.

Alesina, Alberto, Vittorio Grilli, and Gian Maria Milesi-Ferretti (1993), "The Political Economy of Capital Controls", NBER working paper, National Bureau of Economic Research Inc., Cambridge, MA.

Alfaro, Laura (2004), "Capital Controls: A Political Economy Approach", *Review of International Economics*, September, Vol. 12(4), pp. 571–90.

Alfaro, Laura and Fabio Kanczuk (2004), "Capital Controls, Risk, and Liberalization Cycle", *Review of International Economics*, August, Vol. 12(3), pp. 412–34.

Allen, Franklin and Douglas Gale (2007a), "Systemic Risk and Regulation", Chapter 7 in *The Risks of Financial Institutions*, edited by Mark Carey and Rene M. Stulz, University of Chicago Press, Chicago, pp. 341–75.

Allen, Franklin, and Douglas Gale (2007b), *Understanding Financial Crises*, Oxford University Press, New York.

Altinkemer, Melike (2005), "Recent Experiences with Capital Controls: Is There a Lesson for Turkey?", *Central Bank Review*, July, Vol. 5(2), pp. 1–38.

Amin, Fouzia and Sanmugam Annamalah (2013), "An Evaluation of Malaysian Capital Controls", *Journal of Economic Studies*, Vol. 40(4), pp. 549–71.

Andreasen, Eugenia, Martin Schindler, and Patricio Valenzuela (2015), "Capital Controls and the Cost of Debt", *Working Paper, Wharton School*, University of Pennsylvania: Weiss Center.

Araujo, Juliana, Povilas Lastauskas, and Chris Papageorgiou (2015), "Evolution of Bilateral Capital Flows to Developing Countries at Intensive and Extensive Margins", *Cambridge Working Papers in Economics 1502*, University of Cambridge. http://www.econ.cam.ac.uk/research/repec/cam/pdf/CWPE1502.pdf.

Arisoy, Ibrahim (2012), "The Impact of Foreign Direct Investment on Total Factor Productivity and Economic Growth in Turkey", *Journal of Developing Areas*, Spring, Vol. 46(1), pp. 17–29.

Asiedu, Elizabeth (2004), "The Determinants of Employment of Affiliates of US Multinational Enterprises in Africa", *Development Policy Review*, July, Vol. 22(4), pp. 371–79.

Athukorala, Prema-chandra and Juthathip Jongwanich (2012), "How Effective Are Capital Controls? Evidence from Malaysia", *Asian Development Review*, Vol. 29(2), pp. 1–47.

Azman-Saini, W.N.W., Ahmad Zubaidi Baharumshah, and Siong Hook Law (2010), "Foreign Direct Investment, Economic Freedom and Economic Growth: International Evidence", *Economic Modelling*, September, Vol. 27(5), pp. 1079–89.

Baek, In-Mee (2006), "Portfolio Investment Flows to Asia and Latin America: Pull, Push or Market Sentiment?", *Journal of Asian Economics*, April, Vol. 17(2), pp. 363–73.

Bahmani, Sahar (2012), "Wage-Price Flexibility, Exchange Rate Flexibility, Capital Controls, and the Adjustment Speed in the Money Market", *Journal of Developing Areas*, Spring, Vol. 46(1), pp. 359–66.

Bai, Yan, and Jing Zhang (2010), "Solving the Feldstein-Horioka Puzzle with Financial Frictions", *Econometrica*, Vol. 78(2), pp. 603–32.

Baldursson, Fridrik Mar, and Richard Portes (2013), "Gambling for Resurrection in Iceland: The Rise and Fall of the Banks", *Centre for Economic Policy Research (CEPR) Discussion Papers: 9664*. London, UK.

Baliamoune-Lutz, Mina N. (2004), "Does FDI Contribute to Economic Growth?", *Business Economics*, Vol. 39(2), pp. 49–56.

Barba Navaretti, G., D. Castellani, and A. C. Disdier (2010), "How Does Investing in Cheap Labour Countries Affect Performance at Home? Firm Level Evidence from France and Italy", *Oxford Economic Papers*, Vol. 62(2), pp. 234–60.

Barclay, Lou Anne A. (2004), "Foreign Direct Investment-Facilitated Development: The Case of the Natural Gas Industry of Trinidad and Tobago", *Oxford Development Studies*, Vol. 32(4), pp. 485–505.

Barry, F., and C. Kearney (2006), "MNEs and Industrial Structure in Host Countries: A Portfolio Analysis of Irish Manufacturing", *Journal of International Business Studies*, May, Vol. 37(3), pp. 392–406.

Barry, F., and John Bradley (1997), "FDI and Trade: The Irish Host-Country Experience", *Economic Journal*, Vol. 107(445), pp. 1798–811.

Bartokova, Ludmila (2011), "Portfolio Investments in the Selected European Transition Economies", *Journal of Advanced Studies in Finance*, Summer, Vol. 2(1), pp. 4–17.

Bartram, Sohnke M., and Gunter Dufey (2001), "International Portfolio Investment: Theory, Evidence, and Institutional Framework", *Financial Markets, Institutions and Instruments*, August, Vol. 10(3), pp. 85–155.

Belloumi, Mounir (2014), "The Relationship between Trade, FDI and Economic Growth in Tunisia: An Application of the Autoregressive Distributed Lag Model", *Economic Systems*, Vol. 38(2), pp. 269–87.

Beltratti, Andrea, and René M. Stulz (2012), "The Credit Crisis around the Globe: Why Did Some Banks Perform Better?", *Journal of Financial Economics*, July, Vol. 105(1), pp. 1–17.

Ben Naceur, Sami, Damyana Bakardzhieva, and Bassem Kamar (2012), "Disaggregated Capital Flows and Developing Countries' Competitiveness", *World Development*, February, Vol. 40(2), pp. 223–37.

Bencivenga, V. R., and B. D. Smith (1991), "Financial Intermediation and Endogenous Growth", *Review of Economic Studies*, Vol. 58(2), pp. 195–209.

Bengoa, Marta and Blanca Sanchez-Robles (2003), "Foreign Direct Investment, Economic Freedom and Growth: New Evidence from Latin America", *European Journal of Political Economy*, September, Vol. 19(3), pp. 529–45.

Benigno, Gianluca, Huigang Chen, Christopher Otrok, Alessandro Rebucci, and Eric R. Young (2014), "Optimal Capital Controls and Real Exchange Rate Policies: A Pecuniary Externality Perspective", *Center for Economic Policy Research (CEPR) Discussion Papers: 9936*. London, UK.

Benzing, Cynthia (2001), "Capital Flows and Financial Crises: Theory versus Reality: Review Article", *Atlantic Economic Journal*, March, Vol. 29(1), pp. 107–12.

Bernanke, Ben (2008a), Speech Titled "Liquidity Provision by the Federal Reserve", At the *Federal Reserve Bank of Atlanta Financial Markets Conference*, Sea Island, Georgia (via satellite). http://www.federalreserve.gov/newsevents/speech/bernanke 20080513.htm.

Bernanke, Ben (2008b), Speech Titled "Reducing Systemic Risk", At the *Federal Reserve Bank of Kansas City's Annual Economic Symposium*, Jackson Hole, Wyoming. http://www.federalreserve.gov/newsevents/speech/bernanke20080822a.htm.

Bernanke, Ben (2009), Speech Titled "Reflections on a Year of Crisis", At the *Federal Reserve Bank of Kansas City's Annual Economic Symposium*, Jackson

Hole, Wyoming. http://www.federalreserve.gov/newsevents/speech/bernanke20090821a.htm.

Bernanke, Ben (2014), Speech Titled "The Federal Reserve: Looking Back, Looking Forward", At the *Annual Meeting of the American Economic Association*, Philadelphia, Pennsylvania. http://www.federalreserve.gov/newsevents/speech/bernanke20140103a.htm.

Berument, M. Hakan, Zulal S. Denaux, and Furkan Emirmahmutoglu (2015), "The Effects of Capital Inflows on Turkish Macroeconomic Performance", *Empirica*, November, Vol. 42(4), pp. 813–24.

Bhattacharya, Sharad Nath, and Mousumi Bhattacharya (2012), "Capital Inflows and Economic Growth: An Indian Perspective", *Bogazici Journal: Review of Social, Economic and Administrative Studies*, Vol. 26(2), pp. 93–114.

Bibow, Jorg (2008–2009), "Insuring against Private Capital Flows: Is It Worth the Premium? What Are the Alternatives?", *International Journal of Political Economy*, Winter, Vol. 37(4), pp. 5–30.

Bijsterbosch, Martin, Matteo Falagiarda, Gurnain Pasricha, and Joshua Aizenman (2015), "Domestic and Multilateral Effects of Capital Controls in Emerging Markets", ECB *Working Paper Series: 1844*. European Central Bank, Eurosystem. Frankfurt, Germany.

Binici, Mahir, Michael Hutchison, and Martin Schindler (2010), "Controlling Capital? Legal Restrictions and the Asset Composition of International Finance Flows", *Journal of International Money and Finance*, Vol. 29, pp. 666–84.

Bitzer, Jurgen, and Holger Gorg (2009), "Foreign Direct Investment, Competition, and Industrial Performances", *The World Economy*, February, Vol. 32(2), pp. 221–33.

Blanchard, Olivier, Gustavo Adler, and Irineu de Carvalho Filho (2015), "Can Foreign Exchange Intervention Stem Exchange Rate Pressures from Global Capital Flow Shocks?" *NBER Working Papers: 21427*, National Bureau of Economic Research. Cambridge, MA.

Bodman, Philip, and Thanh Le (2013), "Assessing the Roles That Absorptive Capacity and Economic Distance Play in the Foreign Direct Investment-Productivity Growth Nexus", *Applied Economics*, March, Vol. 45(7–9), pp. 1027–39.

Boero, Gianna, Kostas Mavromatis, and Mark P. Taylor (2015), "Real Exchange Rates and Transition Economies, *Journal of International Money and Finance*, September, Vol. 56, pp. 23–35.

Bohn, Henning, and Linda L. Tesar (1996), "U.S. Equity Investment in Foreign Markets: Portfolio Rebalancing or Return Chasing?", *American Economic Review*, May, Vol. 86(2), pp. 77–81.

Bordo, Michael D., Alberto F Cavallo, Christopher M. Meissner (2010), "Sudden Stops: Determinants and Output Effects in the First Era of Globalization, 1880–1913", *Journal of Development Economics*, Vol. 91(2), pp. 227–41.

Bordo, Michael D., B. Eichengreen, D. Klingebiel, and M. Martinez-Peria (2001), "Is the Crises Problem Growing More Severe?", *Economic Policy*, April, pp. 53–82.

Bordo, Michael D., and John Landon-Lane (2010), "The Lessons from the Banking Panics in the United States in the 1930s for the Financial Crisis of 2007–2008", *NBER Working Paper No. 16365*, National Bureau of Economic Research. Cambridge, MA.

Borenszrein, E., J. De Gregorio, and J-W. Lee (1998), "How Does Foreign Direct Investment Affect Economic Growth?", *Journal of International Economics*, Vol. 45, pp. 115–35.

Boucekkine, Raouf, Aude Pommeret, and Fabien Prieur (2013), "On the Timing and Optimality of Capital Controls: Public Expenditures, Debt Dynamics and Welfare", *International Journal of Economic Theory*, March, Vol. 9(1), pp. 101–12.

Braconier, H., K. Ekholm, and K.H.M. Knarvik (2001), "In Search of FDI-Transmitted R&D Spillovers: A Study Base on Swedish Data", *Review of World Economics*, Vol. 137(4), pp. 644–65.

Brink, Nicola, and Wilma Viviers (2003), "Obstacles in Attracting Increased Portfolio Investment into Southern Africa", *Development Southern Africa*, June, Vol. 20(2), pp. 213–36.

Brooks, Robin (2004), "Exchange Rates and Capital Flows", *European Financial Management*, September, Vol. 10(3), pp. 511–33.

Brunnermeier, Markus K., and Yuliy Sannikov (2015), "International Credit Flows and Pecuniary Externalities", *American Economic Journal: Macroeconomics*, January, Vol. 7(1), pp. 297–338.

Buss, Adrian (2013), "Capital Controls and International Financial Stability: A Dynamic General Equilibrium Analysis in Incomplete Markets", ECB *Working Paper Series: 1578*, European Central Bank. Eurosystem, Frankfurt, Germany.

Callen, Timothy, and Paul Cashin (2002), "Capital Controls, Capital Flows and External Crises: Evidence from India", *Journal of International Trade and Economic Development*, March, Vol. 11(1), pp. 77–98.

Calomiris, Charles W. (2009), "Banking Crises and the Rules of the Game", *NBER Working Paper No. 15403*, National Bureau of Economic Research. Cambridge, MA.

Calomiris, Charles W., and Doron Nissim (2007), "Activity-Based Valuation of Bank Holding Companies", *NBER Working Paper No. 12918*, National Bureau of Economic Research. Cambridge, MA.

Calomiris, Charles W., and Doron Nissim (2014), "Crisis-Related Shifts in the Market Valuation of Banking Activities", *Journal of Financial Intermediation*, Vol. 23(3), pp. 400–35.

Calvo, Guillermo A., Alejandro Izquierdo, and Ernesto Talvi (2003), "Sudden Stops, the Real Exchange Rate, and Fiscal Sustainability: Argentina's Lessons", *NBER Working Papers: 9828*, National Bureau of Economic Research. Cambridge, MA.

Campion, Mary Kathryn, and Rebecca M. Neumann (2003), "Compositional Effects of Capital Controls – Theory and Evidence", *World Economy*, July, Vol. 26(7), pp. 957–73.

Campos, Nauro F., and Yuko Kinoshita (2002), "Foreign Direct Investment as Technology Transferred: Some Panel Evidence from the Transition Economies", *Manchester School*, June, Vol. 70(3), pp. 398–419.

Cardoso, Eliana, and Ilan Goldfajn (1998), "Capital Flows to Brazil: The Endogeneity of Capital Controls", *International Monetary Fund Staff Papers*, March, Vol. 45(1), pp. 161–202.

Ceh, Ana Maria, and Ivo Krznar (2008), "Optimal Foreign Reserves: The Case of Croatia", *Financial Theory and Practice*, Vol. 32(4), pp. 421–60.

Chakraborty, Debasish, and Vigdis Boasson (2013), "Capital Flows, Degree of Openness and Macroeconomic Volatility", *Indian Journal of Economics and Business*, April, Vol. 12(1), pp. 1–12.

Chamon, Marcos and Márcio Garcia1 (2016), "Capital Controls in Brazil: Effective?", *Journal of International Money and Finance*, Vol. 61, pp. 163–87.

Chang, Chia-Ying Chang (2010), "Capital Flows, Financial Intermediaries, and Economic Growth", *Journal of International and Global Economic Studies*, Vol. 2(2), pp. 47–60.

Chang, Chia-Ying Chang (2012), "Can a Home Country Benefit from FDI: A Theoretical Analysis", *SEF Working Papers*, Victoria University of Wellington, New Zealand.

Chang, Chia-Ying Chang (2013a), "Banking Crises, Sudden Stops, and the Effectiveness of Short-term Lending", *SEF Working Papers*, Victoria University of Wellington, New Zealand.

Chang, Chia-Ying Chang (2013b), "Capital Controls, Capital Flows, and Banking Crises", *SEF Working Papers*, Victoria University of Wellington, New Zealand.

Chang, Chia-Ying Chang (2015), Interbank Repo, Reverse, and Regulations: The Roles on the run", *SSRN Working Papers 2587545*. http://dx.doi.org/10.2139/ssrn.2587545.

Chang, Chun, Zheng Liu, and Mark M. Spiegel (2015), "Capital Controls and Optimal Chinese Monetary Policy", *Journal of Monetary Economics*, September, Vol. 74, pp. 1–15.

Chang, Yanqin, and R. Todd Smith (2014), "Feldstein-Horioka Puzzles", *European Economic Review*, November, Vol. 72, pp. 98–112.

Chen, Shikuan, and Ming-Jen Chang (2015), "Capital Control and Exchange Rate Volatility", *North American Journal of Economics and Finance*, July, Vol. 33, pp. 167–77.

Chen, Shyh-Wei, and Chung-Hua Shen (2015), "Revisiting the Feldstein-Horioka Puzzle with Regime Switching: New Evidence from European Countries", *Economic Modelling*, Vol. 49, pp. 260–69.

Cheung, Yin-Wong, and Risto Herrala (2014), "China's Capital Controls – Through the Prism of Covered Interest Differentials", *Pacific Economic Review*, February, Vol. 19(1), pp. 112–34.

Choi, Changkyu (2004), "Foreign Direct Investment and Income Convergence", *Applied Economics*, June, Vol. 36(10), pp. 1045–49.

Choong, Chee-Keong, Siew-Yong Lam, and Zulkornain Yusop (2010a), "Private Capital Flows to Low-Income Countries: The Role of Domestic Financial Sector", *Journal of Business Economics and Management*, Vol. 11(4), pp. 598–612.

Choong, Chee-Keong, Zulkornain Yusop, and Siong-Hook Law (2010b), "Private Capital Flows to Developing Countries: The Role of the Domestic Financial Sector", *Journal of the Asia Pacific Economy*, November, Vol. 15(4), pp. 509–29.

Choudhry, Moorad (2011), "Effective Bank Corporate Governance: Observations from the Market Crash and Recommendations for Policy", *Journal of Applied Finance and Banking*, June, Vol. 1(1), pp. 179–211.

Chung, J. -H., and S. Ni (2002), "An Empirical Analysis on Government Capital Controls and International Capital Flows in Korea", *Applied Economics Letters*, November, Vol. 9(14), pp. 919–23.

Cipollina, Maria, Giorgia Giovannetti, Filomena Pietrovito, and Alberto F. Pozzolo (2012), "FDI and Growth: What Cross-Country Industry Data Say", *World Economy*, November, Vol. 35(11), pp. 1599–629.

Claessens, Stijn, and M. Ayhan Kose (2013), "Financial Crises: Review and Evidence", *Central Bank Review*, September, Vol. 13(3), pp. 1–23.

Coakley, Jerry, Farida Kulasi, and Ron Smith (1996), "Current Account Solvency and the Feldstein-Horioka Puzzle", *Economic Journal*, Vol. 106(436), pp. 620–27.

Concha, Alvaro, Arturo Jose Galindo, and Diego Vasquez (2011), "An Assessment of Another Decade of Capital Controls in Colombia: 1998–2008", *Quarterly Review of Economics and Finance*, November, Vol. 51(4), pp. 319–38.

Corbin, Annie (2001), "Country Specific Effect in the Feldstein-Horioka Paradox: A Panel Data Analysis", *Economic Letters*, Vol. 72(3), pp. 297–302.

Costinot, Arnaud, Guido Lorenzoni, and Ivan Werning (2014), "A Theory of Capital Controls as Dynamic Terms-of-Trade Manipulation", *Journal of Political Economy*, February, Vol. 122(1), pp. 77–128.

Damasceno, Aderbal Oliveira (2011), "Financial Integration, Foreign Savings and Income Convergence: Theory and Evidence", With English Summary, *Brazilian Journal of Political Economy*, December, Vol. 31(5), pp. 751–70.

Dang, Tri Vi, Gary Gorton, Bengt Holmström, and Guillermo Ordonez (2014), "Banks as Secret Keepers", *NBER Working Paper No. 20255*, National Bureau of Economic Research. Cambridge, MA.

Darku, Alexander Bilson (2010), "Consumption Smoothing, Capital Controls and the Current Account in Ghana", *Applied Economics*, August, Vol. 42(19–21), pp. 2601–16.

Das, Khanindra C. (2013), "Home Country Determinants of Outward FDI from Developing Countries", *The Journal of Applied Economic Research*, February, Vol. 7(1), pp. 93–116.

David, Antonio C. (2007), "Revisiting Price-Based Controls on Capital Inflows in a 'Sophisticated' Emerging Market", *World Development*, August, Vol. 35(8), pp. 1329–40.

David, Antonio C. (2008), "Controls on Capital Inflows and the Transmission of External Shocks", *Cambridge Journal of Economics*, November, Vol. 32(6), pp. 887–906.

David, Antonio C. (2009), "Are Price-Based Capital Account Regulations Effective in Developing Countries?", *Applied Economics*, November–December, Vol. 41(25–7), pp. 3375–88.

De Jonghe, Olivier, Mustafa Disli, and Koen Schoors (2012), "Corporate Governance, Opaque Bank Activities, and Risk/Return Efficiency: Pre- and Post-crisis Evidence from Turkey", *Journal of Financial Services Research*, April, Vol. 41(1–2), pp. 51–80.

de Mello, Luiz, Pier Carlo Padoan, and Linda Rousova (2012), "Are Global Imbalances Sustainable? Shedding Further Light on the Causes of Current Account Reversals", *Review of International Economics*, August, Vol. 20(3), pp. 489–516.

de Roure, Calebe, Steven Furnagiev, and Stefan Reitz (2015), "The Microstructure of Exchange Rate Management: FX Intervention and Capital Controls in Brazil", *Applied Economics*, July–August, Vol. 47(34–6), pp. 3617–32.

da Silva, Guilherme Jonas Costa, and Marco Flavio da Cunha Resende (2010), "The Effectiveness of Capital Controls in Brazil: A Theoretical Approach and Empirical Alternative", With English Summary)", *Estudos Economicos*, July–September, Vol. 40(3), pp. 617–49.

de Vita, Glauco, and Khine S. Kyaw (2009), "Growth Effects of FDI and Portfolio Investment Flows to Developing Countries: A Disaggregated Analysis by Income Levels", *Applied Economics Letters*, January–February, Vol. 16(1–3), pp. 277–83.

Debaere, P., H. Lee, and J. Lee (2010), "It Matters Where You Go: Outward Foreign Direct Investment and Multinational Employment Growth at Home", *Journal of Development Economics*, Vol. 91, pp. 301–9.

Debbiche, Imene, and Oubeid Rahmouni (2015), "Does Foreign Capital Enhance Economic Growth in Emerging Countries: Flow Decomposition Approach?", *Journal of Applied Business Research*, January–February, Vol. 31(1), pp. 221–29.

Dell'Erba, Salvatore, and Dennis Reinhardt (2015), "FDI, Debt and Capital Controls", *Journal of International Money and Finance*, November, Vol. 58, pp. 29–50.

Demirgüç-Kunt, Asli, Edward J. Kane, and Luc Laeven (2014), "Deposit Insurance Database", *NBER Working Paper No. 20278*, National Bureau of Economic Research. Cambridge, MA.

Dermine, Jean (2013), "Bank Corporate Governance, beyond the Global Banking Crisis", *Financial Markets, Institutions and Instruments*, Vol. 22(5), pp. 259–81.

Diamond, Douglas. W., and Phillip H. Dybvig (1983), "Bank Runs, Deposit Insurance, and Liquidity", *Journal of Political Economy*, Vol. 91, pp. 401–19.

Diamond, Douglas W., and Phillip H. Dybvig (1986), "Banking Theory, Deposit Insurance, and Bank Regulation", *Journal of Business*, Vol. 59(1), pp. 55–68.

Diamond, Douglas W., and Raghuram G. Rajan (2012), "Illiquidit Banks, Financial Instability, and Interest Rate Policy", *Journal of Political Economy*, June, Vol. 120(3), pp. 552–91.

Ding, Ding, and Yothin Jinjarak (2012), "Development Threshold, Capital Flows and Financial Turbulence", *North American Journal of Economics and Finance*, Vol. 23, pp. 365–85.

Dooley, Michael P. (2002), "Responses to Volatile Capital Flows: Controls, Asset Liability Management and Architecture", *Journal of Emerging Market Finance*, May–August, Vol. 1(1), pp. 99–124.

Doytch, Nadia, and Merih Uctum (2011), "Does the Worldwide Shift of FDI from Manufacturing to Services Accelerate Economic Growth? A GMM Estimation Study", *Journal of International Money and Finance*, April, Vol. 30(3), pp. 410–27.

Driffield, N., J. H. Love, and K. Taylor (2009), "Productivity and Labour Demand Effects of Inward and Outward FDI on UK Industry", *The Manchester School*, Vol. 77(2), pp. 171–203.

Duasa, Jarita, and Paul Mosley (2006), "Capital Controls Re-Examined: The Case for 'Smart' Controls", *World Economy*, September, Vol. 29(9), pp. 1203–26.

Duasa, Jarita, and Salina H. Kassim (2009), "Foreign Portfolio Investment and Economic Growth in Malaysia", *Pakistan Development Review*, Summer, Vol. 48(2), pp. 109–23.

Edison, Hali J., and Francis E. Warnock (2008), "Cross-Border Listings, Capital Controls, and Equity Flows to Emerging Markets", *Journal of International Money and Finance*, October, Vol. 27(6), pp. 1013–27.

Edwards, Sebastian (2001), "Capital Mobility and Economic Performance: Are Emerging Economies Different?" *NBER Working Paper No. 8076*, National Bureau of Economic Research. Cambridge, MA.

Edwards, Sebastian (2004), "Financial Openness, Sudden Stops, and Current Account Reversals", *American Economic Review*, Vol. 94(2), pp. 59–64.

Edwards, Sebastian (2007a), "Capital Controls, Sudden Stops, and Current Account Reversals", in *Capital Controls and Capital Flows in Emerging Economies: Policies, Practices, and Consequences*, edited by S. Edwards, University of Chicago Press, Chicago, pp. 73–119.

Edwards, Sebastian (2007b), "Capital Controls, Capital Flow Contractions, and Macroeconomic Vulnerability", *Journal of International Money and Finance*, Vol. 26(5), pp. 814–40.

Edwards, Sebastian (2009a), *Capital Controls and Capital Flows in Emerging Economies: Policies, Practices, and Consequences*, The University of Chicago Press, Chicago and London.

Edwards, Sebastian (2009b), "Sequencing of Reforms, Financial Globalization, and Macroeconomic Vulnerability", *Journal of Japanese International Economics*, Vol. 23, pp. 131–48.

Edwards, Sebastian (2012), "The Federal Reserve, the Emerging Markets, and Capital Controls: A High-Frequency Empirical Investigation", *Journal of Money, Credit, and Banking*, Supplement December, Vol. 44, pp. 151–84.

Eichengreen, Barry (2004), *Capital Flows and Crises*, MIT Press, Cambridge, MA.

Eichengreen, Barry, and Andrew Rose (2014), "Capital Controls in the 21st Century", *Journal of International Money and Finance*, November, Vol. 48, pp. 1–16.

Eichengreen, Barry, Poonam Gupta, and Ashoka Mody (2008), "Sudden Stops and IMF Supported Programs", Chapter 7, in *Financial Markets Volatility and Performance in Emerging Markets*, edited by Sebastian Edwards and Marcio G. Garcia, University of Chicago Press, Chicago, pp. 219–77.

Eichengreen, Barry, and Richard Portes (1987), "The Anatomy of Financial Crises", *NBER working paper series No. 2126*, National Bureau of Economic Research. Printed in *Threats to International Financial Stability*, edited by Richard Portes and Alexander K. Swoboda, Cambridge University Press, New York, pp. 10–58.

Elia, Stefano, Ilaria Mariotti, and Lucia Piscitello (2009), "The Impact of Outward FDI on the Home Country's Labour Demand and Skill Composition", *International Business Review*, Vol. 18, pp. 357–72.

El-Shagi, Makram (2010), "Capital Controls and International Interest Rate Differentials", *Applied Economics*, Vol. 42, pp. 681–88.

El-Shagi, Makram (2012a), "The Distorting Impact of Capital Controls", *German Economic Review*, Vol. 13(1), pp. 41–55.

El-Shagi, Makram (2012b), "Initial Evidence from a New Database on Capital Market Restrictions", *Panoeconomicus*, Vol. 59(3), pp. 283–92.

Errunza, Vihang (2001), "Foreign Portfolio Equity Investments, Financial Liberalization, and Economic Development", *Review of International Economics*, November, Vol. 9(4), pp. 703–26.

Esaka, Taro, and Shinji Takagi (2013), "Testing the Effectiveness of Market-Based Controls: Evidence from the Experience of Japan with Short-Term Capital Flows in the 1970s", *International Finance*, Spring, Vol. 16(1), pp. 45–69.

Federico, Stefano, and Gaetano Alfredo Minerva (2008), "Outward FDI and Local Employment Growth in Italy", *Review of World Economics/Weltwirtschaftliches Archiv*, Vol. 144 (2), pp. 295–324.

Feibelman, Adam (2015), "The IMF and Regulation of Cross-Border Capital Flows", *Chicago Journal of International Law*, Winter, Vol. 15(2), pp. 409–51.

Feldstein, Martin (1983), "Domestic Saving and International Capital Movements in the Long Run and the Short Run", *European Economic Review*, Vol. 21(1–2), pp. 129–51.

Felix, David (2003), "The Past as Future? The Contribution of Financial Globalization to the Current Crisis of Neo-Liberalism as a Development Strategy", *Working Papers (51 pages)*, Political Economy Research Institute, University of Massachusetts at Amherst.

Fernandez, Andres, Michael W. Klein, Alessandro Rebucci, Martin Schindler, and Martin Uribe (2015), "Capital Control Measures: A New Dataset", *NBER Working Papers: 20970*, National Bureau of Economic Research. Cambridge, MA.

Fernando de Paula, Luiz, and Daniela Magalhaes Prates (2015), "Capital Account and Foreign Exchange Derivatives Regulation: The Recent Experience in Brazil",

(With English Summary), *Investigacion Economica*, January–March, Vol. 74(291), pp. 79–115.

Ferreira Gabriel, Luciano, and Jose Luis da Costa Oreiro (2008), "Capital Flows, External Fragility and Currency Regimes: A Theoretical Review", With English Summary, *Revista de Economia Politica/Brazilian Journal of Political Economy*, April–June, Vol. 28(2), pp. 331–57.

Forbes, Kristin J. (2005), "Capital Controls: Mud in the Wheels of Market Efficiency", *Cato Journal*, Winter, Vol. 25(1), pp. 153–66.

Forbes, Kristin J. (2007), "One Cost of the Chilean Capital Controls: Increased Financial Constraints for Smaller Traded Firms", *Journal of International Economics*, Vol. 71, pp. 294–323.

Forbes, Kristin J. (2012), "The 'Big C' Identifying and Mitigating Contagion", *MIT Sloan Research Paper No. 4970–12*. SSRN: https://ssrn.com/abstract=2149908.

Forbes, Kristin J., and Francis E. Warnock (2012), "Capital Flow Waves: Surges, Stops, Flight, and Retrenchment", *Journal of International Economics*, Vol. 88, pp. 235–51.

Forbes, Kristin J., Marcel Fratzscher, and Roland Straub (2015), "Capital-Flow Management Measures: What Are They Good for?", *Journal of International Economics*, Vol. 96, pp. S76–S97.

Forbes, Kristin J., Marcel Fratzscher, Thomas Kostka, and Roland Straub (2016), "Bubble Thy Neighbour: Portfolio Effects and Externalities from Capital Controls", *Journal of International Economics*, Vol. 99, pp. 85–104.

Forbes, Kristin J., and Michael W. Klein (2015), "Pick Your Poison: The Choices and Consequences of Policy Responses to Crises", *IMF Economic Review*, Vol. 63(1), pp. 197–237.

Forssbaeck, Jens, and Lars Oxelheim (2006), "On the Link between Exchange-Rate Regimes, Capital Controls and Monetary Policy Autonomy in Small European Countries, 1979–2000", *World Economy*, March, Vol. 29(3), pp. 341–68.

Fortanier, Fabienne (2007), "Foreign Direct Investment and Host Country Economic Growth: Does the Investor's Country of Origin Play a Role?", *Transnational Corporations*, August, Vol. 16(2), pp. 41–76.

Forte, Rosa, and Rui Moura (2013), "The Effects of Foreign Direct Investment on the Host Country's Economic Growth: Theory and Empirical Evidence", *Singapore Economic Review*, September, Vol. 58(3), pp. 1–28.

Fortin, Rich, Gerson M. Goldberg, and Greg Roth (2010), "Bank Risk Taking at the Onset of the Current Banking Crisis", *Financial Review*, November, Vol. 45(4), pp. 891–913.

Fratzscher, Marcel (2012), "Capital Controls and Foreign Exchange Policy", (With English Summary), *Economia Chilena*, August, Vol. 15(2), pp. 66–98.

Freixas, Xavier (2010), "Post-Crisis Challenges to Bank Regulation", *Economic Policy*, April, Vol. 62, pp. 375–99.

Frost, Jon, and Ruben van Tilburg (2014), "Financial Globalization or Great Financial Expansion? The Impact of Capital Flows on Credit and Banking Crises", *DNB Working Papers*, The Netherlands Central Bank.

Fukuda, Shin-ichi (2001), "The Impacts of Bank Loans on Economic Development: An Implication for East Asia from an Equilibrium Contract Theory", in *Regional and Global Capital Flows: Macroeconomic Causes and Consequences*, NBER-EASE Volume 10, edited by Takatoshi Ito and Anne O. Krueger, University of Chicago Press, Chicago, pp. 117–45.

Furceri, Davide, Stephanie Guichard, and Elena Rusticelli (2012), "Episodes of Large Capital Inflows and the Likelihood of Banking and Currency Crises and Sudden Stops", *International Finance*, Spring, Vol. 15(1), pp. 1–35.

Gambacorta, Leonardo (2008), "How Do Banks Set Interest Rates?", *European Economic Review*, Elsevier, Vol. 52(5), pp. 792–819.

Gamberger, Dragan, and Tomislav Smuc (2013), "Good Governance Problems and Recent Financial Crises in Some EU Countries", *Economics: The Open-Access, Open-Assessment E-Journal*, Vol. 7, pp. 1–21.

Garcia, Marcio G. P., and Alexandre Barcinski (1998), "Capital Flows to Brazil in the Nineties: Macroeconomic Aspects and the Effectiveness of Capital Controls", *Quarterly Review of Economics and Finance*, Fall, Vol. 38(3), pp. 319–57.

Garcia, Marcio G. P., and Marcus Vinicius F. Valpassos (2000), "Capital Flows, Capital Controls, and Currency Crisis: The Case of Brazil in the 1990s", in *Development and Inequality in the Market Economy Series*, edited by Larrain B., Felipe, University of Michigan Press, Ann Arbor, pp. 143–91.

Garg, Reetika, and Pami Dua (2014), "Foreign Portfolio Investment Flows to India: Determinants and Analysis", *World Development*, July, Vol. 59, pp. 16–28.

Gatev, Evan, Til Schuermann, and Philip Strahan (2007), "How Do Banks Manage Liquidity Risk? Evidence from the Equity and Deposit Markets in the Fall of 1998", in *The Risks of Financial Institutions*, edited by Mark Carey and René M. Stulz, University of Chicago Press, Chicago, pp. 105–31.

Gertler, Mark, and Nobuhiro Kiyotaki (2015), "Banking, Liquidity, and Bank Runs in an Infinite Horizon Economy", *American Economic Review*, Vol. 105(7), pp. 2011–43. http://dx.doi.org/10.1257/aer.20130665

Ghosh, Atish R., and Mahvash Qureshi (2016), "What's in a Name? That Which We Call Capital Controls", *IMF working Paper 16/25*. International Monetary Fund, Washington, DC.

Giofre, Maela (2014), "Domestic Investor Protection and Foreign Portfolio Investment", *Journal of Banking and Finance*, September, Vol. 46, pp. 355–71.

Goh, Soo Khoon (2005), "New Empirical Evidence on the Effects of Capital Controls on Composition of Capital Flows in Malaysia", *Applied Economics*, July, Vol. 37(13), pp. 1491–503.

Goldstein, Itay, and Assaf Razin (2006), "An Information-Based Trade Off between Foreign Direct Investment and Foreign Portfolio Investment", *Journal of International Economics*, September, Vol. 70(1), pp. 271–95.

Gopinath, Munisamy, and Weiyan Chen (2003), "Foreign Direct Investment and Wages: A Cross-Country Analysis", *Journal of International Trade and Economic Development*, September, Vol. 12(3), pp. 285–309.

Grabel, Ilene (2015), "The Rebranding of Capital Controls in an Era of Productive Incoherence", *Review of International Political Economy*, February, Vol. 22(1), pp. 7–43.

Graham, Michael, Jarkko Peltomaki, and Hildur Sturludottir (2015), "Do Capital Controls Affect Stock Market Efficiency? Lessons from Iceland", *International Review of Financial Analysis*, October, Vol. 41, pp. 82–8.

Grittersova, Jana (2014), "Non-market Cooperation and the Variety of Finance Capitalism in Advanced Democracies", *Review of International Political Economy*, April, Vol. 21(2), pp. 339–71.

Gropp, Reint, and Jukka Vesala (2004), "Deposit Insurance, Moral Hazard, and Market Monitoring", *Review of Finance*, Vol. 8(4), pp. 571–602.

Gros, Daniel, and Cinzia Alcidi (2015), "Country Adjustment to a 'Sudden Stop': Does the Euro Make a Difference?", *International Economics and Economic Policy*, March, Vol. 12(1), pp. 5–20.

Gu, Xinhua, and Li Sheng (2010), "A Sensible Policy Tool for Pareto Improvement: Capital Controls", *Journal of World Trade*, June, Vol. 44(3), pp. 567–90.

Gur, Nurullah (2015), "Financial Integration, Financial Dependence and Employment Growth", *International Journal of Economics and Financial Issues*, Vol. 5(2), pp. 493–500.

Han, Xuehui, and Shang-Jin Wei (2014), "Policy Choices and Resilience to International Monetary Shocks", *Global Economic Review*, December, Vol. 43(4), pp. 319–37.

Hanlon, Michelle, Edward L. Maydew, and Jacob R. Thornock (2015), "Taking the Long Way Home: U.S. Tax Evasion and Offshore Investments in U.S. Equity and Debt Markets", *Journal of Finance*, February, Vol. 70(1), pp. 257–87.

Hanson, Samuel G., Andrei Shleifer, Jeremy C. Stein, and Robert W. Vishny (2015), "Banks as Patient Fixed-Income Investors", *Journal of Financial Economics*, Vol. 117(3), pp. 449–69.

Hart, Oliver, and Luigi Zingales (2014), "Banks Are Where the Liquidity Is", *NBER Working Paper No. 20207*, National Bureau of Economic Research. Cambridge, MA.

Hartmann, Philipp, Stefan Straetmans, and Casper de Vries (2007), "A Cross-Atlantic Perspective", in *The Risks of Financial Institutions*, edited by Mark Carey and René M. Stulz, University of Chicago Press, Chicago, pp. 133–92.

Hartwell, Christopher A. (2014), "Capital Controls and the Determinants of Entrepreneurship", *Finance a Uver/Czech Journal of Economics and Finance*, Vol. 64(6), pp. 434–56.

Hassen, Soltani, and Ochi Anis (2012), "Foreign Direct Investment (FDI) and Economic Growth: An Approach in Terms of Co-integration for the Case of Tunisia", *Journal of Applied Finance and Banking*, August, Vol. 2(4), pp. 193–207.

Hau, Harald, and Marcel Thum (2009), "Subprime Crisis and Board (In-)Competence: Private versus Public Banks in Germany", *Economic Policy*, October, Vol. 60, pp. 701–43, 750–52.

Hegerty, Scott W. (2011), "Openness and Capital Flow Volatility: Comparisons between Transition Economies and Latin America", *Applied Economics Letters*, July–August, Vol. 18(10–12), pp. 1177–80.

Hellmann, Thomas F., Kevin C. Murdock, and Joseph E. Stiglitz (2000), "Liberalization, Moral Hazard in Banking, and Prudential Regulation: Are Capital Requirements Enough?", *The American Economic Review*, March, Vol. 90(1), pp. 147–65.

Herzer, D. (2008), "The Long-Run Relationship between Outward FDI and Domestic Output: Evidence from Panel Data", *Economics Letters*, Vol. 100, pp. 146–49.

Herzer, D. (2010), "Outward FDI and Economic Growth", *Journal of Economic Studies*, Vol. 37(5), pp. 476–94.

Herzer, D. (2011), "The Long-Run Relationship between Outward Foreign Direct Investment and Total Factor Productivity: Evidence for Developing Countries", *Journal of Development Studies*, Vol. 47(5), pp. 767–85.

Herzer, D. (2012), "Outward FDI, Total Factor Productivity and Domestic Output: Evidence from Germany", *International Economic Journal*, Vol. 26(1), pp. 155–74.

Hijzen, A., S. Jean, and T. Mayer (2011), "The Effects at Home of Initiating Production Abroad: Evidence from Matched French Firms", *Review of World Economy*, Vol. 147, pp. 457–83.

Hooks, Linda, and Kenneth Robinson (2002), "Deposit Insurance and Moral Hazard: Evidence from Texas Banking During the 1920s", *The Journal of Economic History*, September, Vol. 62(3), pp. 833–53.

Hoshi, Takeo, Anil Kashyap, and David Scharfstein (1993), "The Choice between Public and Private Debt: An Analysis of Post Deregulation Corporate Financing in Japan", *NBER working Paper 4421*, National Bureau of Economic Research. Cambridge, MA.

Hovakimian, Armen, Edward J. Kane, and Luc Laeven (2015), "Tracking Variation in Systemic Risk at US Banks During 1974–2013", *NBER Working Paper No. 18043, May 2012, Revised August 2015*, National Bureau of Economic Research. Cambridge, MA.

Hsu, Chun-Pin (2013), "The Influence of Foreign Portfolio Investment on Domestic Stock Returns: Evidence from Taiwan", *International Journal of Business and Finance Research*, Vol. 7(3), pp. 1–11.

Hsu, Chun-Pin, Chin-Wen Huang, and Alfred Ntoko (2013), "Does Foreign Investment Worsen the Domestic Stock Market during a Financial Crisis? Evidence from Taiwan", *The International Journal of Business and Finance Research*, Vol. 7(4), pp. 1–12.

Hsu, Hsiao-Tang (2005), "Capital Control and Domestic Interest Rates: A Generalized Model", *Contemporary Economic Policy*, July, Vol. 23(3), pp. 456–64.

Hutchison, Michael M., Gurnain Kaur Pasricha, and Nirvikar Singh (2012), "Effectiveness of Capital Controls in India: Evidence from the Offshore NDF Market", *IMF Economic Review*, Vol. 60(3), pp. 395–438.

Ibrahim, Mansor H. (2006), "Integration or Segmentation of the Malaysian Equity Market: An Analysis of Pre- and Post-Capital Controls", *Journal of the Asia Pacific Economy*, November, Vol. 11(4), pp. 424–43.

Imbriani, C., R. Pittiglio, and F. Reganati (2011), "Outward Foreign Direct Investment and Domestic Performance: the Italian Manufacturing and Services Sectors", *Atlantic Economics Journal*, Vol. 39, pp. 369–81.

Inagaki, Kazuyuki (2016), "Population Aging, Retirement Policy, and Current Account Reversals", *Working Paper*, Nagoya City University, Japan.

Inoguchi, Masahiro (2009), "Did Capital Controls Decrease Capital Flows in Malaysia?", *Journal of the Asia Pacific Economy*, February, Vol. 14(1), pp. 27–48.

International Monetary Fund (2012a), "The Liberalization and Management of Capital Flows: An Institutional View", November 14.

International Monetary Fund (2012b), March 28th.

Iyer, Rajkamal, Manju Puri, and Nicolas Ryan (2013), "Understanding Bank Runs: Do Depositors Monitor Banks?" *NBER Working Paper 19050*, National Bureau of Economic Research. Cambridge, MA.

Jeanne, Olivier (2016), "The Macro-prudential Role of International Reserves", *American Economic Review*, May, Vol. 106(5), pp. 570–73.

Jinjarak, Yothin, Ilan Noy, and Huanhuan Zheng (2013), "Capital Controls in Brazil – Stemming a Tide with a Signal?", *Journal of Banking and Finance*, August, Vol. 37(8), pp. 2938–52.

Johnson, Simon, Kalpana Kochhar, Todd Mitton, and Natalia Tamirisa (2007), "Malaysian Capital Controls: Macroeconomics and Institutions", in *Capital Controls and Capital Flows in Emerging Economies: Policies, Practices, and Consequences*, edited by Sebastian Edwards. University of Chicago Press, Chicago and London, pp. 529–74.

Jones, Charles I. (1999), "Growth: With or without Scale Effects?", *The American Economic Review*, Papers and Proceedings of the One Hundred Eleventh Annual Meeting of the American Economic Association, May, Vol. 89(2), pp. 139–44.

Jongwanich, Juthathip, and Archanun Kohpaiboon (2012), "Effectiveness of Capital Controls: Evidence from Thailand", *Asian Development Review*, Vol. 29(2), pp. 50–93.

Jongwanich, Juthathip, Maria Socorro Gochoco-Bautista, and Jong-Wha Lee (2011), "When Are Capital Controls Effective? Evidence from Malaysia and Thailand", *International Economic Journal*, December, Vol. 25(4), pp. 619–51.

Jorion, Philippe (2007), "Bank Trading Risk and Systemic Risk", in *The Risks of Financial Institutions*, edited by Mark Carey and René M. Stulz, University of Chicago Press, Chicago, pp. 29–57

Joseph E. Stiglitz, Amartya Sen, and Jean-Paul Fitoussi (2010), *Mis-measuring Our Lives: Why GDP Doesn't Add Up*, The New Press Publisher, New York.

Joshi, Vijay (2001), "Capital Controls and the National Advantage: India in the 1990s and Beyond", *Oxford Development Studies*, October, Vol. 29(3), pp. 305–20.

Joyce, Joseph P. (2011), "Financial Globalization and Banking Crises in Emerging Markets", *Open Economies Review*, November, Vol. 22(5), pp. 875–95.

Joyce, Joseph P., and Malhar Nabar (2009), "Sudden Stops, Banking Crises and Investment Collapses in Emerging Markets", *Journal of Development Economics*, November, Vol. 90(2), pp. 314–22.

Kanayo, Ogujiuba, and Obiechina Emeka (2012), "Foreign Private Capital, Economic Growth and Macroeconomic Indicators in Nigeria: An Empirical Framework", *International Journal of Economics and Finance*, October, Vol. 4(10), pp. 111–24.

Kandil, Magda (2011), "Financial Flows to Developing and Advanced Countries: Determinants and Implications", *International Journal of Development Issues*, Vol. 10(1), pp. 60–91.

Karolyi, G. Andrew (2002), "Did the Asian Financial Crisis Scare Foreign Investors Out of Japan?", *Pacific-Basin Finance Journal*, September, Vol. 10(4), pp. 411–42.

Kashyap, Anil K, Dimitrios P. Tsomocos, and Alexandros P. Vardoulakis (2014), "How Does Macroprudential Regulation Change Bank Credit Supply?" *NBER Working Paper 20165*, National Bureau of Economic Research. Cambridge, MA.

Kasibhatla, Krishna M., David B. Stewart, and Mak Khojasteh (2008), "The Role of FDI in High Medium, Low Medium and Low Income Countries during 1970–2005: Empirical Tests and Evidence", *Journal of Business and Economic Studies*, Fall, Vol. 14(2), pp. 60–72.

Kawai, Masahiro, and Li-Gang Liu (2015), "Trilemma Challenges for the People's Republic of China", *Asian Development Review*, March, Vol. 32(1), pp. 49–89.

Kim, Iljoong, Inbae Kim, and Yoonsen Han (2014), "Deposit Insurance, Banks' Moral Hazard, and Regulation: Evidence from the ASEAN Countries and Korea", *Emerging Markets Finance & Trade*, November–December, Vol. 50(6), pp. 56–71.

Kim, Soyoung, and Doo Yong Yang (2012a), "Are Capital Controls Effective? The Case of the Republic of Korea", *Asian Development Review*, Vol. 29(2), pp. 96–133.

Kim, Soyoung, and Doo Yong Yang (2012b), "International Monetary Transmission in East Asia: Floaters, Non-floaters, and Capital Controls", *Japan and the World Economy*, December, Vol. 24(4), pp. 305–16.

Kim, Wi Saeng, Esmeralda Lyn, and Edward Zychowicz (2003), "Is the Source of FDI Important to Emerging Market Economies? Evidence from Japanese and U.S. FDI", *Multinational Finance Journal*, September–December, Vol. 7(3–4), pp. 107–30.

Kinda, Tidiane (2012), "On the Drivers of FDI and Portfolio Investment: A Simultaneous Equations Approach", *International Economic Journal*, March, Vol. 26(1), pp. 1–22.

Kitano, Shigeto (2011), "Capital Controls and Welfare", *Journal of Macroeconomics*, December, Vol. 33(4), pp. 700–10.

Kitano, Shigeto, and Kenya Takaku (2015), "Capital Controls, Monetary Policy, and Balance Sheets in a Small Open Economy", *Kobe University, Discussion Paper Series*: DP2015–10, 33 pages. Kobe, Japan.

Kiyotaki, Norbuhiro, and John Moore (1997), "Credit Cycles", *Journal of Political Economy*, Vol. 105(2), pp. 211–48.

Kiyotaki, Norbuhiro, and John Moore (2002), "Balance-Sheet Contagion", *American Economic Review*, Vol. 92(2), pp. 46–65.

Klein, Michael W. (2012), "Capital Controls: Gates versus Walls", *Brookings Papers on Economic Activity*, Fall, pp. 317–55.

Klein, Michael W., and Jay C. Shambaugh (2015), "Rounding the Corners of the Policy Trilemma: Sources of Monetary Policy Autonomy", *American Economic Journal: Macroeconomics*, October, Vol. 7(4), pp. 33–66.

Knill, April M. (2005), "Taking the Bad with the Good: Volatility of Foreign Portfolio Investment and Financial Constraints of Small Firms", *Policy Research Working Paper Series: 3797*, The World Bank. Washington, DC.

Knill, April M. (2013), "Does Foreign Portfolio Investment Reach Small Listed Firms?", *European Financial Management*, March, Vol. 19(2), pp. 251–303.

Knill, April, and Bong Soo Lee (2014), "The Volatility of Foreign Portfolio Investment and the Access to Finance of Small Listed Firms", *Review of Development Economics*, August, Vol. 18(3), pp. 524–42.

Komulainen, Tuomas (2004), Essays on Financial Crises in Emerging Markets, Series Bank of Finland *Studies E:29*, Bank of Finland, Helsinki, Finland.

Korinek, Anton (2011), "The New Economics of Prudential Capital Controls: A Research Agenda", *IMF Economic Review*, Vol. 59(3), pp. 523–61.

Korinek, Anton, and Damiano Sandri (2016), "Capital Controls or Macro-prudential Regulation?", *Journal of International Economics*, Vol. 99, pp. S27–S42.

Kornecki, Lucyna (2008), "Foreign Direct Investment and Macroeconomic Changes in CEE Integrating into the Global Market", *Investment Management and Financial Innovations*, Vol. 5(4), pp. 124–32.

Kose, M. Ayhan, and Eswar Prasad (2012), "Capital Accounts: Liberalize or Not?" *Finance & Development, International Monetary Fund, March 28th.* http://www.imf.org/external/pubs/ft/fandd/basics/capital.htm.

Kotrajaras, Polpat, Bangorn Tubtimtong, and Paitoon Wiboonchutikula (2011), "Does FDI Enhance Economic Growth? New Evidence from East Asia", *ASEAN Economic Bulletin*, August, Vol. 28(2), pp. 183–202.

La Porta, Rafael, Florencio Lopez-de-Silanes, Andrei Shleifer, and Robert W. Vishny (1998), "Law and Finance", *Journal of Political Economy*, Vol. 106(6), pp. 1113–55.

Laeven, Luc, and Ross Levine (2009), "Bank Governance, Regulation and Risk Taking", *Journal of Financial Economics*, Elsevier, August, Vol. 93(2), pp. 259–75.

Lajuni, Nelson, Ooi Ai Yee, and Mohd Fahmi Ghazali (2008), "Capital Controls: Impact on Foreign Direct Investment and Portfolio Investment in Malaysia 1991–2004", *Global Journal of Business Research*, Vol. 2(1), pp. 17–24.

Leblang, David (2010), "Familiarity Breeds Investment: Diaspora Networks and International Investment", *American Political Science Review*, August, Vol. 104(3), pp. 584–600.

Lee, C. G. (2010), "Outward Foreign Direct Investment and Economic Growth: Evidence from Japan", *Global Economic Review*, Vol. 39(3), pp. 317–26.

Lee, Gwanghoon (2007), "Long Run Equilibrium Relationship between Inward FDI and Productivity", *Journal of Economic Development*, December, Vol. 32(2), pp. 183–92.

Lee, Hsiu-Yun, Kenneth S. Lin, and Hsiao-Chien Tsui (2009), "Home Country Effects of Foreign Direct Investment: From a Small Economy to a Large Economy", *Economic Modelling*, Vol. 26(5), pp. 1121–28.

Lee, Hyun-Hoon, Cyn-Young Park, and Hyung-Suk Byun (2013), "Do Contagion Effects Exist in Capital Flow Volatility?", *Journal of the Japanese and International Economies*, December, Vol. 30, pp. 76–95.

Lee, Hyun-Hoon, and Donghyun Park (2013), "The Financial Role of East Asian Countries in Global Imbalances: An Econometric Assessment of Developments after the Global Financial Crisis", *Global Journal of Economics*, June, Vol. 2(2), pp. 1–29.

Levchenko, Andrei A., and Paolo Mauro (2007), "Do Some Forms of Financial Flows Help Protect against 'Sudden Stops'?", *World Bank Economic Review*, Vol. 21(3), pp. 389–411.

Li, Jie, and Ramkishen S. Rajan (2015), "Do Capital Controls Make Gross Equity Flows to Emerging Markets Less Volatile?", *Journal of International Money and Finance*, December, Vol. 59, pp. 220–44.

Liljeblom, Eva, and Anders Loflund (2005), "Determinants of International Portfolio Investment Flows to a Small Market: Empirical Evidence", *Journal of Multinational Financial Management*, July, Vol. 15(3), pp. 211–33.

Lipsey, Robert E. (2004), "Home and Host Country Effects of FDI", in *Challenges to Globalization*, edited by Robert E. Baldwin and L. Alan Winters, University of Chicago Press, Chicago, pp. 333–82.

Liu, Zheng, and Mark M. Spiegel (2015), "Optimal Monetary Policy and Capital Account Restrictions in a Small Open Economy", *IMF Economic Review*, Vol. 63(2), pp. 298–324.

Ma, Guonan, and Robert N. McCauley (2008), "Efficacy of China's Capital Controls: Evidence from Price and Flow Data", *Pacific Economic Review*, February, Vol. 13(1), pp. 104–23.

Magud, Nicolas, and Carmen M. Reinhart (2007), "Capital Controls: An Evaluation", Chapter 14, in *Capital Controls and Capital Flows in Emerging Economies: Policies, Practices, and Consequences*, edited by Sebastian Edwards, University of Chicago Press, Chicago, pp. 645–74.

Manova, Kalina, Shang-Jin Wei, and Zhiwei Zhang (2015), "Firm Exports and Multinational Activity under Credit Constraints", *Review of Economics and Statistics*, July, Vol. 97(3), pp. 574–88.

Marin, D. (2004), "A Nation of Poets and Thinkers – Less so with Eastern Enlargement? Austria and Germany", *Centre for Economic Policy Research (CEPR) Discussion Paper No. 4358*, Centre for Economic Policy Research, London, UK.

Martin, A. (2006), "Liquidity Provision vs. Deposit Insurance: Preventing Bank Panics without Moral Hazard", *Economic Theory*, Vol. 28, pp. 197–211.

Masciandaro, Donato, and Alessio Volpicella (2016), "Macro Prudential Governance and Central Banks: Facts and Drivers", *Journal of International Money and Finance*, Vol. 61, pp. 101–19.

Masciandaro, Donato, Rosaria Vega Pansini, and Marc Quintyn (2013), "The Economic Crisis: Did Supervision Architecture and Governance Matter?", *Journal of Financial Stability*, December, Vol. 9(4), pp. 578–96.

Masso, Jaan, Urmas Varblane, and Priit Vahter (2008), "The Effect of Outward Foreign Direct Investment on Home-Country Employment in a Low-Cost Transition Economy", *Eastern European Economics*, November–December, Vol. 46(6), pp. 25–59.

Mayer-Foulkes, David, and Peter Nunnenkamp (2009), "Do Multinational Enterprises Contribute to Convergence or Divergence? A Disaggregated Analysis of US FDI", *Review of Development Economics*, May, Vol. 13(2), pp. 304–18.

McCoy, Patricia A. (2007), "Moral Hazard Implications of Deposit Insurance: Theory and Evidence", *IMF Working Paper*, International Monetary Fund, Washington, DC.

Mencinger, Joze (2003), "Does Foreign Direct Investment Always Enhance Economic Growth?", *Kyklos*, Vol. 56(4), pp. 491–508.

Mendoza, Enrique G., and Marco E. Terrones (2012), "An Anatomy of Credit Booms and their Demise", *The Chilean Economy*, Central Bank of Chile, Vol. 15(2), pp. 4–32.

Michaud, Amanda, and Jacek Rothert (2014), "Optimal Borrowing Constraints and Growth in a Small Open Economy", *Journal of International Economics*, November, Vol. 94(2), pp. 326–40.

Minton, Bernadette A., René Stulz, and Rohan Williamson (2009), "How Much Do Banks Use Credit Derivatives to Hedge Loans?", *Journal of Financial Services Research*, Springer, February, Vol. 35(1), pp. 1–31.

Mishkin, Frederic S. (2001), "Financial Policies and the Prevention of Financial Crises in Emerging Market Economies", *The World Bank, Policy Research Working Paper Series: 2683*, The World Bank, Washington, DC.

Mitchener, Kris James, and Kirsten Wandschneider (2015), "Capital Controls and Recovery from the Financial Crisis of the 1930s", *Journal of International Economics*, March, Vol. 95(2), pp. 188–201.

Molnar, Margit, Nigel Pain, and Daria Taglioni (2008), "Globalisation and Employment in the OECD", *OECD Journal: Economic Studies*, Vol. 2008, pp. 83–116.

Molnar, Margit, Yusuke Tateno, and Amornrut Supornsinchai (2013), "Capital Flows in Asia-Pacific: Controls, Bonanzas and Sudden Stops", *OECD Development Centre Working Papers: 320*, OECD Publishing, Paris, France.

Montiel, Peter, and Carmen M. Reinhart (1999), "Do Capital Controls and Macroeconomic Policies Influence the Volume and Composition of Capital Flows? Evidence from the 1990", *Journal of International Money and Finance*, Vol. 18, pp. 619–35.

Moudatsou, Argiro (2003), "Foreign Direct Investment and Economic Growth in the European Union", *Journal of Economic Integration*, December, Vol. 18(4), pp. 689–707.

Nachum, L., G. G. Jones, and J. H. Dunning (2001), "The International Competitiveness of the UK and Its Multinational Enterprises", *Structural Change and Economic Dynamics*, September, Vol. 12(3), pp. 277–94.

Narula, Rajneesh, and Nigel Driffield (2012), "Does FDI Cause Development? The Ambiguity of the Evidence and Why It Matters", *European Journal of Development Research*, February, Vol. 24(1), pp. 1–7.

Neely, Christopher J. (1999), "An Introduction to Capital Controls", *Federal Reserve Bank of St. Louis Review*, November–December, Vol. 81(6), pp. 13–30.

Neumann, Rebecca M. (2006), "The Effects of Capital Controls on International Capital Flows in the Presence of Asymmetric Information", *Journal of International Money and Finance*, October, Vol. 25(6), pp. 1010–27.

Nunnenkamp, Peter (2004), "To What Extent Can Foreign Direct Investment Help Achieve International Development Goals?", *World Economy*, May, Vol. 27(5), pp. 657–77.

O'Brien, James M., and Jeremy Berkowitz (2007), "Estimating Bank Trading Risk: A Factor Model Approach", Chapter 2, in *The Risks of Financial Institutions*, edited by Mark Carey and René M. Stulz, University of Chicago Press, Chicago, pp. 59–101.

Orlov, Alexei G. (2005), "Pros and Cons of Capital Controls in the Presence of Incomplete Markets", *American Economist*, Spring, Vol. 49(1), pp. 79–93.

Osazee, Frank Ogieva, and Eseoghene Joseph Idolor (2014), "Testing Day of the Week Effect in Nigerian Stock Market Returns", *Indian Journal of Economics and Business*, Vol. 13(3), pp. 419–32.

Ostry, Jonathan D., Atish R. Ghosh, Marcos Chamon, and Mahvash S. Qureshi (2011), "Capital Controls: When and Why?", *IMF Economic Review*, Vol. 59(3), pp. 562–80.

Pandey, Radhika, Gurnain Pasricha, Ila Patnaik, and Ajay Shah (2015), "Motivations for Capital Controls and Their Effectiveness", *Working Papers*, 59 pages, Bank of Canada, Ottawa, Ontario, Canada.

Park, Daekeun (2013), "Cross-Border Bond Investment and Foreign Exchange Market Stability in Emerging Market Economies", *Journal of Economic Research*, November, Vol. 18(3), pp. 293–319.

Pasricha, Gurnain Kaur (2012), "Recent Trends in Measures to Manage Capital Flows in Emerging Economies", *North American Journal of Economics and Finance*, December, Vol. 23(3), pp. 286–309.

Pasricha, Gurnain, Matteo Falagiarda, Martin Bijsterbosch, and Joshua Aizenman (2015), "Domestic and Multilateral Effects of Capital Controls in Emerging Markets", *NBER Working Papers: 20822*, National Bureau of Economic Research, Cambridge, MA.

Pelizzon, Loriana, and Stephen Schaefer (2007), "Pillar 1 versus Pillar 2 under Risk Management", in *The Risks of Financial Institutions*, edited by Mark Carey and René M. Stulz, University of Chicago Press, Chicago, pp. 377–415.

Peni, Emilia, and Sami Vahamaa (2012), "Did Good Corporate Governance Improve Bank Performance during the Financial Crisis?", *Journal of Financial Services Research*, April, Vol. 41(1–2), pp. 19–35.

Peni, Emilia, Stanley D. Smith, and Sami Vahamaa (2013), "Bank Corporate Governance and Real Estate Lending during the Financial Crisis", *Journal of Real Estate Research*, July–September, Vol. 35(3), pp. 313–43.

Poon, Jessie P. H., and Edmund R. Thompson (1998), "Foreign Direct Investment and Economic Growth: Evidence from Asia and Latin America", *Journal of Economic Development*, December, Vol. 23(2), pp. 141–60.

Popov, Alexander (2014), "Credit Constraints, Equity Market Liberalization, and Growth Rate Asymmetry", *Journal of Development Economics*, March, Vol. 107, pp. 202–14.

Poshakwale, Sunil S., and Chandra Thapa (2009), "The Impact of Foreign Equity Investment Flows on Global Linkages of the Asian Emerging Equity Markets", *Applied Financial Economics*, November–December, Vol. 19(22–4), pp. 1787–802.

Poshakwale, Sunil S., and Chandra Thapa (2010), "Foreign Investors and Global Integration of Emerging Indian Equity Market", *Journal of Emerging Market Finance*, April, Vol. 9(1), pp. 1–24.

Poshakwale, Sunil S., and Chandra Thapa (2011), "Investor Protection and International Equity Portfolio Investments", *Global Finance Journal*, Vol. 22(2), pp. 116–29.

Qian, Xingwang, and Andreas Steiner (2014), "International Reserves and the Composition of Foreign Equity Investment", *Review of International Economics*, May, Vol. 22(2), pp. 379–409.

Ramos-Tallada, Julio (2013), "The IMF and Management of Capital Flows: The Long Road towards a Pragmatic Approach", *Quarterly Selection of Articles*, Autumn, Vol. 31, pp. 63–85.

Ratanamaneichat, Chiratus (2008), "The Financial Crises and Their Associated Output Loss in Emerging Markets", Dissertation, Claremont Graduate University.

Raza, Hamid, Gylfi Zoega, and Stephen Kinsella (2015), "Capital Controls, Financial Crisis and the Investment Saving Nexus: Evidence from Iceland", *Working Papers: 201518*, 19 pages, University College Dublin, Ireland.

Razin, Assaf (2003), "FDI Flows and Domestic Investment: Overview", *CESifo Economic Studies*, Vol. 49(3), pp. 415–28.

Rodrik, Dani, and Andres Velasco (1999), "Short-Term Capital Flows", NBER working paper 7364, National Bureau of Economic Research Inc., Cambridge, MA.

Romero-Avila, Diego (2009), "Liberalization of Capital Controls and Interest Rates: Restrictions in the EU–15: Did It Affect Economic Growth?", *Applied Financial Economics*, October–November, Vol. 19(19–21), pp. 1625–48.

Sarisoy Guerin, Selen (2006), "The Role of Geography in Financial and Economic Integration: A Comparative Analysis of Foreign Direct Investment, Trade and Portfolio Investment Flows", *World Economy*, February, Vol. 29(2), pp. 189–209.

Schaling, Eric (2009), "Capital Controls, Two-Tiered Exchange Rate Systems and Exchange Rate Policy: The South African Experience", *South African Journal of Economics*, December, Vol. 77(4), pp. 505–30.

Schularick, Moritz, and Alan M. Taylor (2012), "Credit Booms Gone Bust: Monetary Policy, Leverage Cycles, and Financial Crises, 1870–2008", *American Economic Review*, American Economic Association, April, Vol. 102(2), pp. 1029–61.

Sghaier, Imen Mohamed, Zouheir Sghaier Abida, Imen Mohamed, and Zouheir Abida (2013), "Foreign Direct Investment, Financial Development and Economic Growth: Empirical Evidence from North African Countries", *Journal of International and Global Economic Studies*, June, Vol. 6(1), pp. 1–13.

Shawa, Moses Joseph, and Yao Shen (2013), "Causality Relationship between Foreign Direct Investment, GDP Growth and Export for Tanzania", *International Journal of Economics and Finance*, September, Vol. 5(9), pp. 13–19.

Shen, Chung-Hua, Chien-Chiang Lee, and Chi-Chuan Lee (2010), "What Makes International Capital Flows Promote Economic Growth? An International Cross-Country Analysis", *Scottish Journal of Political Economy*, November, Vol. 57(5), pp. 515–46.

Sigurgeirsdottir, Silla, and Robert H. Wade (2015), "From Control by Capital to Control of Capital: Iceland's Boom and Bust, and the IMF's Unorthodox Rescue Package", *Review of International Political Economy*, February, Vol. 22(1), pp. 103–33.

Singh, Rajesh, and Chetan Subramanian (2008), "Temporary Stabilization with Capital Controls", *Economic Theory*, March, Vol. 34(3), pp. 545–74.

Sinn, Stefan (1992), "Saving-Investment Correlations and Capital Mobility: On the Evidence from Annual Data", *Economic Journal*, Vol. 102(414), pp. 1162–70.

Solomon, Edna Maeyen (2011), "Foreign Direct Investment, Host Country Factors and Economic Growth", *Ensayos: Revista de Economia*, May, Vol. 30(1), pp. 41–70.

Song, Zheng, Kjetil Storesletten, and Fabrizio Zilibotti (2014), "Growing (with Capital Controls) Like China", *IMF Economic Review*, Vol. 62(3), pp. 327–70.

Stehrer, Robert, and Julia Woerz (2009), " 'Attract FDI!' – A Universal Golden Rule? Empirical Evidence for OECD and Selected Non-OECD Countries", *European Journal of Development Research*, February, Vol. 21(1), pp. 95–111.

Steiner, Andreas (2013), "The Accumulation of Foreign Exchange by Central Banks: Fear of Capital Mobility?", *Journal of Macroeconomics*, December, Vol. 38, pp. 409–27.

Stiglitz, Joseph E., and Andrew Weiss (1981), "Credit Rationing in Markets with Imperfect Information", *The American Economic Review*, June, Vol. 71(3), pp. 393–410.

Straetmans, Stefan T. M., Roald J. Versteeg, and Christian C. P. Wolff (2013), "Are Capital Controls in the Foreign Exchange Market Effective?", *Journal of International Money and Finance*, June, Vol. 35, pp. 36–53.

Stulz, René M. (2014), "Governance, Risk Management, and Risk-Taking in Banks", *NBER Working Paper No. 20274*, National Bureau of Economic Research Inc., Cambridge, MA.

Suliman, Adil H., and Mohammad I. Elian (2014), "Foreign Direct Investment, Financial Development, and Economic Growth: A Cointegration Model", *Journal of Developing Areas*, Summer, Vol. 48(3), pp. 219–43.

Suzuki, Kenji, Kanji Tanimoto, and Ari Kokko (2010), "Does Foreign Investment Matter? Effects of Foreign Investment on the Institutionalization of Corporate Social Responsibility by Japanese Firms", *Asian Business and Management*, September, Vol. 9(3), pp. 379–400.

Tabova, Alexandra (2013), "Portfolio Diversification and the Cross-Sectional Distribution of Foreign Investment", *International Finance Discussion Papers: 1091*, Board of Governors of the Federal Reserve System, Washington, DC.

Tamirisa, Natalia T. (2006), "Do the Macroeconomic Effects of Capital Controls Vary by Type? Evidence from Malaysia", *ASEAN Economic Bulletin*, August, Vol. 23(2), pp. 137–59.

Thapa, Chandra, and Sunil S. Poshakwale (2012), "Country-Specific Equity Market Characteristics and Foreign Equity Portfolio Allocation", *Journal of International Money and Finance*, March, Vol. 31(2), pp. 189–211.

Tirole, Jean (2002), *Financial Crises, Liquidity, and the International Monetary System*, Princeton University Press, Princeton, NJ.

Todea, Alexandru, and Anita Plesoianu (2013), "The Influence of Foreign Portfolio Investment on Informational Efficiency: Empirical Evidence from Central and Eastern European Stock Markets", *Economic Modelling*, July, Vol. 33, pp. 34–41.

Tuan, Chyau, Linda F. Y. Ng, and Bo Zhao (2009), "China's Post-Economic Reform Growth: The Role of FDI and Productivity Progress", *Journal of Asian Economics*, May, Vol. 20(3), pp. 280–93.

Uctum, Merih, and Remzi Uctum (2011), "Crises, Portfolio Flows, and Foreign Direct Investment: An Application to Turkey", *Economic Systems*, December, Vol. 35(4), pp. 462–80.

Vannapanich, Kunlavee (2009), "Essays on Crises and Risk Management in Emerging Markets", Dissertation, Claremont Graduate University.

Verdier, Geneviève (2008), "What Drives Long-Term Capital Flows? A Theoretical and Empirical Investigation", *Journal of International Economics*, Vol. 74, pp. 120–42.

Vithessonthi, Chaiporn, and Jittima Tongurai (2013), "The Perils of a Central Bank's Capital Control: How Substantial Is the Effect on Firm Value?", *Journal of International Financial Markets, Institutions and Money*, February, Vol. 23(1), pp. 111–35.

Wallace, N. (1988), "Another Attempt to Explain an Illiquid Banking System", *Federal Reserve Bank of Minneapolis Quarterly Review*, Vol. 12(4), pp. 3–16.

Wallace, N. (1996), "Narrow Banking Meets the Diamond-Dybvig Model", *Federal Reserve Bank of Minneapolis Quarterly Review*, Vol. 20, pp. 3–13.

Wang, Miao (2009), "Manufacturing FDI and Economic Growth: Evidence from Asian Economies", *Applied Economics*, March–April, Vol. 41(7–9), pp. 991–1002.

Wang, Miao, and M. C. Sunny Wong (2009a), "Foreign Direct Investment and Economic Growth: The Growth Accounting Perspective", *Economic Inquiry*, October, Vol. 47(4), pp. 701–10.

Wang, Miao, and M. C. Sunny Wong (2009b), "What Drives Economic Growth? The Case of Cross-Border M&A and Greenfield FDI Activities", *Kyklos*, Vol. 62(2), pp. 316–30.

Wang, Miao, and M. C. Sunny Wong (2011), "FDI, Education, and Economic Growth: Quality Matters", *Atlantic Economic Journal*, June, Vol. 39(2), pp. 103–15.

Weinstein, Harris (1992), "Moral Hazard Deposit Insurance and Banking Regulation", *Cornell Law Review*, Vol. 7(5), Article 33, pp. 1099–104.

Wibaut, Serge (2014), "An E.U. Financial Transaction Tax and the Unintended Consequences for Risk Management", *Journal of Financial Perspectives*, July, Vol. 2(2), pp. 45–53.

Williams, Barry (2014), "Bank Risk and National Governance in Asia", *Journal of Banking and Finance*, December, Vol. 49, pp. 10–26.

Wong, Chin-Yoong, and Yoke-Kee Eng (2015), "Surviving Asymmetry in Capital Flows and the Business Cycles: The Role of Prudential Capital Controls", *Review of Development Economics*, August, Vol. 19(3), pp. 545–63.

Wright, Mark L. J. (2006), "Private Capital Flows, Capital Controls, and Default Risk", *Journal of International Economics*, June, Vol. 69(1), pp. 120–49.

Yepez Albornoz, Juan Francisco (2012), "Essays on the Effectiveness of Capital Controls", Dissertation, May, University of Notre Dame, Indiana, IN.

You, Yu, Yoonbai Kim, and Xiaomei Ren (2014), "Do Capital Controls Enhance Monetary Independence?", *Review of Development Economics*, August, Vol. 18(3), pp. 475–89.

Young, Alwyn (1998), "Growth without Scale Effects", *Journal of Political Economy*, February, Vol. 106(1), pp. 41–63.

Zajc Kejzar, Katja, and Andrej Kumar (2006), "Inward Foreign Direct Investment and Industrial Restructuring: Micro Evidence – The Slovenian Firms' Growth Model", *Journal of Economics and Business*, Vol. 24(2), pp. 185–210.

Zhang, Kevin Honglin (2013), "Outward FDI and Economic Growth in Home Countries: Evidence from 59 Countries in 1980–2010", *International Economics*, February, Vol. 66(1), pp. 113–22.

Index

For Product Safety Concerns and Information please contact our EU representative GPSR@taylorandfrancis.com Taylor & Francis Verlag GmbH, Kaufingerstraße 24, 80331 München, Germany

Printed and bound by CPI Group (UK) Ltd, Croydon, CR0 4YY
01/05/2025
01858450-0001